Joshua Girling Fitch

Lectures on Teaching Delivered in the University of Cambridge

During the Lent Term, 1880

Joshua Girling Fitch

Lectures on Teaching Delivered in the University of Cambridge During the Lent Term, 1880

ISBN/EAN: 9783337036430

Printed in Europe, USA, Canada, Australia, Japan

Cover: Foto ©Paul-Georg Meister /pixelio.de

More available books at **www.hansebooks.com**

LECTURES ON TEACHING

DELIVERED IN THE

UNIVERSITY OF CAMBRIDGE

DURING THE LENT TERM, 1880,

BY

J. G. FITCH, M.A., LL.D.

HER MAJESTY'S INSPECTOR OF TRAINING COLLEGES; AND
ASSISTANT COMMISSIONER TO THE LATE
ENDOWED SCHOOLS COMMISSION.

FOURTEENTH THOUSAND.
STEREOTYPED ENGLISH EDITION.

CAMBRIDGE:
AT THE UNIVERSITY PRESS
1887

[*The Right of Translation and Reproduction is reserved.*]

Cambridge

PRINTED BY C. J. CLAY M.A. AND SONS
AT THE UNIVERSITY PRESS

PREFACE.

IN 1879 the Senate of the University of Cambridge in compliance with numerous memorials from Headmasters and others determined to take measures with a view to encourage among those who intended to adopt the profession of teaching, the study of the principles and practice of their art. In furtherance of this design a "Teachers Training Syndicate" was appointed, and that body shortly afterwards put forth a scheme of examination in the history, the theory and the practice of Education. The first examination under this scheme was held in June 1880. The Syndicate also resolved to provide that courses of lectures should be given during the academical year 1879-80. The introductory course on the History of Education, and the life and work of eminent teachers, was delivered by the Rev. R. H. Quick in Michaelmas Term. In the following Easter Term, Mr James Ward, Fellow of Trinity College, lectured on Mental Science in its special relation to teaching; and the second course, which fell to my own share, was delivered in the Lent Term, and related mainly to the practical aspects of the schoolmaster's work.

It has been considered by some of those most interested in this experiment that this, the first course of lectures on the Art of Teaching specially addressed to the members of an English University, might properly be placed within reach of a somewhat wider circle of students. In carrying out this suggestion, I have not thought it necessary to abandon the free and familiar forms of address appropriate to a lecture, or attempted to give to what is here said the character of a complete treatise. Nor did I deem it advisable, out of regard to the supposed dignity of an academic audience, to keep out of view those simple and elementary considerations, which though usually discussed in their relation to the lower class of schools lie really at the basis of all sound and skilful teaching whether in high schools or low.

Some explanation may seem to be needed of the nomenclature which is here used in distinguishing different classes of Schools. It would doubtless be an advantage to employ in England the same terminology which is adopted throughout the Continent. But the term 'Secondary School' in France, Germany and Switzerland covers all the institutions which lie between the Elementary School and the University; and it is manifest that within these wide limits some further distinction is needed, in England at least, to mark the different aims of schools so far asunder as Winchester or Clifton, and a humble commercial school. Such phrases as 'Enseignement Supérieur' and 'Enseignement Moyen' would hardly indicate this distinction with sufficient accuracy, and I have given on page 48 my reasons for thinking that the terms 'First, Second and Third Grade,' suggested by the Schools Inquiry Commissioners, will not find permanent acceptance in this country. So I have been fain to fall back upon the words Primary, Secondary and High School, not because I think them necessarily the best; but because they mark with tolerable clearness the practical distinctions I have tried to make; because they are equally appropriate to schools for boys and for girls; and because they do not, like such words as Classical, Commercial, and Technical, connote any theory defining the kind of study specially suited to a particular age or rank in life.

It seems right to add that this book is not, and does not profess to be, a manual of method. Indeed it may well be doubted whether at the present stage of our educational experience any body of rules whatever could be safely formulated and declared to be the best. Nor is it certain, even though the best conceivable methods could be put forth with authority, that more harm than good would not be done, if by them teachers were deterred from exercising their own judgment, or became less sensible of the responsibility which lies upon them of adapting methods to their own special circumstances and needs. I cannot regret, even though the book proves profoundly disappointing to those—if any such there be —who suppose teaching to be a knack or artifice, the secret of which may be acquired, like that of dancing or swimming, in a short course of lessons. All that has been attempted here has been to invite intending teachers to look in succession at each of the principal problems they will have to solve; to consider what subjects have to be taught, and what are the reasons for teaching them; and so by bringing together a few of the plainer results of experience to place readers in a position in which it will be a little easier for them to devise and work out methods for themselves. No one can be more conscious than I am of the incomplete and provisional character of these first lectures; but I cannot doubt that the University, in seeking to promote investigations into the philosophy and the practice of the teacher's art, is entering on an honourable and most promising field of public usefulness, and that, under her sanction, future explorers in this field will do much to make the work of honest learning and of noble teaching simpler, more effective, and more delightful to the coming generations.

January, 1881.

CONTENTS.

I. THE TEACHER AND HIS ASSISTANTS.

	PAGE
Introduction	1
Relation of the University to the teaching profession	3
Teaching not to be stereotyped	5
Teaching both an Art and a Science	7
Qualifications of the ideal Teacher	9
Knowledge of the thing to be taught	10
Preparation	11
Extra-professional Knowledge	13
Temper	15
Activity and Cheerfulness	17
Avoidance of Pedantry	20
Power of describing and narrating	22
Freshness of mind	23
Sympathy	24
The work of Assistants	26
Limits to their responsibility	29
School Councils	29
Student-teachers	32
The Teacher's aims	33

II. THE SCHOOL, ITS AIMS AND ORGANIZATION.

	PAGE
Limits to School-work	37
Five departments of School-instruction	38
Their relative importance	39
Primary, Secondary and High Schools	42
The studies appropriate for each	43
What is a liberal education?	45
The grading of Schools	46
Day and boarding Schools	48
True relation of the School to the Home	49
Bifurcation and modern departments	52
Girls' Schools	55
Distribution of time	57
Classification	59
Entrance Examination	60
Fees	62

III. THE SCHOOL-ROOM AND ITS APPLIANCES.

The physical conditions of successful teaching	64
Space and light	65
Desks	67
Ventilation and Warmth	69
Furniture and Apparatus	71
Comeliness of a School	73
Registration and School book-keeping	74
Tabulated Reports of progress	75
Note-books for Teachers and Scholars	77
Text-books	81
Tests of a good School-book	83
School libraries	84
School museums	88
Costly apparatus not always the best	89

IV. DISCIPLINE.

	PAGE
The Teacher as a ruler and administrator	91
Commands to be well considered before they are given	93
Over-governing	95
Right and wrong uses of mechanical drill	96
Corporate life of a School	98
Child-nature to be studied before insisting on rules	99
School-time to be filled with work	100
The law of Habit	102
Its bearing on School life and work	103
Recreation and gymnastics	104
Sunday discipline in boarding schools	107
Rewards: how to use and to economize them	108
Happiness of children	111
Punishments and their purpose	112
Principles to be kept in view	113
The sense of shame	114
Tasks as punishments	115
The discipline of consequences	117
Why inadequate for the purposes of the State	119
And inadequate for School purposes	119
The best kinds of punishment	121
Corporal punishment	121
How to dispense with punishments	123

V. LEARNING AND REMEMBERING.

The law of mental suggestion	124
Different forms of association	126
The process of remembering	127
Modes of establishing permanent associations	128
(1) Frequent Repetition, (2) Interest in the thing learned	129
Verbal and rational memory	131
Learning by heart when legitimate	132
How to commit to memory	135
Memory to be supplemented by reflection	137
And strengthened by exercise	137

	PAGE
Tests of a good *memoriter* lesson	138
Printed catechisms	141
Relations of memory to intelligence	143
The uses of forgotten knowledge	145
Oral instruction—its advantages and its dangers	146
Self-tuition	149
Book-work, its advantages and shortcomings	150
Home and written exercises	152
Conditions to be fulfilled by them	154
Illustrative examples	155

VI. EXAMINING.

Purposes to be served by questioning	158
A Socratic dialogue	160
The Socratic method in its application to Schools	163
Characteristics of good oral questioning	164
Clearness, Terseness, Point	165
Simplicity, Directness, Continuity	167
Different forms of answer	169
Collective answering deceptive	171
Mutual questioning	172
The inquisitive spirit	173
Books of questions	175
Written examinations, their use and abuse	176
Dishonest preparation	179
Legitimate preparation	181
How to frame a good Examination paper	182
And to estimate the answers	187
Venial and punishable blunders	189
The morality of Examinations	190

VII. PREPARATORY TRAINING.

The training of the Senses	192
Principles to be kept in view in Infant discipline	193
The Kindergarten	195

	PAGE
Its merits	196
Limits to its usefulness	198
The art of Reading	201
Anomalies of the English Alphabet	202
Proposals to reform it	203
Modes of teaching Reading	206
Reading books	209
Spelling	211
Dictation and Transcription	213
Words to be used as well as spelled	215
Thoughtful and effective reading	216
Oral expression	219
Writing and the mode of teaching it	220
Locke's directions	223

VIII. THE STUDY OF LANGUAGE.

	PAGE
Language long the staple of school instruction	225
Reasons for this	226
Greek and Latin	228
Purposes once served by the learning of Latin	230
Some of these no longer useful	231
'Classical' Schools	233
The true place of Latin in the schools of the future	234
In High Schools, and in Secondary Schools	235
Comparison of Latin with English forms	237
How much Grammar should be learned by heart	240
Exercises in translation from the first	242
Literature to be studied early	244
The place of Latin in a primary school	246
Etymology—Prefixes and Affixes	248
Modern foreign languages	249
Purposes and methods of teaching them	250
Audition	252
The choice of foreign teachers	254

IX. THE ENGLISH LANGUAGE.

	PAGE
The relation of English to other linguistic studies	256
Grammar as an Art, not to be acquired by technical rules	257
Grammar as a Science	259
A vernacular language to be studied analytically	261
Classification of English words	262
Logical and Grammatical Analysis	266
Example of Analysis	268
Verbal Analysis	271
Composition	273
Paraphrase; examples	275
Précis-writing	278
Versification	278
The study of English Literature	279
Principles and Methods to be kept in view	280
Critical analysis not destructive of literary enjoyment	282
The history of literature	284

X. ARITHMETIC AS AN ART.

Why Arithmetic should be taught	286
It is both an Art and a Science	287
Robert Recorde's Arithmetic	289
The place of Arithmetic among school studies	291
Its practical uses	293
Skill in Computation, how to obtain it	294
The discipline of an Arithmetic class	295
Exercises in words as well as in figures	296
Answers to be kept out of sight	297
Oral or Mental Arithmetic	299
Its uses and abuses	300
Examples of its legitimate use	302
Exercises in weighing and measuring	304
Rapidity and exactness	307
Exercises in ingenuity and invention	308
Practical applications of Arithmetic	310
Decimalizing English money	311
Visible relation to business no test of real utility	312
Practical Geometry	313

XI. ARITHMETIC AS A SCIENCE.

	PAGE
Its disciplinal value	315
Inductive and deductive methods of reasoning	317
Arithmetic a training in deductive logic	318
Our artificial notation	321
Methods of elucidating it	322
Other Scales of Notation	324
The *Système Métrique*	325
Methods of demonstrating simple rules—Subtraction	327
Arithmetical parsing	329
The teaching of Fractions	331
Illustration of demonstrative exercises	332
The use of *formulae*	333
Proportion	335
Extraction of Roots	336
Synthesis before Analysis	337
Analogous truths in Arithmetic and Geometry	340
True purpose of mathematical teaching	342

XII. GEOGRAPHY AND THE LEARNING OF FACTS.

Objects to be kept in view in teaching geography	344
Its use (1) as information, (2) as mental discipline	345
Home Geography	347
Lessons on earth and water	348
Order of teaching geographical facts	349
No necessary sequence of difficulty or importance	350
The use of a globe	352
Measurement of approximate distances	353
Physical Geography	354
Its influence on national character and history	356
Maps	358
Verbal description of phenomena	359
Fact-lore	361
Object-lessons	362
Their use and their abuse	363
Lessons on general information	364
Subjects suited for such lessons	364
A basis of fact needed for future teaching of science	365
Technical terms	367

XIII. HISTORY.

	PAGE
Purpose of historical teaching	370
Text-books, and their legitimate use	371
The Bible a model of history	373
Great epochs to be studied first	375
Chronology	377
Right and wrong ways of teaching it	378
Mnemonic methods of learning Chronology	379
Biography	381
Lessons on great writers	384
Historical readings	385
The poetry of History	387
Picturesque teaching and its relation to detail	389
Lessons on the Government and Constitution	390
The training for citizenship	391

XIV. NATURAL SCIENCE.

The place of Physical Science among school studies	393
Its claims to rank as part of a liberal education	396
The utilities of physical truths	398
Their beauty and intellectual attractiveness	399
The disciplinal value of the inductive process	400
The search for the causes of phænomena	402
Reasons and explanations not discoverable, but only facts	403
Large truths instead of small ones	404
What are 'laws' of Nature?	405
Application of the methods of inductive investigation to the business of life	406
The relation of science to skilled industry	407
Technical and Trade Schools	409
Subjects of physical enquiry suited to form part of general education	411
Scientific terminology	413
Lessons on common things not necessarily scientific	415
General not special training	417

XV. THE CORRELATION OF STUDIES.

	PAGE
Review of the curriculum of school studies	420
Multum non multa	421
Distribution of time not necessarily proportioned to the importance of subjects	422
The contending claims of numerous subjects	423
The convertibility of intellectual forces	424
Adaptation of the school course to individual wants and aptitudes	425
Religious and moral instruction	426
Moral teaching latent in school discipline	429
Indirect moral teaching in school lessons	431
The ideal life and work of a school	430
The vocation of the true teacher	434

UXORI DILECTISSIMÆ,

CUI OPERA ET CONSILIIS ADJUVANTI

SI QUID UTILE VEL HODIE SCRIPSI

VEL UNQUAM EGI

ACCEPTUM REFERO,

D.

I. THE TEACHER AND HIS ASSISTANTS.

Introduction. THAT the University of Cambridge should institute a course of lectures on the Art and Method of teaching is a significant fact in the history of Education in England. We have in this fact a recognition on high authority of a principle which has hitherto been but imperfectly admitted, in relation to the higher forms of school life and instruction, although it has been seen in most beneficial application to the elementary schools. That principle I take to be, that there is in the teacher's profession the same difference which is observable in all other human employments between the skilled and the unskilled practitioner, and that this difference depends in large measure, on a knowledge of the best rules and methods which have to be used, and of the principles which underlie and justify those rules. It is easy to say of a schoolmaster '*nascitur non fit*,' and to give this as a reason why all training and study of method are superfluous. But we do not reason thus in regard to any other profession, even to those in which original power tells most, and in which the mechanic is most easily distinguishable from the inspired artist. For when in the department of painting you meet with a heaven-born genius, you teach him to draw; and you know that whatever his natural gifts may be, he will be all the better *pro tanto*, for knowing something about the best things that have been done by his predecessors; for studying their failures and their successes, and the reason why some have succeeded and others have failed. It is not the office of professional training in art, in law or in medicine, to obliterate the natural distinctions which are the result of special gifts; but rather to bring them into truer prominence, and to give to each of them the best opportunities of development. And if it be proved, as indeed I believe it to be demonstrable, that some acquaintance with the theory, history and rules of teaching may often serve to turn one who would be a moderate teacher into a good one, a good one into a finished and accomplished artist, and even those who are least qualified by nature into serviceable helpers, then we shall need no better vindication of the course on which we are about to enter.

Teaching not to be best learned by practice only.

It seems scarcely needful to reply to the contention of those who urge that the art of teaching is to be learned by practice, that it is a matter of experience only, that a man becomes a teacher as he becomes a swimmer, not by talking about it, but by going into the water and learning to keep his head above the surface. Experience it is true is a good school, but the fees are high, and the course is apt to be long and tedious. And it is a great part of the economy of life to know how to turn to profitable account the accumulated experience of others. I know few things much more pathetic than the utterances of some Head Masters at their annual conferences, at which one after another, even of those who have fought their way to the foremost rank of their profession, rises up to say, "We have been making experiments all our lives; we have learned much, but we have learned it at the expense of our pupils; and much of the knowledge which has thus slowly come into our possession might easily have been imparted to us at the outset, and have saved us from many mistakes." The truth in regard to the office of a teacher is that which Bacon has set forth in its application to the larger work of life, "Studies perfect nature and are perfected by experience: for natural abilities are like natural plants that need pruning by study. And studies themselves do give forth directions too much at large, except they be bounded in by experience." There is here, I think, a true estimate of the relation between natural aptitude, the study of principles and methods, and the lessons of experience. Each is indispensable, you cannot do without all three, you are not justified in exalting one at the expense of the rest. It is in the just synthesis of these three elements of qualification, that we must hope to find the thoroughly equipped schoolmaster, the teacher of the future. And of these three elements, it is manifest that it is the second only which the University can attempt to supply. She cannot hope to give the living power, the keen insight into child-nature, which distinguish the born teacher, the man of genius from the ordinary pedagogue. The University does not need to be reminded that the best part of a teacher's equipment is incommunicable in the form of pedagogic lectures; and that when she undertakes to give a professional diploma to the schoolmaster, some of the most important qualifications of the office—as zeal, faithfulness, self-consecration, and personal fitness—will escape her analysis and defy her power to test them. She is conscious of the inevitable limitations under which she works, in regard to this, as indeed to all other of the learned professions. It suffices for her to say that she will attempt to communicate only that which is communicable; and to test so much as

What a University may do to improve it.

in its nature is capable of being tested, and no more. Nor can the University to any appreciable extent supervise the actual professional practice of her sons and daughters, or follow them into the schoolroom, the laboratory and the home, to see how well they do their work, and lay to heart the lessons which experience has to teach. But she can help to call attention to principles of teaching; she can record for the guidance and information of future teachers, the details of the best work which has been done aforetime; she can accumulate rules and canons of the didactic art, can warn against mistakes, can analyse the reasons why so much of scholastic work has often been joyless, dull and depressing, can set up year by year a higher standard of professional excellence, can "allure to brighter worlds and lead the way."

The Art of Teaching, the proper concern of a University.

Shall we attribute this newly awakened ambition to nothing but the restless spirit of modern academic life; to discontent with the old plain duty of encouraging learning, devotion and research, to a morbid and uneasy hankering after "fresh woods and pastures new?" I think not. The great function of a University is to teach; and to supply the world with its teachers. The very title of Doctor, which marks the highest academic distinction in each of the faculties of Law, Divinity and Physic implies that the holder is qualified to teach the art which he knows. And if the experience of these later times has brought home to us the conviction that the art of communicating knowledge, of rendering it attractive to a learner, is an art which has its own laws and its own special philosophy; it is surely fitting that a great University, the bountiful mother whose special office it is to care alike for all the best means of human culture and to assign to all arts and sciences their true place and relation should find an honoured place for the master science, a science which is closely allied to all else which she teaches—the science of teaching itself. It is not good that this science, or indeed any other science, should be mainly pursued *per se*, in separate training institutions or professional colleges, where the horizon is necessarily bounded, and where everything is learned with a special view to the future necessities of the school, or the class-room. It is to the Universities that the power is given in the highest degree of co-ordinating the various forms of preparation for the business of life; of seeing in due proportion the study and the practice, the art and the science, the intellectual efforts which make the man, as well as those which make the lawyer or the divine. It is to the Universities that the public look for those influences which will prevent the nobler professions from degenerating into crafts and trades. And if the schoolmaster is to become something more than a mere pedant; to know the rules and formulae of his art, and at the same time to estimate them at their true value, it is to his University that he ought to look for guidance; and it is from his University that he should seek in due time the attestation of his qualifications as a teacher; because that is the authority which can testify that he is not merely a teacher, but a teacher and something else.

Even at the risk of lingering a little longer at the threshold, I am tempted to refer briefly to one other objection which is often felt by thoughtful people, and which is doubtless present in the minds of some of you, to the trial of the novel experiment in which we who are assembled here are all interested. Teaching is an art it may be said, which especially requires freshness and vigour of mind. The ways of access to the intelligence and the

Independence not discouraged by the study of method.

conscience of learners are manifold; different circumstances and intellectual conditions require different expedients. Variety and versatility are of the very essence of successful teaching. If by seeking to formulate the science of method, you encourage the belief that one mode of teaching is always right and all others are wrong, you will destroy the chance of new invention and discovery, and will do much to render teaching more sterotyped and lifeless than ever. And even if it be admitted that a perfect set of rules for practice is desirable and attainable; we are not yet in a position to lay them down; and any attempt to fix educational principles and to claim for them an authoritative or scientific character, is at present premature, and therefore likely to prove mischievous. This is an argument on which I, for one, should look with special seriousness; if it were not practically answered by every day's observation and experience. It has been my lot to see schools of very different ranks and pretensions, from the highest to the lowest; and the one thing which impresses me most is that the schools under untrained persons, who have given no special attention to the theory of their art, are curiously alike. There is nothing more monotonous than ignorance. It is among those who have received no professional preparation, that one finds the same stupid traditional methods, the same habit of telling scholars to learn instead of teaching them; the same spectacle of a master sitting enthroned at one end of a room and calling up two or three at a time to say their lessons, while the rest, presumably occupied in preparation, are following their own devices. Let us appeal on this point to the experience of other professions. Is it the effect of good professional training in medicine or in law to produce a hurtful uniformity either in opinion or practice? Is it not on the contrary true that the most original methods of procedure, the most fruitful new speculations, come precisely from the men who have best studied the philosophy of their own special subject, and who know best what has been thought and done by other workers in the same field? So in teaching, the freshest and most ingenious methods originate with those men and women who have read and thought most about the *rationale* of their art.

And if in this place we are in any degree successful in laying down principles of action, and in evolving a few of the simpler practical deductions from those principles; the truest test of our success will be found in bringing home to every earnest student the conviction, that good teaching is not an easy thing; that those who undertake to call out the intelligence and fashion the character of children are undertaking to deal with the most complex and wonderful phenomena in the world; that the philosophy of the teacher's art, is yet in its infancy; that the best results we are yet able to attain are only provisionally serviceable until they are absorbed or superseded by something better; and that it is part of the duty of every one who enters the profession to magnify his office, to look on each of the problems before him in as many lights as possible; and to try by his own independent experiments to make the path of duty, easier, safer and happier for his successors. *Independent thought more important than any rules.*

The question is often asked, "Is Education an Art or a Science?" and at present the answers to this question are not unanimous. But in truth no compendious reply is possible. The object of Science is the investigation of principles, of truth for its own sake, considered as an end, not as a means to any further end. But it is obvious that this view alone will not carry us very far. It may help us to analyse mental processes and laws of *Teaching both an Art and a Science.*

human development, but it may leave us very impotent in the presence of the actual problems of school-keeping and of professional work. And the object of Art is simply the accomplishment of a given result by the best means. Hence we are justified in speaking of Education as an Art; because it has a complex practical problem to solve. But this view of it alone would be inadequate; for in fact teaching is both an Art and a Science. It aims at the accomplishment of a piece of work and is therefore an Art. It seeks to find out a rational basis for such rules as it employs, and is therefore a Science. Down very deep at the root of all our failures and successes, there lie some philosophic truths—it may be of ethics, or of physiology, or of psychology—which we have either heeded or disregarded, and the full recognition of which is needed to make us perfect teachers. The more these underlying truths are brought to light the better; and it is satisfactory to know that the University has made other and very effective provision for the discussion both of the philosophy and the history of the teacher's work. Here however our task is humbler. We have to gather together a few of the plainer lessons of experience, and to apply them to the actual requirements of the class-room and the school. Yet, if while thus regarding Education as an Art we lose sight of the fact that it is also a Science, we shall be in danger of becoming empirics, and of treating our work as if it were a mere knack, a collection of ingenious artifices for achieving a certain desired end. This is a danger not less real than would be incurred by those who in their zeal to vindicate the claims of Education to the name and character of a Science resolved it merely into a series of speculations into the relative value of different forms of human knowledge, or into the constitution of the human mind. Those who ask us to think of Education as a Science must remember that it is an Applied Science, whose principles are largely derived from experiment and observation, and need to be constantly reduced to practice and brought to the test of utility. And we on the other hand who are seeking for some rules and counsels by which we may guide our practice and economize our resources must not forget that such rules and counsels have no claim upon our acceptance, except in so far as they have their origin in a true philosophy, and can be justified by reason and by the constitution of human nature.

Now in regard to all the duties of life there has to be considered the correlation between the thing to be done and the doer of it; the qualities of the agent largely determine the character and the results of the work. In all mechanical labour, in which matter alone has to be acted on, the physical strength and tactual skill of the artizan are the determining forces; his motives and moral qualifications have little to do with the result. But in the case of the schoolmaster, as in that of the priest, or of the statesman, mind and character have to be influenced; and it is found that in the long run nothing can influence character like character. You teach, not only by what you say and do, but very largely by what you are. Hence there is a closer correspondence in this department of human labour than in others between the quality of the work and the attributes of the workman. You cannot dissociate the two. And because in the profession of teaching the ruler or agent comes into closer contact with the person ruled than in any other profession, it becomes here specially needful to enquire not only what is the character of the work to be done, but what manner of men and women they should be

The qualifications of a perfect teacher.

who undertake to do it. We may then, I think, usefully employ some of our time in considering rather the artist than his art—the qualifications which the ideal teacher should bring to his work.

Ample and accurate knowledge of the thing taught.

It seems a trite thing to say that the teacher of a given subject should first of all possess a full and exact knowledge of the subject which he essays to teach. But I am not sure that the full significance of this obvious maxim is always recognized. Some of us imagine that if we keep a little ahead of our pupils, we shall succeed very well. But the truth is that no one can teach the whole, or even the half of what he knows. There is a large percentage of waste and loss in the very act of transmission, and you can never convey into another mind nearly all of what you know or feel on any subject Before you can impart a given piece of knowledge, you yourself must not only have appropriated it, you must have gone beyond it and all round it; must have seen it in its true relations to other facts or truths; must know out of what it originated, and to what others it is intended to lead. A person cannot teach a rule of Arithmetic—say division—intelligently, without having himself mastered many advanced rules, nay, without some knowledge of Algebra as well. Your own experience, if you watch it, will force this truth upon you. You hear a story, or you receive an explanation of a new fact. The thing seems perfectly intelligible to you, and you receive it with satisfaction and without a suspicion that anything more is wanting. But you try to tell the story or reproduce the explanation, and you find quite unexpectedly that there are weak points in your memory, that something or other which did not seem necessary when you were receiving it, is necessary to your communicating it: and that this something lies outside and beyond the truth or incident itself. Or you are giving a lesson on some subject on which your information is limited, or has been specially prepared for the occasion, and you give it under a consciousness that you are very near the boundary of your own knowledge, and that if certain further explanations were asked for you could not supply them. Is it not true that this latent consciousness begins to shew itself in your teaching; that you falter and speak less positively, and that your scholar who shews curious acuteness in discerning whether you are speaking from a full mind or not finds out the truth directly, and so your lesson is a failure? And the moral of this is that if a certain amount of accuracy, or a certain strength of conviction is necessary for a learner much greater accuracy, and a still stronger conviction, is needful for the teacher: if you want to teach well the half of a subject, know first for yourself the whole, or nearly the whole of it: have a good margin of thought and of illustration in reserve for dealing with the unexpected questions and difficulties which may emerge in the course of the lesson, and look well before beginning, not only at the thing you want to teach, but at as much else as possible of what lies near it, or is akin to it.

And if this be true there arises the necessity for looking into ourselves and carefully guaging our resources before we begin to give even the humblest lesson. Before undertaking a matter so simple as hearing a class read, we should glance over the passage and determine on what words it will be well to dwell by way of explanation and what form of illustration should be brought to bear upon it. Even if you are going to give an exposition of a rule in Arithmetic, or of the use of the Ablative, it is wise to select beforehand and mentally to rehearse your illustrative examples; to see that the instances

Preparation.

chosen, have no irrelevant factors in them, but are calculated to furnish the most effective examples of the particular truth which you wish to explain. However simple the subject of a lesson, it is never so good when unpremeditated as it would be with a little pre-arrangement and forethought. And for all lessons which do not lie in the ordinary routine, the careful preparation of notes is indispensable; it is only by such preparation that you can determine how much can fairly be attempted in the prescribed time, what is the order in which the parts should be taken up, how they should cohere, at what points you should recapitulate, and how you can give unity and point to the general impression you desire to leave.

The teacher should always be a learner.

And further, a true teacher never thinks his education complete, but is always seeking to add to his own knowledge. The moment any man ceases to be a systematic student, he ceases to be an effective teacher; he gets out of sympathy with learners, he loses sight of the process by which new truth enters into the mind; he becomes unable to understand fully the difficulties experienced by others who are receiving knowledge for the first time. It is by the act of acquiring, and by watching the process by which you yourself acquire, that you can help others to acquire. It is not intended by this that the thing thus acquired should be merely a greater store of what may be called school learning, or of what has a conscious and visible bearing on the work of school. It is true that we can never know all that is to be known, even about the subjects which we teach in schools. Mathematics, History, Philology are constantly subject to new developments, are stretching out into new fields, and becoming capable of new and unexpected applications to the needs and to the business of life. There should never be a time in the history of a teacher at which, even in regard to these purely scholastic subjects, he is content to say "I know now all that needs to be known for my purpose. I have an ample store of facts and illustrations at my command, and may now draw freely upon it." Still the question, 'What has this or that study to do with the main business of my life? How far will this kind of reading *tell* upon my professional work in school?' though it naturally occurs to a conscientious man, is narrowing and rather ignoble. The man is something greater than the teacher. The human needs crave to be satisfied even more than the professional. Our work makes the centre of our world no doubt; but life needs a circumference as well as a centre, and that circumference is made up of sympathies and tastes which are extra-professional. And in relation to the tastes and reading of your own leisure I would say: When your more strictly professional work is done, follow resolutely your own bent; cultivate that side of your intellectual life on which you feel that the most fruitful results are to be attained, and do not suppose that your profession demands of you a cold and impartial interest in all truth alike, or that what to others is a solace and delight, to you is to be nothing but so much stock in trade. If when I see a school, and ask the teacher what is its special feature, or in what subject the scholars take most interest, he replies, "O, there is nothing distinctive about our course, we pay equal attention to all subjects," I know well that his heart is not in his work. For over and above the necessary and usual subjects every good school ought to reflect in some way the special tastes of the teacher. The obvious demands of your profession and of the public must first be satisfied. And when they are satisfied, one mind will be drawn to the exact

Not of scholastic lore only.

sciences, another to poetry and the cultivation of the imaginative faculty, another to the observation of the phenomena of nature, a fourth to the sciences of history and of man. Be sure that no study thus honestly and affectionately pursued can be without important bearings on your special work. Everything you learn, even in matters like these, will tell in ways you little suppose on the success of your lessons, will furnish happy digressions, or will suggest new illustrations. 'Tout est dans tout,' said Jacotot, by which I suppose he meant that all true knowledge is nearly akin, and that any one fact honestly acquired sheds light on many others, and makes every other fact easier to acquire. The one thing you dread most in your pupils, dread most in yourself—stagnation, acquiescence in routine, torpor of mind, indifference to knowledge. When your own soul loses the receptive faculty, ceases to give a joyous welcome to new truth, be sure you have lost the power of stimulating the mental activity of others, or of instructing them to any real purpose.

Old Roger Ascham in his *Scholemaster*, the oldest educational book in England, describes his ideal student and teacher as *Philoponos*, 'one who hath lust to labour,' and *Zetetikos*, 'one that is always desirous to search out any doubt, not ashamed to learn of the meanest, nor afraid to go to the greatest, until he be perfectly taught and fully satisfied.' And these qualities are still as indispensable as ever. There must be in the perfectly successful teacher a love of work for its own sake. The profession is no doubt laborious; but as it has been well said, "It is not labour, but vexation that hurts a man." Trouble comes from mismanaged labour, from distasteful labour, from labour which we feel ourselves to be doing ill, but not from labour itself when it is well organized and successful.

Then there arises a positive delight in the putting forth of power, and in the sense that difficulties are being overcome.

Familiar as the truth is, it is worth reiterating that *Temper.* while teaching is one of the professions which most tries the patience, it is one in which the maintenance of a cheerful and happy temper is most essential. Some of us are conscious of a tendency to hasty unguarded words, to petulance, and to sudden flashes of injustice. Such a tendency may become a great misfortune to a teacher, and lead to consequences he may regret all his life. And I have known those who, having chosen the vocation of a teacher and being at the same time aware of their own infirmity in this respect, have so guarded and watched themselves, that their profession has become to them a means of moral discipline, and has sweetened and ennobled tempers naturally very hasty or very sour. But be this as it may, unless we are prepared to take some pains with ourselves and cultivate patience and forbearance, we are singularly out of place in the profession of schoolmaster. We want patience, because the best results of teaching come very slowly; we want habitual self-command, because if we are impulsive or variable and do not obey our own rules we cannot hope scholars will obey them. Chronic sullenness or acerbity of temper makes its possessor unhappy in any position, but it is a source of perpetual irritation and misery in a school. "That boy," said Dr Johnson when speaking of a sulky and unhappy looking lad, "looks like the son of a schoolmaster, which is one of the very worst conditions of childhood. Such a boy has no father, or worse than none, he never can reflect on his parent, but the reflection brings to his mind some idea of pain inflicted or of sorrow suffered.". Poor Johnson's own scholastic experiences, which, both as learner and as teacher, had not been delightful ones, led him no doubt to an exaggerated view of the misery of school-keeping as he had seen it. But he did not exaggerate the mischievous effect of a *régime* of brute force, and of a hard and ill-tempered pedagogue on the character of a child. Injustice breeds injustice. Every act of petulance or ill-temper will have some effect in deteriorating the character of the pupils, and will be reproduced in their own conduct towards their juniors or inferiors. Dr Channing has well said that "a boy compelled for six hours a day to see the countenance and hear the voice of a fretful, unkind, hard or passionate man is placed in a school of vice."

Cheerfulness. The need of constant cheerfulness on the part of a teacher becomes more apparent when we consider the nature of childhood. In some professions an artificial gravity of demeanour is not inappropriate. The clergyman or the surgeon has much to do at the bedside, in the house of mourning, with the sick and the suffering, where anything approaching to levity would often be unbecoming. But the intercourse of a teacher is with the young, the strong and the happy, and he makes a great mistake if he thinks that a severe and forbidding manner is required by the dignity of his calling. A good fund of animal spirits puts the teacher at once into sympathetic *rapport* with his pupils, because it shews them that seriousness of purpose need not mean dulness, and that the possession of learning is not incompatible with a true enjoyment of life. We must not forget that to a little child the teacher is the possessor of unfathomable erudition, the representative and embodiment of that learning which he himself is being urged to acquire. And if he sees that the acquirement of it has rather made the teacher's life gloomy than bright or joyous, he may not put his inference into the form of a proposition, but he will none the less surely acquire a dislike for knowledge, and arrive at the conclusion that it cannot be such a cheering and beautiful thing after all. It is well-known that the men and women most influential in the school-room are those who know how to share the enjoyment of their scholars in the playground; who at least do not frown at children's play, but shew an interest in it, recognize it as a proper and necessary employment of time, and indeed can play heartily themselves when the proper occasion comes. Many of the influences which surround a teacher's life have a special tendency to encourage a sedentary and physically inactive habit, and it is also observable that persons are not unfrequently attracted to the profession of teaching because they are not strong, and are studiously inclined. But it ought never to be forgotten that bodily activity is a very valuable qualification in a teacher and should be cultivated as far as possible; not rapidly lost as it too often is. That eminent schoolmaster shewed a true appreciation of his work who said, "Whenever the day comes in which I find I cannot run up stairs three at a time I shall think it high time to retire."

And among other merely physical qualifications necessary in a teacher one cannot overlook the need of great quickness both of eye and of ear. These are indispensable. In standing before a class, whether it be large or small, it is essential to stand so that every member of it should be brought into focus so to speak, that the eye should take in all that is going on, and that no act or movement should escape notice. I am more and more struck as I look at schools, with the importance of this. I often see teachers who either

Quick perception of eye and of ear.

place themselves so that they can not see every pupil, or who, by keeping the eye fixed either on the book, or on one particular part of the class, fail to check indifference or inattention simply because they do not see it and are not instantly conscious of it. No real intellectual drill or discipline is possible in such a class. It is a great thing therefore to cultivate in yourself the habit of glancing rapidly, of fixing the gaze instantly on any child who is wandering or disobedient, and applying a remedy without delay. And the need for a remedy will steadily diminish as your own vigilance increases. Let scholars know that every deviation from rule, every wandering look, every carelessly written letter in a copy is sure to be at once recognized by your quick glance, and they will cease very soon to give you much to detect. But let them see always before them a heavy eye, an unobservant manner, which permits let us say two out of every three faults to pass undiscovered, and they are skilful enough in the doctrine of chances to know well in effect what this means. It means that the probability is two to one against the detection of any given fault, and you will find that in this way, the chances being largely in favour of the disobedient one, disobedient acts will be multiplied in far greater proportion still. The teacher's ear too should be trained to a sensitive perception, of all discordant or unpermitted sounds. It should be acute to distinguish between the legitimate noise of work and the noise which impedes work or is inconsistent with it. Obvious as this is, many schoolmasters and mistresses waste much time and add greatly to the difficulties of their duty by disregarding it. Quick sensibility, both of ear and of eye, are special natural gifts with a few; but they may be acquired with the help of cultivation, even by those who have not been gifted by nature, if they only believe them to be worth having and take a little pains to obtain them. I may add that if a teacher possesses enough knowledge of the art of drawing to enable him to make impromptu rough diagrams illustrative of his lessons, the accomplishment is one which will add much to his effective power.

And may we not enumerate among the physical attributes which go to make a perfect teacher a gentle, and yet an authoritative voice. There is necessarily a great expenditure of voice in teaching, and it is of much importance to know how to economize it. As years go on, those whose profession obliges them to talk much *ore rotundo*, begin to find the vocal organs weak and overworked, and to regret all useless exertion of vocal power. And thus it should be borne in mind from the first that simply from the point of view of one's bodily health it is not good to shout or cry or lift up the voice unnecessarily. It is a great point in what you may call the dynamics of teaching to effect the maximum result with the minimum of effort. And it happens that in regard to the voice, a low tone not only effects as much as a loud one, but it actually effects more. The key at which the teacher's voice is habitually pitched determines the tone of all the school work. Children will all shout if you shout. On the other hand, if you determine never to raise your voice when you give a command they will be compelled to listen to you, and to this end to subjugate their own voices habitually, and to carry on all their work in quietness. The moral effect of this on the character of the pupils is not insignificant. A noisy school is one in which a great opportunity of civilizing and softening the manners is habitually lost. And a school whose work is always done on a low tone, is one in which not only is the teacher healthier, and better able to economize the

Voice.

resources of his own life, but as a place of moral discipline it is far more effective.

Pedantry. Touching the matter of speech, which among the minor conditions of effective and happy school-keeping is of far more significance than it may at first appear, I should like to add that some teachers seem to think it necessary to affect a studied precision in language, and to cultivate little crotchets as to elegant pronunciation, which are unknown outside of the school world. The perfection of language is the perfection of a transparent glass; it is the virtue of self-effacement. By it and through it one mind should look right into another and see exactly the thing which has to be seen; but if the medium is itself visible, if it challenge attention to itself, it is, in just that degree, an imperfect medium, and fails to fulfil its highest purpose. *Ars est celare artem.* The moment our speech becomes so precise and so proper that its precision and propriety become themselves noticeable things, that moment we cease to be good speakers in the best sense of the word. Ours is the one profession in which there is the greatest temptation to little pedantries of this kind, and it may therefore not be unfitting to refer to it. He whose speech or manner proclaims him to be a schoolmaster is not yet a perfect adept in his art. We may not conceal from ourselves that in society those whose manners and speech betray them thus are not popular, and that they are not unfrequently spoken of as pedants. Now what is it to be a pedant? It is to have our vision so narrowed by the particular duty we have in hand that we see it and other peoples' duties, so to speak, in false perspective, and mistake the relative importance of our own doings and theirs. In this sense there are pedants in all professions, and it must be owned that they are often the people most devoted to their work. But the profession of teaching is more often credited with this particular vice than any other, and for a very obvious reason. "We are never at our ease," says Charles Lamb, "in the presence of a schoolmaster, because we know he is not at his ease in ours. He comes like Gulliver from among his little people, and he cannot fit the stature of his understanding to yours. He is so used to teaching that he wants to be teaching you." The truth is that the one exceptional circumstance of a teacher's life, the necessity of passing many hours a day with those who know so much less than ourselves, and who, because of their own youth and ignorance, look up to us as prodigies of learning is very unfavourable to a perfectly just estimate of ourselves, and is calculated to make us put a higher value than it deserves on the sort of knowledge which gives us this accidental ascendancy over the little people. We ought to know this and to be on our guard against it. And after all, if there be a certain faulty tone of mind and character produced by the habit of spending much time with our intellectual inferiors, the true remedy is obvious, it is to take care that out of school we spend our time as much as possible with our intellectual superiors. We may seek them in society, or if they are not easily accessible there, we may always have recourse to the great shadowy companions of our solitude, the wise and the noble who speak to us from our libraries, and in whose presence we are no longer teachers, but reverent disciples.

To be corrected by liberal studies,

Another corrective to the special danger of the scholastic profession, is to have some one intellectual interest—some favourite pursuit or study—which is wholly unprofessional, and bears no visible relation to school work. I have known many teachers who have been saved from the narrowness and pedantry to which

and by work out of School.

their duties would have inclined them, by their love of archæology or art, or their interest in some social or public question. This extra-scholastic interest has brought them into contact with other people whom they meet on equal terms; it has helped them to escape from the habit of using the Imperative Mood, and to see their own professional work in truer relations with the larger world of thought and action, of which after all a school is only a small part. We all need, in playing our part in life, to perform some at least of it, in the presence of an audience which habitually demands our best.

Power of describing and narrating.

I have spoken of the necessity for laying all your private reading under contribution, and for bringing it to bear by way of illustration or otherwise in vivifying the teaching given in a class. But to do this well it is essential that the skilled teacher should cultivate in himself the rather rare gift of telling a story well. There are some who are good *raconteurs* by nature or by instinct. They know how to seize the right point, to reject what is irrelevant, and to keep up by their mode of telling it, the hearer's interest in any narrative they relate. But even those who have no natural aptitude of this kind may acquire it by practice, and such an aptitude when acquired is most serviceable in teaching. Watch therefore for good pieces of description which come in your way in books or newspapers, or for effective stories which you hear; and practice yourself often in reproducing them. Observe the effect of telling such a story when you give it to a class, see when it is that the eye brightens, and the attitude becomes one of unconscious fixedness and tension; and observe also when it is that the interest languishes, and the attention is relaxed. A very little experience of this kind, if superadded to thoughtfulness, to some care in the choice of materials, and to a genuine desire to interest the scholars will go far to make any one of ordinary intelligence a good narrator; and therefore to give him a new and effective instrument for gaining their attention and for doing them good.

There is indeed an abiding necessity for the application of fresh thought to every detail of school work. There is no method, however good, which does not want to be modified and reconstructed from time to time; no truth, however true, which does not need to be stated now and then in a new form, and to have fresh spirit infused into its application. It is true of rules of teaching as of higher matters, "The letter killeth, the spirit giveth life." But even this is not the whole truth. For the spirit is constantly tending to fix and embody itself and to *become* the letter, unless we are ever on our guard. We know how often it has happened in the history of religion that a great reforming movement, which has begun in the shape of a protest, and perhaps a very effective protest, against formalism and mechanical religion, has in time, come to have its own watchwords and stereotyped usages, and has ended by being just as cold and unspiritual as that which it has sought to supersede. And this has been no less true in the history of education. The new thought, the bright rational method seeks to embody itself in a rule of action. While this process is going on, all is well. But when it is at an end, and the rule is arrived at, then comes the relapse into verbalism. Routine is always easier than intelligence. And some of the most worthless of all routine is—not the traditional routine of the mediæval schools, which is known to be mechanical, and is accepted as such—but the routine at first devised by enthusiasts, and afterwards adopted by dull uninspired people, who think that they can learn the method of Socrates, of Arnold, or of Fröbel as they could learn a

Freshness of mind.

system of calisthenics or of short-hand. *Corruptio optimi pessima est.* It is very touching to read M. Michel Bréal's account of a visit to Pestalozzi, at the end of his career. He describes the old man, pointing with his finger to the black-board, to his diagrams and to the names of the qualities of objects, while the children repeated mechanically his favourite watchwords, which they had learned by heart. Those words had once been full of meaning. But they had ceased to represent real intellectual activity on the children's part, or on his. They had become dead formulas, though he knew it not. And so it will ever be, with you and with me, if we lose the habit of looking at all our methods with fresh eyes, of revising them continually, and impregnating them anew with life. It would be a melancholy result of the humble and tentative efforts, which under the encouragement of the University, we are now seeking to make, after an Art of teaching, if by them, any of us were led to suppose that it was an art to be acquired by anybody once for all. In truth though we may enter on the inheritance of some of the stored up experience of others, each of us must in his own experience, begin at the beginning, and be responsible for the adaptation of that experience to the special needs of his pupils, as well as to the claims of his own idiosyncracies and convictions. Nothing can ever be so effective as the voice, the enthusiasm, the personal influence of the living teacher. Without these, apparatus, pictures, helps, methods, degenerate soon into mere processes and a sterile mnemonic. And no set of rules however good, can ever release us from the necessity of fashioning new rules, each for himself.

Sympathy. And it need hardly be said here that the one crowning qualification of a perfect teacher is sympathy—

sympathy with young children, with their wants and their ways; and that without this all other qualifications fail to achieve the highest results. The true teacher ought to be drawn towards the profession by natural inclination, by a conviction of personal fitness, and by a wish to dedicate himself and the best powers and faculties he has to this particular form of service. That conviction, if it once dominates the mind of a person in any walk of life does much to ennoble and beautify even work which would otherwise be distasteful; but I know no one calling in which the presence of that conviction is more necessary, or its absence more disheartening than that of a schoolmaster. Teaching is the noblest of all professions, but it is the sorriest of trades; and nobody can hope to succeed in it who does not throw his whole heart into it, and who does not find a positive pleasure as he watches the quickened attention and heightened colour of a little child as he finds a new truth dawning upon him, or as some latent power is called forth. There is no calling more delightful to those who like it; none which seems such poor drudgery to those who enter upon it reluctantly or merely as a means of getting a living. He who takes his work as a dose is likely to find it nauseous. "The good schoolmaster," says Fuller, "minces his precepts for children to swallow, hanging clogs on the nimbleness of his own soul, that his scholars may go along with him." This means that he has enough of imaginative sympathy to project his own mind, so to speak, into that of his pupil, to understand what is going on there, and to think not only of how his lesson is being imparted, but also of how it is being received. But nobody can do this who is not fond of his work. That which we know and care about, we may soon learn to impart; that which we know and do *not* care about we soon cease to know at all, to any practical purpose.

Assistants. It is obvious that in selecting assistants you should seek to find as far as possible, those who possess the qualifications you would most desire in yourselves.

It is also clear as the result of modern experience that the head teacher in every school ought to be responsible for the choice of each of his own assistants. But having secured him, what is the best use to make of him? There are two opposite views on this point. There is one which gives the assistant the care of the whole work of a class, and another which makes him the teacher of a particular subject and sends him from class to class to give lessons on it. Both systems may be seen in operation in very good schools, and it would be hard to say that all the truth lies necessarily on one side, or that one mode of dividing the labour is necessarily and always right. It is here as in governments:

> That which is best administered is best.

One system gives scope for special ability, and assigns to each the work for which he is presumably fittest. But the disadvantages are serious. In the first place, the teacher of one subject only—the French or Arithmetic master—is generally without influence. When a man confines himself to one subject he is apt to see his one subject in a false light, and to lose sight of its relation to the general culture of the pupil. Perhaps too if he has a stronger will than his colleagues he demands proficiency in his one subject at the expense of others. The class system avoids this particular danger, but it has the obvious disadvantage of setting each of your assistants to teach several subjects, of which it may fairly be assumed he can teach some much better than others.

There must be a compromise between these two systems. I believe that which in the long run secures best the unity and coherence of the school work is to assign to an assistant a definite portion of responsibility, not to move him about from place to place, but to attach him to a class for a sufficient time to make it clear that the progress or backwardness of the class is to be distinctly attributed to him. Each assistant should be clearly identified with the work of particular scholars and mainly responsible for it. On the whole a distribution of assistants among classes, effects this purpose better than their distribution among subjects. Experience is not favourable to the plan of making one teacher take the exclusive charge of arithmetic, another of writing, and another of literature. The class system calls out more varied power, prevents the mind of the teacher from always running in the same groove; and is more interesting to himself. He wants a change of occupation and of subject as much as his pupils. At the same time while this seems to be the best general rule, it is clearly important to utilize any special gift possessed by an assistant and to find out in the case of every one such assistant what is the subject he can teach best, or in what work he feels most interest. If over and above his proper and ordinary work in his class, an assistant who is fond of drawing, or who sings well, or who is skilful in the book-keeping and supervision of registers, has appropriate special work assigned to him,—work which belongs rather to the whole school than to the class, such work will be a clear gain, not only to the school which will thus turn all its best resources to account, but also to the assistant himself, whose interest in the prosperity of the school as a whole will thus be much augmented.

So we may conclude from these considerations that on the whole the class-master plan should prevail in the lower classes, and the plan of employing specialists in the higher, but that the evils of too exclusive a dependence upon either plan should be carefully guarded against throughout the school.

Another form of compromise between the two systems succeeds well in some good schools. To each class of from 30 to 40 pupils two teachers are attached— a senior and a junior. The class is divided into two for arithmetic, languages, reading, and a good deal of *viva-voce* questioning, and each teacher is responsible for his own section. For all lecture lessons the sections are thrown together and the class is one. The most important lectures are given by the senior teacher, others by the junior; but both teachers are present at all lectures, and responsible for seeing that their respective sections understand and profit by them. This plan has the further advantage of putting a younger teacher under the supervision and practical training of an elder; and also of relieving the younger teacher occasionally for his own studies or for higher lectures.

Responsibility to be confided to Assistants, But though it is well to confide responsibility to assistants it is essential to watch its exercise carefully. The principal teacher should hold frequent periodical examinations to see what progress is being made, should himself stand by and listen to the teaching, should make himself thoroughly acquainted with the methods employed by his assistant, and with the sort of influence he exerts. I once knew a large private school in which this was done by the cunning device of letting a small pane of glass into the wall of each class-room; and the principal prided himself on being able to pervade the whole establishment at all times, and peep in when it was least suspected. But this is not what I recommend. It is not *espionage*, for this always destroys the self respect of those who are subject to it. Nor is it the half-apologetic way which some head-masters have of coming into the class of an assistant with some pretext, as if they felt they were intruding. It is the frank recognition of such oversight as one of the conditions under which the work is to be done, and under which alone responsibility can be properly concentrated in the hands of the principal. It is indispensable that there should be *unity* in a school, that the plans and methods in use in the various classes should harmonize and be mutually helpful. And to this end the occasional presence of the principal in the lower classes should be part of the recognized order of the school. He will not interrupt or criticize of course in the presence of the scholars. He will in their eyes rather appear as in friendly co-operation with the assistant than as a critic. But he will criticize nevertheless. He will carefully note mistakes, negligences and ignorances; and make them the subject of private counsel to the assistants afterwards. *yet concentrated in the Head.*

In many large schools, it is the custom to have every week a short conference among the teachers, in which they and the head-master compare notes and consult together about the work and about the pupils. Whether the number be small or great, some such comparison of experience is absolutely necessary if the school is to be at unity with itself, and if its parts are to fit together. I once visited an Endowed Grammar School, in which the head-master and the usher, both clergymen, both on the Foundation, both separately appointed, carried on their duties in separate rooms. They had not spoken to each other for fifteen years. The head-master explained to me that the low state of *School Councils.*

his own department was attributable to the worthless character of the preparation obtained in the usher's class; and the usher with equal frankness, told me that it was of no use to take any pains with boys, who were to come under so foolish a *régime* as that of the Upper Department. These cases it may be hoped are rare, but instances of practical isolation, and want of harmony in the work of classes, are not rare, and I hold it to be indispensable, that the principal of the school should know everything that is going on in it; and should habitually test and observe the work of his subordinates, not because he suspects them, but because thorough and intelligent co-operation towards a common end is impossible without it.

Youthful assistants. No general rule can be laid down about the age of assistants; the whole question is a personal one, to be settled by the individual characteristics of the people within your reach, and not by any fixed rules. But I may confess to a strong sense of the services which may often be rendered by young teachers as assistants. Much experience in elementary schools of the working of the pupil teacher system has not led me, as it appears to have led many others, to distrust that system, and to wish to see it universally superseded by an organization dependent on adult teachers alone. You know that by the regulations of the Council Office, one grown up assistant master or mistress is allowed to count as two pupil teachers in assessing the sufficiency of the staff. They are about equal to one such assistant in point of cost, but I have come to the conclusion that in a great many cases the two pupil teachers do more work than one assistant. And I have no doubt that in secondary schools the system of student teachers might often be adopted with much advantage, and that you may get very valuable work out of young people of seventeen or eighteen who are drawn to the profession by choice and aptitude and who wish to become trained for it. What they lack in maturity and experience they often make up in enthusiasm, in freshness of mind and in tractability. You can easily direct them, and mould their work so as to fit your own plans. Only it is worth while to bear in mind two or three conditions. They should not at first be put to the care of the youngest children. It is a very common fault to suppose that your rawest and least trained teacher should be put to your lowest class, whereas it is in the lowest class that the highest professional skill is often wanted. To awaken the interest and intelligence of very young children is often a much harder task than to direct the work of elders. The easiest part of the work of a school is the supervision of the more mechanical lessons, such as reading and writing, or the correction of sums and of home exercises in the middle classes of a school, where scholars may be presumed to have already been drilled into good habits of work. And this therefore is the department of duty which should first be confided to a young teacher. The function which is known in the French schools as that of *repetiteur*, who has charge of the minor and more mechanical parts of the teaching is the proper function of such a teacher, not the sole charge of any one department of a school. Then by degrees he may be called upon to give a lesson perhaps on some rule of arithmetic in the presence of a class, and afterwards to teach in succession other subjects properly graduated in difficulty. It is a mistake to exact so much, as is often demanded from young teachers. While in the stage of probation or partial studentship they should not give more than half the day to teaching, and reserve the rest for their own studies. If we expect a young assistant to spend the whole of the ordinary school-hours in charge of young children, and to pursue his own studies when school is over we expect what is unreasonable, and we go far to disgust him and make him feel the task to be drudgery. On the other hand an alternation of teaching and learning, of obeying and governing is very pleasant to an active mind; and I think by trying the experiment of what may be called the 'half time system' the principal of a school may often get better, fresher work—work which he can more completely control and bring into harmony with his own views and plans—out of student teachers than out of adult ushers of the ordinary type.

Student-teachers. There is great advantage, whenever possible, in securing assistants of your own training, those whom you have manufactured on the premises, so to speak. And the system of student-teachers lends itself well to the adoption of this course. But we must not overlook the demerits and dangers of this system on the other hand. A youth selected from among your most promising pupils and trained under your own eye with a view to taking office as an assistant, may indeed be expected to be familiar with your own methods and in sympathy with your aims. But it is essential that in the interval between the time of quasi-apprenticeship and that in which he takes permanent office as assistant he should go out either to the University or to some other school for that important part of his education which you cannot give him. In the elementary schools young people are chosen early as pupil teachers, go out at eighteen for two years to a training college and return to an elementary school as assistants before they are qualified to take the sole charge of schools. In theory this is unexceptionable. And if at the training colleges they were enabled to obtain a broader view of their profession and of life little more could be desired. Unfortunately however at the Normal college they are associated only with others who have had precisely the same training, who come from the same social class, and have been subject to the same early disadvantages. They are therefore from the beginning to the end of their career always moving in the same rut, always bounded by the traditions and the experience of the elementary school, and they know too little of the outer world, or of what in other professions passes for a liberal education. Hence the narrower views and the more obvious faults which often characterize the elementary teacher. For a successful teacher of a higher school we may indeed desire in some cases the early training analogous to pupil-teachership; and some special preparation, either as assistant or otherwise, in the duties of a schoolmaster. But it is important that a substantial part of his training, at any rate, should be obtained in other places than the school in which he intends ultimately to teach ; and among persons who are not intending to follow the same profession as himself.

And for the teacher and for all his assistants, the one thing needful, is a high aim, and a strong faith in the infinite possibilities which lie hidden in the nature of a young child. One hears much rhetoric and nonsense on this subject. The schoolmaster is often addressed by enthusiasts as if he were more important to the body politic than soldier and statesman, poet and student all put together; and a modest man rebels, and rightly rebels, against this exaggeration, and is fain to take refuge in a mean view of his office. But after all, we must never forget that those who magnify your office in ever so bad taste, are substantially right. And it is only an elevated ideal of your profession which will ever enable you to contend against its inevitable discouragements — the weary repetitions, the dulness of some, the wilfulness of others, the low aims of many parents, the exactions of governors and of public bodies, the ungenerous criticism, the false standards of estimation which may be applied to your work. What is to sustain you in these circumstances, in places remote from friends, or in the midst of uncongenial surroundings? Nothing, except the faith which removes mountains, the strong conviction that your work after all, if honestly and skilfully done, is some of the most fruitful and precious work in the world. The greatest of all teachers, in describing his own mission once said, "I am come that they might have life and that they might have it more abundantly." And may we not without irreverence say that this is, in a humble and far-off way the aim of every true teacher in the world? He wants to help his pupil to *live* a fuller, a richer, a more interesting and a more useful life[1]. He wants so to train the scholar, that no one of his intellectual or moral resources shall be wasted. He looks on the complex organization of a young child, and he seeks to bring all his faculties, not merely his memory and his capacity for obedience, but also his intelligence, his acquisitiveness, his imagination, his taste, his love of action, his love of truth, into the fullest vitality;

> "That mind and soul according well
> May make one music."

No meaner ideal than this ought to satisfy even the humblest who enters the teacher's profession.

---

[1] "Qu'on destine mon élève a l'epée, a l'Eglise, au barreau, que m'importe! avant la vocation des parents, la nature l'appelle a la vie humaine. Vivre est le métier que je lui veux apprendre."
ROUSSEAU.

From considerations so high and far-reaching does it seem to you a rather steep descent to come down to the details of school organization, to books and methods, to maps and time tables? I hope not, for it is only in the light of large principles that little things can be seen in their true significance; and a great aim is often the stimulus to exertions which were otherwise petty and wearisome.

II. THE SCHOOL: ITS AIMS AND ORGANIZATION.

The business of a School.
WE are to consider now the nature and functions of a School generally. The Art of Teaching or *Didactics* as we may for convenience call it falls under two heads, general and special. And before seeking to investigate the several subjects usually included in a school course, one by one; and the methods appropriate to each, it seems right to take a *vue d'ensemble* of the whole work of a School, and to ask ourselves what it ought to aim at, and what it cannot do. We shall not gain much from any preliminary speculation as to what Education is. Nothing is more easy than to define it as the awakening and training of faculty, the co-ordinate development of all the powers both passive and active of the human soul, the complete preparation for the business of life. In the view of many who have written on this subject there is no one element of perfectibility in the human character, no one attribute, physical, intellectual, or spiritual, which it is not the duty of a teacher to have in mind, and which does not form part of the business of education. We may leave for the present all such speculations. They are unquestionably true; because all the experience of life is a training, and men are educated from infancy to the grave, by all the sights and sounds,

the joys and sorrows which they encounter, by the character and behaviour of their friends, the nature of their surroundings, and by the books they read. But we have to ask which and how many of these formative influences are within the control of professional teachers. The home and the family influence do much, and these have to be presupposed. The out-door life, and the contact with its facts and experience will do still more; and this also must be taken into account. The school comes in between these, and seeks to control some of the forces which act on the young life from seven years old to 15 or 18; and for a very limited number of the hours of each day. It is for a school to supplement other means of training, not to supersede them; to deal with a part and not with the whole even of youthful life. It can never safely seek to relieve parents of their own special moral responsibilities; or to find for the child fit surroundings in the home or in the world. The teacher may properly set before himself the ideal perfection of a life. He will do well to study Herbert Spencer's description of the purpose of Education as a means of forming the parent, the worker, the thinker, the subject, and the citizen. But the practical question for him is what portion of the vast and intricate work of attaining such perfection is to be done in a school, and under the special limitations and conditions to which a professional teacher is subject. After all, he is not and cannot be to his pupil, in the place of the parent, the employer, the priest, the civil ruler, or the writer of of books, and all these have in their own way educative functions not inferior to his. It is well also to remember that some of the most precious teaching of life comes to us *obiter*, and without special provision or arrangement, while other knowledge can hardly come to us at all

The limits of its work.

except we get it at school. We cannot therefore measure the claim of a given kind of knowledge to become a part of a school course, by considering merely its worth *per se*. We must also consider whether it is a kind of knowledge which is capable of being formulated into lessons and imparted by a teacher. For otherwise, however valuable it may be, it is for the purpose now in view no concern of ours.

Its true functions. Now a school can operate on the education of a scholar in two ways: (1) by its discipline and indirect training, and (2) by positive instruction. Of discipline in so far as it is moral and affects the growth of character, we have to speak hereafter. But of instruction, and the special intellectual and practical discipline which may be got by means of definite lessons, we may usefully take a brief preliminary view now.

I suppose that if we seek to classify the objects of instruction (*lehr-stoff*), so far as they lie within the purview of a school-teacher, they are these:

Five departments of instruction. (1) The attainment of certain manual and mechanical arts e.g. those of reading, writing, drawing and music. With these you try to train the senses, and to develope a certain handiness and readiness in the use of physical powers, and in the solution of some of the practical problems of life.

(2) The impartation of certain useful facts—of the kind of information which is needed in the intercourse of life, and of which it is inconvenient, and a little disgraceful to be ignorant. Such are the facts of geography, and history, and a good deal of miscellaneous information about common things, and about the world in which we live. It may be safely said that quite apart from all consideration of the intellectual processes by which knowledge of these facts finds entrance into the mind,

and of the way in which it is systematized or made to serve an intellectual purpose, such facts are in themselves useful, and ought to be taught.

(3) Language, including the vocabulary, grammar and literature of our own and other tongues; and all exercises in the meaning, history and right use of words.

(4) Pure Science, including Arithmetic, Mathematics and other studies of a deductive character, specially intended to cultivate the logical faculty.

(5) Applied Science, including Natural History, Physics, Chemistry, and the Inductive Sciences generally.

Now under these five heads may be included nearly all the secular teaching of a school; and I think we may roughly say that, if you take the whole period of a child's school life, supposing it to be prolonged to the age of 18, the time would not be ill-divided if about one-fifth of it were given to each. All five are indispensable. But the proportions of time which you give to them respectively will vary much according to the stage of his career which the child has reached. At first the first second and third will occupy the whole time. As the arts of Reading and Writing are acquired, i.e. after the age of 8 or 9, practice in them will become less and less important; and in a year or two later, exercises in what may be called Art will only be interspersed among the lessons of the school as reliefs from intellectual labour. Thus more time will become available for the subjects of the 2nd, 3rd, 4th and 5th groups. And of these it should always be remembered, that the second is of the smallest value educationally, and that in just the proportion in which you deal wisely and successfully with the other branches, the acquisition of information about history, geography and common things may be safely left to the private reading, and

Their relative importance.

intelligent observation, for which your purely disciplinal studies will have created an appetite. Moreover these classes of knowledge are not quite so sharply divided in fact, as they seem to be in a theoretical scheme. Much depends on the mode of their treatment. For instance, much of the work done under the name of arithmetic, is often taught more in the nature of a knack, or mechanical art, than as a mental discipline. Grammar too, considered as the art of correct speaking is matter of imitation rather than knowledge. And Physical Geography may easily, if well taught, become lifted to the rank of a science, and fall under the fifth rather than the second head. On the whole, the staple of school discipline and instruction will be found in the third, fourth and fifth groups, and you cannot go far wrong, in allotting the best of the time in the case of older pupils, in about equal proportions to these three departments of intellectual effort. We shall have to consider more fully hereafter the reasons which justify the teaching of each of these subjects. At present, it may suffice to say that you teach language in order to enlarge a learner's vocabulary, to give him precision in the use of words, and a greater command over the resources of speech considered as an instrument of thought. And an ancient language, which is fully inflected, a modern language which we learn for purposes of conversation mainly, and our own vernacular speech, all in their several ways conduce to the same end, though each has processes peculiar to itself. And we teach besides arithmetic some branch of mathematical or deductive science, because this furnishes the best training in practical logic, in the art of deducing right inferences from general or admitted truths. And as to the sciences which are not to be investigated deductively; but depend on experience, observation, and a generalization from a multitude of phenomena; we teach them not only because they make the student acquainted with the beauty and the order of the physical world; but because the mode of attaining truth in these matters corresponds more nearly than any other to the mode by which right general opinions are formed about all the principal subjects which for the purposes of practical life it behoves us to know.

You can hardly conceive a completely educated man whose faculties have not been trained in each of these ways. *Their co-ordination.* But while this three-fold division of studies may always be held in view; it does not follow that every one of them should be pursued uniformly and co-ordinately all through a scholar's course. When elements have been learned and the scholar has got to the age of 13 or 14, you will do well, often in a given term or half year to concentrate special attention on two or three subjects, and for a while, to do little more with some others than take measures for keeping up what has already been gained. It is unsafe to specialize too soon, till a good general foundation has been laid for acquirement in all departments; but when this foundation has been secured, it is a great part of education especially in the higher classes, to shew what may be done now and then by a resolute and steady devotion to a particular department of work. It is only by doing so, occasionally, and in doing this, by sacrificing for a time the theory of proportion which ought always to prevail in your scheme of instruction considered as a whole, that you will give to your elder pupils a due sense of their own power, and prepare them for that duty which is so often needed in after life—the duty of bringing the whole faculty, and effort and enthusiasm to bear on one subject at a time. Do not be afraid therefore of giving an extra proportion of time to Latin or to Literature, or to Natural Science; when you find the pupils have just caught the spirit of the work and are prepared to do it unusually well. For though relatively to the particular month or term the distribution of time may seem inequitable, it is not so relatively to the whole period of the school life.

The three kinds of Schools. We have, in fact to keep in view the general principle that every school ought to provide in its own way and measure, instruction and training of several different kinds —the practical arts, so that the pupil learns to *do* something, as read write or draw; the real or specific teaching, so that the pupil is made to *know* something of the facts and phenomena round him; the disciplinal or intellectual exercise whereby he is helped to *think* and observe and reason; and the moral training, whereby he is made to *feel* rightly, to be affected by a right ambition, and by a sense of duty. But in applying this general view to different schools we must make great modifications. Whether a school is intended for girls or for boys, for young children or elder, for boarders or for day scholars, must be first considered before we determine its curriculum. And after all, the most important consideration which will differentiate the character of various schools, is the length of time which pupils are likely to spend in them. Roughly we may say that a Primary School is one the majority of whose scholars leave at the age of 14; a Secondary School, one in which they remain till 16, and a High School one which may hope to retain them till 18 or 19, and to send them direct to the Universities. The problem may be further modified by special professional aims and by the necessary differences in the training of boys and girls, especially in relation to the side of art culture; but mainly we may keep these three divisions in view.

Now the work of a Primary school begins earlier, and is much more usually founded on infant school discipline than the work of either of the other two. From 5 years old to 7, the playful kindly discipline of the Kindergarten, may be made to alternate with short lessons on reading, writing, drawing and counting, and with manual and singing exercises. And during the age from 7 to 14 it is not too much to expect that the child of the poor man who is to earn his living after that age, shall learn to read with intelligence, to write and express himself well, to know something of the structure of his own language, and to understand the meanings of words. The purely logical part of his training will be gained by instruction in the principles and the practice of arithmetic, and the elements of geometry; his knowledge of facts will be mainly that of geography and of history; the scientific side of his training will be obtained through the elementary study of mechanics or chemistry, or physiology, *Erdkunde* or *Naturkunde*, and the æsthetic side by vocal music and drawing, and the learning of poetry. And if to this can be added sufficient instruction in the elements of any foreign grammar, say French, to enable the pupil to pursue the study of another language than his own, by his own efforts after leaving school, the primary school may be considered to have done its work, and to have given him relatively to the limited time, in which he has been under instruction, a complete, coherent, and self-consistent course.

1. *The Primary School.*

The curriculum of the Secondary School, which ex *hypothesi* is to be carried on at least to the age of 16, should from the first aim at all that is attained in the primary, with some additions. It may reasonably include the elements of two languages other than the pupil's own, of which it is expedient that one should be Latin and the other

2. *The Secondary School.*

French or German. It should on the side of pure science, be carried to algebra and geometry; and in the department of applied science should include at least, one such subject as chemistry, physics or astronomy rather fully treated. On the side of the humanities it should recognize the study of a few literary masterpieces, and some knowledge of the history of thought as well as of events. But it should not in my opinion, attempt to include Greek, nor any exercise in Latin versification or composition; simply because it is not possible to carry discipline of this kind far enough within the limits of age to achieve any real intellectual result.

3. The High School.
The public school of the Highest grade necessarily and rightly adjusts its course to the requirements of the University, for which as a rule its pupils are destined. It keeps in view the same broad distinctions, and the same general scheme of the co-ordination of studies; but it may from the first lay wider and deeper foundations; it may proceed more slowly, and may fitly give heed to niceties of scholarship, which would be unsuitable in a shorter course. The scheme put forth by the Oxford and Cambridge Joint Board for the final examination in schools, which is to be regarded either as a *terminus ad quem* relatively to the public school couse, or a *terminus a quo* relatively to the University; and is to serve either for a leaving certificate or for matriculation, arranges studies in four groups on this wise:—

    I. (1) Latin, (2) Greek, (3) French and German,

    II. (1) Scripture knowledge, (2) English, (3) History,

    III. (1) Mathematics (elementary), (2) Mathematics (additional),

IV. (1) Natural Philosophy, (2) Heat and Chemistry, (3) Botany, (4) Physical Geography and elementary Geology,

and requires candidates to satisfy the examiners in at least four subjects taken from not less than three different groups.

Having determined the course of instruction by considering the age to which it is likely to be prolonged, we have to secure that within this probable limit there shall be unity of purpose, and a distinct recognition of the claims of each of the four or five principal means of training. The course should be rounded and complete as far as it goes, on the supposition that, except in the case of schools which are preparing for the University, there is little or no chance that the time of formal school instruction will be prolonged. It is by losing sight of this, that we often commit the grave mistake of conducting the school education of a boy on too pretentious a plan, and on the assumption that he is to make a long stay at school. And the incomplete *frustum* of a higher course is not of the same value as the whole of a scheme of instruction which from the first has a less ambitious aim. The nature and extent of a foundation must be determined by the character of the superstructure you propose to build on it. The course of instruction should be begun with a reasonable prospect of continuing it. Otherwise it may simply come to nothing, and represent a weary waste of time.

Each course rounded and complete.

And thus, we are to have in view, for schools of all kinds, an education which may well deserve to be called 'liberal,' because it seeks to train the man, and not merely the good tradesman or doctor or mechanic. What we may call the 'real' elements of a school course, the acquisition of power to read and write and do certain

And each in a sense a 'liberal' course.

things, and the knowledge of useful facts, will form the largest proportion of the work of the primary school; while the formative elements,—those which seek to give general power and capacity—language, logic and science will be less prominent, simply for the reason that time is limited. But these higher elements should not be absent even from a course of instruction which ended at 10 or 11. And the reason why a High or public school course or a University course better deserves to be called a course of liberal education than the other, is not because it neglects the 'real' elements of manual arts and matters of fact, but simply because a larger proportion of its work is essentially formative and disciplinal; and because every year enables the student to give relatively more attention to those studies, by which taste and power and thoughtfulness are increased. From this point of view, it will be seen how unsatisfactory are such designations as 'Classical' school, *Realschule*, or 'Science' school, which imply that all the intellectual training is to be of one kind, or worse than all 'Commercial' school, which implies that there is to be no intellectual training at all, but that the whole course shall be consciously directed rather to the means of getting a living, than to the claims of life itself.

The gradation of Schools.
And if this be the true principle to be kept in view in the gradation of schools, it follows, that except within certain limits, we must not regard the primary as a preparatory school for the secondary, or the secondary for the high school. We need, no doubt, to construct the ladder of which we have so often heard, from the lower to the highest grades of public instruction. But it is a grave mistake to suppose that the highest step in a primary school corresponds with the lower one in the secondary. Or to change the figure, the three courses of instruction—primary, secondary and higher—may be compared

to three pyramids, of different sizes, though all in their way symmetrical and perfect. But you cannot take the apex of the larger pyramid and set it on the top of a smaller. You may indeed fit on, with a certain practical convenience the top of the higher scheme of education to the truncated scheme of the lower, provided you go low enough. If by means of scholarships or otherwise, we desire to take a promising pupil out of the elementary into the secondary school, it is not expedient to keep him in the first till 14 when the course is ended, and then transfer him for the last two years of his school life into a school of higher pretentions. He should be discovered earlier, say at 11, and placed in the higher school for a sufficiently long period to gain the full advantage of its extended course. And in like manner, if a scholar is to be helped from a secondary school into one which prepares for the Universities, he should not remain to complete the school course, but should be captured, and transferred at 14 or 15 at the latest. Otherwise it will be found that he has something to unlearn, that the continuity of his school life is broken, that some of the books and methods will be new to him, and that the conditions will not be favourable to his learning all which the more advanced school can teach. This principle, if once accepted, will it is clear prove fatal to the very prevalent notion that the higher or more expensive school may be regarded as a sort of finishing school for pupils from the lower. There is still a theory, current especially among parents in regard to girls, that it is worth while to take a pupil from one school, and send her for the last year to some expensive establishment to 'finish.' I know few more pestilent heresies than this—the notion that a little top-dressing of accomplishments is the proper end of a school course. There is a great break in the unity and sequence

The 'finishing' School.

of the school career; and the new books and new aims come much too late to be of any real service, and indeed serve only to unsettle the pupil. When schools are rightly graded each will have its own complete and characteristic course; and for this reason, it is only within certain limits, that is to say, about two years before its natural completion, that any one of these courses can be rightly regarded as preparatory to the other[1].

Day and boarding Schools. In fashioning schemes of instruction, it is well to make up our minds as to the relative advantages of day schools and boarding schools. In this part of our island, a strong preference has long been felt for boarding schools; and it is believed that a more complete as well as a more guarded course of education is attainable in them than in day schools. In Scotland and in most European countries the opposite feeling has prevailed; and wherever good day schools are within reach parents prefer to use them, and to look after the moral discipline of their children at home. I believe that this view is becoming more prevalent among us, and that the establishment of large public day schools in towns, is doing much to reconcile parents especially in regard to girls, to a method of training which a few years ago, was generally

---

[1] The desire of the Schools Inquiry Commission was to make three grades of Schools above the primary:—the Third grade for scholars who would leave at 15, in which the fees should be £4 or £5 a year; the Second grade to take boys to 16 or 17, and to charge fees of £8 or £10; and the First grade to retain scholars till at the age of 18 or 19 they should be able to proceed to the University; and in such schools the fees might be fixed from £15 to £20 a year for tuition only. This theory has proved to be unworkable, (1) because, in fact, it separates three classes rather too rigidly, when two would have sufficed; and (2) because of the unfortunate use of the word 'grade,' which is popularly taken to connote social rather than educational rank.

regarded by the middle and upper classes, as inadequate and just a little lowering from the social point of view. The discipline of an orderly and intelligent home, and the intercourse with brothers and sisters is itself an important part of education. But this cannot be attained, when three-fourths of the year are spent in an artificial community, which is very unlike a home, in which one's companions are all of one sex and nearly of the same age, and in which the child is placed under the discipline of strangers who have no other than a professional interest in his progress. If we consider the matter well, there is a sense in which the custom of relying on the boarding school implies the degradation of the home. It attaches the ideas of duty, order and systematic work exclusively to the school; and of leisure, licence and habitual indulgence to the home. Now the highest conception of the life of youth regards both school and home as places of systematic discipline, and of orderly and happy work. It is after all in the home that much of the serious work of men, and nearly all the serious work of women has ultimately to be done; and the sooner this fact is made evident to the young scholar the better. No parent should willingly consent to part for a large part of the year with the whole moral supervision of his child. That so many parents do thus consent may be attributed partly to the conviction of some, that they are unable owing to other occupations or to personal inaptitude to do the work properly; and partly to the love of social exclusiveness which is a prominent characteristic and not the noblest characteristic of people in the middle and upper ranks. We all know that a day school is often spoken of as an inferior institution, one in which there will be mixture of classes, an object of special dread to the vulgar rich. With a truer

Home should be a place of work.

sense of responsibility on the part of parents and truer notions as to the functions of a school, this difficulty is likely to become less seriously felt. The association of scholars from different ranks of life in classes and lessons, involves no real danger to the manners and habits of a child. On the contrary such association is well calculated to break down foolish prejudice, to furnish the best kind of intellectual stimulus, and to shew the scholar his true place in the world in which he has to play his part. This principle is already widely recognised in regard to boys; but it is for obvious reasons, not so readily admitted in its relation to girls, although it is not less true and sound in their case. Ere long, I hope it will be admitted even by the most refined of parents that, with reasonable care as to the associations which their daughters form *out* of school; they may not only without risk, but with great advantage, permit them to share all the advantages of good public day schools; and need feel no greater misgiving as to the results of association for school purposes, than they do in respect to the meeting together on Sundays in the same place for public worship.

The boarding-school.
In the boarding-school, however, habits and personal associations are necessarily formed. And since partly from necessity and partly from the preference of parents, boarding-schools will always exist; it is well to bear in mind that the reasons which render them desirable, and which should control their organization differ much in the case of boys and of girls. The great public school has much to teach besides what is learned in the form of lessons, much which could not be learned by boys at home. It is a moral gymnasium, an arena for contest, a republican community in which personal rights have both to be maintained for oneself and respected in

others; it should be a microcosm; a training ground for the business and the struggle of life, and for the duties of a world in which men have to work with men and to contend with men. But a big conventual boarding-school for girls is unlike any world which they are ever likely to enter. It has no lesson to teach and no discipline to furnish, which bears at all on the future claims of society and of home. Hence while the ideal boarding-school for boys may be large and stately; with its strong sense of corporate unity, its traditions, its contests, its publicity, its representation on a small scale of municipal and political life; the ideal boarding-school for girls is an institution large enough indeed as to all its teaching arrangements to admit of perfect classification, right division of duty among teachers and abundant intellectual activity; but organised as to all its domestic arrangements, on the principle of small sheltered boarding-houses in separate communities of not more than 20, each under the care of a mistress who shall stand *in loco parentis*. And in each of such boarding-houses it is well that care should be taken to gather together under the same roof scholars of very different ages, in order that relations of helpfulness and protection may be established between the elder and the younger, and that in this way something analogous to the natural discipline of a family may be attained.

We may not forget too that all large boarding establishments when limited to pupils of one particular class, clergy-orphan schools, schools for officers' daughters, orphan-schools, and the like have a very narrowing influence on the formation of character and are essentially wrong in principle. Any disadvantages which belong to the children of any one such class become intensified by the attempt to bring them up together. Experience has

Class boarding-schools.

shewn us that the worst thing to do with pauper children is to bring them up in pauper schools; and that the wise course is as soon as possible to let their lives be passed in ordinary homes, and in schools frequented by children whose parents are not paupers. So the happiest thing for the orphan daughter of a clergyman is that she should be placed in a school where the children do not all come from parsonages, and where some at least of her associates are not orphans.

Bifurcation.

To what extent are the principles we have laid down consistent with a system of bifurcation, or division of the upper part of the school, into two branches, according to the special bent or probable destiny of the scholars? On this point there has been much discussion. Even in the greatest and most ancient of our schools, it has come to be recognized that the traditional classical discipline is not equally suited for all the pupils; that what are called modern subjects—modern languages and sciences—have a right to recognition; and that for all boys who are not likely to go to the University, as well as for all, who, when they enter an academic life, mean to pay special attention to science, an alternative course should be offered; and they should be permitted to substitute modern languages for ancient, or chemistry and physical science for literature. And hence the establishment in so many of the great schools of what are called "modern departments," or "modern sides." It is impossible to declare that this experiment has been wholly successful. There is often a complete separation, say at the age of 15, of the boys in this department from those of the "classical." The "moderns" are sometimes placed under the care of a class of teachers of inferior academic rank. It is understood that the work is rather easier,

Modern departments.

and that boys of inferior abilities gravitate to it. So it
comes to be regarded as less creditable to belong to it;
and those who keep in the ancient traditional groove, in
which all·the former triumphs of the school have been
won, consider themselves, not only intellectually, but
socially superior to those who avail themselves of the
locus pœnitentiæ provided by the modern department.
What is worse, the masters themselves, often encourage
this feeling, and let it be seen that they think the more
honourable school career is to be found in exclusive devotion to classics. We shall never give a fair chance to
other forms of intellectual discipline, while this state of
academic opinion lasts. We shall, I hope, ere long,
come to the conclusion that the true way to recognize
the claims of what are called modern subjects, is not by
the erection of separate modern departments, but rather
by taking a wiser and more philosophical view of the
whole range and purpose of school education. It is not
good that the boy who is to be a classical scholar, should
grow up ignorant of physical laws. Still less is it good
that the boy who shews a leaning for the natural sciences
should be debarred from the intellectual culture, which
literature and language give. And it may well be doubted
whether it is desirable to recognize too early, the differences
of natural bent, or probable professional career, at all.
Up to a certain point, it is good for all of us to learn
many things, for which we have no special aptitude. Unless we do this, we do not give our faculties a fair chance.
We do not know until our minds have been directed to
particular forms of study, whether they will prove to be
serviceable to us or not. You and I know many persons
whose intellectual training has been completely one-sided;
scholars, *e.g.* who have never given a moment's study to
the sciences of experiment and observation in any form.

With some of them, the result of this is seen in the lofty contempt with which they regard the kind of knowledge, which they themselves do not possess. With others, the result is seen in a highly exaggerated estimate of chemistry or civil engineering, and an absurd and ultra-modest depreciation of that form of mental culture to which they themselves owed so much. Both states of mind are mischievous. And they may be guarded against by taking care that our school-course gives at least the elements of several different kinds of knowledge to *every* learner. There comes a time no doubt, when it is quite clear that we should specialize; but this time does not arrive early; and until it arrives, it is important that we should secure for every scholar, a due and harmonious exercise, of the language faculty, of the logical faculty, of the inductive faculty; as well as of the powers of acquisition, and of memory. Let arrangements be made by all means for dropping certain studies, when experience shall have made it clear that they would be unfruitful. Let German be the substitute for Greek, or higher proficiency in physics be aimed at as an alternative to the closer perception of classic niceties. But you do not want distinct courses of instruction, existing side by side, to provide for these objects. And if modern departments are to exist at all in our great schools, they can only justify their existence by fulfilling these very simple conditions:

Conditions of their success.

(1) That the student of language shall not neglect science, nor the student of science neglect language, even after the bifurcation has begun.

(2) That in each department, the same general curriculum including the humanities as well as science and mathematics shall be pursued; the only difference being in the proportion of time devoted to each, and

possibly in the particular language or science selected, *e.g.* German for Greek; chemistry for applied mathematics.

(3) That as far as possible, so much of the instruction as is common to the scholars in both departments—and this should be by far the larger portion—should be given to them in common, and not in separate departments or by separate teachers.

(4) That there shall be no pretext for regarding the modern course as intellectually inferior to the other; but that both courses should rank as equivalent, exact the same amount of effort; and should even from the schoolboy's point of view be equally honourable.

Now how far ought this general scheme of division into five departments, of which the first two—the real—gradually yield the chief importance to the other three, the formative or disciplinal, to be modified for the sake of girls' schools? Probably to a very small extent indeed. We may indeed postulate one special condition, for which we men have all good reason to be thankful, that a larger portion of a woman's life than of ours is spent in giving pleasure to others; and that to charm and beautify the home is accepted by her, as the chief—one might almost say the professional—duty which she feels to be most appropriate. Hence the greater importance in her case of some form of artistic training. The elements of instrumental music and of drawing should be taught to every girl; and these studies should be carried far enough to give her faculties for them a fair chance of revealing themselves, and to discover whether she is likely to excel. And as soon as it becomes clear in respect to either, that she has no special aptitude, and no prospect of attaining excellence, the subject should be dropped.

Nothing adds more to the charm of life, than good music, but nothing is more melancholy than to reflect upon the wasted hours spent by many a girl in the mechanical practice of music, from which neither she nor any hearer derives real enjoyment. But this admission once made, and the just claims of art and taste as part of a woman's education duly recognized, there seems no good reason for making any substantial difference between the intellectual training of one sex and that of the other. The reasons which have been urged for a co-ordinate development of faculty apply to the human, and not to any specially masculine needs.

We are bound to make a practical protest against that view of a girl's education which prevails so widely among ignorant parents. They often care more for the accomplishments by which admiration is to be gained in early years, than for those qualities by which it is to be permanently retained, and the work of life is to be done. In the long run, the usefulness and happiness of women and their power of making others happy depends more than on any thing else, on the number of high and worthy subjects in which they take an intelligent interest. Some day perhaps we may be in a position to map out the whole field of knowledge, and to say how much of it is masculine, and how much of it is feminine. At present the data for such a classification are not before us. Experience has not yet justified us in saying of any form of culture or useful knowledge that it is beyond the capacity of a woman to attain it, or that it is unsuited to her intellectual needs. Meanwhile the best course of instruction which we can devise ought to be put freely within the reach of men and women alike. We may be well content to wait and see what comes of it; for we may be sure that no harm can possibly come of it.

As to the distribution of time, it is impossible to lay down any rigid rule, applicable to schools of different characters and aims. Specimen time-tables might easily be given, but they would probably be very misleading. It may be useful, however, to keep in view some general directions for the fabrication of your own time-table :—

Distribution of time.

(1) Calculate the total number of hours per week available for instruction, and begin by determining what proportion of these hours should be devoted respectively to the several subjects.

(2) In doing this contrive to alternate the work so that no two exercises requiring much mental effort or the same kind of effort come together, *e.g.* let a lesson in translation, in history or arithmetic, be followed by one in writing or drawing; one in which the judgment or memory is most exercised by one in which another set of faculties is called into play. It is obvious that the exercises which require most thinking should generally come earliest in the day.

(3) Have regard to the character and composition of your teaching staff; and to the necessity for continuous yet well-varied and not too laborious employment for each of them; particularly for those who are specialists, or teachers of single subjects.

(4) As a rule do not let any lesson last longer than three-quarters of an hour. It is unreasonable to expect continuous and undivided attention for a longer time, and with very young children even half an hour is enough. Thus a three hours' school in the morning should be divided into four parts, and a two hours' attendance in the afternoon into three.

(5) An interval of ten minutes may fitly be provided in the middle of each school-time, for recreation in playroom or ground. So a morning will give three lessons of

three-quarters of an hour each, one of half an hour, which is quite long enough say for a dictation or a writing lesson, and a little break beside.

(6) Let the plans be so arranged as to provide movement and change of position at each pause in the work. One lesson a day may very properly be given to the scholars standing.

(7) Let one short period be reserved in every day for the criticism of the preparatory or other lessons which have been done out of school. We shall see hereafter, that some forms of home lessons admit of very effective and expeditious correction, in class.

(8) Reserve also a short period, for some purpose not comprehended in the routine of studies, say the last half hour of the week, for gathering the whole school together addressing them on some topic of general interest, or reading an extract from some interesting book.

(9) Do not so fill up your own time, if you are the principal teacher, and have assistants, as to be unable to fulfil the duty of general supervision. Provide for your own inspection and examination of the work of the several classes, at least once in every two weeks, and take care that the work of all youthful teachers, and of those who are not fully trained goes on in your sight.

(10) Punctuality should be the rule at the end as well as the beginning of a lesson, otherwise you do not keep faith with your scholars. The time table is in the nature of a contract between you and them. Do not break it. The pupils are as much entitled to their prescribed period of leisure, as you are to your prescribed time of lecturing and expounding.

I cannot tell you how much a school gains by possessing a thoroughly well considered time-table, and adhering closely to it. In the elementary school as you know, the time-table once sanctioned and approved by the Inspector, and duly displayed becomes the law of the school, and must not in any way be departed from. And I feel sure that you will gain by putting yourselves under a *régime* just as severe. For the habit of assigning a time for every duty, and punctually performing everything in its time, is of great value in the formation of character. And every good school is something more than a place for the acquirement of knowledge. It should serve as a discipline for the orderly performance of work all through life, it should set up a high standard of method and punctuality, should train to habits of organized and stedfast effort, should be "an image of the mighty world."

In separating a school into classes two conditions have to be fulfilled—that the scholars shall be near enough in ability and knowledge to work well together, to help and not hinder one another, and that there shall be a sufficient number of scholars in one class to secure real emulation and mental stimulus. A large school in which the ages range from 10 to 15, may for the former purpose have five classes. Indeed it may be roughly said that there should be as many classes as there are years in the school-life of the scholars. Otherwise, you will be mingling children in the same class, whose attainments and powers differ so widely that either some of them will be held back, or others will be urged to progress too rapidly. On the other hand, it is essential that classes should be of a certain size, and I believe that every teacher who understands his business prefers large classes to small ones. There are advantages in the fellowship and sympathy which are generated by numbers, in the self-knowledge which the presence of others gives to each, and especially in the stimulus which a dull or

Classification.

commonplace child receives from hearing the answers and witnessing the performances of the best in the class. And these advantages cannot be gained in a small class. In fact I believe it is as easy to teach 20 together as 10; and that in some respects the work is done with more zest and more brightness. So it will be seen that the two conditions we have laid down cannot both be fulfilled except in schools of a certain size. There is in fact an inevitable waste of resources and of teaching power in any school of less than 100 children; and a very serious waste in small schools of 20 or 30. In all of them you must either sacrifice the uniformity of the teaching, or you must at considerable cost, have a teacher for every group of six or seven scholars, and in such classes must sacrifice the intellectual life and spirit which numbers alone can give. For the sake of this intellectual life, I should be prepared to make some sacrifices of other considerations, and even to incur the risk in small schools, of keeping back one or two elder scholars, or pushing now and then a backward scholar, a little farther on than would otherwise be desirable. The most joyless and unsatisfactory of all schools are those in which each child is treated individually, is working few or no exercises in common with others, and comes up to be questioned or to say a lesson alone.

Entrance Examination. In examining a scholar on entrance, before the age of ten it is well to determine his position mainly by his reading and by his arithmetic. Above that age, especially in a school in which language forms the staple of the higher instruction, an elementary examination in Latin, in Arithmetic and in English will suffice to determine his position. These are the best rough tests for choosing the class in which he should be placed. If you are in doubt, it is safer and better to put him low at first rather than too high. It is always easy as well as pleasant to promote him afterwards, if you have at first under estimated his powers; and it is neither easy nor pleasant, to degrade him if you begin by making a mistake in the other direction. I do not think it desirable to have separate classification for different subjects, except for special subjects such as drawing or music in which the individual gifts and tastes, of children otherwise alike in age and standing, necessarily differ considerably. But for all the ordinary subjects of class instruction, language, history, reading, writing, and lessons on science, it is well to keep the same scholars together. A little latitude may perhaps be allowed for scholars in the same class, who have made different degrees of progress in Arithmetic, and it will not always be possible or desirable that all the scholars in a class should be working exactly the same sums. Yet even here we have to ask ourselves what we mean by progress? It does not mean hurrying on to an advanced rule; but a fuller mastery over the applications of the lower rules. I would therefore resist the very natural desire of the more intelligent scholars, who may have got on faster, and perhaps finished all the exercises in the text-book under a particular rule, to go on to a new rule before their fellows. It is much better to let them occupy their time either in recapitulation, or in doing exercises you have specially selected from a more difficult book, and in dealing with rather more complex exemplifications of the lower rules. When a new rule is taken the whole class should begin it at once; because as we shall hereafter see the oral exposition of a new rule is an essential part of class-work; and it is one in which you cannot dispense with that kind of intellectual exercise which comes from questioning, cross-questioning and mutual help. And if this be true of

Arithmetic then certainly it is true of every other subject which is usually taught in schools.

Fees.   A word or two may be properly added on the subject of fees. They will have a necessary tendency to increase, as the value of money alters, and the public estimation of good teaching rises. Already the sums mentioned on p. 48, which were recommended by the Schools' Inquiry Commission in 1867, have often proved to be insufficient for the satisfactory conduct even of schools provided with good buildings for which no interest has to be paid. Much will depend on the size of the schools—for the cost per head is reduced when numbers are large,— and much also upon the character of the place and its surroundings, and upon the value, if any, of the endowment the school possesses. But whatever the fees prescribed, they should be inclusive of all the school charges, and of all the subjects taught in it. There is no harm in graduating fees by age; or in imposing a heavier charge on those who come into the school late. But there should be no graduation by subjects,—no extras; except perhaps for instrumental music, or other special subject requiring quasi-private instruction. Nothing is more fatal to the right classification of a school, and to its corporate unity, than the necessity of appealing to the parent at each stage of a pupil's career, to know if this or that particular subject can be afforded or sanctioned. A school is not a mart, in which separate purchases may be made for each scholar at discretion of so much French, or Latin or Mathematics; but an organized community for the purposes of common instruction; in which no other distinction should be recognized among the scholars than the fitness of each to enter a particular class, or to commence a new study. And of this fitness the principal teacher should be the sole judge. There may be in special circumstances good reasons for reducing the fee to the holders of scholarships or exhibitions; but the fee prescribed by regulation for those who have no special privilege should always be such as shall honestly avow to the parents the true market value of the education imparted, and as shall place within the reach of every scholar who is admitted, without exception, the full advantage of all the instruction which the school can furnish.

III. THE SCHOOL-ROOM AND ITS APPLIANCES.

The physi-cal con-ditions of successful teaching.

WE may fitly devote one of our meetings to the consideration of the physical conditions under which school work should be carried on; and the merely material equipments and appliances, which are needed in teaching. Such considerations are of great importance. No effective teaching is possible when children are in a state of physical discomfort. We cannot afford to despise one of the artifices which science and experience have adopted, for making our scholars more at ease, and putting them into a more receptive attitude for instruction. What then are the most favourable external conditions under which the work of a school can be carried on?

Space.

There is first the necessity for sufficient space. In the elementary schools it is an imperative requirement that at least eight square feet of floor area shall be provided for every child, and this in a room ten feet high means a total space of 80 cubic feet. This is the minimum; and in schools provided by the rates it has of late been the practice to require a larger space—ten superficial feet or 100 cubic feet. But a more liberal provision still is needed in good secondary schools. For you have not only to provide sitting-room at a desk for each scholar, but room for each class to stand up and means

for combining two or more classes for collective lessons.
It is obvious that the space-requirement must be mainly
determined by the nature of the organization of the
school, whether in separate class-rooms, or in one large
room. As a general rule there is no harm in providing
an isolated class-room for every class for which you are
also able to provide a responsible adult teacher who
does not need constant supervision. And many modern
schools are constructed on the theory that all the work
is to be done in class-rooms, and that all the space
needed is a sufficient number of such rooms, to seat all
the scholars. But there are occasions on which it is
desirable that all the scholars should assemble together;
for morning or evening prayer, for singing, or for collective addresses. Without a central hall large enough
to contain the whole of the scholars, the corporate life
of a school cannot be properly sustained and many
opportunities are lost of making the scholars conscious
of their relations to each other and to the general repute
and success of the school. And it is manifest that if
such a central hall is used for these public purposes
alone, and not for teaching, much space is wasted, and
the estimate of area already given must be multiplied
by two. In some modern schools the various class-
rooms are arranged in the four sides of a quadrangle
which is covered in, and which serves the double purpose
of a central hall and of a common entrance to all the
rooms. In this way you economize space and dispense
altogether with the necessity for a corridor. Moreover
such an arrangement renders the assembling of all the
scholars from their separate rooms, and the dismissal of
all to their work after the roll-call or the prayers of
the morning, a simpler and easier process. On the
whole, experience shews that in a well-planned, lofty

room, two or three or even more different classes may work apart without any disadvantage; and this arrangement is a very convenient one for securing due supervision over younger teachers, and especially for the occasional junction of two or three classes for some lecture or special exercise which may be given collectively. Of course, if you are in circumstances which make you indifferent to cost, it is a good thing to have class-room accommodation enough for the whole school; and a central hall for no other than quasi-public gatherings. Even then some of the adjacent class-rooms should be so divided by moveable partitions that two of them may be readily thrown into one when occasion requires. But when circumstances render it important to economize space or money, one large room which will hold the entire school for collective purposes, and class-rooms enough to hold half the scholars, will suffice. This arrangement presupposes that, for ordinary class work, one half of the classes will meet and receive their lessons side by side in the principal room. Thus, taking 100 as the unit, there should be one room of 45 ft. by 20, in which all can sit, but in which half are habitually taught; and two class-rooms, about 15 by 17, each sufficiently large to provide accommodation for 25 scholars. Class-rooms should be adjacent and should have glass doors, not necessarily for easier supervision, though that is important, but for increase of light.

Light.   As to light, we have to remember that all glare should be avoided, and that therefore southern windows are not the best. It is well to have one southern window for cheerfulness, but the main light should be the steadier and cooler light from the north. I need hardly say that though sunshine may easily be in excess in a school-room, you cannot have too much of it in a play-ground.

The best light for working purposes is from the roof; but sky-lights are often hard to open, and in snowy weather are apt to become obscured. They should not therefore be the only windows. You secure a better diffusion of light throughout a room and avoid shadows by having all windows high up, the lowest part being 6 or 7 ft. from the ground. But this is not, owing to the structure of rooms, always possible. When windows are low side light is preferable both to that from behind, which causes the pupil to sit in his own shadow, and to that from the front, which is apt to distress his eyes. And of side lights that from the left hand is always the best; otherwise the pupil's writing is done at a disadvantage and in the shadow of his own pen.

In planning desks, you have to consider several *Desks.* requirements: (1) They should be comfortable, with a height of 2 ft. for little children, and 2 ft. 6 in. to 3 ft. for older scholars; the seat in both cases being about as high from the ground as the length of the leg from the knee to the foot. There should be a back rail not more than 10 inches high, and for very young children about 7 inches high, to give support just at that portion of the back where it is most needed. Most backs to seats and pews are too high. (2) They should be easy of access; for in writing lessons, half the work of the teacher consists in going round the class pointing out the errors, correcting and pencilling them; and this is impossible, if the desks are long or too crowded. At least 1 ft. 8 in. should be allowed for each child. In some of the American schools access is facilitated by giving to each scholar a separate desk and seat, the latter revolving on a pivot and having its own back like a chair. But this is a very expensive arrangement. In the schools of the School Board for London, the desks are called 'dual.' Each of these measures about 3 ft. 4 in. long and accommodates two children. They are constructed with a hinge, so that the front half can be lifted up when standing exercises are given. (3) The seats of scholars should be compactly arranged; so that for teaching the whole class may be brought well into one focus, and not spread over too wide an area for thorough supervision and economy of voice. This requirement appears to conflict in some measure with the first-named conditions. Yet it seems so important that, for the sake of it, I should be inclined to sacrifice some other advantages. The desks should be so arranged that the angle of vision for the teacher does not exceed $45°$. It is a mistake to have more than five desks deep. If there are six the scholars behind are too far off for effective oversight or perfect hearing. (4) Desks should be very slightly sloped, nearly flat and about 1 foot wide; it will suffice if the seats have a width of 8 inches[1]. There should be a shelf-space underneath for books or slates, and when each scholar has a fixed place allotted to him this space may be kept for all his own books and belongings. But except for a very limited number of the eldest and most trustworthy scholars in a High school, it is not well to have lockers; all pigeon-holes and covered spaces which are appropriated to the use of individual scholars should be open or easily openable; there should be no secrets or private hoards, and the occasional and frequent inspection of them is itself a useful discipline in neatness. (5) I would have you distrust all contrivances by which desks like Goldsmith's "bed by

---

[1] For fuller details on this subject, and indeed on most of the topics treated in this chapter, the reader will do well to consult an excellent work, Robson's *School Architecture*, and also an American work by Barnard on the same subject.

night and chest of drawers by day" undertake to serve two purposes, e.g. to turn over and furnish a back suited for older people in a lecture-room, or to be fixed horizontally two together to make a tea-table. All such devices are unsatisfactory and involve a sacrifice of complete fitness for school purposes. The desks should be so arranged that the teacher from his desk should command the whole group. There are two ways of effecting this. If his own desk is on the floor, the fourth and fifth rows of desks at the back should be raised by two steps, so that each shall be higher than that in front. If, on the other hand, all the scholars' desks are on the same level floor, he himself should have his desk on a mounted estrade or platform. (6) We have to remember also that all the work of a scholar has not to be done at a desk. For the due maintenance of life and animation in teaching, it is well, as I have already said, to give some of the lessons to scholars in a standing position. The change of attitude is a relief, and is conducive to mental activity. Do not therefore have so large a portion of your school or class-room encumbered with desks as to make this arrangement impossible. Always have space enough reserved to enable you to draw out the class into the form of a standing semi-circle.

The questions of warmth and of ventilation should always be considered together. They are rather complex, owing to the very different form of buildings, the aspect of the rooms, and the relative position of near and surrounding objects. Teachers have few opportunities of being consulted by architects about the requirements on which they wish to insist, but it is well to have a few principles in view, ready for such an opportunity when it occurs. We have to remember that each of us breathes

Ventilation.

about 16 times a minute or 960 times an hour, and that every time we do this the air in any confined room is partly vitiated. The indispensable thing is that every room should have some means of admitting fresh and emitting foul air. There are several ways of attaining this. When rooms open out into a corridor, a good place for a ventilator is over the door; when a group of gas burners is in the centre of the room, there should be a ventilating shaft above it to carry off the products of combustion. In some cases a ventilating opening in the wall of the chimney above the fireplace is useful. And for the admission of fresh air, a Tobin ventilating shaft in the corner of the room, communicating below with the outer air and open about 7 feet above the floor, so as to introduce a current of air where no draft will be felt by the head, is often an effective experiment. But all windows should be made to open, both at the top and bottom; and in any interval which occurs in the work of the class, they should be opened. A very slight opening both at the top and the bottom of a window at the same time is often found to be effectual as a ventilator; for you have here what the engineers call an upward and a downward shaft, the colder air coming in at the bottom, and passing upwards so as to expel the bad air at the upper opening. And if owing to the defective supply of means for attaining this purpose, you have any reason to suppose that the air is likely to become bad in a three hour's sitting of the school, it is a good plan to break up the class for ten minutes when half the morning's or afternoon's work is over, and in this short interval to throw open all the windows and introduce a fresh supply, even in the coldest weather, of pure air. The little sacrifice of time will be more than compensated.

As to warmth, we have to remember that the tempe- *Warmth.*
rature, if work, especially sedentary work, is to be carried on in comfort, should not in any school-room be lower than 60°. But it is bad policy to get warmth by vitiating the air, e.g. by gas-stoves, by stoves not provided with flues, by steam, or by large heated metal surfaces. On the whole, except for very large schools, open fires, if judicious arrangements are made to surround them with proper reflecting surfaces and also to diffuse an equable temperature through the room and to prevent waste of fuel, are best for the purposes of heat and ventilation as well as of cheerfulness. It may be added that a grey colour is better for the walls, than either a more pronounced and strong colour or simple white.

Of the teaching appliances in the room, no one is *Appara-* more important than the Black-board. We may not *tus.* perhaps go so far as the enthusiastic Charbonneau, who says 'Le tableau noir, c'est la vie de l'enseignement,' but we may safely say that no school or class-room is complete without one, that there is no single subject of instruction wherein constant recourse should not be had to it; and that it and all its proper appurtenances of chalk, sponge, and duster should always be within easy reach, that there may be no excuse for dispensing with its aid whenever it is wanted. Perhaps there is no one *crux* by which you may detect at once so clearly the difference between a skilled and an unskilled teacher, as the frequency and tact with which he uses the blackboard. In some American schools there is a blackboard all round the room, 4 or 5 ft. wide; and the black surface close to the teacher's desk extends nearly to the ceiling. This surface is more often of slate than of wood, and is sometimes of a material known as liquid slating. It is occasionally of a green colour instead of black, as offering a pleasanter surface to the eye; but diagrams and writing are apt to be less clear when any colour but black is adopted.

Furniture of a State school in Belgium.

I will give you from the official regulations of the Belgian Government the list of objects required to be provided in every State school:

A bust or portrait of the King, some religious pictures, a small shelf or case for the teacher's own books of reference, a collection of weights and measures, a set of diagrams or pictures for each of the subjects taught.

A map of Europe, a map of Belgium, a globe, a special map of the province, and a cadastral plan (ordnance map) of the commune in which the school is situated.

A small collection of objects of natural history illustrative, as far as possible, of the flora, fauna, and physical products of the district.

A clock; a thermometer; and a collection illustrative of the principal geometrical forms.

A frame or board on which to affix all programmes and special rules, as well as the permanent time-table of the class.

To this one might add that an easel on which maps or diagrams may be displayed is useful, and that all books, slates, and other objects in use in the class should be kept in an easily accessible cupboard in the room itself, not only because all these things should be at hand—otherwise there is a pretext sometimes for trying to do without them—but also because all fetching and carrying from store cupboards at a distance increase the risk of loss and destruction.

Care of furniture important as discipline in habits.

We are to remember that over and above the convenience and economy which have to be secured in regard to all school-material, there are important incidental purposes to be served by care and method in all these material arrangements. We have to teach respect for public property, care in handling things which are not our own or which have no visible owner. It is notorious that this is much disregarded in higher schools for boys, and that the aspect of the desks and school furniture in them is such as would be simply disgraceful in a school for the poor. There seems no good reason for this difference. I would therefore never permit the schoolroom to be used for play, or to be open as a common room out of school-hours when there is no supervision. Remember too that every time you enlist the services of the scholars in some little effort to render the schoolroom and its surroundings more comely and attractive, you are doing something to encourage the feeling of loyalty and pride in the school, and are doing still more to educate them into a perception of beauty, and a desire for refined and tasteful surroundings. In schools for the poor, this aim is especially important; but in schools for children of every rank, it must be borne in mind that the careful and artistic arrangement of all the school material, and of all pictures and illustrations, is a silent but very effective lesson in good taste; and will go far to make children love order and neatness. Whoever carries into his own home, a feeling of discomfort and of æsthetic rebellion against dirt, vulgarity and untidiness, has learned a lesson which is of considerable value as a foundation for an orderly life. Old Joseph Lancaster's rule, "A place for everything and everything in its place," is of universal application.

The registration of admission and of attendance in elementary schools subsidized by government grants demands a special and minute care, owing to the fact that a portion of the grant is assessed according to the attendance; some of the payments made being dependent

Registration.

on the average attendance of scholars and some on the aggregate of attendances made by the particular scholars presented for examination. Hence, for the elementary schools the strictest rules are laid down (1) for the marking of every attendance, (2) for the computation of the number of attendances registered for each child in every year and in every separate school term, (3) for the computation of averages in each class, and of the whole school: the total number of all the registered attendances being of course for this purpose divided by the number of times in which the school has been open. No erasures are ever allowed. An exact estimate is thus easily arrived at as to the degree in which the work of the school has been interrupted by irregularity of attendance, and as to the proportion of the actual attendance to the number of those whose names appear on the school registers. Nothing so elaborate is needed in the case of higher schools, partly because no grant of public money is involved, and partly because in such schools the scholars attend much more regularly. But I am sure that the importance of careful registration is insufficiently recognized in our secondary and high schools; and I think that even in the best of them it is essential that there should be a systematic record for each pupil of these particulars: (1) the date of admission and the exact age; (2) the date of promotion to a higher class or of the entry on a new study; (3) absence; (4) lateness; (5) the result of each examination; (6) any punishment, or failure of duty.

Communication to parents. You want all these particulars for your own satisfaction; and also for reference when you send to the parent of each scholar, at the end of the term, a tabulated statement shewing his precise position as to attendance, conduct, and progress. The particulars which parents have a right to expect from a well-ordered school, and which may easily be recorded and summarized at the end of the term wherever the habitual book-keeping is careful, are these :

The number of times in which the scholar has been absent from a lesson or late in attendance.

The result of any examinations which may have been held within the term.

The number of scholars in the class to which he belongs.

His standing, in order of merit, in regard to each subject of instruction.

His place in the form or class, as determined by the collective result of his work.

A general estimate of his conduct.

So long as these particulars are held in view, it matters little what form the report takes. You will of course preserve a duplicate of every such report. Each teacher will do well to adopt his own form, and to determine on his own particular mode of estimation, whether arithmetical, by the use of mere figures or marks; or more general, by the use of such symbols as Excellent, Good, Fair, Moderate, and Imperfect. The thing to be chiefly borne in mind in the choice of your system of marking is to reduce to a minimum the chance of caprice and guess-work, and not to attempt to record anything unless you have carefully preserved the data by which you can assure yourself that the record is thoroughly accurate. Some teachers, in their zeal for comprehensiveness of statement, have columns for deportment, for politeness, and for other moral qualities which are in their nature very difficult to estimate, and in respect to which hap-hazard and therefore somewhat unjust estimates are almost necessarily made. For

Tabulated reports of progress.

example I have seen in some foreign schools columns for registering 'moralité d'élèves,' 'dispositions naturelles,' and other impossible data. Here the rule is a good one: Do not pretend to measure with arithmetical exactness qualities and results which are essentially incapable of such measurement.

In the French Lycées, the system of registration is often very elaborate. There is (1) Registre d'inscription, (2) Registre d'appel or attendance, (3) Registre des Compositions, and (4) Registre des bons points, in which marks are recorded for conduct, and for the results of every class or other examination. The whole of these marks are added up and tabulated at the end of every month, a copy being kept by the pupil, and one sent to his parents or guardians.

School diaries. One of the requirements in the public elementary schools, which at first appeared to many of the teachers to be a needless addition to the routine and burden of their lives, is the keeping of what is called a Log-book or School Diary. It is a thick volume, such as will last for a good many years, and is generally fastened with a Bramah lock. The Code requires that entries shall be made in this book at least once a week, and that thus a record shall be kept of the Inspector's report, of changes in the staff, of visits of managers, and other facts concerning the school and its teachers. It is not permitted to enter reflections or opinions of a general character. Now the practice thus enforced by authority, has come to be generally approved and liked on its own merits, and has been found of considerable value. Many little circumstances in the history of a school which appear of no importance at the moment, require to be recalled afterwards, and are seen to have unexpected value when referred to. The date of the entry of a new teacher on his duty, the introduction of any new school-book, or plan, or piece of apparatus; the starting of a new series of lessons; the result of a periodical examination; special occurrences in relation to the discipline of the school; promotion of scholars from one class to another; any unusual circumstance which affects the attendance; the visit of a stranger or a governor—all these are matters which are easy to jot down at the time of their occurrence; and which serve to make up the history of the school, and to give continuity and interest to its life. The adoption of the plan may be strongly recommended in schools of all grades.

It may be well also to remember that, especially in schools of any size in which the number of books and the quantity of school material given out is large, there should always be a Stock-book, in which a ledger is kept, shewing how and when books and stationery are given out, and to whom. The office of keeping the needful record is a very simple one, which may well devolve on an assistant, or even on an elder scholar; and it will be found that the practice conduces to economy and order; and enables you to know exactly in what direction to look, if you have reason to suspect negligence or waste. *School book-keeping.*

I spoke in the first lecture of the importance of the habit of preparing the notes of many and indeed most of the lessons you give. To this I may now add that such notes should not be on fugitive scraps, but should always be made in a book and carefully preserved. Unless a teacher does this habitually he squanders much time and effort, and has the weary task of preparing many of his lessons over again. Suppose you keep a brief record of the plan and order of each lesson, of the books or authorities you consulted in getting it up; suppose you *Teachers' note-books.*

add a little note after giving it, stating whether it proved too long or too short, too easy or too difficult; and indicating for your own private information how it might be more effectively given next time: and lastly suppose you leave a blank space at the end of each, and enter in it from time to time, as new information comes in your way, other facts or references which will be helpful whenever you go over the same ground again; you will find the practice easy and well calculated to economize time and power. It will bring all your wider reading and added experience to bear on the enrichment of your professional resources; it will aid you in gathering up the fragments of life's teaching "that nothing be lost."

Scholars' note-books. In the higher classes, and for all lessons which take the form of lectures, it is a good practice to let the scholars have note-books, to take down at the moment any details which are likely to escape the memory. But such note-taking is of no value whatever, unless the notes are used afterwards as helps to the writing out of an amplified and careful summary of the contents of the lesson. Mere note-taking is often one of the most delusive and unfruitful of practices. Consider for a moment, what is the purpose which the taking of notes ought to serve. I have seen students in reading Froude's history, or Mill's Logic, sit down with the book on one side of them and a large note or common-place book on the other into which they have laboriously made copious extracts. There seems to be a good deal to shew for this effort; but the result often is that the author's thoughts have merely been transferred out of one book into another; and the proportion of these thoughts which have actually found a lodgment in the student's intelligence is very small indeed. There has been a mechanical process of appropriation, not a rational one[1].

Note-taking generally. The true way to make notes of a book when you read it is—if it is your own—to mark in the margin the passages which you feel to be of most value, and to make at the end a little index of references, which will differ from the printed index, in being specially suited to you, and calculated to help you in consulting the book hereafter. But except for these purposes, I would not read with a pencil in hand, or copy out extracts. It is far better to read through an entire chapter or section, while the whole faculty is bent on following the reasoning or understanding the facts. Then when you have closed the book, and while your memory is fresh, sit down, and reproduce in your own words as much of the contents of the chapter as you please. By this means you will have been forced to turn the subject over in your own mind, to ruminate a little, and so to make it your own. But unless this process of rumination goes on, there is no security that any of the knowledge you are trying to acquire is actually assimilated. And the same rule applies to the use of note-books during lectures. Many students make a great effort to seize rapidly whole sentences and to set them down at the time; but while they are writing one down, another follows which gravely modifies the first, and this escapes them. Thus they get a few disjointed fragments, torn from their proper connexion, and they fail to gain any true

---

[1] "Men seldom read again what they have committed to paper, nor remember what they have so committed one iota the better for their additional trouble. On the contrary, I believe it has a direct tendency to destroy the promptitude and tenuity of memory by diminishing the vigour of present attention and seducing the mind to depend on future reference."—SYDNEY SMITH.

intellectual advantage from the whole. I am aware that the judicious use of a note-book depends a good deal on the special character of the teaching; and that a good many lecturers in the Universities and elsewhere expressly adapt their prelections to the case of students who take notes. I have heard very able lectures which took the form of measured, brief but very pregnant sentences, in which the lecturer had been at the pains to concentrate as much thought as possible; these sentences being slowly uttered, with a sufficient pause at the end of each, to allow quick writers to take down the whole *verbatim*. Undoubtedly the note-book result in such cases seems to have considerable value. But it may well be doubted whether the most effective teaching ever takes the form of a dictation lesson; still more may it be doubted whether when this method is adopted enough is done to make the students thinkers as well as receivers, on the subject which they learn. Whenever the object of the lecture is to expound principles, to illustrate them in an ample and varied way, and to shew the learner rather the processes by which the results are arrived at, than the formulated results and conclusions themselves; you fail to derive any real advantage from very copious note-taking. It is distracting, not helpful. You get a few detached sentences perhaps, which in an unqualified way and out of their true perspective, are no fair representation of the lecturer's meaning: the continuity of his argument is broken, while you are picking out these fragments; and you fail wholly to get the particular kind of stimulus and help which the lecturer wants to give. If, on the other hand, you will listen attentively, seek to follow the reasoning, and to possess yourself not only of the aphorisms and conclusions, but of the processes by which they have been arrived at; and perhaps now and then jot down a characteristic phrase, a heading or some hint as to the order of the thought; and then, on getting home revolve the whole matter in your mind, and write down in your own words an orderly summary of your recollections, there will be a genuine acquisition. You will be sure that some at least of what you have tried to learn has been actually assimilated. And I would counsel the adoption of the same rule in permitting your scholars the practice of note-taking. Teach them how to use note-books. Do not let them suppose that the reproduction of your phrases is of any use. Do not mistake means for ends. It is a chemical not a mechanical combination you want. It is the writing out of memoranda *after* the lecture which serves this purpose and is of real intellectual value; not the notes taken during the lecture itself. And of these notes you have no assurance that they have served any good purpose unless they are ultimately translated out of your phraseology into the student's own language.

On the larger subject of School-books and Manuals *Text-books.* much might be said. But it would obviously be beside the main purpose of these lectures if I were to take upon myself to recommend particular books; and so possibly to do injustice to the authors and publishers of many excellent books which I have never seen. The truth is that goodness and fitness in a school-book are not absolute but relative terms. They depend entirely on the person who uses it. That book is the best for each teacher which he feels he can use best, and which suits best his own method and ideal of work. Even if the best conceivable criticism could be brought to bear on all the innumerable manuals now in use, and they could be arranged in the order of abstract merit, such criticism might not help you much. There would

F. L.

still remain for each of you the responsibility of making your own choice. Indeed some of the best and most vigorous teaching I have ever heard has been given by teachers who were consciously using a very bad book, and who were goaded by it into remonstrance and criticism, which were in themselves very instructive and stimulating to the learner. I remember well my own teacher of mathematics, Professor De Morgan, and his animated polemic against Dilworth and Walkinghame, and especially poor Robert Simson's edition of Euclid. His anger, his pitiless sarcasm, as he denounced the dulness of these writers and exposed the crudeness of their mathematical conceptions, were in themselves well calculated to sharpen the perceptions of his students. The bad book in the hands of a skilful teacher proved to be better than the best book in the hands of an ordinary practitioner. I am not, however, prepared to recommend the use of bad books as a general expedient. But it cannot be too clearly understood that the right choice of a book depends entirely on the use you mean to make of it.

If you are, as every teacher ought to be, fluent and skilful in oral exposition, you will need very little of the sort of explanation which school-books contain; your chief want will be supplied by books of well-graduated exercises, by which your oral teaching may be supplemented, fixed, thrust home, and brought to a point. But if, on the other hand, you want explanations, rules, and a knowledge of principles, mere books of exercises will not suffice. You need the treatises more or less full,—say of grammar, of arithmetic, of geography —and I will not promise that when you have got the best of them, your pupils will be able to make progress with their help alone. The best explanations in school-books are concise, and therefore generally inadequate. They need expansion and much comment. The Educational Reading Room at South Kensington is a great resource. In it you will always find very easy of access all the newest and best school-books; which you can sit down and examine, and from which it is not difficult to determine what form of manual will suit your purpose best.

Some of the tests by which the goodness of a school-book may be determined are not however difficult to lay down. Take a Reading-book for example. You have here to secure:—that it is well-printed and attractive, that it is not silly and too childish, that the passages selected are not too short and scrappy, but continuous enough to be of some value in sustaining thought, and that every lesson contains a few—a very few—new words which are distinct additions to the reader's vocabulary. Above all it concerns you to be much more anxious about the style than about the amount of information which is packed into the book. So also of a book of History or Science, I should not choose that which comprised in it the greatest mass of facts, but that which was best written and most likely to encourage the student to desire a larger and fuller book. As to French, Latin and English Grammars, to books on Arithmetic and Geography, it concerns us much more to secure a good logical arrangement of rules; proper distinction of type between important and unimportant facts, between typical rules and exceptional rules; with good searching and well-arranged exercises, than anything else. One good test of a Grammar or delectus or of a manual of any kind is this: Does it, as soon as it has helped the student to *know* something, instantly set him to *do* something which requires him to use that knowledge, and to shew that he

Some tests of a good school-book.

has really acquired it? E.g. If it explains a new term, does it require the learner soon to use that term? If it states a rule, does it give him instantly occasion to put the rule in practice? If it points out a new logical or grammatical distinction, does it challenge him forthwith to find new instances and illustrations of that distinction? These seem to me to be the chief purposes which a book can serve—to supplement oral teaching, not to furnish an excuse for dispensing with it. I suppose the task of making compendiums, and trying to reduce the essence of a good many books into a cheap school manual is a depressing one. At all events school-books must, I fear, as a rule be placed in the category—let us say—of uninspired writings. Their authors often evince a great want of imagination and a curious incapacity to discriminate between the significant and insignificant, between the little and the great. That is precisely the deficiency which a good teacher has to supply, and it can only be supplied by vigorous oral teaching.

Libraries. The usefulness and need of School Libraries depend very much on the character of the school. In every Boarding School they are indispensable; as children have leisure to be filled and tastes to be formed, and a life to live which is not wholly that of the school. But even in Day Schools, there is great need for such adjuncts to the materials for instruction, and this need is becoming more and more recognised. Until a good library is attached as a matter of course to every one of our elementary schools, a great opportunity of refining the taste and enlarging the knowledge of the young will continue to be wasted, and the full usefulness of those institutions will remain unattained. After all, it is the main business of a primary school, and indeed a chief part of the business of every school, to awaken a love of reading, and to give children pleasant associations with the thought of books. When once a strong appetite for reading has been excited the mere money difficulty of providing the library in a school for the poor is already half overcome. For subscriptions from children and their parents, gifts from kindly friends, are obtainable without much difficulty, whenever a teacher makes up his mind that the object is worth attaining, and casts about in earnest for the means of attaining it.

Now granting that you have to form a school library, or that your advice is asked by those who desire to purchase or give one, what sort of books will you select? That is a question worth thinking about. In the first place, you will get books of reference, good manuals, such as you need for amplifying a school lesson. You constantly have to say in teaching: 'There is a fuller account of this incident in such a book.' 'There are some anecdotes about this animal, or a poem descriptive of this place, by such a writer.' Or 'I should like you to read up the life of this eminent man before we have our next lesson.' And for purposes like these it is of great importance to have the best books of reference —books fuller and larger than mere school-books— within reach. This remark applies to all schools alike. But besides this, it adds to the value of a child's school-life, if something can be done by it to direct his reading and to teach him how to fill his leisure profitably. In a secondary day-school, to which pupils come from orderly and intelligent homes, this particular purpose is of less importance than elsewhere, because it may be presumed that educated parents will look after the leisure reading of their children. It is in schools for the poor, and in all boarding-schools, that a general library is most needed.

How to choose them.

Not always children's books.

Yet, in making the selection I would not, in the first place, fill the library with *children's* books, though of course there should be a good many of them. Children often rebel, and with good cause, against books written purposely for them as a class. Such books are often too obviously written down to the level of a child's understanding. The childishness and simplicity which are affected by many persons who write children's books have a falsetto ring about them which an intelligent child soon detects. He is no more content to confine his reading to books written specially for him as a child than you or I would be to read such books as are considered specially appropriate to persons of our age and profession. We want, and a child wants, to read some books, not specially meant for *us* or the class to which we belong, but which are good and interesting in themselves, and were meant for the whole world.

Nor "good books."

Nor is it well to confine your selection to what are technically called good books. I mean to books which are consciously instructive and moral. You do not want to be always reading such books yourselves. You know, even those of you who are most earnest in efforts after self-improvement, that you do not regulate *all* your reading with the distinct intention of getting instruction and improving your mind. Assume this to be true of a child. Remember, if he is ever to love reading, he must have room left to him to exercise a little choice. Think how rich the world is, how much there is to be known about it, its structure, its products, its relation to other worlds, its people, the great things that have been done in it, the great speculations that have been indulged in it, the very varied forms in which happiness has been enjoyed in it. And do not forget that, beyond the region of mere information about these things, there is the whole domain

of wonderland, of fancy, of romance, of poetry, of dreams
and fairy tales. Do not let us "think scorn of that pleasant
land," or suppose that all the fruit in the garden of the
Lord grows on the tree of knowledge. Wonder, curiosity,
the sense of the infinite, the love of what is vast and
remote, of the strange and the picturesque—all these
things it is true are not knowledge in the school sense
of the word. But they are capable in due time of being
transformed into knowledge,—nay, into something better
than knowledge—into wisdom and insight and power.

So let us abstain from any attempt to direct a child's *Large
tolerance
should be
shewn for
different
mental
appetites.*
general reading in accordance with our own special tastes.
Let us remember that all children have not the same
intellectual appetites, and that the world would be a very
uninteresting world if they had. We need not be disappointed if even our favourite pupils shew reluctance to
read the books which we specially recommend, and to
admire what we admire. Of course, we have first to take
care that all lessons are diligently finished, and that all
due use is made of the library for legitimate school purposes. But when this is done, and you come to consider
the kind of service which a library should render to a
child in his hours of leisure, and for his own enjoyment,
I think the true rule of action is first to make your library
as full and varied as you can, then to exclude from it
resolutely all books which you yourself are sorry you ever
read, or would be ashamed to be seen reading—all books
which for any reason you believe to be harmful; and
when you have done this, Turn the scholar loose into the
library and let him read what and how he likes. Have
faith in the instincts of a child, and in the law of natural
selection. Believe that for him, as for yourself, it is true,
that any book which is really enjoyed, which enlarges the
range of the thoughts, which fills the mind with sweet

fancies or glowing pictures, which makes the reader feel happier and richer, is worth reading, even though it serves no visible purpose as part of school education.

School museums. The uses to which School Museums may be put are manifold, but are not all obvious at first sight. It is manifest that if Botany is taught, a collection of the wild flowers of the district, properly pressed and classified, will be a useful resource. But even if this subject is not systematically taught, such a collection, with carefully prepared specimens of the leaf, the flower, the fruit, of the trees, ferns and grasses, and cereals of the district, when properly named, will have scarcely less interest and value. Specimens of the insects to be found in the district, of the stones and shells from the sea-shore, of the material employed in some local manufacture, and of its condition in its successive stages; illustrations of the geological formation of the district; a clay or plaster model shewing the conformation of the neighbouring hills and valleys; drawings or specimens illustrating the antiquities and historical associations of near places, will all have their place in such a collection. When once a suitable receptacle has been provided for such things, and arrangements have been made, by the appointment of curators or otherwise, for keeping it in seemly condition, it is surprising to observe what pride the scholars often feel in it, how it serves to keep their eyes open to find new and suitable objects, and how glad they are to contribute to it. A museum of this kind cannot be purchased or set up all at once, it must grow, and be the product of willing workers and observers. Its purpose need not be wholly scientific or even instructive. It may with advantage be made the depository for any little work of invention or art which the scholars can themselves produce. One may contribute a drawing, another a piece of needlework unusually well finished, another an effort at design, a model of a neighbouring church or castle, or a set of illustrations of some form of manufacture in which his father is engaged. Every scholar may be encouraged to leave behind him before quitting school some little memorial of himself, his doings, or his special tastes. A mere general museum of odds and ends which anybody chooses to present to the school, and with which the scholars have no associations, is of little worth. However small your collection, it should be characteristic of the school and of its special studies, its history and its surroundings. And if it fulfils this condition, it will not only be found a useful adjunct to your scientific teaching, but also a means of encouraging the development of any special gift the scholars may possess, and of increasing their loyalty to the school.

We shall, in connexion with each of the subjects of instruction hereafter discussed, refer to the particular form of apparatus or material aid which lends itself best to the furtherance of the teacher's objects. But one general observation may be made here. New and ingenious forms of mechanical aid for teaching are being devised every day, and publishers and instrument-makers are interested in multiplying them. It may occur to some of us that the material equipments of a good school are thus becoming more complex, and threatening to be very costly. It may partly console us to remember that the elaborate illustrations which cost most money are not necessarily the most effective. A good copy set by a writing-master is often more useful than an engraved copy. A rough black-board drawing of the particular river or county which you are describing impresses and interests scholars more than a painted map. A rude model in sand or clay, made up in sight of the scholars,

Costly illustrations not always the best.

will illustrate the set of a glacier or the formation of a lake better than any purchased model. To count the panes of glass in a window, or the pictures on the wall, is not less instructive, and much more interesting than to count the balls on an abacus or frame. In short, illustrations made *pro hâc vice*, and visibly contrived by the teacher's own ingenuity for the elucidation of the particular truth he wants to teach, are often found to serve their purpose much more effectually than the manufactured illustrations which you buy at shops.

It is, after all, but a few detached suggestions as to the material surroundings of a teacher, and as to school equipment generally, that we have thus been able to offer you. But the general impression which it has been sought to convey is that no amount of care and inventiveness and forethought which you are able to devote to these little things will be wasted, and that whatever tends to make the school-room brighter, healthier, comelier, more orderly, tends to economize time and temper, and to diminish the friction inseparable from a laborious school life. Above all, you cannot, by putting yourself into the hands of publishers, instrument-makers, or even of lecturers on teaching, escape from the responsibility of looking at each of these problems with fresh eyes; and of determining how far the helps and contrivances which other people have used are available for your own special aims and special needs, and in what way they may be best adapted to them.

IV. DISCIPLINE.

I HAVE thought it right to dedicate one of these lectures to the consideration of a teacher's character rather as a ruler and administrator than as an instructor. For it need not be said that he who can teach but cannot govern works at an enormous disadvantage. Perfect discipline in a class or a school is an indispensable condition of successful teaching. It is necessary for the pupils, not only because by it they will learn in a given time twice as much and twice as easily; but because one of the things they come to school to acquire over and above certain arts and accomplishments which are generally termed education, is the practice of obedience. The habit of subjugating one's own impulses, of constantly recognizing the supremacy of law, and bringing our actions into harmony with it, is one of the first conditions of an orderly and well-disciplined life. He who does not at least acquire that at school, has been under instruction to little purpose, whatever progress he may have made in technical learning. And it is of no less consequence to the teacher. His own health, his temper, and his happiness suffer grievously if he cannot command perfect obedience. One may secure it by personal influence and another by force, and it will be easy for us to see which is the better method

The teacher as an administrator and ruler.

of the two. But by some means or other it must be had: it is better to gain it by force than not at all. For without it the school is a place of torment to all concerned, and must always remain inefficient for every purpose which it professes to serve.

Obedience not to be had by demanding it.

It may clear the ground a little if I say how obedience is not to be gained. You cannot get it by demanding or claiming it; by declaring that you will have it; or even by explaining to your scholars how useful and indispensable it is. Obedience is a habit, and must be learned like other habits, rather by practice than by theory; by being orderly, not by talking about order. There are some things on which it is well to draw out the intelligence and sympathies of a child, and to make him understand the full reason and motive of what you do. But on this point, I would not, except on rare and special occasions, enter into any discussions, or offer any explanations. All entreaty—'Now *do* give me your attention;'—all self-assertion—'I *will* have order;'—all threats—'If you don't attend to me, I will punish you;' are in themselves signs of weakness. They beget and propagate disobedience; they never really correct it. All noise and shouting aggravate the evil, and utterly fail to produce more than a temporary lull at best.

"He who in quest of silence 'silence' hoots,
Is apt to make the hubbub he imputes."

All talk about discipline in a school is in fact mischievous. To say 'I ought to be obeyed' is to assume that a child's knowledge is to be the measure of his obedience, to invite him to discuss the grounds of your authority, perhaps to dispute it. A nation, we know, is in an abnormal state while its members are debating the rights of man or the fundamental principles of government. There should be underlying all movement and political activity, a settled respect for law and a feeling that law once made must be obeyed. So no family life of a right kind is possible, if the members ever treat the authority of the parent as an open question. The duty of obeying is not so much a thing to be learned *per se*. It must be learned before the learning of anything else becomes possible. It is like food or air in relation to our bodily lives; not a thing to be sought for and possessed for itself, but an antecedent condition, without which all other possessions become impossible. So it is not well in laying down a school rule to say anything about the penalty which will fall upon those who transgress it. Shew that you do not expect transgression; and then, if it comes, treat it—as far as you can with perfect candour and honesty do so—as something which surprises and disappoints you; and for which you must apply some remedy rather for the scholar's sake than your own.

Now the first way to secure obedience to commands is to make every rule and regulation you lay down the subject of careful previous thought. Determine on the best course and be sure you are right. Then you will gain confidence in yourself, and without such confidence authority is impossible. Be sure that if you have any secret misgiving as to the wisdom of the order you give or as to your own power ultimately to enforce it, that misgiving will reveal itself in some subtle way, and your order will not be obeyed. An unpremeditated or an indefinite command—one the full significance of which you yourself have not understood—often proves to be a mistake, and has to be retracted. And every time you retract an order your authority is weakened. Never give a command unless you are sure you can enforce it, nor unless you mean to see that it is obeyed. You must

Commands to be well considered before they are given.

not shrink from any trouble which may be necessary to carry out a regulation you have once laid down. It may involve more trouble than you were prepared for; but that trouble you are bound to take, in your scholar's interest and in your own. We must not evade the consequences of our own orders, even when we did not foresee or even desire all of them. The law once laid down should be regarded as a sacred thing, binding the lawgiver as much as the subject. Every breach of it on the scholar's part, and all wavering or evasion in the enforcement of it on your own, puts a premium on future disobedience and goes far to weaken in the whole of your pupils a sense of the sacredness of law.

And when rules and orders descend to details, your supervision should be so perfect, that you will certainly know whether in all these details the orders have been obeyed or not. Unless you can make arrangements for detecting a breach of law with certainty, do not lay down a law at all. It may be replied to this, that an attitude of habitual suspicion is not favourable to the cultivation of self-respect in a scholar; and that you want often to trust him, and shew you rely on his honour. True. The development of the conscience and of the sentiment of honour is one of your highest duties; but in cases where you can safely appeal to the sense of honour, it is not a command which is wanted, but a wish, a principle, a request. You explain that a certain course of action is right or desirable or honourable in itself; and you say to your scholar, 'Now I think you see what I mean; I shall trust you to do it.' That is, you part in some degree with your own prerogative as a governor, and invite him to take a share in his own government. But you do not put your wishes into the form of a command in this case. Commands are for those in whom the capacity for self-command is imperfectly developed; and in their case vigilance does not imply suspicion: it is for them absolutely needful to know that when you say a thing has to be done, you mean for certain to know whether it is done or not. Involuntary and mechanical obedience has to be learned first; the habit of conscious, voluntary rational obedience will come by slow degrees.

And let us not forget that admirable rule so often quoted from Jean Paul Richter, "Pas trop gouverner;" we should not over-govern, we should never multiply commands, nor needlessly repeat one. Our governing force should be regarded by us as a bank reserve, on which we should be afraid to draw too often, because it may become exhausted. Every good ruler economizes power, and never puts it all forth at once. Children should feel, when they see us exercising authority, that there is a great reserve of unused strength and resolution behind, which they can neither see nor measure. It is not the visible exercise of power which impresses children most, but the unseen, which affects their imagination, and to which they can assign no limit. And this is most fully felt when the manner of putting forth strength is habitually calm and quiet, when you abstain from giving commands in regard to things which are indifferent, and when such commands as you give are few and short. "Even a grown man," says Richter, "whom some one should follow all day long with moveable pulpit and stool of confession, from which to hurl sermons and anathemas, could never attain any real activity and moral freedom. How much less then a weak child, who at every step in life must be entangled with a 'stop,' 'run,' 'be quiet,' 'do this, do that'? Your watch stops while you wind it up, and you everlastingly

Over-government to be avoided.

wind up children and never let them go." We have not to think of a scholar merely as material put into our hands to mould and manipulate, but rather as a responsible human being, whom we are so to help, that as soon as possible he may regulate his own life, and be a law unto himself. Keep clearly in view your own responsibilities, but the less display you make of your disciplinary apparatus, and the more freedom you can leave to the pupil, the better. Reduce as far as possible the number of formal rules; and remember that the perfection of government is to effect the maximum result with the minimum of visible machinery.

Drill and mechanical discipline. And yet you will gain much in a school by cultivating the habit of order and exact obedience about little things. There are right and beautiful ways and there are clumsy and confused ways—of sitting down at a desk, of moving from one place to another, of handling and opening books, of cleaning slates, of giving out pens and paper, of entering and leaving school. Petty as each of these acts is separately, they are important collectively, and the best teachers habitually reduce all these movements to drill, and require them to be done simultaneously, and with finished and mechanical exactness. Much of this drill is conducted in some good schools by signs only, not merely because it is easy so to economize noise and voice-power, but also because it makes the habit of mechanical obedience easier. And children once accustomed to such a *régime* always like it—nay even delight in it. I have seen many schools, both small and large, in which all the little movements from class to class were conducted with military precision; in which even so little a thing as the passing of books from hand to hand, the gathering up of pens, or the taking of places at the dinner table, of hats or bonnets from their numbered places in the hall was done with a rhythmical beauty, sometimes to musical accompaniment, which not only added to the picturesqueness of the school life, and to the enjoyment of the scholars, but also contributed much to their moral training and to their sense of the beauty of obedience. And I have no doubt that it is a wise thing for a teacher to devise a short code of rules for the exact and simultaneous performance of all the minor acts and movements of school life, and to drill his scholars into habitual attention to them.

Does it seem to some of you that there is a little inconsistency between the last two counsels I have ventured to give you—the one, that you should not waste power by a needless multiplication of rules, the other, that you should turn the little ones into machines, even in regard to such matters as sitting and standing at a desk, or opening a book? There is indeed, if you will look at it, no inconsistency between these two views of your duty. There is a sphere of our life in which it is desirable to cultivate independence and freedom; and there is another in which it is essential that we should learn to part with that independence for the sake of attaining some end which is desirable for others as well as for ourselves. In the development of individual character and intelligence, the more room we can leave for spontaneous action the better; but when we are members of a community, the healthy corporate life of that community requires of us an abnegation of self. The soldier in an army must *quâ* that army forego his personal volition, and become part of a great machine, which is working towards some greater end than could possibly be achieved, if he retained complete autonomy. And every one among us is called, as citizen, as member of a council or municipality, or public company, to work with others

Limits to its usefulness.

towards ends which require unity of action, and which are incompatible with the assertion of our individual rights. It is then for this class of duties that school should in some measure prepare every child. He is in an artificial community which has a life and needs of its own, and in so far as he contributes to make up this school life, he may be well content to suppress himself and to become a machine. There are times in life for asserting our individuality, and there are times for effacing it. And a good school should provide means whereby it may be seen when and how we may do both.

The corporate life of a school. This sense of corporate life and responsibility so essential to the making of a good citizen may be further cultivated by providing, as far as possible, that the school shall have something in it for the scholar to be proud of; some function or ritual in which he shall be specially interested, and in which he can sustain an honourable part. I do not like a needless multiplication of unmeaning offices in a school, but every little function, such as that of curator of the books, or the copies, or the apparatus of a class is in its way useful, if it makes the elder scholar feel that he can be helpful to the younger, or that he can contribute something to the beauty or to the repute of the school as a whole. It is here, as with the games in which the victory is not for an individual, but for the side, the company or the school to which the player belongs; the very act of putting forth effort on behalf of the community tends powerfully to check selfishness and egöism, and to make the scholar conscious that the community has interests into which for a time, it is both a duty and a privilege for him completely to merge his own.

Difference between Some there may be who as they hear me now are saying to themselves, This may be true in the case of large schools, but mine is a small sheltered establishment, *school discipline and that of home.* where we take great pains with the formation of individual character, and where we seek to make the discipline more like that of a family. Now let us try to clear our minds of illusions. It is not well to make believe that a school, even a small school, is a family; because it is not one. Your relations to your pupils can never be those of a parent, and any pretence that they are has an unreality about it, which very soon becomes evident both to them and to yourself. The fact is that a child is sent to school to obtain a kind of discipline which is impossible in a family, and to learn many things which he could not learn at home. The moral basis of family life is affection. The moral basis of school life, as of that of all large communities is justice. It is not difficult in a well-ordered home to learn courtesy, kindness, the sanctity and the happiness of self-sacrifice, because those virtues have to be exercised towards those whom we know and love. But in a school we are called on to respect the rights and consult the feelings of people whom we do not love, and whom we scarcely know. And this is a great part of education. It can only be attained when the corporate spirit is rightly called forth, when the equal claims of others are fully recognized, and when opportunities are offered for losing the sense of personal claims in that of comradeship, and for evincing pride in the perfection and prosperity of the school as an institution.

And in governing, it is of the last importance that we should well consider the nature of the being whom we want to control, and not demand of him an impossible standard of virtue. A little child has not your seriousness, nor your sense of duty, nor your capacity for sitting still. He would be a very curious, almost an unpleasant *Child nature to be studied before insisting on rules.*

phænomenon if he had. On the contrary, nature makes him physically restless, very curious, mobile, and inquisitive, and exceedingly deficient in reverence. And these qualities should be taken for granted and allowed for, not set down as faults. Provision should be made for giving lawful vent to his personal activity, and if such provision be not made, and he is called on to maintain a confined posture for an unreasonable time, his restlessness and disobedience are the teacher's faults, not his. Let us take for granted that in every fault of a child there is an element of good, 'would men observingly distil it out,' that every act of mischief he is guilty of, is only an example of perfectly healthy and legitimate activity, accidentally misdirected. And above all let us take care not to measure his fault by the inconvenience which it causes us, but rather by considering the motive and the causes of it. Some of the little wrong acts of a child which bring the most annoyance to a teacher and try his temper most are precisely those which from the point of view of a moralist, are least blameworthy—talking at unreasonable times, destructiveness, untidiness, noise. These things have to be checked of course. But do not let us confuse the conscience of a child by exaggerating their seriousness, or by treating offences against school rules, as if they were breaches of the moral order of the universe. Consider what are the natural instincts of a child, and how unformed his moral standard is, and you will see that relatively to him offences of this kind are not crimes, though relatively to you and to the school they may be serious annoyances.

Fill the time with work. After all the great safeguard for good and happy discipline in a school is to fill the time with work. If a child is to have an interval of leisure, let it be in the play-room or ground, where relaxation is permissible, and even noise is not a sin. But let him have no intervals of leisure in school. There, and in school time, where play is not permitted, let work be systematically prescribed. You will of course take care that the work is duly varied, that it does not put too great a strain on one set of muscles, or on one set of faculties; you will see that light mechanical work alternates duly with serious intellectual application. But work of some kind—work which is duly superintended, and which cannot be evaded, should be provided for every minute of the school day. 'Let every child have,' said Joseph Lancaster, 'at all times, something to do and a motive for doing it.'

No doubt this business of maintaining discipline comes more easily to some than others. There are some who seem qualified and designed by nature to exercise ascendency over others. They are born like Hamlet's father with

The faculty of command; natural or acquired.

"An eye like Mars, to threaten and command,"

or better still they are naturally endowed with that sweet graciousness and attractiveness of manner which at once win confidence, and predispose the hearers to listen and obey. Of such a teacher her pupil may often say as Richard Steele once said in the finest compliment ever paid to a lady, "That to love her is a liberal education." And yet those of us who are not thus equipped by nature have no right to be discouraged. Every one may acquire the power of ruling others by steadily setting himself to do so, by thinking well over his orders before he gives them, by giving them without faltering or equivocation, by obeying them himself, by determining in every case, and at whatever cost, to see them obeyed, and above all by taking care that they are reasonable and right, and properly adapted to the nature of childhood, to its weaknesses and its needs.

The law of habit. Since obedience and fixed attention are habits, they are subject to the same law which is found to regulate all other habits. And this law is very curious and worth attention. In virtue of it we find that any one act which we perform to-day is easier to perform to-morrow, and easier still next day, and afterwards becomes so mechanical by frequent repetition that in due time it is difficult for us not to do it. We may observe this in ourselves, in all the little manual acts which we perform every day: they become exactly like one another even without any conscious desire on our part that they should be like. Our handwriting for instance becomes so fixed, that it is positively difficult for us to disguise it. And on the other hand all acts which we leave undone become daily more difficult; the habit of not doing becomes as confirmed as that of doing. Bishop Butler has analysed this law of habit at much length, and with great subtlety; and he proves that all our habits whether mental, bodily or moral are strengthened by repeated acts. The practice of speaking the truth, of temperance, of charity, or of prompt obedience, becomes strengthened every time it is put into action. The question is as old as Aristotle, Does character produce actions, or do actions produce character? Is for example a man a temperate man because he abstains from excessive indulgence; or does he so abstain because he is a temperate and virtuous man? Now no doubt either of these questions might in a sense be answered in the affirmative; because habit and character act and react on each other. But in the long run it is far truer to say that habits make character, than to say character makes habits. Character has been not improperly called a bundle of habits. We are what we are not so much because of what we wish to be, nor of any sentiments we have formed, but simply

The law of habit. 103

by virtue of what we are doing every day. And if as is probably true of all of us, we are constantly saddened by noticing how far we fall short of our own ideal; there is but one remedy; it is to place ourselves in new conditions, to brace ourselves up to some new effort, and to form a new set of habits. Mere meditation on what we wish to be, good resolutions, clear perception of the difference between right and wrong, are of little use unless they shew themselves in acts. Nay they are worse than useless. Hear Butler: "Going over the theory of virtue in one's mind, talking well and drawing fine pictures of it: this is so far from necessarily or certainly conducing to form a habit of it in him who thus employs himself that it may harden the mind in a contrary course. * * For from our very faculty of habit, passive impressions, by being repeated grow weaker. Thoughts by often passing through the mind are felt less sensibly. Being accustomed to danger begets intrepidity, i.e. lessens fear, and to distress lessens the emotion of pity. And from these two observations together, that practical habits are formed and strengthened by repeated acts and that passive impressions grow weaker by being repeated, it may follow that motives and excitements (to right action) are continually less and less consciously felt, even as the active habits strengthen."

Now, I know of no truth more fruitful or far-reaching *Its bearing* in its relation to a teacher's work than this, nor one on *on school* which he will do well oftener to reflect. I say nothing of *work*. its bearing on your own personal character, on your capacity for work, on the steadiness and the method of your reading; but think for a moment what it means in relation to the pupils who come to you for instruction. It means that every time they come into your presence the habit of obedient attention is being either confirmed or weakened. It means that every unregarded counsel or order of yours falls more ineffectually on the ear than the last. It means that prompt and exact obedience if insisted on in little things, becomes available for great things; it means in short that on the daily *régime* of your school depends the whole difference for life, in the case of your pupils, between a wandering loose slipshod style of thinking and of reading, and an orderly and observant mind, one accustomed to put forth all its best powers and to bring them to bear on any object worthy of pursuit. And what a profound difference this is! It is only when we try to realize it and to see it in relation to our own life, and to the lives of the people who are struggling and failing around us, that the true significance of early drill and discipline becomes apparent to us.

Recreation. The sports and recreations of childhood come fairly within the province of a schoolmaster and deserve his careful thought. But it would be easy to err on the side of over-regulation and too minute direction on this point. It is of the essence of healthy and really useful play that it should be spontaneous. What children are learning—and they are learning much—in play, ought to be learned unconsciously, and without any suspicion that they are being drilled and disciplined. Their own fresh instincts are here the safest guides to you, when you want to supply them with recreation. The toys which they like best, are not merely objects to look at; such as would gratify the taste of older persons. The capacity for admiration is soon exhausted in children. They like best something to handle, to arrange, to derange, and to re-arrange; a doll which can be dressed and undressed, a house of bricks which can be built up and pulled down; a tool which can be actually used; a machine model or a puzzle which will take to pieces. It is not the beauty or the costliness of a toy which gives permanent pleasure to a child; but the possession of some object however rude, which calls into exercise his faculties of invention, of tactual and physical activity, and even of destructiveness. For destructiveness is not wholly a vice. It is in its way a symptom of curiosity and of inquisitiveness, of desire to know what a thing is made of, and how it is made. And this after all is the true philosophic instinct; without it, we should have no great inventors, and make little or no advance in science. We must not repress this instinct because some of its manifestations are apt to be inconvenient to us. It is our business to take the instinct for granted, to recognize its usefulness and to provide due scope for its exercise. This is now often done in great public schools, by attaching to them workshops, in which boys who have a mechanical turn are allowed to learn the use of tools and a turning-lathe, to make the apparatus used in the lessons on science as well as boxes and other useful articles for themselves.

Gymnastics. Regular gymnastic and calisthenic exercises, graduated and arranged on a system, have their value, though they are for several reasons less in favour in English than in French and German schools. A covered gymnasium, with cross-bars, ropes and poles for leaping and climbing is a useful appendage to every school. But it is not well to rely too much on this artificial help. Most good English teachers prefer to let nature have freer play, and suggest her own form of gymnastics. The movements of a healthy child in running, in leaping, in rowing, in swimming, in throwing a ball, in achieving some object which he cares to attain, are quite as valuable, as the regulated preconcerted set of movements of a professor of gymnastics, and much more interesting. Taking a constitutional walk, for walking and for exercise sake, is as we all know, less enjoyable, and even less invigorating than walking to some place we want to go to. So a child likes better to achieve some result, to overcome some difficulty; than to go through a set of exercises which are of no value except as exercises, and which lead to nothing in which he is interested.

Over-estimate of athletic exercises for boys.
The need of free animal pastime is already so fully recognized in Boys' schools, that there is some danger of over-estimating its importance as an element in school life. Considering that it is, at any rate the first business of a school to encourage learning, and develop mental power, it is rather a discredit to some of our great schools that so large a proportion of time and thought should be devoted to athletics; and that success in cricket and football and rowing should so often be valued as much as intellectual distinction. We are in danger of presenting boys with a false ideal of manliness, when we lead them to suppose that they come to school merely to become healthy and robust. Let us by all means place scholars in conditions favourable to the highest physical activity and development, but do not let us so mistake the true proportions of things as to exalt mere healthy animalism into a school-accomplishment or a moral virtue. The publicity and show often attendant on the exhibition of athletic sports in a school may easily be carried to a mischievous extent.

More of them needed for girls.
It need not be said that we are in no such danger in schools for girls. There, the great fault is the frigid propriety, the languor and inaction, which too often fill up the leisure time. Girls need the free exercise of their limbs, as much as their brothers, but they are not nearly so conscious of this need; and exercises must therefore

be devised for them. Tennis, fives, and even cricket are among the out-door games which would serve the purpose well; something more is wanted than mere dawdling in the open air over such a game as croquet; and as to the prim and solemn promenade two and two, under the severe scrutiny of an assistant mistress, it is hardly to be called relaxation in any sense.

One of the hardest of the disciplinal problems of a boarding-school is the regulation of the employments for Sunday. You want that the day shall have a special character, that its religious associations shall be respected, and above all that it shall be felt by all the scholars to be a day of rest, refreshment and enjoyment. It must not be passed in mere idleness, so one or two lessons of an appropriate kind must be devised; but with these there should be required as little as may be of irksome effort. The religious services should be short, varied, and interesting, and if possible such as to enlist the aid of the scholars in the choir. And for the rest, leave as much liberty as you can, both as to the reading and the occupations of the day. Let the claims of the higher life be recognized, and do what you can, rather by opportunity and by the general calm and order of the day's arrangements, to shew that you regard those claims as paramount. But do not map out your Sunday scheme on the assumption that a day full of devotion or of religious reading or exercises, can be delightful to a boy, or is appropriate to so early a stage in his moral and spiritual progress. Any attempts to enforce upon him the behaviour and the tastes of older and serious people are apt to defeat their own purpose. They produce a sense not only of unreality but of weariness and disgust in those who rebel; or worse still, they sometimes generate insincerity and religious

Sunday in a boarding-school.

conceit, in those who submit. Whatever else is done, let Sunday exercises be such as can be reasonably enforced and honestly enjoyed.

Rewards. We have to consider now the influence of rewards and punishments on the discipline of a school, and on the formation of individual character. Now a child may be stimulated to exertion by very different motives:

(1) By the desire to get something: or by the hope of some tangible reward.

(2) By the desire of distinction and the wish to excel his fellows.

(3) By the desire to win approbation from parents or teachers.

(4) By the simple wish to improve, and to do the right thing because it is right.

Now here is a whole gamut of motive, and I have put first that which is clearly the lowest, and have arranged them according to their degrees of worthiness. You may feel that so long as you can get right conduct and intellectual exertion, you will be well content, whichever of these motives prevails. But at the same time you are conscious that it is a much nobler result of your discipline to get them from the last motive than from any one of the others. For the first has an element in it of selfishness and covetousness, the second is nearly akin to vanity, and even the third is not perfectly pure. And one rule of action will be anticipated at once by all who follow me in this classification of motive forces. Never appeal to the lower form of inducement if you can make the higher suffice. But it is notorious that we do appeal very much in England to the hope of reward. Our whole educational plans both for boys and for men are pervaded through and through with the prize system. We have rewards, exhibitions, money prizes, scholarships, fellowships—an elaborate system of bribery, by which we try to stimulate ambition and to foster excellence. A recent traveller in England, Dr Wiese, the late director of public instruction in Prussia, a man of keen insight, and strongly predisposed to admire British institutions, expresses great surprise at this. "Of all the contrasts which the English mode of thinking and acting shews, none has appeared to me so striking and contradictory as the fact that a nation which has so great and sacred a sense of duty makes no use of that idea in the school education of the young. It has rather allowed it to become the custom, and it is an evil custom, to regard the prospect of reward and honour as the chief impulse to industry and exertion." This is to be found, he goes on to say, at all stages of instruction from the University to the Elementary School. Prizes and medals are given not only for progress in learning but also for good conduct. "If any one in England wishes to benefit an institution the first thing always is to found prizes and scholarships, which in this way have enormously increased in some schools." And he then expresses his amazement not only at the large proportion of scholars who at a breaking-up day are found to have been *couronnés* or rewarded in some way, but at the heap of gift-books which often falls to the lot of a single scholar. Now Dr Wiese has here hit an undoubtedly weak point in our English education. We use rewards somewhat lavishly. We rely on them too much, as furnishing the motive to excellence, and we thus do not give a fair chance to the development of purer and nobler motives. There are many reasons for this. I have seen schools in which prizes were numerous and costly, out of all proportion to the merits of the scholars, and have been told that the parents expected it, that they would be offended if the children brought nothing home at Christmas, and that therefore it was necessary under some pretext or other that nearly every child should have a prize. Then rich people of kindly instincts who take an interest in a school often know no other way of gratifying those instincts than by establishing a prize. The immediate result is so pleasant, the gratification of the receiver of the prize is so evident, that it is very hard for the generous giver to believe that he has done any harm.

Prizes should be carefully economized.
But harm is done nevertheless. It is here as with charity to the poor, about which so much has been said of late. We have no right to gratify our kindly sensibilities at the expense of the manliness and strength of those whom we wish to benefit. What we see in both cases is pleasure, gratitude, very agreeable things to recognize; but what we do *not* see is some enervation of the character, the silent encouragement of a false and lowered estimate of duty. Hence I venture to offer this general counsel. Use rewards sparingly. Do not rely on their influence too much. Do not give them for ordinary obedience, or fair average application; but let them be felt as real distinctions; reserve them for cases of special effort or excellence; and do not feel bound to accept every gift or endowment, by which an amiable friend of the school may propose to enrich it, unless you see that there is likely to be genuine merit to correspond to the gift.

And commendation also.
And in like manner I would urge upon you to economize your praise. People of kindly natures who are much in contact with children are apt to be profuse in little expressions of satisfaction, "Very well done," and the like. And if such phrases are habitually used, one of two things will happen; either they will be taken at their real worth—as amiable but rather feeble utterances, and not true criticisms—in which case the teacher's influence will be diminished, and he will have no means left for

giving praise when the special occasion for it arises; or they will be really valued by the scholars who will learn to expect it and to rely on it, and so will lose something of their moral strength. It is not good to get a habit of relying on constant encouragement. It is a great part of the discipline of a school to train a child into doing what is right without commendation. Do not therefore let a false amiability cause you to waste your praise. "Even distinguished merit," says Mr Bain, "should not always be attended with pæans." And the merit you are most concerned to encourage is not cleverness, nor that which comes of special natural gifts, but rather the merit of conscientious industry and effort.

By all means let us respect the happiness of children. *Happiness of children.* Cheerfulness—joyousness—the atmosphere of love and of well-ordered liberty—these things make the heaven in which a little child lives, and in which all that is gracious and beautiful in his character thrives the best. Let him have as much of this as you can. But do not confound it with enjoyments, with what are called pleasures, with entertainments, with spectacles, with prizes, with things that cost money[1]. These are not what a child wants. Let us keep them in reserve till the evil days come when the zest of life needs to be sustained by these poor devices. "Life would be very tolerable," said Sir George Lewis, "were it not for its pleasures." A schoolmaster cannot accept for himself or his scholars quite so cynical a theory as this, but he will none the less admit that it is a poor thing even in childhood to be dependent for a substantial part of our happiness on treats, on *menus plaisirs* and exceptional gratifications. In the long run we should find our chief delight in the ordinary pursuits and duties of life rather

[1] See Jean Paul's *Levana oder Erzieh-lehre*, 44.

than in occasional release from them. And if school is to provide in this respect a training for after life, it should establish in the young scholar's mind happy associations with the duties and employments of every day, and not exclusively or even mainly with fêtes and holidays.

Punishments.

The saddest part of a schoolmaster's experience lies in the necessity for punishments. It is impossible but that offences will come. But if we are to deal rightly with them when they come, we must first understand in what light we ought to look on all sin and wrong-doing, especially that of a child. And it is surely essential to learn to treat it without harshness, yet without levity or indifference; with full recognition of the sanctity of the law which has been broken, and yet with sympathy for the weakness which led to the breach of it. If we begin by viewing faults in this light, we shall be better prepared to look this difficult question in the face.

Different purposes of punishment.

Now I can conceive three possible purposes which punishment may serve. It may (1) be purely retributive or vindictive, and intended to shew the necessary and righteous connexion between wrong-doing and suffering; or (2) be purely exemplary, designed to warn others and to prevent the repetition of the fault; or (3) be designed for the reformation of the offender. If you consider the punishments inflicted by the State for the violation of its laws, you will see that they are to be defended mainly, almost exclusively on the second of these grounds. It is not simply for the vindication of the eternal principles of right and wrong, or for avenging evil deeds as such, that the State punishes. Else it would deal with the vices which degrade men and dishonour their nature as well as with the crimes which injure society. Still less is it purely with a view to the reformation of the wrong doer that the community punishes its members. Of course when the miscreant is once in our hands, and the State assumes the responsibility of regulating his life, it is right to make the discipline as useful and reformatory as is consistent with due severity in the punishment. But this is not the first object. We do not keep up our costly and elaborate system of police and prisons mainly as an educational institution on behalf of that class of persons which least deserves the nation's solicitude. The object of the whole system of punishment is the protection of society by the prevention of crime. "You are not sent to prison," said a magistrate to a thief, "for picking a pocket, but in order that pockets may not be picked." Now it is evident that in this respect the School and the State are essentially different. The one concerns itself with the act done and its effect on the rights and welfare of the community; but the other concerns itself chiefly with the doer of the act. That which is to the lawgiver only a secondary and subordinate object, is to the ruler of the school the first object, the discipline or improvement of the offenders. If he punishes, he cannot of course keep out of view the moral effect of the punishment on those who might otherwise be tempted to do wrong; but his main object is to bring the pupil who has strayed, back again into the right path—the path of obedience and of duty.

There are two principal forms of punishment—those *Kinds of* which consist in the actual infliction of pain, or the de-*punishment.* privation of some enjoyment; and those which derive their force from the fact that they are meant to be punishments, and are known to be so. A glance of rebuke, a word or tone of anger, disgrace or degradation in the eye of others, loss of office or of confidence, a low place in a list of marks for merit; all these are forms of punishment belonging to the second class; while detention from play, the loss of holidays or of entertainments, the withholding of some pleasant ingredient from a meal, confinement, the imposition of unpleasant tasks, and actual castigation belong to the first class. And as we enumerate these, and perhaps think of others which our own ingenuity has devised, the first thought which occurs to us all, is how happy we should be if we could rid ourselves altogether of this kind of duty; and how great an object it is in all good discipline to reduce the necessity for punishment to a minimum. All these instruments of torture are in our hands. But it is obvious that we should never use the more formidable instrument if the less formidable can be made to serve the purpose. While the eye commands respect, the voice is unnecessary; while a gentle rebuke will suffice, the harder tones of indignation and remonstrance should not be used. And it is not till the voice ceases to be obeyed at all, that we should resort to severer measures. It is one of the first objects of a wise ruler to dispense with the necessity of inflicting punishment altogether. But as this cannot always be accomplished, one or two principles about its infliction may be usefully kept in view.

The sense of shame. Remember that secondary punishments intended to work upon the sense of *shame* seldom succeed. One reason is that they are so unequal. They fall so differently on different natures. The kind of disgrace which wounds a sensitive child to the quick and weakens his self-respect for years, falls harmless on a bolder, harder nature; and gives no pain at all. Many very good teachers, though, I am glad to say, a decreasing number, think it possible to produce a salutary effect on children by humiliating them in the eyes of others. Joseph Lancaster, who shewed a shrewd insight into many matters of education, was curiously unwise in this respect. He invented a number of penalties, designed expressly to make wrong doing ridiculous. He would tie a boy who had broken a rule to one of the pillars of the school. He had a pulley fixed in the roof, and a rope and a basket, and would put an offender into the basket, and let him be drawn up in the sight of the whole school, and remain there suspended for its amusement. All such devices are happily extinct. Fools' caps and stools of repentance in schools have gone the way of the stocks, of the pillory, and of public floggings in the criminal code of the nation; because they were all founded on the same vicious principle, of trying to prevent wrong doing by making fun of it, and by exposing the offender to scorn and ridicule. You degrade an entire community when you enable its members to get any amusement out of the procedure of justice, or out of the sufferings of a criminal.

And I think the use of sarcasm and of ridicule in the treatment of children, even when we do not punish them, is equally out of harmony with a wise and high-minded moral discipline. Some of us have a natural gift for satire and for wit; and it is very hard to abstain from the exercise of this weapon, whenever there is anything in a child's conduct to excite our scorn or sense of the ridiculous. But it is a dangerous weapon nevertheless, and we should put a severe restraint upon ourselves in the use of it. We must not so treat wrong doing as to weaken the self-respect of the scholar, and to make the way to reformation steeper or more thorny than it is. *Ridicule.*

Is it needful that I should warn any one here against setting tasks for punishments? I believe, however, that they are still sometimes used for this purpose, and I am astonished to find in a modern book containing so much that is wise and philosophical as Mr Bain's *Education as* *Tasks as punishments.*

a Science, a recognition of tasks and impositions as legitimate punishments, because "the pain of intellectual *ennui* is severe to those that have no liking for books in any shape." One might have hoped that this doctrine at least would ere this have been swept away 'into the limbo large and broad' of obsolete heresies. For what possible effect can be produced by all our homilies as to the profit and pleasantness of learning if by our own act we admit that a lesson may serve as a punishment? "Because you have disobeyed me you shall have a harder or a longer lesson to night." What is this but to reveal that you think learning a lesson is a kind of penal servitude? And this is a thing we should never even tacitly admit. First because it ought not to be true, and secondly, because it will soon become true if you shew that you believe it to be so. Of course this remark does not apply to the making up for some neglect by finishing a lesson in play hours. It is a legitimate thing, if a duty of any kind is not performed at the proper time, to insist on its finished performance before the scholar begins to enjoy his leisure. And in this sense, detention in doors to go over again some neglected lesson, though it looks like a punishment, is right and lawful. For it is not the lesson in this case which constitutes the punishment, but the expenditure of time needed to make up for former waste. And this, as you will see, is a very different thing from setting the lesson itself as a penalty for wrong doing of some other kind.

Blame should be specific, not general.
And in punishing never let your indignation betray you into making your blame too comprehensive, or out of proportion to the particular act which called it forth. Treat every separate case of negligence by itself, but do not call a boy a dunce. Censure, and if needful, punish, a deliberate untruth, but do not say to a child, "You are a liar." Regard each separate wrong act, as far as you can

honestly do so, as exceptional, not typical, as one which may be atoned for, and the memory of which may be obliterated by a right act. To call a child by an evil name is to assume that his character is formed, and this happily is not true even of your worst scholars. If it were true, what could be more discouraging, more fatal to the success of any poor struggles he may make to set himself right, and to regain your approbation?

May I add also that punishments should never be inflicted on too many at a time, on a whole class for instance. They lose all their force if they are thus indiscriminate; it is very improbable that all the children in a group should be equally guilty; and unless each one feels that the loss or disgrace inflicted on him is duly and properly proportioned to his own personal fault, he is conscious of injustice, and your punishment fails to produce any moral effect.

Rousseau and Mr Herbert Spencer have said much, and have said it well, about the evil of arbitrary punishments, which have no intelligible fitness or relation to the nature of the fault committed. And I strongly recommend every teacher to read what is said in *Emile*, and in the chapter on Moral Education in Mr Spencer's well-known book. Those authors point out that nature punishes faults in a very effective way. If one goes too near a fire he is burnt; if he plays with a knife he hurts himself; and in like manner, if a child carelessly loses something belonging to him, he should feel the inconvenience of going without it, and not have it at once replaced by a kind but injudicious parent. If he is unpunctual he should not be waited for when any walk or pleasure is to be had, but should be left behind; if he is untidy and makes a litter he should be made to gather it up. When in this way, the inconvenience suffered is seen to be the

The discipline of consequences.

direct consequence of the fault, a child cannot rebel as he could, for example, if for doing any one of these things he was sent to bed. You eliminate altogether the feeling of personal resentment and the sense of injustice if you make the punishment thus, whenever possible, obviously appropriate to the fault and logically its sequel. The principle, once seen, covers a good many school offences. The obvious punishment for late coming is late going; for doing an exercise ill is to do it again well; for wasting the time in school is to forfeit some of the hours of leisure; for all invasion of the rights and comforts of others is to find one's own privileges or comforts restricted; for injury to the property of others, restitution at one's own cost. And from this point of view it will be seen how unsatisfactory is the discipline when for telling a lie one has to learn a hundred lines of Virgil; or for confounding the perfect with the pluperfect tense to receive a flogging. In the former cases the discipline commends itself to the conscience of the child. In the latter his moral sense rebels, and rightly rebels, against it.

Why inadequate. But unfortunately for the theory of Rousseau and Mr Spencer, nature does not provide a sure and visible penalty for every offence. Truly I know no more impressive lesson for a child than to shew him how wrong doing produces evil consequences; how pitiless and inexorable are the laws in virtue of which all sin brings harm and misery with it in the long run; how intemperance enfeebles the body; how idleness begets poverty; how the liar is not trusted; how ignorance brings dishonour; how improvidence breeds crime, and leads to loss of character, and loss of happiness. And I think that the utilitarian philosophers are right in urging us to teach in our schools some of the simpler truths of economic science, the laws of industrial and social life, which will enable the scholars thus to trace out the connexion between conduct and well being, between all faults and their natural penalties. But valuable as such teaching is, experience proves to us that it is wholly inadequate as a theory of moral government either for a school or for a State.

The reasons why it is inadequate are not the same in the two cases. A civil ruler cannot rely on the discipline of natural consequences, because they are too remote and too dimly seen to serve as effective deterrents. It needs an effort of imagination, of which a criminal is generally incapable, to realize such consequences at all. And in fact, you cannot demonstrate to his satisfaction that any consequences which he dreads will certainly occur. You take a thief and explain to him that honesty is conducive to the public welfare. But in most cases he knows that as well as you. You prove to him that nine thieves out of ten are detected and come to ultimate ruin. Your demonstration fails to affect him. Why? Because he means to be the tenth. He knows that consequences are sometimes avoided, and he thinks he will be skilful enough to avoid them. And as to your proof that dishonest acts will bring about slow deterioration of character and certain loss of friends, of position, and of general esteem; the man with criminal tendencies who is subject to strong temptation is generally inaccessible to such considerations; and society for its own protection is justified in interposing with its artificial penalties, which are sharper and more effective. *Because not severe enough for the purpose of a State.*

And while the State cannot rely wholly on natural punishments, because for her purpose they are too light, the parent or the teacher has exactly the opposite reason for not depending upon them. They are for his purpose far too severe. You want by timely interposition with a *Because too severe for the purpose of a school.*

small arbitrary punishment to save the child from the cruel Nemesis which nature has provided for wrong doing. He is, it may be, inclined to gluttony, and you know that if you leave him alone Nature will avenge the violation of her laws by enfeebling his constitution and depriving him prematurely of health and vigour. But because you are chiefly concerned with the formation of his character, this is precisely the penalty you wish to avoid; and you subject him to some painful restraint, in order that you may substitute a light penalty for a heavy one. You see a man rushing towards a precipice, and you knock him down. What justifies this act of violence? Nothing, except that by the infliction of a small and wholly arbitrary injury, you have helped him to escape from the greater injury which would have been the natural penalty of his own imprudence.

The certainty not the severity of a punishment deters.

It is a familiar conclusion from experience that in a school, as in a State, it is the certainty rather than the severity of a punishment which has a deterring effect. If an offender could feel that detection was absolutely certain, the dread of consequences, whether natural or arbitrary, would be much more potent. "Because," said Solomon, "sentence against an evil work is not executed speedily, therefore the hearts of the sons of men are fully set in them to do evil." That was his experience as an administrator. As a matter of fact, every child knows that though lying is wrong, there are lies which serve their purpose and are never found out; that there are cases in which dishonesty seems for a time at least to be good policy; and it is the knowledge of these and the like facts which will always leave something more to be desired, when you are seeking to deter children from evil, by the utilitarian method of tracing out that evil to its consequences. And what is that something? I believe it to lie in the constant reference of moral questions to higher considerations than those of expediency and of results—to the inward sense of right and of moral fitness, to the sentiment of honour "which feels," as Burke finely says, "a stain like a wound," to a perception of the beauty of holiness, to the desire to do what our heavenly Father meant us to do and to be what he fitted us to be, whether happiness and prosperity come of it or not.

And as you succeed in cultivating the sentiment of honour and the habit of referring school merits and offences to the standard of what is in itself right and fitting, and worthy of your scholar's best self, it will come to pass that your most effective punishments—indeed almost your only punishments, will consist in the loss of honour. Bad marks, a low place in the class, the withholding of office and responsibility, and of all signs of esteem and confidence;—these after all fulfil in the best way, the two most important conditions of all right punishment. For there is nothing arbitrary or capricious about them, since they are the natural and appropriate consequences of the faults to which they pertain. And at the same time they are eminently reformatory; for they indicate clearly the way to repentance and improvement. So my counsel to all schoolmasters is: Look in this direction for the punishments which you may lawfully and wisely use: and be dissatisfied with yourself and with your own plan of discipline so long as you find it needful to employ any others. *The best kinds of punishment.*

·Yet we must not omit a brief reference to corporal punishment, the *ultima ratio* of the puzzled and baffled schoolmaster when all other means fail. Shall we begin by denouncing it altogether? I think not. The punishment of the body for certain offences is nature's way of discipline, and it is not necessarily degrading to young *Corporal punishment.*

children, nor unsuited to the imperfect state of their mental and moral development. Arnold, though I suspect that his views on this subject would have altered in later years, was not wholly wrong when he vindicated flogging in certain extreme cases. "The proud notion of independence and dignity which revolts at the idea of personal chastisement is not reasonable and is certainly not Christian," he said. After all it is sin which degrades and not the punishment of it. So if there be certain forms of vice which can be cured more readily by the infliction of such chastisement than by any other means, the chastisement will need no other vindication. And yet while allowing full weight to this view of the case, I am convinced that corporal punishment is almost wholly unnecessary, that it does more harm than good, and that in just the proportion in which teachers understand their business they will learn to dispense with it. In boarding schools it seems to me wholly indefensible; for there, where the whole discipline of the life and the control of leisure is in the teachers' hands, there are many other ways open to him of imposing penalties. And there is scarcely less necessity for it in day schools. The largest and one of the best day schools I ever examined, where the whole tone of the discipline is singularly high, manly, and cheerful, has never once during its whole history had a case of corporal punishment. But the master, when I was reporting on the school, begged me not to mention this fact. "I do not mean to use it," he said, "but I do not want it to be in the power of the public or the parents to say I am precluded from using it. Every boy here knows that it is within my discretion, and that if a very grave or exceptional fault occurred I might exercise that discretion." I believe that to be the true attitude for all teachers to assume. They should not have their discretion narrowed by any outward law, but they should impose a severe law on themselves. And in carrying it out I venture to make two or three suggestions only:

(1) Never inflict corporal chastisement for intellectual faults; for stupidity or ignorance. Reserve it exclusively for vices, for something morally degrading. (2) Never inflict it while under the influence of heat or passion. (3) Never permit an assistant or an elder scholar to inflict it in any circumstances. (4) Do not let any instrument of punishment be included as part of the school furniture, and as an object of familiar sight, or flourished about as a symbol of authority. (5) Do not strike with the hand.

On this whole subject of the mode and manner of inflicting punishment you will find some useful hints in Jeremy Bentham's *Chrestomathia*, which I advise every teacher to read.

But we return finally to this consideration. The great triumph of school discipline is to do without punishments altogether. And to this end it is essential that we should watch those forms of offence which occur oftenest, and see if by some better arrangements of our own, temptation to wrong may be diminished and offences prevented. If your government is felt to be based on high principles, to be vigilant and entirely just, to be strict without being severe, to have no element of caprice or fitfulness in it; if the public opinion of the school is so formed, that a scholar is unpopular who does wrong, you will find not only that all the more degrading forms of personal chastisement are unnecessary, but that the need of punishment in any form will steadily disappear.

How to dispense with punishments.

V. LEARNING AND REMEMBERING.

Practical rules must be ultimately dependent on philosophy.

THERE is no one department of educational work in which the difference between skilled and unskilled teaching is so manifest as in the view which is taken of the faculty of memory, the mode of training it, and the uses to which different teachers seek to put it. We are here at the meeting point of practice and of speculative psychology; and it is impossible for you or me to arrive at entirely right rules of action in reference to this subject unless our attention is also directed to the nature of the intellectual process which we call remembering, and to the laws which determine its action. I shall however abstain from encroaching on the domain of my successor here, whose duty it will be to expound to you the philosophy of memory. But it may be well to say that this line of enquiry will prove very fruitful, and that some study of what Locke, Reid, Dr Thomas Brown and Professor Bain have said on the laws of association; of what Dr Carpenter and Dr Maudsley have said respecting the physical basis of memory; and of the wise and practical distinction which Mr Latham in his book on Examinations has drawn between what he calls respectively the "portative," the "analytical," the "assimilative," and the "index" memory would be of great value in forming your own judgment upon it.

For my present purpose it must suffice to mention one or two very simple truths as a basis for the few practical rules which we hope to arrive at on this important matter. By a wonderful process, which is sometimes called mental suggestion or association, we find that every thought and action in our life links itself with some other thought or action. No piece of mental or spiritual experience is thoroughly isolated. No act, even of sensible perception, takes place without associating itself with some previous thought, or suggesting a new one. When we come to analyse these phænomena we find that there are, roughly distinguishable, two classes of associations. We may, when we are told of a fact, think also of the reason or consequence of that fact; and two distinct ideas may come before our minds together, because we perceive the logical *nexus* which unites them. Thus the thought of a good vintage in France suggests to me that claret may be cheaper; the history of Caxton and the early printers may make me think of the revival of learning; heavy war expenditure suggests national debt; bad government suggests revolution. In like manner a particular problem in Euclid reminds me of the axioms and postulates on which its solution depends; and a solecism in speech makes me think of the grammatical rule which has been violated. In all these cases the character of the associations which are formed and the ease with which they may hereafter be recalled together, depend on the degree in which the judgment and the reflective power have been cultivated on the subjects to which they relate.

But besides these logical and natural associations as we may call them, there are many others which are purely

The law of mental suggestion.

arbitrary, in which there is no special appropriateness in the connexion formed. Such are the associations between names and persons, between dates and facts, between words and ideas, between weights or measures and the figures representing their ratios, between contemporaneous events in different countries. Now in all these cases no judgment or reflection will help me to strengthen the association. If the link between the things thus related exists at all it must be forged by some mechanical process. I am told that Columbus discovered America in 1492, but there is no reason in the world which my understanding can recognize why the date should not have been 1452. The books tell me that there are $5\frac{1}{2}$ yds. in a pole, and I think of the word pole and these figures together, but I do not establish this association by any rational process. It is established, if at all, by some other means. The suggestion is one of words rather than of thoughts.

Different forms of associations.
Now, if we will consider it, the main differences in the mental calibre and character of men depend largely upon the sort of ideas which habitually or most readily coalesce in their minds. To a man of strong or lofty imagination a very common incident may suggest some hidden moral analogies, or far-reaching truth:

> "To him the meanest flower that blows doth give
> Thoughts that do often lie too deep for tears."

And such a man we call a poet. In the case of another man, every striking scene in the phantasmagoria of life sets him reflecting on its antecedents and consequences; and such a man has the philosophic temper, he is the reasoner, the moralist, the sage. To a third the sound of a word suggests only some grotesque simile, some remote allusion, some idea, which though essentially different, has a superficial resemblance. And such a person is the man of fancy or of wit. But when on hearing a word, or being reminded of a scene, the mind at once passes to the other words or actions which were linked with it when we recognized it at first; when it simply recalls a certain group of words or thoughts in the same sequence as that in which they were before presented; then we say the man has a good memory. He can in fact reproduce readily former associations, whether logical or not.

Consider for a moment the process which goes on when we try to remember a fact. You ask me the name of the statesman who tried so hard to set poor Louis XVI.'s finances in order, and I cannot remember it. Of course, if I knew the first letter of the name, that would give me a clue, and I should wait till that initial suggested to me a number of names, should fasten with special attention on likely names, and dismiss as fast as I could other names, which, though beginning with the same letter, were not, I know, what were wanted. But I do not remember the initial. So I let my mind dwell for a moment on Louis XVI. As I do so, the names of Calonne, of La Fayette, even of Burke and Pitt occur to me. They are not what I want, and I refuse to let my mind dwell on them. I think of Madame de Stael. Stop, she was the daughter of the statesman whose name I seek. Of Gibbon: that reminds me that he had sought the same lady in marriage. Then Geneva and Lausanne and Ferney and Voltaire, all names which are connected come rapidly through my mind, and in the midst of them *Necker's* name is suggested, and I fasten on it at once. It is what I wanted.

The process of remembering.

Now you will observe here that it is not by any conscious act that I have remembered this name. I cannot be said to have found it, or dug it up from the stores of my memory. These metaphors are very misleading. What I have done is simply this, I have waited for the laws of association to operate, and for the wonderful spontaneous power of mental suggestion to help me. An effort of will served to bring my attention to bear on those suggestions which, as they emerged, seemed most hopeful; I withdrew my attention from all unpromising trains of association, and in due time the particular name of which I was in search came back. If I had had a better memory it would have come back sooner, or with less effort.

Now this faculty of remembering is one which we constantly want to use in our teaching. What would be the worth of any teaching without it? We desire of course to stimulate the power of fresh thought, to make children observers, reasoners, thinkers. But the first thing we demand of them is that they should recollect what we teach. If we have been at the pains to link together two things, say a word and its meaning, a fact and a date, or two thoughts by way of comparison or contrast, we want the process of linking them to be so effective, that whenever afterwards, the one is presented to the mind, the other shall come with it. Unless the associations of thought and words which we seek to establish are permanent, there is imperfect memory; and if the memory is imperfect, our labour is lost.

Modes of establishing permanent associations.

So it is obvious that we ought to enquire into the conditions which give permanence to associations once brought before the mind. How are we to fix them? There are two obvious ways:

(1) Frequent repetition.

The first of them is that of frequent repetition. We learn to fix many pairs of associated words or ideas together, not because we try to do so; but simply because circumstances bring them constantly before us in juxtaposition[1]. Thus we learn the names of the people about us, the sequence of words in familiar texts and verses, the collocation of objects in the houses and streets we see every day. Suggest any one of these to the mind, and instantly, those which are related to it by mere contiguity come up before us in connexion whether we care to recall them or not. I might to-day by simply reiterating the same sentence fifty times make such an impression on your mind that you would never forget it. The effect of mere frequency of repetition, in fastening together even the most incongruous associations, is so familiar to you that it needs no further illustration.

The second condition of remembering is the interest or sympathy with which we regard the things associated. I go to hear a lecture on English Literature, and incidentally there are mentioned in the course of it two facts, the one

(2) *Interest in the thing learned.*

[1] "That which has existed with any completeness in consciousness leaves behind it, after its disappearance therefrom, in the mind or brain, a functional disposition to its reproduction or reappearance in consciousness at some future time. Of no mental act can we say that it is 'writ in water.' Something remains from it whereby its recurrence is facilitated. Every impression of sense upon the brain, every current of molecular activity from one to another part of the brain, every cerebral reaction which passes into movement, leaves behind it some modification of the nerve-elements concerned in its function, some after-effect, or, so to speak, memory of itself in them, which renders its reproduction an easier matter, the more easy the more often it has been repeated, and makes it impossible to say that, however trivial, it shall not in some circumstances recur. Let the excitation take place in one of two nerve-cells lying side by side, and between which there was not originally any specific difference, there will be ever afterwards a difference between them. This physiological process, whatever be its nature, is the physical basis of memory, and it is the foundation of our mental functions."—Dr MAUDSLEY.

that Phineas Fletcher wrote the *Purple Island*, the other that James Thomson wrote Rule Britannia in a masque of his called *Alfred*. Well it probably happens that the one fact interests me and the other does not. I never heard of Fletcher before, and have not cared to enquire what the Purple Island meant. But I have often heard Rule Britannia sung and perhaps it never occurred to me to enquire who wrote it. That a rather vain-glorious, noisy, patriotic song, should have been written by James Thomson, whose name I have been accustomed to associate with pastoral musings, and sweet luxurious fancies about the Castle of Indolence, comes to me as a surprise. A month later, it is found that I have forgotten all about the Purple Island, but I remember vividly the origin of Rule Britannia. And the reason is plain. It is true, I heard both facts once only. But then the one fact excited my attention and interest and the other did not; and this accounts for the difference.

Now the obvious conclusion from this is, that if you want to have a thing remembered you may do it in either of two ways. You may fasten it by dint of frequent repetition into the memory of one who does not care to retain it; or you may get the thing remembered simply by exciting in your pupil a strong wish to remember it. And the labour involved in the two processes may be stated in inverse proportion; the more you use the one expedient the less you want of the other. The act of remembering may be a mechanical—almost an automatic process, or it may be an intelligent process. But in just the proportion in which you make it intelligent, it ceases to be mechanical, and conversely. Every emotion of sympathy and interest you can awaken will render less necessary the wearisome joyless process of learning a task by heart. Let it be kept in your own view, and in that

Abstract and concrete memory.

of your pupils, that the first condition of easy remembering is that we care to remember, that if we have a bad memory, it is not nature's fault, but it is simply because we do not put sufficient force of will into the act of tying together the ideas which we propose to keep associated. Promise children some pleasure, and they will find no difficulty in remembering it. To say that we do not recollect a thing is simply to say that we did not pay sufficiently close attention to it, when it was first brought before our minds.

And what is the kind of memory we want most to cultivate? Is it the memory of words, or of the things and facts represented by those words? Is it the concrete memory which carries accurate impressions of visual pictures or of sounds, or is it the abstract memory which retains the gist and meaning of what has been heard and seen? No doubt it is good to secure each of these kinds of power. Some people who are keen at remembering the relations between events, and the substance of what they hear, have a difficulty in remembering mere names and words. But if we were to choose, and could only secure one, we should prefer to have the memory for things, their causes, effects, and mutual relations, rather than the power of mere verbal reminiscence. In schools however, we want both, and it is a great point in education to know when to cultivate the one, and when to aim at the other. If you hear a pupil demonstrate a proposition in Euclid, you want memory of course, but it is the memory of a logical sequence, and not of particular words. In fact, if you have any reason to suspect that he has learned it by heart, you at once change A, B, C on the diagram to X, Y, Z, or adopt some other device to baffle him. For to turn what is meant as a discipline in ratiocination, into

Verbal and rational memory.

an exercise of purely verbal memory destroys the whole value of the lesson, and makes nonsense of it. And if you have been giving a lesson on History, and have described say the period of the English Revolution—the attempt at the dispensing power, the trial of the seven bishops, the bigotry of James II. and the final catastrophe: you want all these facts to be linked together in their due correlation as causes and effects; and when they are reproduced to come up again as facts, in words supplied by your pupil and representing his own thoughts, not in the particular words which you happened to use in teaching. In these cases Montaigne's aphorism applies with special force, *Savoir par cœur n'est pas savoir.* Nothing would be gained, but much would be lost, if instead of requiring him thus to recall the events in his own way, you set him to learn by heart some sentences from a history book in which those facts were summarized. The associations you want to fix in the memory here are of events, not of words or phrases.

Learning by heart, when legitimate.

Are there then no occasions on which it is wise and desirable to establish verbal associations and to require them to be committed to memory, or to use a common expression, to be learned by heart? Undoubtedly there are. Let us look at them.

(1) There are in arithmetic and in all the exact sciences certain formulae which are frequently in use, which have constantly to be referred to, and which we want to use at a moment's notice. The multiplication table for example. 7 times 9 make 63. The association between these figures is apparently arbitrary. Reflection and reasoning would not help me much to know that they do not make 53; and when I am working a problem in which the fact is available, I do not want to reason or reflect at all. The two figures should suggest 63 instantaneously by

a mechanical process, and without a moment's thought. So it is good to know that the relation of the diameter to the circumference of a circle is expressed by the figures 1 and 3·14159, because this fact is often wanted in working out problems in mensuration, and furnishes a key to the rapid estimation of the sizes of familiar things. In the case of each of these terse and fruitful formulae, we observe that there is one thing right and everything else is wrong; there should be no mistake at all in our minds in regard to the exact truth; and the frequency with which the formula becomes of use fully justifies us in the labour of committing it to memory.

(2) There are some things which we want to remember in substance, but which are best remembered in one particular form. Geometrical definitions and axioms, and some rules in Latin syntax are of this kind. They have been carefully reduced to the simplest form of expression, it is specially necessary that they should be applied with perfect accuracy, and we therefore do well to have them in our mind in one fixed and concise form.

(3) Again, there are some things which deserve to be remembered as much on account of the special form they assume as on that of the truths they embody. If the language in which a truth is conveyed has any special authority, any historic significance, or any poetical beauty, the language itself becomes a thing worth appropriating, over and above the thoughts conveyed in that language. So verses of poetry, passages from great writers and orators, formularies of faith, wise maxims in which, as Lord Russell said, the wisdom of many has been fixed and concentrated by the wit of one—all these are worth learning by heart. The memory is enriched by a store of strong thoughts or of graceful expressions;—a great and

pregnant passage from Shakespeare, a few fervid and finished sentences from an oration of Burke, a piece of jewelled eloquence from one of Jeremy Taylor's sermons, a quaint aphorism from old Fuller, a sweet restful poem by Wordsworth, or some devout spiritual utterance of George Herbert or Keble, has a preciousness of its own which depends rather on its artistic excellence as a specimen of language, than on its value as a statement of truth. And it is this very artistic excellence which gives it its special claim to lie garnered in the store-house of memory. The possessor of such a store has a resource in hours of weariness or dulness, when thoughts are sluggish and imagination is weak. He goes back and finds that by recalling such utterances his thoughts are stimulated and his emotions ennobled[1]. But this would not happen if the words themselves were not felt to have a fitness and beauty of their own.

There is therefore a right use and a wrong use of what I have for my present purpose called by the rather unscientific name of the 'verbal memory,' or what is generally known as 'learning by heart.' This too is not a felicitous phrase, for of all conceivable employments for the human understanding, this kind of task work has the least 'heart' in it. No doubt many teachers have been accustomed to rely too much on the power of remembering words. It is the easiest of all forms of school-keeping to say "Go and learn that lesson, and then come and say it to me," and accordingly, setting tasks to be learned by heart is the chief, almost the only, resource of teachers who cannot teach, and are content to be mere pedagogic machines. But then the opposite of wrong is not always

[1] "What we want for ready use is a well-turned sentence form, or a suitable designation or phrase for some meaning that we are at a loss to render." BAIN.

right; and in the reaction against a system which relied wholly on the memory and never appealed to the judgment, we may very easily make another mistake equally great by discrediting and undervaluing the memory, by treating it as the Cinderella in the household of the human faculties, useful merely as a drudge.

We are, I hope, prepared now to come to a true conclusion as to the right use of this great educational instrument. And this is the conclusion. When the object is to have thoughts, facts, reasonings reproduced, seek to have them reproduced in the pupil's own words. Do not set the faculty of mere verbal memory to work. But when the words themselves in which a fact is embodied have some special fitness or beauty of their own, when they represent some scientific datum or central truth, which could not otherwise be so well expressed, then see that the form as well as the substance of the expression is learned by heart. *General principle to be kept in view.*

And, having once determined that this is worth doing, see that it is thoroughly done. It is of no value to learn a thing by heart unless it is learned so thoroughly that it can be recalled without the least mistake and at a moment's notice. Other lessons, in which the understanding is chiefly concerned, may be only partially successful, and yet be of some use. A lesson half understood is better than no lesson at all. But a *memoriter* lesson half learned—said with a few promptings, and blundered through just well enough to escape serious blame—is sure to be forgotten directly afterwards, and simply comes to nothing. Yes, it does come to something. It leaves behind it a sense of wasted time and a disgust for the whole subject to which it relates. That is all. *Thoroughness.*

Grant also that for some such good reason as I have named, you determine to set certain lessons to be learned *How to commit to memory.*

by heart, it is well to give pupils a hint as to the conditions under which the memory lays hold of a lesson best. Sitting down immediately after a lesson to commit a task to memory is a bad plan, for the mind is not then in its most receptive state. All persons do not commit tasks to memory under precisely the same conditions, so no universal rule can be laid down. To many, the morning when the mind is fresh is the best time. As a rule, the cerebral activity is said to be at its height within two or three hours after the first meal of the day. Many find the easiest way of learning by heart is to con over the lesson just before going to bed, and then they discover that in the morning it all comes to them with much greater clearness. Some philosophical writers have pointed out that there is such a thing as unconscious cerebration, a process of mind going on in sleep, and at other times when we are not conscious, whereby impressions made before are not only fixed but even more clearly apprehended. We cannot now discuss this theory; but it is certain that to many minds the expedient of learning a thing over night is found exceedingly helpful in economizing the conscious effort of the brain, and causes the thing you want to remember to come up with curious vividness in the morning[1].

---

[1] "Whatever the organic process in the brain, it takes place, like the action of other elements of the body, quite out of the reach of consciousness. We are not aware how our general and abstract ideas are formed; the due material is consciously supplied, and there is an unconscious elaboration of the result. Mental development thus represents a sort of nutrition and organisation; or, as Milton aptly says of the opinions of good men, that they are truth in the making, so we may truly say of the formation of our general and complex ideas, that it is mind in the making. When the individual brain is a well-constituted one and has been duly cultivated, the results of its latent activity, rising into consciousness

Again, a lesson learned in school, or a book read *Memory to be supplemented by reflection.* and dismissed from the mind the moment the reading is over, or the particular purpose is served is very apt to be forgotten, and often needs to be learned over again. But a lesson which is turned round and round in the mind again, and made the subject of rumination, even for a few minutes, is sure to become part of the permanent furniture of the mind. We do not want to let school-work encroach on the whole domain of life, and haunt a thoughtful scholar in all his hours of leisure. But we may not forget that the old way in which the Jews were exhorted to teach their children the commandments of the Lord in ages when there were no books, was a true way. "Thou shalt teach them diligently to thy children, and shalt talk of them when thou sittest in thy house, and when thou walkest by the way, and when thou liest down, and when thou risest up." Whatever we make a subject of reflection at odd times, when the thoughts are at leisure, is sure to be remembered. If a scholar can only be trained to the habit of giving ten minutes a day, in a walk, or in a quiet evening, to asking himself, "What have I learned, and why have I learned it?" and to the act of trying to recall it, and to think out some illustration of it, he is sure to make great and true progress.

There is one very common excuse often urged *Memory strengthened by exercise.* by those who make an excessive use of task-work in

suddenly, sometimes seem like intuitions; they are strange and startling as the products of a dream ofttimes are to the person who has actually produced them. Hence it was no extravagant fancy in Plato to look upon them as reminiscences of a previous higher existence. His brain was a brain of the highest order, and the results of its unconscious activity, as they flashed into consciousness, would shew like revelations, and might well seem intuitions of a higher life quite beyond the reach of present will." Dr CARPENTER.

teaching. You complain of their setting poor scrappy little passages of grammar, history, or geography to be learned by heart. You point out to them that sentences of this kind would be worthless even to an educated man. And the answer is they are useful because they strengthen the memory That is quite true. So it would strengthen my memory if I learned the leading article of this morning's *Times* by heart, or the names of all the Senior Wranglers in regular order from the beginning of the century. Moreover it is just conceivable that some day these acquisitions would turn out to be of value. In like manner, it would strengthen the muscles of a man's arm if he were on every alternate morning to dig a hole in his garden, and on the second morning regularly and laboriously fill it up again. But it is better perhaps that he should get this exercise in digging up something that needs to be dug. The truth is that life is not long enough, and our faculties are not potent enough to justify us in strengthening the memory by learning what is not worth remembering. You may get the same discipline for your faculties by learning something which has a value of its own; and unless what you propose to lay up in store in a child's mind has such real value, and is of such a kind that you yourself would find it fruitful and well worth possessing in after life, the use you mean to make of the faculty is illegitimate and unwise.

Tests of right and wrong forms of memory lesson.

Now in the light of the principles thus laid down let me ask myself one or two questions. Shall I learn by heart a list of the prepositions which govern a dative, and of the prepositions which govern an ablative in Latin? Yes. For these are idiomatic laws which are essential to me in Latin composition as well as in translation; they are largely arbitrary, and I could not recall them easily by any effort of reflection. Shall I learn the definitions of the parts of speech given by grammarians? No. 'An article is a word placed before a noun to shew the extent of its meaning.' If I did not know what an article is without the help of this definition, I should never tell it by means of it. Moreover, there are a good many other ways of defining parts of speech quite as good as those in any given grammar, and so long as I know thoroughly the distinction itself, the more varied is the form in which I can define it the better. Shall I learn the number of yards in a mile, the formula for the square of $(a+b)$ or the trigonometrical expression for the area of a triangle in terms of its sides? Yes. For these are central and most serviceable truths, constantly wanted in the solution of problems, and often wanted in a hurry. Will it be well to learn the logarithms of all numbers up to 100, the number of pints in a hogshead, or the number of inches in a Flemish ell? No, I think I will not encumber my memory with facts so seldom wanted, so little known outside of a school-room, and so very easy to find, if by chance there should be any occasional need for them. Shall I set my pupil to learn by heart, an extract from Scott's Marmion? Well I think not. For it is not likely to have any unity of its own. It is a fragment of a longer narrative, and is unintelligible without the rest; and since it is unreasonable to expect that the rest will be remembered, the fragment will soon drop out of recollection altogether. Shall I set him to learn part of Goldsmith's Traveller, or Gray's Elegy, or Wordsworth's Ode on Immortality? Yes. For every couplet here is a picture or thought in itself. Any one line will help to recall the lines related to it; and even if it does not do so, it has a value and suggestiveness of its own. Shall I learn the dates of the English kings, the latitude of

London, and at least approximately, the size of this island, and the population of its five or six largest towns? Yes, because England is my home, because it interests me more than any other place in the world, and because all these facts will be useful as fixed points of comparison round which all my constantly increasing acquaintance with it and its history, and with other places, will cluster and arrange itself. Shall I learn the dates of the Popes, a list of the departments of France, the figures which give me the length of the Mississippi, or the latitude and longitude of Timbuctoo? No. I think I would rather not know these things. I should like to know where the book is, where I can find them on the rare occasions on which I may want them, and I should also like to know how to consult it. What Mr Latham calls the Index memory is all I want here, the knowledge of where to look for what I want, and how to look for it. But as to carrying such lumber about as part of my mental furniture through life, I will certainly not do it, unless you compel me, and if you force me to learn it, I will try to forget it as soon as I am out of your reach. Shall I learn the Creed, the Lord's Prayer and the Ten Commandments by heart? Well—assuming of course that I accept them as true representations of my faith and duty—certainly. For they are venerable formularies, which come to us with very sacred associations and with a great weight of authority. They have shaped the conduct and guided the devotions of my Christian forefathers for centuries, and they are presumably expressed in the choicest, tersest, and most weighty words, which tradition has been able to bestow upon us. Shall I learn by heart the historical compendium of the ingenious Mangnall? Not if I can help it. Let me read to you two or three questions and answers from that author.

Printed Catechisms.

What became of the Druids? They were almost entirely extirpated when the Roman general Suetonius Paulinus took the island, or Anglesea in the year 61, and Agricola a second time in 78.

How were the public events transmitted to posterity when the Britons were ignorant of printing and writing? By their bards or poets, who were the only depositaries of national events.

What Roman emperor projected an invasion of Britain, gathered only shells upon the coast, and then returned to Rome in triumph? Caligula, in the year 40.

What British generals distinguished themselves before the Saxon Heptarchy was formed? Cassivelaunus defeated by Julius Cæsar in 54 B.C. and Caractacus defeated and taken by Ostorius in 51 A.D., and sent a prisoner to Rome in the following year.

What was the exclamation of Caractacus when led in triumph through Rome? How is it possible that a people possessed of such magnificence should envy me a humble cottage in Britain!

Now suppose I learn this lesson by heart, you observe that every answer consists of about one-third or fourth of a statement, of which all the rest lies in the question. And the question is not learnt by heart. So the fragment actually committed to memory is incomplete and means nothing. Even if the question were remembered, the separate facts thus learned are incoherent, and unrelated, and so, though concerned with one of the most interesting of all subjects, are made profoundly uninteresting. To print a book of questions and answers is to assume that there is to be no real contact of thought between scholar and master, that all the questions which are to be asked are to take one particular form, and that they all admit of but one answer. There is no room for inquisitiveness on the part of the learner, nor for digression on the part of the teacher, no room for the play of the intelligence of either around the subject in hand; the whole exercise has been devised to convert a study which ought to awaken intelligence, into a miserable mechanical performance; and two

Books of question and answer.

people who ought to be in intimate intellectual relations with each other, into a brace of impostors—the one teaching nothing, the other learning nothing, but both acting a part and reciting somebody else's words out of a book. It is said that there are schools in existence in which Mangnall's Questions is actually still in use as a task-book to be learned by heart, and that new editions of it are in constant demand. It is appalling to think of the way in which whole generations of English girls and boys have been stupified by this book and by others like it.

Memory not a receptacle to be filled.

It will be seen on further consideration that many of the metaphors we are accustomed to use about memory are like all metaphors when applied to the region of our inner and spiritual life—a little misleading. To speak of memory as a receptacle which may be filled, or as a chain which may draw treasure up from a well, is to imply that memory is a limited power. And this is not true. It is capable of indefinite increase and improvement by exercise. Nevertheless, minds which are differently constituted will develop in different ways, and when we have subjected them all to the same discipline there will remain great diversities of result. To some the memory will be specially retentive in regard to names and words, to some the recollection of places and persons will be easier than that of the names which designate them. An unreasoning person may catch up by ear the words of a foreign tongue with far greater readiness than one whose habits of mind lead him to be always on the watch for the laws of language and for illustrations of comparative philology. We need not seek to obliterate these distinctions. Even a deficiency in the power of carrying a truth in the exact form in which we first received it may coexist with the power of recording that truth by a process of reflection in some other, and possibly better form. Thucydides and Lord Bolingbroke went so far as to complain of the possession of a memory so prodigious, so indiscriminately tenacious, that it was rather a hindrance than a help to their intellectual activity. "Some people," says Archbishop Whately, "have been intellectually damaged by having what is called a good memory. An unskilful teacher is content to put before children all they ought to learn, and to take care that they remember it; and so, though the memory is retentive, the mind is left in a passive state; and men wonder that he who was so quick at learning and remembering should not be an able man, which is as reasonable as to wonder that a cistern, if filled, should not be a perpetual fountain. Many men are saved by the deficiency of their memory from being spoiled by their education; for those who have no extraordinary memory are driven to supply its place by thinking If they do not remember a mathematical demonstration they are driven to devise one. If they do not remember what Aristotle or Bacon said, they are driven to consider what they are likely to have said, or ought to have said."

Thus, while we do well to mark deficiencies in any one particular form of memory among our pupils, and to supply appropriate exercises for removing them, we may be consoled to remember that there are compensations for these deficiencies. It is most undesirable that all minds should conform, or be made to conform, to the same type, and so long as by some process or other—the verbal association or the logical association—the mind can be led back to the truth once known, and that the truth can be so recovered for the purpose for which it is now required, we may be well content. Only let us in teaching anything always give the impression that it will be wanted again. Let us remember that our minds refuse

Why memory lessons do not always serve their purpose.

to retain mere isolated facts which are not associated with something which we knew before, or which we hope to know hereafter. It is by frequent recapitulation, by recalling the work of other lessons, by shewing the relation between the past, the present and the future stages of learning that we encourage the student to make that effort of attention which is indispensable to remembering. This is why so many of the memory exercises which are given in schools are so barren of result. They lead to nothing of which the scholar can see the value.

The fruit-bearing stage earlier in some subjects than in others. Up to a certain time in the course of learning any subject its details seem dry and uninteresting, and are learned by a conscious and not always agreeable effort. But there comes a moment, say in the learning of a language, when the learner catches its spirit, receives a new idea through its means, actually uses it as an instrument of thought. From that moment all the gerund-grinding, the weary exercises in vocabulary and grammar have a new meaning and value. Knowledge has passed into the form of culture, and the memory exercises all prove to have served their purpose. So in arithmetic and mathematics, the moment the student perceives the principle of a rule, the process ceases to be mechanical and becomes intelligent. Here the fruit-bearing stage of the study comes earlier than in language, and it may be said that an elementary knowledge in this department, even if it stop short at the elements, is worth something. But if the fruit-bearing stage is not reached, if the study is not carried far enough to enable a student to receive or express a thought by means of the language, much of the time spent in acquiring the rudiments is absolutely wasted. There is nothing in the future life of the student to recall to him what he has learned, and much of it comes to nothing.

Yet it would not be right to conclude that all knowledge which is forgotten has failed to serve a useful purpose. It may be forgotten in the form in which it has been received, but it may reappear in another. What is true in the vegetable world is often true in the world of spirit and of thought: "Except a corn of wheat fall into the ground *and die*, it abideth alone." It comes to nothing. The condition of its germinating and giving birth to something better than itself is that it shall die; and that it shall cease to retain the exact shape and character which it had at first. It is true that what is hastily acquired is hastily lost. What is consciously got up for some temporary purpose drops out of the mind and leaves no trace. Like Jonah's gourd, it comes up in a night and perishes in a night. It is not of this I speak. But all knowledge once honestly acquired and made a subject of thought germinates, even though in time it becomes unrecognizable, and seems to disappear altogether. It has fulfilled its purpose, has deepened a conviction, has formed the legitimate ground for some conclusion on which in turn something else has been built; and it gives to the learner a sense of freedom and of elbow-room when in after life he is dealing with it and cognate subjects, such as he could not possibly experience if the subject were wholly new to him. Rules serve their purpose if they form our habits of speech or of action, even though these habits are not consciously obedient to the rules, and although the rules themselves could not be re-stated in an explicit form. A demonstration in mathematics has done its work if, for the time, it gave an insight into the true method of reasoning, even though in later life we utterly fail to remember the theorem or the proof. So the exact character of a set of experimental illustrations in physics may be entirely forgotten;

yet if the truth they illustrated was by their help fastened on the mind, and has subsequently been seen in wider and more varied application, we have no right to say that the original effort has been wasted.

· The thoughts and experiences which make up the sum of our mental life in different years vary as much as the particles that compose the body. Some disappear and others take their place. But the life is the same so long as there is continuity and health. Personal identity consists, not in sameness of substance, but in continuity of life. So the relation of what you teach to the permanent thoughts and work of the pupil consists in its capacity for development into something not itself, but akin to itself, better than itself. Here then is one of the tests of our school-lessons. Grant that as school-lessons they will be forgotten. Let us reconcile ourselves to this as inevitable, and ask in relation to everything which we teach: "Is it germinating and fruit-bearing, or not? When the husk and shell shall have decayed, will there be anything left? If so, what? Will this bit of knowledge drop wholly out of the memory and leave no trace? If so, I will not teach it, though it is in the text-book. Or will it, even though it looks crabbed and unpractical, make the perception of some larger and more useful truth easy; will it leave some effect in the form of improved taste, truer judgment, or increased power to balance opposing facts? If so, I will have it learned, even though I know it will be forgotten; and I will feel thankful that there is an art of wisely forgetting, as well as one of useful remembering."

Chief instruments of learning. (1) *Oral instruction.* The main instruments for obtaining knowledge and storing the memory are three: oral exposition; self-tuition and reflection; and book or task-work. Of the reaction in modern times against the too frequent use of books and tasks I have already spoken. And there can be little doubt that this reaction is right, and that as people get a worthier and truer perception of the nature of teaching, oral instruction comes to be more valued. It is chiefly by means of the living voice that scholars can be really inspired; it is only when the eyes meet and expression and gestures are seen, and tones are heard, that there arises that subtle and indefinable sympathy between teacher and taught, which is so essential to the intellectual life of the scholar. Then only can there be that adaptation of the matter to his wants; the light glancing over unimportant details, the rest and repetition over the more significant facts, the pause after what is exceptionally difficult, the happy illustration, the *argumentum ad hominem*, the brisk and pointed question by which the teacher assures himself that he is being followed, and understood. For all this the teacher wants fluency, fertility and quickness of resource, care in the choice of his language, a *lucidus ordo* in his arrangement; a power of putting the same truth in several different lights; a quick insight in discovering what are the difficulties in the learner's mind, and in removing each difficulty when it occurs; a certain tact which tells him when he may safely hasten, when he ought to linger, how fast he should go, and where he ought to stop. *Its advantages.*

There is room then for something in the nature of a lecture, for the collective or class lesson, in connexion with every subject you teach.

But while such teaching is after all the great vitalizing instrument in education, we may not forget that, if too exclusively relied on, it has its drawbacks. There is first the danger lest the teacher should mistake the signs of collective animation for individual progress. The whole may seem interested, and yet the units composing the *Its dangers.*

whole may be very imperfectly taught. The sympathetic influence arising from the presence of numbers, all of whom are working together to the same end, has the effect of awakening interest; but it has also the disadvantage of making this result seem greater than it is. Then a skilful oral teacher often anticipates difficulties, seeks to exemplify and explain everything, and in this way leaves the scholar too little to do for himself. He stimulates attention, but he does not strengthen the habit of independent research. Too great reliance on the lecture system is apt also to lead pupils to reproduce everything which has been taught in the teacher's own words. Besides, in the desire to make things interesting the teacher is fain to indulge in generalizations, in picturesque statements, which though true and right as the result of a knowledge of *data*, are extremely pretentious and unreal without such data. And the effect on a learner's mind of letting him see the whole without shewing him the parts, and of encouraging him to accept a general induction without knowing the particulars on which it has been based, is sometimes very mischievous.

These are dangers inseparably connected with the lecturing or expository system. They beset in a special way the most earnest and sympathetic teachers. They are to be guarded against (1) by the incessant use of oral questions during the lesson; (2) by requiring that notetaking during the lesson shall be limited to a few significant headings or technical words, and shall not reproduce the phrases or sentences of the teacher; (3) by causing the substance of the whole lesson to be thought out, and in part written out after the delivery of it is finished; (4) and, above all, by taking care to leave something substantial for the learner to do, to find out, or to arrange for himself.

For after all we may not, in our zeal for the improvement of schools as places of instruction, forget that some of the best work of our own lives has taken the form of self-tuition. Consider the multitude of great and famous men who have struggled to master problems without any external aid, and consider too how precious and abiding knowledge won by our own efforts always is. It is true boys and girls do not come to school mainly for what is called self-tuition, but for help and guidance; nevertheless, it is a good rule never to tell them what you could make them tell you; never to do for them what they could do for themselves. Your teaching is not to supersede books, but rather to lead them to the right use of books. You have been studying *e.g.* for a time the history of Edward III.; you want to gather it all up, and to give unity to the impression of that particular period left on the mind of the learners. You give therefore a short catechetical lecture on the life of Wyclif, whom you select as a representative man of the time. But you would not do well even to try to make such a lecture exhaustive. Something should be left for the pupils to hunt out by themselves. A good teacher will say: "I have tried to sketch out the main incidents and drift of Wyclif's life, and I want you in the course of next week to write a biography, as complete as you can. You will find additional information in Longman's book, and in Chaucer's Prologue, in Pauli's *Pictures of Old England*, and in Palgrave's *Merchant and the Friar*. Do not think it necessary to follow the order I have sketched, or to make the same estimate of his character which I have given, if you find any facts which seem to tend the other way." Be sure that if, as the result of your teaching, your pupils seem indisposed to read for themselves, if they get the impression that all that needs to be known will be told

(2) *Self-tuition.*

them by yourself, then there is a fatal flaw even in the most animated oral lessons, and your methods need to be revised.

(3) Book-work.

Book-work for lessons has obvious advantages. It is definite. It puts into a concise and rememberable form,—it focusses, so to speak, much of what is treated discursively in oral lessons. It can be revised again and again, as often as is necessary, until it is understood. Just as oral teaching is the main instrument for awakening intelligence, so book-work is the chief safeguard for accuracy, clearness of impression, and permanence. We cannot do without either. It is however the best teachers who are most in danger of undervaluing set lessons from books. It is the worst, or at least the common-place, the indolent, the uninspired teachers who have a constant tendency to overvalue them. As I have already said, it is the easiest of all forms of teaching to set a book-lesson, and to say, "Go and prepare it." It is because it is so easy that a good teacher will always exercise special watchfulness over himself, and ask before setting a lesson, "Is this really the best way of effecting my purpose?"

Its shortcomings.

Before descending to detail and offering rules as to task and book-work, it may be well to go back a long way for a few moments, to ask you to consider how the relation of written work to intellectual exertion is illustrated in the *Phaedrus*, one of the dialogues of Plato. Socrates is pointing out to one of his disciples how easy it is for a student to mistake means for ends, and to make the art of writing rather a substitute for mental effort than an aid to it.

"I will tell you a story, my dear Phaedrus. Theuth was one of the ancient gods of Egypt, who was the first to invent arithmetic and geometry, and draughts and dice, but especially letters. Now Thamus was at this time the king of Egypt, and dwelt in the great city of Thebes. To him Theuth went and shewed him all the arts which he had devised, and asked him to make them known to the rest of the Egyptians. Thamus asked him what was the use of each. But when they came to the letters, 'This knowledge, O king,' said the deity, 'will make thy people wiser, for I have invented it both as a medicine for memory and for wisdom.' But the king answered: 'Most ingenious Theuth, it is for you to find out cunning inventions, it is for others to judge of their worth and their nobleness. But methinks you, out of fondness for your own discovery, have attributed to it precisely the opposite effect to that which it will have. For this invention will produce forgetfulness on the part of those who use it, since by trusting to writing, they will remember outwardly by means of foreign marks, and not inwardly by means of their own faculties. You are providing for my people the appearance rather than the reality of wisdom. For they will think they have got hold of something valuable when they only possess themselves of written words, and they will deem themselves wise without being so.' What say you, my Phaedrus, did the king speak truly?

"'I think, Socrates, that you can make up stories from Egypt or any other country you please, when you want to prove anything.'

"Nay, but my dear Phaedrus, consider not where the story comes from, but whether it is true. For in the old days men were ready in the groves of Dodona and in other places, to listen to an oak or a stone, provided it spoke the truth. And consider further, my Phaedrus, that written discourses have this disadvantage, they seem as if they were alive and possessed some wisdom, but if you ask them to explain anything they say, they preserve a solemn silence, or give at best but one and the selfsame answer. And once written, every discourse is tossed about and read alike by those who understand it and by those whom it in nowise concerns, and it knows not to whom to speak, and to whom to be silent. But after all, if writing is to be of any service, it must be to recall that which is already known and understood; and unless knowledge is shaped and fixed in a learner's soul, it is of no value at all."

Perhaps this old Greek apologue may not be without a useful bearing upon the next practical question before us. "What are the conditions on which book-work and written exercises, especially those done out of school, are most likely to serve a useful educational purpose?"

Characteristics of good home exercises.

They should not be long.

The first of these conditions is that the exercises should not be too long. Children under twelve should not be asked to do home work which takes more than an hour, nor scholars of any age to do more than can be fairly done in two hours. A good teacher will ask the parents to inform him if the time devoted to home exercises exceeds this limit, and if it proves to do so, the lesson should be diminished in amount. Nor should lessons given to be prepared at home be such as require or presuppose intelligent assistance. It is not fair for a teacher to relegate much of his own work to the parent. It may be that your pupil is so circumstanced that he has no access at home to scholarly help; and in that case you impose an unreasonable burden on him, and your task will not be done. And if he has access to such help, the beneficent influence of an intelligent home will produce far more effect in ordinary intercourse, than if father or mother is reduced to the *rôle* of a school assistant. Home has its own sacredness, and its own appropriate forms of training. Do not let the school exercises encroach too far upon it.

They should be very definite.

Home lessons should be very definite, and admit of easy correction. They have no value, and they encourage carelessness, unless they are thoroughly examined. Think well then before setting them whether you have leisure and teaching power enough to examine them critically. And to this end let an exercise of this kind be as far as possible such as admits of only one way of being right, so that it may be perfectly clear if it is wrong how and why it is wrong. Remember that exercises may be very easy to set, but very difficult to examine and test. Nothing is easier after a lesson than to say, "Write me to-night an account of what has been said to-day." But when the exercises come in you will find that there are a dozen different forms of right and a hundred ways in which it is possible to be wrong; and that to bring the merits and defects clearly before the mind of your pupils implies discussion and lengthy personal interviews with each child, which, however valuable, take too much time. And unless you have the time to spare, do not try it; but keep to lists, names, definitions, facts, of which you can say at once whether they are right or wrong.

One great advantage of very definite lessons is that they often admit of being expeditiously corrected in class, by the method of mutual revision. The exercise books change hands, and each scholar takes a pencil for the marking of mistakes, while the teacher publicly goes through the questions, causing the answers to be read, and criticizing them when they are wrong. After errors have been marked, they are handed back to the original writers. This is not the only way of correcting exercises, and many occasions arise when more minute personal supervision is needed on the part of the teacher. But it economizes time, it furnishes the occasion for a most effective form of recapitulatory lesson, and it awakens interest by putting the scholars into a new attitude of mind—that of critics. Moreover, it is far more effective as a means of correction than the laborious marking of exercise books by the teacher after hours. For such commentaries as there is time to write on the margin are necessarily very concise and incomplete, and not unfrequently remain unread. It is obvious however that this plan of mutual correction in class, though I believe it might be more largely adopted with advantage, presupposes that the exercises are very definite in their character, such as memory-work, translation, and arithmetic, and is inapplicable to essays or general composition.

They should admit of ready correction.

They should be supplementary rather than preparatory.

Two distinct objects may be contemplated in the setting of home tasks. The one that the lessons so learned shall be preparatory, and give the materials for to-morrow's lesson; the other, that they should be supplementary, and should have a bearing on the school-teaching of the previous day. There is an obvious sense in which any given lesson may be said to fulfil both purposes. Nevertheless, your minds should be clearly made up as to the purpose which you think the more important of the two. One view on this point is well expressed by Mr D. R. Fearon in his very able and useful work on School Inspection. He says of geography and history, that "matters of fact should be acquired by pupils out of school, in readiness for the lessons. It is a deplorable waste of teaching power, and is ruinous both to teacher and taught to let the teacher's time and vigour be spent in telling the children mere rudimentary facts which they can gain from a text-book......At Marlborough and Rugby the scholars are expected to get up those mere elements out of school, and the business of the master is one which presupposes in his scholars an acquaintance with such rudiments; it is to test, illustrate, amplify and give interest to such presupposed elementary knowledge."

Now grant that the distinction here made is a right one, that all the interesting and intelligent work has to be done in school, and all the drudgery out of it, it is still an open question whether the task of learning names and facts may not be greatly lightened by coming after rather than before your lesson. It is rather hard on a child to expect him to deal thus with all the dry bones, until you come and clothe them with flesh and with life. I hold that however judicious this method may be in some exceptional cases, it is a safe general rule that out of door exercises should be designed less often to prepare the way for a coming lesson than to deepen and fix the memory of a past lesson. Children learn with much more zest and interest that of which they can see the bearing and the use than that which they are merely told will have a bearing and a use hereafter.

So if I were going to give a lesson on the geography of Switzerland, I would not require the scholars the day before to get up a list of the towns, the cantons, or the mountains. But I would give a general oral description, would describe by map or model its physical configuration, would try to awaken some interest in the hardy, thrifty, liberty-loving people who lived in it; and then at the end of the lesson would require a map of the country and a few written data about it to be prepared as a home lesson. So in arithmetic, I would not, if to-morrow's lesson were to be on reducing fractions to a common denominator, say to the scholars, " Now to-night you are to learn by heart a new rule, and I will explain it and shew you how to apply it to-morrow." It is in my judgment a better plan to begin by taking a problem and working it out inductively on the black-board, to shew as you go on the need of each process and its fitness for the end proposed; and then at the end of it to say: "What we have thus found is contained in a rule which I want you to learn and write out. Here also are three examples to be worked in the same manner, which you will do to-night." So with a new grammatical distinction, say the ablative absolute, I would give an explanation, seek to make it clear by a few striking examples, and then give out as a home lesson the task (1) of learning the rule or definition by heart—provided it were such a rule or definition as fulfilled the conditions we have already

Illustrative examples.

laid down—and (2) of finding out in a given page or chapter as many examples of the ablative absolute as possible.

I am far from saying that there are no cases in which it is good to give out a home exercise in anticipation of to-morrow's work. You want *e.g.* to have an ode of Horace or a fable of La Fontaine prepared to-morrow. Now if you say to a child, "Learn this, and be prepared to-morrow with a complete translation of it;" and you expect then to find him able to account for all the idioms and allusions, what you are asking is somewhat unreasonable. The complete understanding of the whole passage is precisely that which your teaching is meant to give him. You must not throw upon him so much responsibility. But it is well to say: "We are going to take to-morrow the twelfth ode of the second book, and we shall read it in class together. Find out therefore to-night from the dictionary all the words you do not already know." That is a perfectly legitimate requirement. If that is fulfilled, you have some material to work with. You read it line by line, you elicit by questioning as much grammar and idiom as is known, you supply the new facts, the illustration of new grammatical difficulties, the allusions, the significance of the metaphors, the turns of happy expression; and then, when you have done this, you say, "To-night I shall expect you to write me a full and careful translation of the whole; and here are a dozen words—proper names, idioms, or allusive phrases—which you will underline, and on each of which you must write a special comment or explanation."

Thus you will see, the home or evening work which may legitimately be set is partly preparatory and partly supplementary to your class teaching. But the best part of it is supplementary. And I have no doubt that, as a general rule, the chief value of written exercises is to give definiteness to lessons already learned, and to thrust them home into the memory rather than to break new ground. Kindle interest and sympathy first. Let the scholars see what you are aiming at, and catch something of your own interest and enthusiasm in the pursuit of truth, and then they will be prepared to take some trouble in mastering those details which they see to be needed in order to give system and clearness to their knowledge. But he who expects children to master with any earnestness details of which they do not see the purpose, is asking them to make bricks without straw, and will certainly be disappointed.

VI. EXAMINING.

Examinations.   THE whole subject of Examinations looms very large in the vision of the public and is apt to be seen out of its true proportions, mainly because it is the one portion of school business which is recorded in newspapers. We shall perhaps arrive at right notions about it more readily, if we first consider the business of examining as wholly subordinate to that of education, and as part of the work of a school. If we are led to just conclusions on this point, we may then hope to consider with profit the effect of the tests and standards applied to school work by outside bodies, by University Examiners, or in competitions for the public service.

The art of putting questions.   First, however, we may be fitly reminded that the art of putting questions is one of the first and most necessary arts to be acquired by a teacher. To know how to put a good question is to have gone a long way towards becoming a skilful and efficient instructor. It is well therefore to ask ourselves what are the conditions under which catechizing can be most effective.

The object of putting questions to a child whom we are instructing may be:—

(1) To find out what he knows, by way of preparing him for some further instruction.

(2) To discover his misconceptions and difficulties.

(3) To secure the activity of his mind and his cooperation while you are in the act of teaching him.

(4) To test the result and outcome of what you have taught.

So that interrogation is not only a means of discovering what is known, it is itself a prime instrument in imparting knowledge. In the employment of all our faculties, we want not only the dynamic power, but the guiding sensation to tell us what we are doing. If a man is deaf, he soon becomes dumb. Unless he can hear himself, he ceases to know how to talk, and he soon leaves off caring to talk. So as we go on giving a lesson, we are completely in the dark, unless by means of constant questioning we keep ourselves *en rapport* with our pupil, and know exactly whether and how far he is following us.

Hence the first object of questioning is to awaken curiosity, to conduct the learner, so to speak, to the boundaries of his previous knowledge, and thus to put his mind into the right attitude for extending those boundaries by learning something new. And we all know that the one person who is generally reputed to be the master of this art, and who has in fact given his name to one particular form of catechizing, was Socrates. Now what is the Socratic method of questioning? Socrates was, as you know, a philosopher who lived in the golden age of Greece, when intellectual activity in Athens was at its highest point; and the function he assigned to himself was a very unique one. He saw around him a people who thirsted for knowledge, and were very fond of speculation. He saw also that there was a large class of men, Sophists, Rhetoricians, and others, who sought to satisfy

The questions of Search.

this appetite. And what struck him most forcibly was the haste with which people generalized about things which they had imperfectly examined, the heedlessness with which they used certain words before fixing their meaning, and generally the need of more self-examination and self-knowledge. Hence it was the chief purpose of the dialogues which have been handed down to us by his affectionate disciples Xenophon and Plato, to clear men's minds of illusions, and of the impediments to learning; and rather to put them into the best attitude for receiving knowledge and for making a right use of it, than to give to them definite dogmas, or authoritative statements of truth. I should have been well content if the plan of these lectures had allowed of our devoting one of our meetings exclusively to a consideration of his remarkable career, and to the effect of his method of teaching in awakening enquiry, and in purging and disciplining the faculties of his hearers. But it must suffice if I say even to those of you who do not read Greek that by devoting a little time to the perusal of some of the dialogues as given by Whewell or Jowett in their editions of Plato, or to a translation of the *Memorabilia* of Xenophon, or to Mr Grote's or Professor Maurice's account of the teaching of Socrates and the Sophists of his day, you will acquire some very valuable hints. Meanwhile I should like to give you one short and free translation of a little dialogue from Xenophon which is characteristic of his method.

A Socratic dialogue. There was a young man named Euthydemus in whom he took much interest, and who was fired with a very strong ambition to distinguish himself as a thinker and a philosopher. So Socrates placed himself in his way and said:

"They say, my Euthydemus, that you have collected many of the writings of those men whom we call wise: Is it so?"

"Most undoubtedly it is, and I shall not cease to collect them, for I value them very highly. I covet knowledge most of all."

"What sort of knowledge do you desire most?" He then enumerates one after another the principal professions—that of a physician, an architect, a geometrician, and receives negative answers in each case.

"Perhaps then you desire that kind of knowledge which makes the able statesman and the good economist, which qualifies for command and renders a man useful to himself and others."

"That indeed is what I sigh for and am in search of," replied Euthydemus with no small emotion.

Socrates commends this resolve and by a few more questions elicits from his catechumen, the declaration that what men want is a stronger sense of justice, and that he hopes to be useful in making them understand their duties better. "Assuredly," he says in reply to Socrates's request for a definition of justice, "there can be no practical difficulty in pointing out what is just and what is unjust, in actions about which we are conversant daily."

"Suppose then," says Socrates, "we draw a line and set down an Alpha here and an Omega there, and arrange under these two heads the things that belong to justice and injustice respectively."

"You may do so, if you think there will be any use in such a method."

"Now" (having done this) " Is there any such a thing as lying?"

"Most certainly."

"And on which side shall we place it?"

"Under Omega, the side of injustice certainly."

"Do mankind ever deceive each other?"

"Frequently."

"And where shall we place this deceit?"

"On the same side of the line."

"Selling people into slavery who were born free?"

"Still the same certainly."

"But suppose one whom you have elected to command your armies should take a city belonging to your enemies, and sell its inhabitants for slaves. Shall we say he acts unjustly?"

"By no means."

"May we say he acts justly?"

"We may."

"And what if while he is carrying on the war he deceiveth the enemy?"

"He will do right by so doing."

"May he not likewise, when he ravages their country, carry off their corn and their cattle without being guilty of injustice."

"No doubt, Socrates, and when I seemed to say otherwise I thought you confined what was spoken to our friends only."

"So then, what we have hitherto placed under the letter Omega may be carried over and arranged under Alpha."

"It may."

"But will it not be necessary to make a further distinction, Euthydemus, and say that to behave in such a manner to our enemies is just, and to our friends unjust, because to these last the utmost simplicity and candour is due?"

"You are in the right, Socrates."

"But how, if this general, on seeing the courage of his troops begin to fail, should make them believe fresh succours at hand, and by this means remove their fears; to which side should we assign this falsehood?"

"I suppose to justice."

"Or, if a child refuseth the physic he stands in need of, and the father deceiveth him under the appearance of food, where shall we place this deceit, Euthydemus?"

"With the same, I imagine."

"And, suppose a man in the height of despair should attempt to kill himself, and his friend should come and force away his sword, under what head are we to place this act of violence?"

"I should think under the same head as the former. It is clearly not wrong."

"But take care, Euthydemus, since it seemeth from your answers that we ought not always to treat our friends with candour and perfect truthfulness, which yet we had before agreed should be done."

"It is plain we ought not, and I retract my former opinion, if it is allowable for me to do so."

"Most assuredly, for it is far better to change our opinion than to persist in a wrong one. However, that we may pass over nothing without duly examining it, which of the two, Euthydemus, appears to you the more unjust, he who deceives his friend willingly, or he who does it without having any such design?"

"By Jove, Socrates, I am not certain what I should answer or what I should think, for you have given such a turn to all I have said as to make it appear very different from what I thought it. I fancied I was no stranger to philosophy, but now it seems to me more difficult, and my own knowledge of it less than I supposed."

Now, by some such method, however humbling, it was Socrates's desire to bring the mind of a disciple into a fit state for further investigation. To shew him that there were latent difficulties in many things which seemed very simple; that plausible and well-sounding general propositions admitted of exceptions and qualifications which were often unsuspected; and that till these things had been recognized and carefully examined, it was premature to dogmatise about them—all this appeared to him a needful part of intellectual discipline. And if, on reading what are called the "dialogues of search," you observe that they end in nothing but mere negative conclusions, and bring you to no definite statement of truth; you may bear in mind that though this result may seem disappointing, and though it undoubtedly disappointed his disciples very often, it would not have disappointed him. For if he could clear away illusions, and make people see the difference between what they knew and what they did not know, and so put them into a better condition for arriving at conclusions for themselves, he thought he had done them a greater intellectual service than if he had provided them with any ready-made conclusions, however valuable.

Socratic questioning.

And, in like manner, I think we shall do wisely as teachers if we seek before giving a new lesson to ascertain by means of questions what previous knowledge exists, and what misconceptions or vagueness are in the minds of our pupils on the subject we want to explain. Doing this serves two purposes. It reveals to you the measure of the deficiency you have to supply, and it

Application of method to school use.

awakens the sympathy and interest of the pupil by shewing him what he has to learn.

Tests of a good question.
Supposing this preliminary work done, you have next to consider how questions may be most effectually used in the course of lessons and at the end of them.

1. *Clearness.*
The first requisite of a question is that it should be in perfectly clear, simple language, the meaning of which admits of no mistake. It should be expressed in as few words as possible. I heard a man questioning a class the other day in physical geography. He said:

"Where do you expect to find lakes? For instance, you know the difference between a chain of mountains and a group, don't you. Well, you know the water comes down the side of a mountain, and must go somewhere. What is a lake?"

Here in this question there are four sentences, and two totally different questions. The questioner knew what he wanted, but while he was speaking it dawned upon him that he might make it clearer, so he interposed a little explanation, and ended by putting a different question from that which he gave at first. It was amusing to see the puzzled and bewildered look of the children as they listened to this, and to many other of the like clumsy and inartistic questions, fenced round by qualifications and afterthoughts, until it was very hard for them to know what was really expected of them. In this particular case he had got hold of a very true notion. He should first have shewn a drawing or a little model of a chain of mountains, and then have asked them to tell him what became of the streams that rolled down into a plain. Soon he would have elicited a good general notion of the course of rivers as determined by a watershed. Then he should have asked what would happen if the mountains were not in a chain but in a group, so that when the water rolled down one side it could not get away but was stopped by another mountain. "What becomes of the water?" It must stop in the valleys. "And when water remains in a valley, what do we call it?" A lake. "Now tell me what a lake is." "How do you expect to find the mountains arranged in the lake country. In a group or in a range? Why?" Each question, you see, ought to be one, and indivisible. There should be no ambiguity about the sort of answer it requires.

Let me warn you also to avoid the habit of surrounding your questions with little expletives and circumlocutions. "Can anyone tell me?" "Which of you knows?" "Will those hold up their hands who can answer?" "Well now, I want some child to answer this." Strip your question, as a rule, of all such verbiage and periphrase, and say plainly what you want. "Which are the verbs in that sentence?" "Why is that noun in the ablative case?" "How many feet are in a mile?" Practise yourself in economizing your words and reducing all such questions to their simplest forms.

2. Terseness.

Generally too, all wide, vague enquiries should be avoided. "What do you think of that?" "What sort of person was Henry VIII.?" "Describe what happened in the civil war." "What are the uses of iron?" I heard a teacher giving a lesson on the atmosphere. He described a man drowning, and brought out that he died for want of air. "Now," said he in triumph, "what is the thought that occurs to our minds?" Well, I am sure I could not have answered that question; a good many thoughts occurred to my mind, but as I had no clear knowledge of the particular thought which was in his, and which he expected from his class, I should certainly have been silent,—and so were his pupils. Questions of this sort, which admit of a good many answers, or of a long

3. Point.

and comprehensive answer, are perfectly legitimate in a written examination, because then there is leisure to answer them fully. But they are unsuited to oral questioning, which should always be brisk and pointed, and should elicit one fact at a time.

4. Not requiring mere affirmative or negative answer. Need I warn you against the use of that style of question in which the whole of what has to be said is said by the teacher, and the scholar is simply called on to assent. Here is an extract from a nice little catechism on 'good manners,' published in Scotland for the use of Board Schools:

> "*Q.*—Is untruthfulness a very common vice in children?
> *A.*—Yes.
> *Q.*—Are children much tempted to the commission of it?
> *A.*—Yes.
> *Q.*—Is untruthfulness or lying a low and degrading vice, repugnant to conscience, punishable by law, and universally abhorred and condemned?
> *A.*—Yes.
> *Q.*—And yet you say children are guilty of it, and greatly tempted to its commission.
> *A.*—Yes.
> *Q.*—Are there instances recorded in Scripture of this sin being instantly visited by the punishment of death?
> *A.*—Yes.
> *Q.*—Ought anyone to respect, or esteem, a known liar?
> *A.*—No.
> *Q.*—Would *you* willingly associate with, or make a companion of, any boy or girl known to be a liar?
> *A.*—No."

I need not say that there is no questioning here, notwithstanding the catechetical form of the book from which I take it. Little children say 'yes' and 'no' quite mechanically as they listen to these admirable sentiments. They know by the very tones of your voice what answer you expect; and they can give it without in the least degree appropriating the idea conveyed by your questions. You may easily test this for yourself; and for the present, take my word for it that the power to give a mere affirmative or negative answer to your questions may co-exist with complete ignorance of the whole subject you are professing to teach.

And in a less degree, I would have you distrust all answers which consist of single words. You explain by a diagram or otherwise to little children, what the line is which passes through the centre, and you say that it is called a diameter. Some teachers would follow up this explanation by saying, "What do we call this line?" A diameter. "What is it?" A diameter. Now the mere echo of the word may readily be given you in this way if you repeat the question a dozen times, and given by children who do not know what it means. The word diameter is part of a sentence. "The line which passes through the centre of a circle or of a sphere is called a diameter." And unless the children have appropriated this whole sentence, they have learned nothing. So the moment you have elicited the word in reply to one question, put a second question in another form, "What is a diameter?" This will make them give you the rest of the sentence. And then afterwards, Now what have we learned? "That a diameter is, &c." Let us remember that every answer we get to an ordinary question is a fragment of a sentence; that it is only the sentence, and not the single word which conveys any meaning; and that the questioner who understands his art turns his question round until he gets from his scholars successively the other parts of the sentence and finally the whole. Indeed one of the best tests of a good question is the relation between the number of words employed by the teacher and the pupil respectively. If the teacher

5. Nor capable of being answered in single words.

does all the talking, and the pupil only responds with single words the questioning is bad. The great object should be with the minimum of your own words to draw out the maximum of words and of thought from him.

6. Nor those to which it is unreasonable to expect an answer.
It will be obvious to you that questions should not be put which you could not answer yourself, or to which you have no reasonable right to expect an answer; nor should they be repeated to those who cannot reply. The Socratic *elenchus* is a mischievous expedient, if it is so used as to worry children for knowledge which they do not possess. For in this case you encourage the habit of guessing, which is clearly a bad habit. So all questions ending in the word "What," and a large number of elliptical questions, in which the teacher makes an assertion, and then stops for the scholar to fill up the last word, are open to the same criticism. And as to the practice of suggesting the first syllable of a word to some one who cannot recollect it, it is one which would never be adopted at all by a skilled questioner.

7. Continuity.
In putting a series of questions, whether in the actual course of teaching, or for purposes of recapitulation and examination, great care should be taken to preserve continuity and order. Each question should grow out of the last answer, or be in some way logically connected with it. Consider the manner in which lawyers who practise at the bar employ the art of questioning. You read in the newspapers the evidence given at a trial, and are struck with the clearness and coherence of the story, especially when you know that it was given by an ignorant witness under all the bewildering excitement of publicity. But in fact, no such story as you read has been narrated. The lawyer has elicited fact after fact by a series of questions, and the reporter has given you the answers only. And the method and clearness, the

absence of all irrelevant matter which strike you so much in the evidence, are due not to the narrative powers of the witness, but to the skill of the barrister who knew exactly what he wanted, and in what order the facts should be evolved. Apply this test to your own work sometimes. Ask yourself when your scholars close their books and you question them on a reading lesson, how the series of answers would look if taken down by an unseen reporter, and printed out in full. Would they be orderly, would they be readable? Would they cover the whole ground, and make a complete summary of what has been learned? Unless your questions would stand this test, you have yet something to learn of the teacher's craft.

And with regard to the answers which either you fail to get, or which when you get, you find to be wholly wrong, or partly wrong and partly right, a word or two must be said. If the answering is bad, either you have been asking for what was not known, or for what had been insufficiently explained, in which case you should go back and teach the subject again. Or there may be knowledge but no disposition to answer, in which case your discipline is bad, and you must fall back upon some way of recovering it. All random and foolish answering is rudeness, and should be dealt with as such. But the wrong answers which come from scholars who want to be right generally require to be met with a question differently shaped. Do not leap to the conclusion that because your question is not answered, nothing is known. Take your question back, alter its shape, or put a simpler one. Perhaps after all, the thing you want to get at is known, but the difficulty is in the mere expression of it. You have been giving a lesson on the pressure of the atmosphere: and you say, 'Why is boiling water not so hot on the top of a mountain as in a valley?'

The answers.

Now if the class is silent, it may be simply because this is a complex question, and a good deal might be said in answering it; and your pupil, though knowing something about it, does not know exactly where to begin. So you keep your question in mind, but for the moment withdraw it. You then ask in succession, "What happens when water begins to boil. What the bubbling means? What would have prevented the bubbling from beginning so soon? Greater pressure of air. What would have caused the bubbling to begin earlier? Less pressure. Whether the water is capable of receiving more heat after it begins to bubble? "What is the state of the air up a mountain as compared with that below?" and so forth; and to all of these detailed questions you will probably get answers. And having got them, it may be well then to go back and to say, 'I asked you at first a hard question including all these particulars. Which of you can now give me a complete answer to that first question?' Do not be impatient, and hasten to answer your own questions, which of course is often the easiest thing to do. It is in the very act of drawing out the knowledge and thought of the scholars, and piecing it together, that you are bringing their intelligence into discipline. You have to shew them that much of what you want them to know, they may find in themselves, and that you can help them to find it. And you can only do this by cultivating very great variety in the form in which you put your questions, and by practising the art of resolving all complex questions which prove too difficult into a series of simple ones. When a good teacher receives a clumsy answer, which is partly wrong and partly right, or which though right in substance is wrong in form, he does not reject it; but either he accepts it as partially true, and stops, and after obtaining a better answer from another scholar, goes back, and asks the first to amend his answer: or else he sees that the full investigation of the difficulty thus revealed, would carry him too far from the main purpose of the lesson and spoil its unity. In this case, he reserves the point, so to speak, says it wants further examination, and promises either at the end of the lesson, or very soon in a new one, to go into the matter and clear the difficulty away. Never treat an honest dilemma or confusion as a fault, but always as something, which you would like to solve, and in the solving of which you mean to ask for the pupil's co-operation.

There are those who in questioning, especially when the class is large, are content to receive replies from such scholars, as by holding up their hands or otherwise, volunteer to answer. This is of course easy, but it is very unsatisfactory. Every scholar should know that he is liable to receive a question, and that the more careless and indifferent he seems, the more liable he will be to be challenged. Fasten your eye on the worst scholar in your class and be sure to carry him with you; and measure your progress by what you can do with him. The eagerness of a teacher who is so impatient of delay that he welcomes any answer he can get, and pushes on at once is somewhat ensnaring to him. We must avoid mistaking the readiness of a few clever children, who are prominent in answering, for the intellectual movement of the whole class. If you find yourself in the least danger of thus mistaking a part for the whole, put your questions to the scholars in turns now and then. It may perhaps help to remove an illusion. Or notice the scholars who fail oftenest, and bring them into the desk nearest you, and take care that they have twice as many questions as any one else.

Collective answering deceptive.

Mutual question-ing.

The art of putting a good question is itself a mental exercise of some value, and implies some knowledge of the subject in hand. You are conscious of this when you yourselves interrogate your class. Bear this in mind, therefore, in its application to the scholars. Let them occasionally change their attitude of mind from that of receivers and respondents, to that of enquirers. Remember Bacon's aphorism, *Prudens quaestio, dimidium scientiae.* You are half-way to the knowledge of a thing, when you can put a sensible question upon it. So I have sometimes heard a teacher towards the end of a lesson appeal to his pupils, and say to them one by one, "Put a question to the class on what we have learned!" To do this, a boy must turn the subject round in his mind a little and look at it in a new light. The knowledge that he is likely to be challenged to do it will make him listen to the lesson more carefully, and prepare himself with suitable questions; and whether he knows the answer or not, there is a clear gain in such an effort. The best teachers always encourage their scholars to ask questions. The old discipline in the Mediæval Universities of posers and disputations, in which one student proposed a thesis or a question, and another had to answer it, was not a bad instrument for sharpening the wits. In a modified way, it may be well to keep this in view, and to set scholars occasionally to question one another.

The inquisitive spirit.

Mr Bain has said, "Much of the curiosity of children is a spurious article. Frequently it is a mere display of egotism, the delight in giving trouble, in being pandered to and served. Questions are put, not from the desire of rational information, but for the love of excitement." And later on, he says that "The so-called curiosity of children is chiefly valuable as yielding ludicrous situations for our comic literature." We have thus, on very high authority a reproof for childish inquisitiveness, and an apology for ignorant nurses, and for *fainéants* and unsympathetic teachers in the use of the familiar formula, "Don't be tiresome and don't ask questions." One might have hoped that this was one of the modes of treating children which was becoming obsolete, and that the teachers of the future would at least try to regard the curious and inquiring spirit among children, as one of the most hopeful of signs; one of the principal things to be encouraged in early training; one of their surest allies in the later development of thought. "For Curiosity," Archbishop Whateley says, "is the parent of attention, and a teacher has no more right to expect success in teaching those who have no curiosity to learn than a husbandman has who sows a field without ploughing it." I doubt whether any one of us can establish for himself a satisfactory code of rules, or a workable theory of discipline, until he shall at least have made up his mind on the point thus raised. Is the childish curiosity a thing to be repressed as an impertinence and a nuisance, or to be encouraged and welcomed as the teacher's best auxiliary? Is the habit of putting questions on what a child does not understand—of saying when a hard word occurs—"If you please will you explain that to me, I want to know"—a good habit or a bad one? For my part, although I am quite aware that as a matter of discipline, mere impudence, and forwardness — the putting of questions for the sake of giving trouble to teachers ought to be sternly discountenanced when they occur; it seems to me nevertheless true that for every time in which they occur, there are ten times in which the question of a child evinces real mental activity and a desire to know.

It seems right to revert for a moment to the printed questions, such as are often found appended to school-books; and to the use of Catechisms. The answers when learned by heart are open to the objections I have already urged: (1) That the language in which they are expressed has seldom or never any special value of its own to justify its being committed to memory at all; and (2) That even when learned by heart and remembered the sentences are generally incomplete; for since part of the sentence lies in the question which is not learned by heart; the other part or the answer is a mere fragment, and is of little or no use; and (3) They assume that every question admits of but one form of answer; which is scarcely true of one question in a hundred. But the worst effect of the use of printed catechisms is that produced upon the teacher. So far from encouraging or helping him in the practice of questioning, the use of the book has precisely the opposite effect. I wish to speak with all respect of catechisms, some of which such as the Church Catechism and the Shorter Catechism of the General Assembly are connected with the history of religion in this country, in a way which entitles them, at least so far as their substance is concerned, to veneration. Moreover for parents and for clergymen, and others who are not teachers by profession it may often be useful to see what is the sort of knowledge which should be imparted to children, and in what order the parts of it should be arranged. But nobody who has the most elementary knowledge of the teacher's art would ever degrade himself by using a catechism, and causing the answers to be learned by heart. I remember with what pious care I was taught the Church Catechism in childhood, and how many hundred times I have recited that formulary.

I remember too that there was one question "What did your godfathers and godmothers *then* for you?" in which I always thought that *then* was a verb. But I never asked. It seemed, though a strange expression, to fit in well with the generally quaint and antiquated character of the rest. And to the best of my recollection, this question was never once turned round, and translated into a form in which it was more intelligible to me. Even the worst of my teachers would, if the responsibility of framing the question had been left to him, have been compelled to ask such a question as I could understand. But the fact that the authorized question was printed in a book released him from this responsibility. He regarded the Church's words when learned by heart as a sort of charm, possessing a value quite independent of any meaning they might actually convey; and the result was that though the lesson was called a catechism, there was no true catechizing, and that instead of an exercise which should appeal to the intelligence and the conscience, there was a barren ceremony, which made no impression on either. And what is true of religion is true of all other subjects. I never once found in examining a school, that a subject—were it astronomy, history, geography or heathen mythology—which had been taught by means of a catechism had been properly understood by the learners.

A similar objection though in a less degree attaches to books on science or history in which an attempt is made to gild the pill by casting the treatise into a conversational form. In such books a good boy and girl are often made to evince a shrewdness and a thirst for knowledge which to say the least are remarkable, to play into the teacher's hands, to ask precisely the questions he wishes to answer, and to start only those

Books in the conversational form.

problems and difficulties which he is specially prepared to solve. There is an unreality about all this which children detect even more readily than their elders, and which causes them as a rule to feel some distrust and not a little resentment at the docile little interlocutors of the 'Evenings at Home,' or 'Sandford and Merton.' Real dialogues have a great charm for children; but not manufactured dialogues, too obviously written to serve the purpose of a lesson.

Written examinations. We have now to consider the use of written examinations. For the moment we will put out of view the fact that they are the chief means whereby outside public bodies estimate the work of schools, and whereby examiners select candidates for the army and for various branches of the public service. We cannot escape the consideration of examination as a means of selection, and of awarding the prizes of life. But we shall do well to think of it first as an aid to education, as a device which we should adopt on its own merits, whether the pupil is likely to be examined by other authorities or not.

What they can test. Now, what is it that a judicious examination in writing does for a pupil? Of course, it tests his knowledge. But it is also a valuable educational instrument. It teaches method, promptitude, self-reliance. It demands accuracy and fulness of memory, concentrated attention, and the power to shape and arrange our thoughts. "Moreover," as Mr Latham well observes, "behind all these qualities lies something which a mental physiologist would call massiveness or robustness of brain, or which we call energy of mind. Of this, so far as it is brought out in dealing with books or ideas, we can judge fairly from a written examination. We see that knowledge has been got, and know that brain-work has been done to get it, and in addition we note indications of strength or feebleness of will, we can find out pretty well from a set of papers whether a man knows his own mind or not." Written work will call out qualities which could not be revealed by *vivâ voce* questions. The oral examination is good for intellectual stimulus, for bracing up the student to rapid and prompt action; for deftness and brightness. But oral answers are necessarily discontinuous and fragmentary. The pupil receives help and suggestion at every moment from the play of the teacher's countenance, from the answers given by his fellows. Whatever of unity and sequence there is in the treatment of the subject is the teacher's work, not the pupil's; and until you subject him to the test of writing, you have no security that he has grasped the subject as a whole, or that he is master of the links that bind one part of that subject to another.

Nevertheless we have to postulate here that there are certain very valuable qualities which are not revealed in a written examination, and which the habit of exclusively relying on such examination does not encourage. Except in so far as diligence and obedience are concerned, examinations do little to test moral qualities, or active power. They do not tell you whether the action of mind has been rapid or sluggish, nor how far the pupil has been influenced by a sense of duty or by strong interest in his work. Still less do they help you to guage those attributes on which success and honour in life so much depend; sympathy with human beings, deference for superiors, the power of working with and influencing others; address, flexibility, manner. Let us once for all acknowledge that either for educational purposes, or for testing and selection, with a view to the requirements of a University or of the public service; the

What they cannot test.

best examinations do not test the whole man, but leave some important elements of character to be ascertained by other means; and we have still to ask, within what limits examinations are valuable, and how we can get the maximum of good out of them. If we get at wrong results by trusting to examinations, it is not because examinations are misleading or inequitable, but because we use them too exclusively, and do not also make a due use of other means of judging.

It often happens that pupils who present themselves for some public examination for the first time are hindered by flurry and nervousness from doing themselves justice. But this is because the conditions of the examination, the silence, the printed paper, the isolation, the utter impossibility of getting a friendly hint, or word of encouragement, or any assurance that they are in the right way, are entirely new to them. But these conditions ought not to be new, for they are in themselves a discipline in self-possession and self-mastery. We do well therefore to accept them, not as a grievance, but as having a value of their own; and if our pupils are looking forward to any public examination, to make that examination subservient to our purposes as teachers; not to allow ourselves to be dominated by it.

False metaphors. In making up our minds on this subject we must beware of being misled by false metaphors. We are told sometimes that the habit of probing children often, either by written or oral examinations is like digging up the root of a flower to see how it grows, and those who talk thus say much as to the value of stillness and meditation, and the importance of leaving scope for silent growth and for the natural action of the child's own mental powers. But there is no true analogy here. The act of reproducing what we know, and giving it new forms of expression is not an act of loosening, but of fixing. We must of course abstain from needless and irritating questions, but we may not forget that with a child, to leave him unquestioned and untested is not to give better room for the spontaneous exercise of his own faculties, but simply to encourage stagnation and forgetfulness.

. There is another still more unpleasant metaphor often *Cram.* used in connexion with the subject of examinations. They are said to encourage *cram;* and this word has come to be currently used as a convenient term to designate any form of educational work which the speaker may happen to dislike or wish to discredit. But we should try to clear our minds of illusions on this point. If by this term we mean dishonest preparation, hasty and crude study, a contrivance by which persons may be made to seem to know more than they actually understand; we are all alike interested in denouncing it. But it is not necessarily encouraged by examinations. On the contrary, this is precisely what every good examination is meant to detect. And every examiner who knows his business can easily discern the difference between the knowledge which is genuine and has been well digested, and that which is superficial and is specially got up to deceive him. Dishonestly prepared men undoubtedly come up for examinations, but they do not pass, and the blame of the transaction rests with those who send them up, not with the examinations themselves.

It is plain that this ugly term cannot properly apply to reading, writing and arithmetic. A child can either perform these acts or he cannot; whether he can perform them or not is ascertainable by a simple test, and if he can perform them well he has acquired an accomplishment of permanent value. He may have been unskilfully taught, or taught by too slow a process, but he cannot have been 'crammed' or dishonestly taught. What is implied by the use of this term is often that the work which has been done is of the wrong sort, that it has been done in an excited eager way, and with too great a consciousness of the imminence of the examination. It is your business to watch any tendency in this direction and to guard against it.

Here however it is to be noted, that if the scholar is permitted to attempt in two months, work which ought to occupy a year, it is the ten months' slackness, and not the two months' exceptional effort which constitutes the evil. Even this is an evil which it is easy to exaggerate. It is good for us, all through life to have in reserve the power of putting special energy into our work at particular emergencies. Such emergencies occur occasionally in after years when we do not think of effort; when we willingly 'scorn delights and live laborious days,' and when the whole faculty and strength are concentrated on the solution of one practical problem, or the achievement of one object of strong desire. So long as the health does not suffer we do not object to see a boy's power strained and concentrated on a cricket-match, or a girl's on some decoration or festival, although we know that the effort is excessive, and could not properly be continued. Nature is very kind to young people, and restores their energies to their proper balance very soon; and she will do it we may be sure quite as readily with the intellectual as well as with the physical powers. For one authentic case of permanent injury to the health of a school-boy or girl from too much mental exercise, there are twenty examples of scholars who suffer from idleness or inaction.

Precautions against

But grant that special pressure of this kind is an unmixed evil; it might easily be avoided in your school

Legitimate preparation.

work if you will bear in mind two or three simple precautions : *the abuse of examinations.*

(1) Do not undertake to prepare the pupils of your school for more than one external examination, and make sure that the scheme selected corresponds to your own aim and ideal of school-work.

(2) Having selected it, look its requirements well in the face a good year beforehand, arrange all your work so that a small but distinct approach shall be made towards your end every day. Refuse to allow any pupil to present himself unless he has had time and opportunity to do his work well.

(3) Do not let any part of the preparation be considered exceptional, but incorporate the whole of it as far as possible into the daily programme of the school.

(4) If you have a few pupils going up for the Oxford or the Cambridge Local Examinations, or any other which offers a considerable variety of alternative subjects, select for them all, the one or two of such subjects which, having regard to your own tastes and to the qualifications of your teaching staff, you feel to be most appropriate. Do not cut up the organization of the school and waste your own teaching power by letting the pupils choose their own alternatives. Of course, it is a good thing to consider the individual bent of each child and to encourage it. But you cannot do this wisely in the matter of examinations except where the pupils have access to private tuition. The interests of every pupil in a school are best consulted in the long run by his learning that which others are learning, and which the school can teach best.

(5) It is a good plan to hold a fortnightly or monthly examination in writing, extending over the principal subjects to be taught and conducted under the same

conditions of silence and complete isolation which are observed in public examinations. Besides this, it is well much more frequently to give, in connexion with each subject, a single question, to be answered fully in writing. The teacher should read some of the answers aloud, and point out their several defects, and then invite his class to watch him while he gives a model answer, as complete as he can make it, both as regards matter and style.

For school purposes it is well often to use a form of examination which would be impossible in public competitions, viz. to give more time, and to allow the use of books. After all, some of the best efforts we make in after life are made under these conditions, and the art of using authorities and of referring to them, is one which a school ought to teach. Some subjects lend themselves better to this form of exercise than others, e.g. biography, the description of a country, the explanation of the theory of a mathematical rule, the preparation of an essay on some familiar subject of fact or moral speculation. Here you do not want to test memory, but the power of using all the resources at one's disposal—books as well as thought. So a teacher may wisely say now and then, "Here is a question which wants a little thinking, I will give you two days to answer it, and you may get the answer where and how you like."

Preparation of written questions. In drawing up a paper of questions, or determining how many you should set, you will be guided by circumstances. If you have to examine a number of persons not your own pupils, it is always well to give more questions than can be answered, and to require the student to choose a limited number of those he can answer best. In the India Civil Service, where the competition is absolutely open, and where it is the business of the examiners to do full justice to men who have different tastes, and have been very differently taught, I have been accustomed to set a long paper, say of 20 questions, and require that no candidate shall take more than six. We thus give a wide range of choice, and at the same time forbid a man to attempt a good many questions, and so to accumulate marks by superficial knowledge. At the University of London, where the curriculum of instruction is more strictly defined, but where the candidates have been taught on very different systems, it is usual at Matriculation to set in most subjects about 15 questions, and to limit the scholar to ten. But in a school where the teacher is himself the examiner, and where he knows exactly what has been taught and what ought to be known, it is not desirable to offer any choice or to set more questions than can be answered easily in the time. It is he, not the pupil, who should choose the questions which have to be answered.

As a rule, it is not desirable to sit down to frame a paper of questions all at once. If the examiner relies on his memory, or general knowledge of the subject, his questions will have a sort of family likeness, will deal with what his pupils know to be his special fancies, and so will probably be anticipated. And if he sits down to prepare a paper by the help of a text-book, he is tempted to select such questions as turn on obscure or isolated details, matters easy to question on, but of little real value. So he should usually have his note-book with him, and from time to time, as experience in teaching suggests to him some good form of question, he should jot it down, so as to have a store of such questions ready for use when they are wanted. You are much more likely to adapt your questions to the actual knowledge of the scholars if you do this, than if you attempt to recall the whole subject at once.

Test of a good paper of questions.

The first requisite of a good paper is that it shall be clear and unmistakeable in its meaning. All obscurity, all pit-falls and all ambiguity should be avoided, for they defeat their own purpose.

The next thing necessary is that the paper should be perfectly fair, i.e. exactly adapted to the scholar's age and attainments; and to what he may reasonably be expected to do. The moment you allow yourself to think of the effect that your questions will have on parents or on the outside public, you are in danger of proving unfair to the scholars. The object of the paper is to draw out their knowledge, not to detect their ignorance. You want to encourage them to do their best with the materials they have, and there is a want of perfect candour towards them, when you present them with a paper which you have framed rather to display your own knowledge than theirs, and rather to impress other people with the width and excellence of your curriculum than to correspond to any reasonable requirements you can make of your pupils. I knew a large private school in Yorkshire, the principal of which used his last paper of examination questions as a printed advertisement, which was exhibited at railway stations and in newspapers, together with a prospectus of the school and a highly idealized wood-cut representing that establishment, though a mean one, as one of palatial elevation and park-like surroundings. I need not say that the questions were of a very formidable kind, and were calculated to astonish and impress ignorant people. But what the boys thought of them, how they had answered them, and what sort of moral influence a master could hope to gain over children whom he caused to be parties to an imposture, the outside public were not informed, though I think some of us can guess.

Then a good proportion of the questions in every *Straight-* paper should be on matters of fact and of memory, *forward-ness.* plain straightforward questions in a familiar form, such as the average scholar, who has merely been diligent, but who has no genius, and not much talent for composition may feel encouraged to answer. Simple questions are always best; for they help you to do full justice to common-place pupils, and yet there is scope enough in them for difference in the manner and substance of the answer, to distinguish between such pupils and the best. Still, over and above these simple questions, I should always put two or three which require a little thought to interpret, and which will afford opportunities to the best scholars to distinguish themselves. Say I draw a paper of ten questions on Arithmetic. I would let seven of them be honest, straightforward sums in the form which the scholar would naturally expect; but I would add three which required an explanation of principles, and which, without being puzzles or conundrums, were designed to call forth the ingenuity and thought of the best scholars. Every paper you set has, it must be remembered, an educational value over and above its office as a mere test. It is liable to be referred to and read again, and it helps to set up among your scholars the ideal at which you are aiming. So let us bear in mind that a good examination, when it has fulfilled its first duty as an honest scrutiny of what the pupils ought to have learned already, has also to fulfil the second purpose of showing what you think they ought to aim at, and in what way you wish their own thoughts to be brought to bear upon their work.

There is a kind of examining which has a sad tendency to beget untruthfulness on the part of both teachers and scholars; I mean that in which young or immature students are encouraged to use language which they do not understand, and which presupposes a speculative and philosophic power which they do not yet possess.

Let me read to you some questions lately set at a public institution to some young people who had been attending a course of lectures;

"What is General History, and how is a scientific treatment of this subject possible?

What are the fundamental principles of the Chinese political and social organisation?

. What do the Vedas contain? How do you account for the development of Brahmanism in India, and what are the analogies between the Indian, Egyptian, and Greek mythologies?

Who were the Persians? Sketch their mythical period, and give the principal incidents of their history, and the causes of their decline.

Who were the Greeks, and what was their influence on the intellectual development of humanity?

Give the principal laws of Lycurgus and Solon, their analogies and differences, and describe their influence on the formation of the Greek character.

Name the most important philosophical schools of Greece.

. What were the chief causes that led to the establishment of the Empire at Rome?

What were the principal causes of the rapid progress of Christianity from an historical point of view?"

I have seen some of the answers to these questions, in which there are no facts, but much vague talk about the philosophic teaching of Thales and Anaximander, and about the static and dynamic forces of humanity. The pretentiousness and falsehood of all this will be apparent to you at once. Here are questions which the most accomplished scholars could not answer without effort, placed in the hands of raw beginners, who are thus tempted to indulge in philosophic generalization while profoundly ignorant of the data on which all such generalization ought to rest.

I will suppose that you have framed your eight or ten questions in view of the actual knowledge, both of the ordinary scholar, and of the best who want an opportunity of distinguishing themselves; it then becomes necessary to estimate the answers. On the whole, the ordinary arithmetical test is the fairest and the least liable to error. You determine on a maximum, say 100, to represent the highest attainable excellence. You then assign a due proportion of marks to each question according to its difficulty. It is a good plan to distribute about 90 in this way, reserving the last ten for style, neatness and finish, and general skill of arrangement. In distributing your 90 marks among, say ten questions, you will give perhaps 12 to one, and 6 to another, according to the amount of knowledge and intelligence required to produce a perfect answer. But I would not tell the scholars which questions carried most marks. It is not good that they should be speculating and enquiring what are the relative values of different answers in your mind. It is enough to tell them to select those questions which they can answer best; and you will judge, if one fastens on the purely memory work, while another chooses to give the best of his time to those questions which require some thought and originality to answer them, how such answers ought to be estimated.

The estimation of written answers.

As you read each answer in turn, you should set down the proportion of the maximum number assigned to that particular question which the answer deserves. It is essential that this should be done with each question, and that there should be no room left for caprice or hasty impression by attempting to mark the value of the paper as a whole. Nevertheless, before passing on to

How to read an examination paper.

another paper, and while your recollections are perfectly fresh, it is well to add up the result and see if the total appears to represent fairly the general merit of the paper considered as a whole. For it may be that the scholar though evidently writing from a full mind, has mismanaged his time, has given needlessly elaborate answers, say to four questions, for which he has the maximum marks, and yet has a smaller total than an inferior scholar who has attempted eight questions, and has scored a fair number for each. This should be set right at once by the addition of a few marks for general ability. It is not safe, or really equitable, to leave the total of each scholar's marks to be added up afterwards.

In mathematics it is not difficult for a student, by doing all the exercises right, both in method and result, to obtain the full number of marks. But in other subjects the maximum will rarely, or ever be attained, as it will represent in the examiner's mind the highest conceivable standard of excellence, and it is very unlikely that this will be attained in every one of a number of questions in History or Literature. So in most subjects I should regard as a good paper that which obtained three-quarters, and as a fair or passable paper that which received half of the marks.

Great care should be taken to keep your own judgment equitably balanced while you are reading. So before marking any, it is well to read over several papers, choosing, if you have any sort of clue, one or two likely to be good, and one or two likely to be indifferent, and so fix the standard of what it is reasonable to expect. With this standard in your mind it will be fair to begin marking the answers one by one. If you are examining for any prize or competition it is needful to give the papers a second reading, comparing not only paper with paper, but answer with answer. For ordinary pass examinations this is not necessary.

It is sometimes asked whether negative marks should ever be given, or marks deducted for ignorance. That depends on the kind of ignorance. Mere absence of knowledge ought not to be counted as a fault, otherwise than as depriving the pupil of the marks which would have been due to knowledge. It ought not, I think, to be punished by the subtraction of marks to which other knowledge would entitle him. But the sort of pretentious ignorance which makes blunders and mistakes them for knowledge, which indulges in grand, sonorous and vague statements carefully constructed to conceal the lack of true information ought to be punished as a fault. A bad and inflated style, false spelling, the use of words which are not understood, may not unreasonably be visited with the forfeiture of marks to which the mere memory work would be entitled. But you must make allowance for a few very innocent blunders, such as will be inevitable among young people who are being put to this sort of test without much previous practice. When a scholar tells you that "we derive a good deal of our early knowledge of English History from an ancient chronicler named Adam Bede," that "Buckingham was at first a friend of Dryden, but that he afterwards became one of his contemporaries," or that "Sir Wm. Temple was a statesman in the time of Charles II. who had a hand in the Triple Alliance, and who in later life acquired some odium by writing Essays and Reviews," you may set it down as mere bewilderment, which does not mean ignorance, which would be corrected by a moment's thought, and should therefore not be counted as a fault. On the other hand, a blunder such as that of the man who, in commenting on the passage in Milton referring to "our

Negative marks.

Venial and punishable blunders.

sage and serious poet Spenser" as ." a better moralist than Scotus or Aquinas," said that these worthies were "two licentious poets of the period;" or that of the student who said that "John Locke was a poet who was knighted by queen Elizabeth," or that of him who wrote that "the Americans were so grateful for the services of George Washington that they made him a peer," ought to be reckoned as a fault to be punished, because in each case it is a mere guess, put out rather dishonestly with the chance of its being right or with the deliberate intention of practising on the possible ignorance or carelessness of the examiner.

Even in class work, the course of oral questioning may sometimes be advantageously interrupted, by requiring the answer to be given by all the students immediately in writing instead of word of mouth. If you want to know whether all the class knows a French verb, or a number of dates, or a group of names, this is an expeditious and very thorough method. And here, when you have examined the note books by the plan of mutual correction or otherwise, the result may well be tabulated in a numerical form. But in ordinary oral questioning of a class and estimating its result, I do not think it is quite possible to adopt the arithmetical mode of measurement with perfect exactness, and therefore I would not use it at all, but employ other symbols such as *Excellent, Good, Fair, Moderate*, which are better fitted to describe general impressions.

The morality of examinations.

And yet now the most important thing remains to be said. This whole problem of examinations and the right way of conducting them and preparing for them touches very nearly the morality of the school life. Look well to the influence which the examinations you use are having on the ideal of work and duty which your scholar is forming. Ask yourself often if that which will enable him to do best in examination is also that which is best for him to learn. Watch how the prospect of the examination tells upon his methods of study, his sense of honour, his love of truth. Determine that whatever happens, you will not pay too heavy a price for success in examinations. Discountenance resolutely all tricks, all special study of past papers, and of the idiosyncracies of examiners, and all speculations as to what it will and what it will not "pay" to learn. It is because sufficient regard is not paid to these considerations, that many thoughtful persons now are fain to denounce examinations altogether, as the bane of all true learning, and as utterly antagonistic to the highest aims of a teacher. There ought however to be no such antagonism. In their proper place, examinations have done great service to education, and are capable of doing yet more. But they can only do this on one condition. Let us make sure that for us, and for our pupils, success in examinations shall not be regarded as an end, but as a means towards the higher end of real culture, self-knowledge and thoughtfulness. And let us keep in mind for them and for ourselves the old sound maxim: "Take care of everything but the examination, and let the examination take care of itself."

VII. PREPARATORY TRAINING.

Preparatory training.

I HOPE the subject of very early instruction will not appear to any one here to be insignificant or beneath notice. In the higher departments of instruction, we want to have at our disposal faculties which have been disciplined and brought into active and systematic exercise; and it would be well if we could presuppose that all this discipline has been obtained in the preparatory school. But there are two very good reasons why teachers in Grammar schools or public schools, should try to form clear notions about elementary and even infant training. First, because that training is often incomplete, and needs to be prolonged into an advanced course. It is not a creditable thing that the simple arts of good reading, spelling, and legible writing, should be so despised and disregarded that youths who have been at public schools are often inferior in these respects to the children of National Schools. Year by year, many young men who come up to be examined for commissions in the army, and in the higher departments of the Civil Service—young men who are presumed to have had a liberal education are rejected for bad spelling; and their writing, as I, an old examiner have good reason to know, is almost ostentatiously slovenly and illegible; the scribble of men who

Why it needs the attention of all schoolmasters.

think good writing a thing for clerks and shopmen, and beneath the consideration of gentlemen. One reason therefore for asking your attention to these elementary matters is because provision ought to be more systematically made in higher schools for teaching them properly, if the preparatory school has failed to do it; and in cases where the preparatory training has been good, care should at least be taken to see that the lessons shall not be lost, but that the higher course shall strengthen rather than destroy the neat and accurate habits which have been once acquired.

Another reason why I hope you will not think these simple matters are beneath your attention, is that even the highest class of teachers are often called on to organize and superintend preparatory departments; or at least to test their work and see that they fulfil their proper purpose. They should therefore make up their own minds as to what is the difference between good and bad early training, and how to discern that difference. They are called on, if not to be the educators of very young children, at least to be the critics and guides of those who undertake this work. They suffer if the preparatory training has been unskilful; and they should be ready when occasion arises to point out to the teachers in preparatory schools, how their work ought to be done.

Now it would be beyond my proper province to attempt here an analysis of the parts respectively to be played by the senses and the intellect in the development of a child. That the way to the understanding is through the senses; that in early childhood the senses are more active than the intelligence, and that the first teaching should therefore be addressed to the eye and the ear rather than to the reflective powers are truisms, on which we need not dwell. The processes by which sensation leads the way

Principles to be kept in view in infant discipline.

to knowledge, and knowledge to inference and reasoning are some of the most fertile subjects of enquiry, and will be duly brought before you by my successor, as parts of mental philosophy in its bearing on teaching. Here however it may suffice to say that one of the first things needed in early training, is to teach a child how to use his fingers, his ears and his eyes; and that whether he does this well or ill makes a great difference to him all through his later course.

The training of the senses. The child who has learned in infancy to look steadily at the forms and aspects of the things near him, is later in life a better observer of nature, and student of physical science. He gets more enjoyment, and more culture from seeing pictures, or fine scenery, than if he had been accustomed to gaze aimlessly and vaguely at the things around him. He who has been taught, by exercises ever so childish, steadiness of hand and precision of touch, is better fitted hereafter to be a good draughtsman or musician. And no training of ear to the finer differences of vocal inflection and expression, is without a very important bearing on literary perception and taste. We need not concern ourselves here with subtle speculations as to the exact priority or interdependence of sensual and intellectual perception. "*Nihil in intellectû quod non prius in sensû,*" may or may not be a tenable dogma in speculative philosophy; but we know at least that the development of greater sensitiveness to sight and sound is accompanied, almost necessarily, with the development of intellectual power; that outward expression is a great help to inward clearness; and that whether we call the quickening of physical sensibility a part of lower or of higher education, it is too important a factor in the life and usefulness of a man to be disregarded by any teacher whether high or low.

In the later stages of education, you do not so much concern yourself with conscious training of the senses, in the form of direct exercises, although you know that some studies, notably botany, chemistry, drawing and music have special value in making observation and hearing accurate. And you should not lose sight of the fact that over and above the practical or intellectual uses of these studies, there is a distinct gain from them in the form of a finer sensibility, and of new capacity for interpreting and enjoying the world your pupil has come to live in. Still, within the ordinary domain of school life, the exercises which specially concern the use of the senses are (1) the discipline of the Infant School, and (2) the arts of reading and writing and drawing as practised later. To these we must confine our present enquiries.

The Kindergarten.

The necessity for more definite and intentional training of the senses has been insisted on with much earnestness by Pestalozzi, by Rousseau, and by George Combe, and you will do well to study, in some detail, what those writers have said on the subject. But it is to Fröbel that we owe the clearest recognition of the main principle, and the most systematic effort to reduce that principle to practical application. His method of infant training, to which the rather fanciful name of *Kindergarten* has been given, has been expounded with much care and clearness by Miss Shirreff, by Miss Maning, and in German by the Baroness Bülow, all of whom have the true spirit of discipleship; for they begin by reverencing their master, and end by interpreting his message to the world more clearly than he was able to explain it for himself.

Fröbel devised a series of exercises for young children beginning at the age of three or four. He knew that the first things children want to do are to see, to handle, to move about and to exercise their senses, and he sought to arrange a set of simple and appropriate employments, with a conscious educational purpose, and in careful obedience to the suggestions of Nature. To the youngest he gives a box of wooden bricks, to arrange, and to build up, in imitation of the model designs, made before him by the teacher. Then come exercises in the careful folding of coloured papers into different forms; the plaiting of straw or strips of paper into patterns, the pricking, or sewing with coloured thread of little pictured diagrams; the tracing of lines gradually increasing in length, number and complexity, so as to develop unexpectedly, new and pleasing geometrical designs. Besides these Fröbel provides organized games, little dramatic performances, dances and physical movements of a rhythmic kind, to simple music, and conversational lessons in which the little ones are made to talk about a picture, to assume and act out their several parts, and to help one another piece together their experiences of a farm yard or a garden, of a street or of a kitchen. I have seen many such little experiments in *Kindergarten* schools, or rather in those infant schools which have a *kindergarten* department; and there is no doubt that the system, in the hands of bright and sympathetic teachers has many very substantial advantages.

Its advantages

Fröbel's method certainly increases the happiness of little children; and this is a clear gain. It greatly diminishes the difficulty of the problem, how to fill up their time at school; for a long day spent in any one of the ordinary forms of instruction is very wearisome to young children; and teachers have long been wanting to know how to vary the employments of infants in a school, so as to keep them under discipline, and at the same time to avoid tiring and overstraining them with lessons, and giving them unpleasant associations with the thought of learning. To such teachers, the little gifts and exercises of Fröbel are a great boon. Interspersed among the graver employments, they absorb the attention and powers of the little ones, without giving them any sense of fatigue. Infants learn obedience, fixed attention, accuracy of eye, steadiness of hand; they learn to count, and to know the nature of colour and of form. They are exercised in imitation, in invention, and in the elements of drawing and design. And all these lessons are learned in the best of all ways; without being considered as lessons; not indeed in the shape of lessons at all, but rather as so much play. They are in fact organized play, with a conscious and direct educational purpose. But this purpose is not obtruded before the children, who think that they are being amused when in fact they are being systematically taught. Experience shews that children who have been disciplined on this system, are found (1) to have got the rudiments of writing, counting and drawing, and to be better prepared for the ordinary subjects of school instruction than others; and (2) to have obtained in an indirect way a good deal of useful training which shews itself in quickened sensibility, and prompter intelligence.

Hence I strongly recommend those of you whose advice is likely to be asked as to the organization of preparatory schools for very young children to make yourselves acquainted with some of the books I have named, and to be ready to take advantage of the good parts of the system. At the same time, I may venture to add two or three cautions, which the writers of books on the system do not give. I do not blame them for this. The best work in the world is not done by criticism but by enthusiasm. The sort of cold-blooded and balanced estimation of the good and bad points in a system, which is appropriate for us in this place, is not to be expected or indeed to be desired on the part of those earnest men and women, who in rebelling against the inert and unintelligent discipline to which little children are often subjected, have perhaps exaggerated the value of Fröbel's method. Let us admit that if they had not seen that method, in a very strong—perhaps even an untrue light,—they would not have made so many converts; or done nearly so much good.

Its success depends on the teacher's personal gifts.

So I would warn you first that it is very useless to try to adopt this system unless you have some one to work it, who has faith in it, and the special aptitude and enthusiasm which will help her to make the best of it. In the hands of spiritless teachers, who look on it merely as a system which anybody can adopt; and who just seek to carry out the methods in a book of diagrams and patterns, which describes Fröbel's gifts and games in regular sequence, the results will be very poor. Much joyousness of nature, versatility and sympathy, and rather unusual power of telling a story, and of encouraging children to talk to her and to one another are indispensable in the teacher, if the system is to have its proper effect.

The limits to its usefulness.

There is one fault to which exactly the opposite kind of teachers—the most sympathetic and enthusiastic, are specially prone; and that is to make too much of the system, and to expect from it more than it can do. Your thorough going *Kindergärtner* is not content to make the Fröbel exercises an element in the school life of a child. He wants to make them the whole. He will keep children up to the age of six or seven engaged all day in straw-plaiting or paper-folding, in dancing round a maypole, and in singing and reciting childish verses. He is apt to mistake means for ends. He has got hold of a novel and pleasing instrument for occupying the attention of the children; and he thinks that so long as they are orderly and attentive, all is well. He keeps the little ones looking at diagrams and pictures, when he might be teaching them to read. He employs them in making marks, of which they see no meaning, when their faculties of imitation might just as well be exercised in a writing lesson. He allows them to spend much time in the manufacture of woven patterns and paper ornaments, which the child sees to have no value in themselves, long after the time when the elementary training of hand and eye might just as well be applied to drawing or sewing or knitting, or something else which the children know to be of real use. Children know very well that they come to school to learn. They want to do something of which they can see the purpose. They are not being well prepared for the serious work of school, or of after life; if all that they are required to do looks like amusement and play. The *Kindergarten* gives them nothing which seems like work; it does not train them to overcome difficulties.

Let us be clear on this point. Do not let us manufacture difficulties under a notion that we have to brace and harden children's natures; but on the other hand, do not let us elaborately keep all difficulties out of sight. This is just as grave an error. Let us admit the paramount necessity of the training of faculties. Nay, let us go farther, and confess that nine teachers out of ten err by overlooking this view of their work, and supposing that the whole of their business is to impart instruction. Nevertheless we must bear in mind that school life is too short to justify us in spending much time in training, *for the sake of training;* and that when we have got a power or faculty into vigorous action the sooner we set it to work on some of the practical problems of life the better.

The habit of observation not of paramount importance.
Besides, though the faculty of observation is a very useful one, it is quite possible to exaggerate its importance. In the long run it is a less valuable factor in the intellectual life than the habit of reflection. And the *Kindergarten* does little or nothing to encourage reflection. It helps children to appreciate more clearly the visible and the concrete; but it scarcely conducts them a step towards the abstract and the invisible. They learn to look, to hear, to act in concert; but all the thinking, and nearly all the talking is done by the teacher for them. This is not a fault in the system, but it is one of the limits to its usefulness, and we must bear it in mind.

Fröbel and his work.
In studying Fröbel's life and doings, you will not fail to respect his enthusiasm, and admire his child-like sympathetic nature. You will not, I think, come to the conclusion that he took a large or very sound view of the purpose of education as a whole. He was not a scholar, and to the last he somewhat undervalued the sort of knowledge which is to be got from books. But he saw with intense clearness certain simple truths which bear on the discipline and happiness of little children. Let us be thankful for such seers and prophets, even if they only give us half-truths. There is something touching in the remark of the Baroness Bülow, one of his most earnest disciples, "The heavenly light given to a man seldom spreads its ray over the whole of his being; but only lights up the field whereon he is called to build." It is well for each of us, if the light is clear and stedfast enough to shew us the duty which we can do best. For Fröbel the field thus illuminated extended over the heart and the life of childhood, the beginnings of

knowing and thinking, the functions and the duties of the primary teacher—a region which indeed has definite frontiers, but is wide and varied enough to satisfy a much more daring ambition than his.

I repeat, then, that whenever you have the opportunity of exercising influence over a preparatory school, you will do well to see that in reasonable measure the methods of Fröbel are adopted. They will have value up to the age of seven if judiciously incorporated with other forms of early instruction, although, for the reasons I have given, I do not think that they should be allowed to supersede such instruction.

And now let us gather together a few of the plainer results of experience in reference to the teaching of the rudimentary arts of reading, spelling and writing.

One of the first difficulties with which we are confronted is the fact that our language presents so many orthographical and phonetic anomalies. In this respect it differs notably from French, in which there are comparatively few, from German, in which there are fewer, and from Italian, in which there are scarcely any. We all know that ours is a composite speech, a conglomerate of many languages; that the portion of it which was spoken before it was written—the purely English portion and the earlier derivatives from Latin and from Norman French—is full of queer and capricious spelling; while other portions of it, the Greek and the Latin derivatives, which have come to us later through the medium of literature, are, on the whole, spelled according to a consistent system, and present little or no difficulty. If we want an exhaustive and very entertaining summary of the chief difficulties presented by our English system of spelling, I may refer you to Prof. Meiklejohn's clever little book: "The problem of teaching to read."

Here it may suffice briefly to indicate the nature of the difficulty which has to be surmounted.

The anomalies of the English Alphabet. There is first of all our anomalous alphabet. And it would be easy to shew that it has every fault that an alphabet can have. A perfect alphabet should, it may well be argued, have a single and fixed character for every single indivisible elementary sound. It should have such compound characters for composite or diphthongal sounds as would indicate clearly the elements of which they are composed. It should also have similar characters for analogous or related sounds. Nothing is easier than to lay down these conditions, and to see that our alphabet violates every one of them. It is at the same time redundant and defective. It has not enough characters, and those which it has it does not make the best of: *e.g.*

(1) A single and indivisible consonant is sometimes expressed by a clumsy combination of two letters instead of one character, as *th*in, *th*ine, *sh*ould.

(2) There are often two or more ways of writing the same sound, as *f*ancy, *ph*ilosophy, and rou*gh*. D*u*ty, n*eu*ter, l*ew*d, and be*au*ty. Na*t*ion, *s*ure, *sh*all, vi*c*ious.

(3) The same letter has many sounds, as f*a*ther, f*a*n, f*a*te, f*a*ll.

(4) The alphabet disguises altogether the true elements of composite sounds; the sound of o*i*l is not made up of *o* and *i*, but of *au* and *ee*.

(5) It fails altogether to indicate the true relations between cognate sounds; the *i* in *pine* is called the long sound of the *i* in *pin;* but these sounds are not related; the true lengthening of p*i*n is into p*ee*n not p*i*ne. So the *p* is related to the *b* in the same manner as the *t* to the *d* or the *s* to the *z*; but there is no such similarity of characters as to represent these relations.

(6) It sometimes gives us a compound sound expressed by a single letter, as Re*j*ect, con*g*eal.

(7) It more often gives a group of letters to represent a single indivisible sound—Daug*h*ter, th*ough*.

(8) The names of the letters are very misleading as representations of their powers, as *Gee* for G. *Aitch* for H. *Double you* for W.

Such is only a part of the indictment against the English Alphabet. Shall we try to get up a society for reforming it? Well, I for one, should not. First, because the task is so formidable. To do it effectually we must have 38 characters instead of 26; we must cease to employ many of the letters we now use, and the whole aspect of the written language must be altered. And even when the written language had been truly conformed to the speech of the capital and of educated persons, it would remain untrue and *non-phonetic* in Yorkshire and Devonshire, and even in Scotland and Ireland, unless all provincialisms and dialectic varieties are to be obliterated; which is neither probable, nor in itself eminently desirable. Then the price we should pay for such a reform would be very heavy. We of this generation, who have been educated in the anomalous system, would learn the new one, I grant, without much difficulty; and for our lifetimes both the old and the new literature would be read. But to the next generation, educated on the more rational principle, our present spelling would be hopelessly unintelligible, and the whole of our past literature, everything that is not worth re-printing would become a foreign language, and would remain unread by our successors. It is not easy to see how such a result could be avoided; yet, if it occurred, the gain would be enormously counterbalanced by the loss.

Proposed reform of the Alphabet.

Again, the difficulties of our present system may

easily be exaggerated, and have been exaggerated. The syllables which are not spelt phonetically are, relatively to the whole language, not very numerous.

Our alphabet also is a historic one, and like the British constitution represents historic growth. Its very anomalies throw a great deal of light on the history and origin of words. No doubt the spelling is occasionally misleading too, on this point. If I lay down a rule, that whenever f is represented by *ph*, or k by *ch*, the word is Greek, or that whenever c represents s and commences a syllable the word is Latin; or that whenever w comes before h it is English, we may find exceptions to the rule; yet in nineteen cases out of twenty the rule is good; and thus the very inconsistencies of our alphabet often furnish a key to the meaning or history of a word.

A somewhat hopeless enterprise.

Lastly, I would not advise spending much time on an effort for a sweeping legal reform in our alphabet, because there is little or no chance of its success. Consider what has happened in the matter of decimalizing our weights and measures. Our present arithmetical tables are far more clumsy and indefensible than our alphabet. They give a great deal more of trouble to teachers, and of mental entanglement to pupils. Moreover it would be a far easier process to reform them. Many proposals for adopting the French *système métrique* or at least for decimalizing and simplifying our present weights and measures have been made from time to time. But the English people and its parliament have steadily opposed all these projects, and we seem at this moment much farther from the adoption of a rational and simple system of compound arithmetic than we were twenty years ago. And we may conclude, in like manner, that though ingenious proposals will be made from time to time, for the amendment, on philosophical principles, of English spelling, those proposals have little chance of being carried out in our time. By the general consent of literary and learned people we may fairly hope that some improvements may be effected and the more grotesque anomalies removed. But the conservative instincts of the nation in matters like this are very strong; and I think it in the highest degree unlikely that for the sake of saving a little trouble to teachers, the nation will put itself to the inconvenience of adopting a new alphabet and making a break in the continuity of its own literary life.

So we may make up our minds that any effort to obtain a complete and scientific reform in the English alphabet, will probably be futile; and that any other than a complete reform would hardly be worth contending for. It may go a little way to reconcile some of us to this conclusion, if we reflect that after all the anomalies and difficulties do not seem so great to a little child as to us. He accepts the spelling you teach him, on your authority, and he is very little impressed by its want of philosophic precision. You spell the word *mat*, and as there are three distinct sounds represented by three distinct letters, which are tolerably uniform in their powers, the word satisfies you. And then you spell the word *through*, and you feel it to be unsatisfactory. The first word is spelt philosophically, the second is spelt unphilosophically. But to the child, though one is a little easier than the other, it is just as arbitrary. He receives them both on your authority. To him it is all alike mysterious. Neither his moral nor his phonetic sensibilities are wounded by unphilosophical spelling. You will have to tell him the one word twice over and the other only once. But when once thoroughly known, it is known for life, and he will

The language, as it exists, has to be taught.

not be troubled by its anomalous character. Nay, he will never know that there *is* any anomaly in it, until in the fulness of time he is old enough to become a member of the Philological Society or the Spelling Reform Association, and to have his critical faculty called into action under its auspices.

Modes of teaching reading. It is, then, the English language as it is, and not as it might be, nor even as it ought to be, that we have to take for better for worse, and to teach in the best way we can. How shall we set about it? There are, as is well known, three different methods :

(1) There is the method of teaching the *Alphabet* first, then proceeding to words of two letters, then to words of three, and so on in order. This is a method of synthesis.

(2) There is what is called the *Look and say method*, which begins by shewing children words, and requiring them to be recognised as a whole and pronounced, before calling attention to the letters of which they are composed. This is a method of analysis.

(3) There is the *Phonic method* which avoids the names of the letters at first altogether, and simply seeks to teach their powers. Groups of words are given in which the same sounds occur, and these words are decomposed into their elementary sounds, which children are taught to utter separately.

Now, in favour of the last method, it may be truly urged that the real composition of the utterances we call words, is better seen by rendering them into their elementary sounds, than by calling those elements by arbitrary names. That is quite true. But the objection to it is that the same letter has so many different sounds, that even if I learn to identify each with a sound and not a name, I shall be constantly making mistakes, e.g. you give the significance of *l*, and illustrate it by *lend*, *lo*, *ill*, and *full*, and then you come to a word like *should*, in which it is not pronounced at all. Writers of Phonic reading books get over this difficulty by printing in italics the letters which are not sounded, and by printing over those vowels or combinations of letters which have an abnormal sound an accent or mark of some kind to indicate their exceptional characters. But the objection to this is that ordinary books are not printed thus, and that therefore the child will have something to unlearn when he goes from his special phonic school-book to any other.

A graver objection to this method, and the real cause of its failure is the extreme difficulty of isolating elementary sounds and pronouncing them apart.

The method would not be unsuited to older people who were learning the written language for the first time, but it pre-supposes that little children are more distressed by orthographic anomalies than they really are. They can in fact, pronounce words, and divide them into syllables; but to them the analysis of syllables into their components is a task much harder than the mere learning of arbitrary characters.

Against the purely Alphabetic method it is easy to urge that the names of the letters do not express their powers; that singly and apart they have no meaning for children, and are held in the mind by no associations; that analysis is always easier than synthesis, and that it would interest a child much more to learn about a word first and examine its parts afterwards, than to begin with the letters which, after all, do not really represent its parts and afterwards to build up the whole.

On the other hand, the 'Look and say method,' which seeks to give a child a picture of a word as a whole, and teaches him to read rather by the general aspect of words than by careful observation of their parts, is open to the objection that many words have a general resemblance in their form, *e.g. form* and *from*, *there* and *three*, *board* and *broad*, which might be misleading, if they were not subjected to close inspection. And this method, if depended on entirely, is apt to encourage loose, careless, visual impressions, out of which mistakes constantly arise.

Again, the philosophers who are so sensible of the incongruity of our alphabet and of the arbitrary and misleading effect of the names of the letters, seem to forget that long before children come under regular instruction, they have actually learned the alphabet in the nursery or in the *Kindergarten;* they have merely in a game handled little wooden letters as toys, talked about them and arranged them in different ways; and they have seen no more difficulty in calling a particular character H. than in calling a horse a horse.

You have therefore to deal with the fact, that in nine cases out of ten the alphabet, with its indefensible nomenclature, is already known, having been learned in fact in the most effectual way, without the child's consciousness that he was learning anything. And after all the art of recognizing printed words ought always to be acquired thus, little by little, in short and playful lessons, while children are very young, and before any appeal is made to their reflection at all. I believe that it is a grave mistake to postpone the first exercises in reading after the fourth year, and that the longer it is postponed the more difficult it becomes. But if this has not been done, and a child of six or seven has to start *de novo*, it is certainly not well to begin by presenting the alphabet. The best way then is to place before him a printed sheet with very easy sentences on it, and to read aloud a whole sentence, pointing to each word as it is pronounced. Next the children should be invited to read it with the teacher aloud; then to read it together without any help; then one and another should be called on to point and identify each single word. So far the Look and Say method is right. But this lesson should be followed up by asking them in turn to count the number of letters in each word, and by writing each of them down, and giving their names. A card containing the alphabet should hang near, and as each letter occurs in the words of the little sentence, it should be pointed out and named. In this way, though the alphabet would not be taught at first as a whole, or as a separate lesson, each letter of it would be learned as it was wanted, and as it occurred in some word previously read.

The requirements of a good reading-book have already been referred to. It may be well to recall attention to them here: *Reading-books.*

(1) It should be well printed and in sufficiently large type to make it very easy for the child to put his finger to each word as he pronounces it.

(2) It should be made attractive by pictures, and by the pleasantness and interest of the subject. This is of the first importance.

(3) The lessons should not be graduated by so mechanical a rule as the mere length of the words and number of syllables. Many words of three letters are harder than those of five; and words like *winter* and *summer* are much easier though they have two syllables in them than words like *eye*, *who*, and *laugh*, though they have one. The real gradation does not depend on the length and number of the syllables, but on the number of anomalies or difficulties in the words. The early lessons

should have no anomalous words at all. But each new lesson should contain two or three combinations harder than those of the previous lesson, and several examples of each.

(4) If possible let a good many of the lessons be narrative and in the form of dialogue, giving some play for changes of voice. Monotony is encouraged by always reading sentences consisting of assertions only.

(5) Again every lesson should contain at least two or three words which are a little beyond the child's own vocabulary, and which therefore when learned will be distinct additions to it. This is very important. One of the first objects of a reading lesson is to enrich the scholar's store of words. A lesson which is so ostentatiously childish that it fails to add anything to this store, or to furnish material for questions, represents a lost opportunity.

(6) Yet it is of very little consequence that the reading lessons should be obviously didactic or instructive, or indeed that they should convey any information whatever. Later on, of course, we regard reading as a means to an end, and that end is instruction or mental culture; but in the early stages, reading is itself an end. And whatever conduces to make it more interesting facilitates the acquisition of the art.

And now suppose a book is found which fulfils these conditions, how is it to be used?

Teaching Reading. First it is well to read the passage aloud very carefully with the proper intonation, requiring the scholars to fix their eyes on the book, and to follow the teacher, pointing out word by word as he utters it.

Next, a simultaneous exercise is often found very useful. The teacher reads the lesson again, and asks the whole class to read it with him slowly, but still with all the proper pauses and inflexions.

The third step is to call upon the class to read the lesson simultaneously without him.

Then he challenges the scholars one after another to read the sentences separately, selecting them by name promiscuously, and causing the worst readers to be appealed to much oftener than the rest.

Afterwards he causes the books to be closed, and proceeds to give a few simple questions on special words, and to require separate little sentences to be turned into others which are equivalent, and of which the words are supplied by the scholars.

As to spelling, it is often the practice to print at the top of a reading lesson the few hardest words, and cause them to be specially spelt. I see no particular use in this. An isolated word has very little meaning or use to children. But they understand sentences. It is far better to read the sentence in which a word occurs, and then ask to have it spelled. And it is a good thing often to cause whole sentences to be spelled, the class taking one word after another.

"The sun sheds light upon the earth."

You have all the words spelled rapidly through, but you halt at the word "Light." You call attention to it. You write it on the black board. You say "I notice this word was difficult. Let us spell it again. I will shew you three or four other words formed like it, *Bright, Might, Fight.* Let us put these into sentences, and spell them."

Thus you encounter the difficulties of spelling, as you encounter all the other difficulties of life, as they come before you, one by one; and try to conquer them in detail. Do not accumulate the difficulties in a menacing and artificial column, and expect them to be dealt with all at once. That is unreasonable. But a difficulty that emerges naturally in the course of a lesson is grappled with willingly, and there is some interest in taking the opportunity of calling attention to a few words of like character, and so of disposing of that particular difficulty once for all. Only in choosing your reading books, and selecting reading lessons, take care that each of the difficulties you want to solve shall occur in its own proper place some time or other.

To be learned incidentally in reading, not in columns of isolated words.

Columns of words arranged alphabetically, dictionary fashion, or according to the number of syllables in them, are open to several objections. They all have to be learned alike, yet some are easy and some are difficult, some are familiar and useful, others wholly technical and unimportant. Moreover standing apart, they are not associated with anything else in the child's mind; whereas if he read them in a sentence he would see their bearing directly. As a general rule all words spelt should be seen in sentences in their proper connexion, not in artificial groups invented by the book-makers.

And with regard to the large number of words which are sounded alike but spelt differently, the simplest way of dealing with them is not to give them separate meanings, but to put them into little sentences, *e.g.*

>The wind *blew* hard; The sky is *blue.*
>I stood by the *sea;* He came to *see* me.
>This is *their* book; He will stay *there* all night.

Spelling is for the eye, not for the ear.

But after all, it is to be borne in mind that spelling is a matter for the eye, not for the ear. If it were not that we had to write, spelling would be an altogether useless accomplishment; and it is only when we write that any deficiency in this respect comes to light. The notion of the extreme importance attached to orthodox spelling is comparatively modern. Our ancestors, as you will easily find if you read the Paston Letters, or old MS. in the British Museum, thought it an accomplishment to spell a word in many different ways, and you will often find the same word in two or three different forms in one document. But since Johnson, with the general consent of the literary men of his time, sought to fix the spelling of the language, there has come to prevail in England an impression that bad spelling is a mark of extreme ignorance, if not worse. Of course this is a very conventional and unreal standard of ignorance; but we must take the world as we find it, and must acquiesce in the fact that whatever else we teach our scholars we shall get no credit for doing anything if they cannot spell. And the person who spells well is simply he who carries in his memory a good visual impression of the picture of the word as it appears in a written or printed book. If he has not this, it is to no purpose that he can, merely as a memory lesson, recall the letters when you exercise him in oral spelling. And if he has this, all else is unnecessary. There are many persons, who, if you ask them how to spell *receive* or how many *s's* there are in *necessary*, would not tell you readily, but would say at once, "Let me write the word down, and I will tell you if it is right." And if it is written down incorrectly, it is the eye which is offended by not seeing the accustomed picture of the word; it is not the verbal memory or the reason which sets them right.

And hence we may infer that it is mainly by writing *Dictation* that spelling is to be taught. And the familiar exercise of Dictation known in all schools is the practical recognition of this obvious truth. But there are skilful and unskilful ways even of conducting a dictation lesson, and I hope it is not beneath the dignity of this place to add a few words on this very simple matter.

In giving out a sentence, some teachers pronounce one word at a time; in a loud monotone. But this method is unsatisfactory, for however loudly and clearly uttered, single words are easily misunderstood. Others read short fragments, and repeat them two, three, and even four times. This plan also leads to mistakes, for when once a word is written, it is distracting and unnecessary to hear it again.

The best way is first of all to read the whole passage through once so as to give its general meaning and purpose; afterwards to read it piecemeal, one member of a sentence at a time, to read it only once, but with the inflection and tone which carries its meaning; and to leave a sufficiently long pause after each fragment to allow the slowest writer time to write it. The pauses should not be determined by the stops, nor by any rule about uniform length; but should come between the logical elements of the sentence, so that each piece to be carried in the memory should have a unity and meaning of its own. Here is an example:

"I was yesterday | about sunset | walking in the open fields | , until the night | insensibly fell | upon me | I at first | amused myself | with all the richness | and variety of colours | which appeared | in the western parts | of heaven."

If it ever becomes necessary to say a word or phrase more than once, the dictator is unskilful, and must either cultivate greater clearness of articulation or more patience.

Transcription. The exercise of copying a passage out of a book, though it should not supersede dictation, is occasionally a useful substitute for it. It is quieter, and more expeditious. It is apt, in the case of a careless child, to reveal exactly the same mistakes, which would have been made in a dictation lesson; since the words are not looked at one by one but dictated to himself two or three at a time. And in the case of more careful learners, who look at the words and try to avoid mistakes, it is evident that this form of exercise is not less effective. When the exercise is finished it may often be examined and corrected by the help of the scholars themselves.

Having observed a particular form of error to occur more frequently than others, you will do well to call attention to it, and to write the two or three difficult words plainly on the board. *Words to be used as well as spelled.* Follow up and thrust home the whole lesson by requiring each scholar to write down the words thus selected, and after this to place each of them in a sentence of his own construction. It is surprising to me to find how seldom this simple expedient is used in schools. It is to no purpose that you explain a new word, discuss its origin and its various shades of meaning, and call attention to the peculiarities of its spelling, so long as the word still remains like the name of some foreign city, outside the range of his own knowledge or experience. The first thing to do with a word which you thus give to your scholar is to teach him to use it. "Put it into a sentence. Make up a little narrative in which this word shall occur." Not till you have done this have you any security that the word in question has been appropriated and become a real part of his vocabulary. We have already said that every new word which we thus add to a child's store, is a new instrument of thought, and does something to widen the horizon of his understanding. So I would say generally, "Never explain or spell a new word, without calling upon the scholar soon after to make use of it in a sentence of his own."

Spelling not to be taught by incorrect examples.

One other caution is needed here, Do not try to teach spelling by the use of incorrect examples. In my school days, it was the custom to set from a printed book, letters and extracts grotesquely misspelled, and to tell us to re-write them without mistake. I believe this practice has nearly died out. But I hope every one here sees the fundamental objection to it and indeed to all such devices. Writing and spelling are imitative arts, and it is essential that the eye should see none but good models for imitation. We have said that to spell a word well is to have an accurate picture of it before the visual memory, so to speak. But if we set a wrong picture before the learner, how do we know that he will not carry that with him instead of the true one? For here there is no absolute right and wrong, nothing in which the judgment can help to set him right. It is all a matter of arbitrary usage and habit; and it is therefore desirable that the only words which meet his eye should be rightly spelt.

Thoughtful and effective reading.

Now assuming that you have taught reading well enough to give to your scholars fluency and readiness and the power to understand a book, is it right to stop there? Most teachers do stop there. They think they have put into the hands of their scholars the instrument of all further acquisitions and that there is an end to it. Reading aloud, considered as a fine art, is very much neglected in schools, especially in the more advanced schools for boys; because there it is undervalued, and thought of far less importance than the attainment of knowledge. Without discussing this, we may affirm that if the attention of teachers was once directed to the extreme usefulness of this art, they would try to find some time for practising it. Consider how rare an accomplishment that of really good reading is. Consider how great an acquisition one person who is a fine and expressive reader is in a household, how much he or she can do to add to the charm, the happiness, and to the intelligence of the home. By fine reading, of course I do not mean pompous stagy elocution, which draws attention and admiration to itself, and is felt by the hearers to be artificial, but reading so clear, so easy, so natural, that one may listen to it for an hour at a time with pleasure, and that no word, no finer shade of the author's meaning, escapes or fails to be conveyed to the mind of the hearers.

We must not regard reading as a merely mechanical art for the reproduction of other people's thoughts. It is itself a discipline in intelligence and taste. It is not only a result but a means of culture. We have said before that to teach is to learn. So also to read aloud, to read for others, to read so as to enlighten, to charm, to move your auditors, is the infallible secret of being enlightened, of being charmed, of being moved yourself. Of many of the best books it may be truly said that they are never thoroughly comprehended, until they are well read or recited. And if you will further consider that the human voice is the most vivid translation of human thought, that it is the most supple, the most docile, the most eloquent interpreter of whatever is best in the reason and in the heart of man, you will see that there is a very real connexion between right thought and right utterance; and that anything you can do to make speech more finished, more exact, more expressive, and more beautiful, will have a very direct bearing on the mental and spiritual culture of your pupils. Finally, let me remind you that of all the arts and accomplishments we possess, this is one of those which come into use most frequently; and that what is done oftenest should be done best.

Chief conditions of good reading.
It would carry us too far to attempt here even a compendium of the rules on which good elocution depends. But three points of paramount importance, you will do well to keep in view: They are

(*a*) *Distinct articulation;* the power to utter clearly every syllable and especially every consonant. You should get together a list of words and of sentences in which there is a special tendency to pronounce three syllables as two, or to elide a consonant, *e.g.* "*nec*essary, distinc*t*ness, Has*t* thou been? An*d* keep his comman*d*ments." Pronounce these words and sentences rapidly, and you will see that a little effort is required to enunciate the letters in italics, with perfect distinctness. Keep your ear open for faults of this kind and correct them at once in reading, before the careless habit of slurred and confused utterance is formed. A former colleague of mine, Mr Brookfield, who was himself a very fine reader, was wont to give this counsel, "Remember your consonants and forget yourself."

(*b*) *Frequent pause.* To form a habit of good reading, it is necessary to begin by reading slowly; and to make habitually many more breaks or pauses than are indicated by the punctuation. The right way of placing these pauses will become clear to any one who has learned to analyse a sentence into subject, predicate, and adjuncts. It is a safe rule that a slight rhetorical pause, hardly a stop, should mark the logical divisions of every sentence, should come, *e.g.* after a nominative, especially when it is formed of two or three words, before every preposition, conjunction and relative, and before any word or phrase which needs to be emphasized.

(c) *Just intonation and expression.* From the first the monotone in which children are apt to read should be discouraged, and they should be trained to read as they speak, putting the same variety of inflections into the printed words, as into their own conversation. This may be secured, partly by the selection of well-varied pieces; partly by challenging pupils whenever they are reading in an artificial tone, to close the book, and tell the substance of what they have read in their own words; and partly by enforcing the rule that the eye should always travel several words in advance of the word actually read, in order that the bearing of the uttered word on its context may be fully known.

Besides the art of reading, or reproducing printed words, you should have in view the usefulness of oral *expression*, or the utterance of the pupil's own thoughts in his own words. This is too much neglected in schools. A scholar is too often expected to say only those things which he has learned, and to say them piece-meal in reply to questions and in nearly the exact form in which he learned them. You will do well to say in the last five minutes of a lesson, "Which of you can give me the best account of what we have learned?" "Who can tell me now the anecdote which I related just now?" There will thus be an exercise in consecutive expression, and in the choice and use of words, such as is not to be had in the mere answering of definite questions. The practice will give a little trouble at first, and pupils will be shy in replying; but once adopted, it will be found very helpful, in giving fluency and confidence, and it will have an excellent reflex action on the reading, especially on the ease and naturalness of the tone. *Oral expression.*

Make provision at certain intervals for a little reading or elocutionary tournament, in which some animated *Special exercises.*

dialogue or dramatic scene is recited in the hearing of the class by some of the best scholars, who have taken special pains to prepare it.

It is well also to cause interesting passages from good orators or poets to be learned by heart, and to be repeated with particular reference to accuracy of pronunciation and just expression.

The teacher's own pattern or model reading.

In many schools it is found a useful and interesting practice to reserve half an hour a week for giving, in the hearing of the scholars, a carefully chosen reading from some good poem or narrative. If you choose such a passage as will awaken the attention; and read it, so that it shall be a treat to the scholars to listen to it, they will not only have a model for imitation, but they will look with more favour on the art of reading itself, as a means of giving and receiving pleasure.

And this, and indeed all my rules, presuppose that the teacher should be himself a good reader. You can never bring your scholars up to your own level. So that if you wish their level to be tolerably high, your own level should be exceptionally high. No pains that you can take with yourself to increase the power, the sweetness, and the flexibility of your own voice will be wasted. Reading is an imitative art, and if you are to teach it well, you must first think careful elocution worth acquiring, and then acquire it for yourself.

Writing.

Writing is one of the subjects on which there seems to be least to say. We all feel that it is a matter of practice mainly, not of theory. In teaching it there are few or no principles to explain, and a great many exercises to do.

As an art it is greatly neglected in high and public schools. The habit of writing many notes, translation and other exercises betrays boys into a scribbling, running hand, before they have taken pains to form single letters well; and very little is done to check this tendency. When it is considered how much a legible handwriting has to do with the comfort of one's correspondents, there seems to be no good reason why young people who are to be brought up as gentlemen and gentlewomen should write a worse hand than the children of a National School, or why some attention to writing *per se* should not be given even in the higher classes at the best schools.

For every good teacher, in addition to the immediate and obvious result contemplated in giving lessons on a given subject, asks himself: "What particular faculties or qualities of mind are being exercised in these lessons?" "What is the incidental effect of the teaching of this subject on the formation of the intellectual character of my scholar?" And when he looks at writing from this point of view, he sees that it may be a training in accuracy of eye, in steadiness and flexibility of hand, in obedience and in cleanliness; and that every time a scholar receives a writing lesson, his habits are either being improved or deteriorated in these respects. *Its indirect importance.*

Now in all good elementary schools it is found easy to have a standard of excellence in this matter, and to make every child conform to it. There are in fact no bad writers in an elementary school of the best class. A good method stedfastly carried out is found to be infallibly efficacious even in the worst cases. And this method is not elaborate. Mulhäuser and others have devised a whole system of writing founded on the analysis of letters into their elements, and have given names to all the parts of which letters are formed, as the *right line*, the *curve line*, the *link*, the *loop*, and the *crotchet;* and I have seen some ingenious lessons given of a synthetic kind, in which models of these various parts having been shewn their names were dictated, so that letters and words emerged one after another. But in practice such systems have not been found of much use, for they make a needless demand on the memory, and they give separate names to things which have no separate value or meaning. The success attained in good elementary schools in teaching the art of writing is due to much simpler methods. A proper graduation of letters according to the difficulty and complexity of the lines composing them is found to fulfil the same purpose as a classification of those lines themselves. There are but 26 letters; and if the *n*, *m*, *l*, *u*, and *i* are formed into one group, the *o*, *c*, *a*, *q*, and *d* into a second, the *r*, *b*, *w*, and *v* into a third, the *g*, *h*, *f*, *j*, *p* into a fourth; and if those letters which do not conform to these types, as *s*, *z*, *k*, *x*, are reserved to the last, the classification suffices for practical purposes, and the teacher gives as copies in succession, not the single letters, but little words which contain them, and which have more interest for children.

A good copy being the first condition, careful supervision, and the prompt correction of each mistake, will do nearly all the rest. Complex oral directions as to how to hold the pen, and how to sit, are not needed. *Gaucherie* and bad attitude may be pointed out in special cases, but there is no harm in allowing different modes of handling a pen or pencil so long as the writing produced is good. The good teacher goes round the writing class to every scholar with a pencil in his hand; he calls attention to each mistake, forms in the next line a letter to be traced over, desires his pupil to complete that line only, and to wait till it has been seen again. He notices each prevalent error in form or proportion, and on a ruled black board in front of the class makes a good pattern of the particular letter, and causes it to be copied several times. He knows that if this is not done children copy their own mistakes. And generally he relies more on incessant watchfulness, on care that the same mistake shall not be made twice over, and on constant use of model writing, than on any theoretical instruction.

The well-known passage from Locke sums up after all the best rules which have to be borne in mind in teaching this subject. He says

Locke on Writing.

"When a boy can read English well, it will be seasonable to enter him in Writing. Not only children, but any body else that would do anything well should never be put upon too much of it at once, or be set to perfect themselves in two parts of an action at the same time, if they can possibly be separated. When he has learned to hold his pen right, * * * the way to teach him without much trouble is to get a plate graved with the characters of such a hand as you like best, but you must remember to have them a pretty deal bigger than he should ordinarily write; for every one comes by degrees to write a less hand than he at first was taught, but never a bigger...Such a plate being graved, let several sheets of good writing paper be printed off with red ink, which he has nothing to do but to go over with a good pen filled with black ink, which will quickly bring his hand to the formation of those characters, being at first shewed when to begin, and how to form every letter. And when he can do that well he may exercise on fair paper, and so may easily be brought to write the hand you desire."

You have here enforced the two principal expedients for securing a good hand; (1) tracing, which is perhaps more effective from the teacher's own pencil-marks than from faint engraved lines; and (2) insisting on large hand, and resisting for much longer than is usual the wish of scholars to write small or running hand. Those who begin small writing too soon are often careless about the formation of single letters, and form a habit of scribbling, which lasts them through life. Those however who are kept writing on a large scale until they can shape every letter well may soon form for themselves without trouble a good and characteristic style of writing. Here, as in so many of the mechanical arts, you must not be impatient at slowness in the earlier stages, and must remember that if accuracy and finish are first gained, rapidity and ease will come afterwards; but yet if these two last are sought for themselves, or too early, the first will never come at all. Here at least it is true that "La gradation et la répétition, sagement entendues, sont l'âme de l'enseignement."

Drawing and Vocal Music. It does not consist with my present plan to comment on the two other chief instruments of Sense-training which fall within the province of a school course. Nor do I feel competent to offer any practical rules for the teaching of either Drawing or Vocal Music. But I have a strong conviction that both should form integral parts of every school course, and should be taught to every scholar. The claims of Music, both in training the voice and in giving cheerfulness to the school-life, are incontestable. And Drawing is not only in a practical sense indispensable to the skilled artizan, and capable of manifold useful applications by scholars of every class; but its indirect effect on the training of the perceptions, on taste, on clearness of vision and firmness of hand, is still more important as an element in a liberal education.

VIII. THE STUDY OF LANGUAGE.

The study of language has held a high place in most systems of education. However far we go back in the history of learning, we find that such subjects as grammar and rhetoric, which concerned themselves with the right use and choice of words, have always formed, if not the chief, at any rate a prominent feature in the scheme of a liberal education. Indeed in the history of our own country and in the practice of our Universities and public schools, linguistic studies have held a place so conspicuous, that they have well-nigh overshadowed all others. *Language, long the staple of instruction.*

So it may be well to ask ourselves at the outset, Why should we study language at all? On what reasons is the universal tradition in favour of philological and grammatical studies founded? Are those reasons valid? And if so, to what extent should they be accepted and acted on, having regard to the just claims of much new and useful knowledge of another kind? Speech we know is the one characteristic distinction of humanity. Every word which has been invented is the record of some fact or thought, and furnishes the means by which facts or thoughts can be transmitted to others. In a sense, every new word represents a new conquest of civilization, a distinct addition to the intellectual resources of the world. To become acquainted with words, in their full significance, is to know much about the things they represent; and about the thoughts which other *The reasons for this.* *Words the records of former thought.*

people have had respecting those things. The enlargement of our vocabulary, whether it be in English or any other language, means the enlargement of our range of thought and the acquisition of new materials of knowledge.

And the instruments of new thought.

Moreover, the words we use are not merely the exponents of notions and thoughts which have existed in the minds of others; they are the very instruments with which we think. We are unable to conceive of any regular consecutive thinking,—any advance from what is known to what is unknown—except by the agency of language. Whatever therefore gives precision and method to our use of words, gives precision to our thoughts. Language as it has been formed by nations, embodied in literature, and formulated into grammar, corresponds in its structure to the evolution of thought in man. Every grammatical rule is, in another form, a rule of logic; every idiom, a representation of some moral *differentia* or characteristic of the people who have used it; every subtle verbal distinction is a key to some logical distinction; every figure of speech, a symbol of some effort of the human imagination to overleap the boundary of the prosaic and the actual, and to pass into the infinite region beyond; every verbal ambiguity is both the effect and the cause of mental confusion. And so the study of language is the study of humanity; the forms of language represent the forms of human thought; the history of language is the history of our race and its development, and great command over the resources of language is only another name for great command over the ideas and conceptions which make up the wealth of our intellectual life.

Extent and variety of vocabulary.

Mr Max Müller estimates the total number of English words at 50,000; he points out that the speaking vocabulary of an ordinary English citizen, who reads his newspaper and books from Mudie's, does not extend beyond 3000 or 4000 words; that accurate thinkers and persons of wide knowledge probably use twice as many; that the Old Testament contains 5642 different words; that in all Milton's works you will find only about 8000; and that Shakespeare, who displayed a greater variety of expression than probably any writer in any language, produced all his plays with 15,000 words. And at the same time he tells us that an uneducated English peasant lives and dies with a vocabulary which scarcely extends beyond 300 words. You cannot reflect on a statement like this, and on all that it implies, without feeling convinced that all investigations into the growth of language, its structure, its history, and the philosophy and reason of its grammatical rules, must have an important bearing on the culture of the understanding, and be very fruitful both of useful knowledge and of mental exercise. It is a shallow thing to say that what the human being wants is a knowledge of things, and not words. Words *are* things; they embody facts. He who studies them is studying much more than sounds and letters. He is gaining an insight into the heart and reality of the things they represent. Let a battle-field or a storm at sea be viewed by a painter, by a poet, by a sailor, and by an ordinary observer;—or say, by a Frenchman and an Englishman. It will be described differently by them all. But he who understands the language of them all, sees it, so to speak, with several pairs of eyes. And he is the richer, and his mind is the larger in consequence.

Some such reasons as these no doubt underlie the very general assumption that a sound and liberal education should pay special regard to the study of language.

And we in England have to deal with this practical question in three distinct forms. We teach (1) the languages of Greece and Rome, which are familiarly called the classic languages; (2) some of the languages of modern Europe; and (3) our own vernacular speech. We shall do well to take this opportunity of noting the special reasons which justify each of these kinds of teaching. On examination we shall find that in each we have a very different object in view. There is, however, a sense in which all are alike valuable, and in which their study may be justified on the general grounds already indicated.

Latin and Greek.

But as we all know, the linguistic and philological culture to which most value has been attached is that which is to be gained in the study of Latin and Greek. We still call the man who is familiar with these languages a scholar *par excellence*, and are inclined to withhold the title from one who, however learned in other ways, has no acquaintance with what are called the classics. Now without denouncing this state of opinion as a superstition as some do, it may be well to ask ourselves, what is the origin of it; and how it ever came to pass that the Latin and Greek languages were regarded as the staple of all learning; almost the only knowledge worth acquiring? Let us look back—to a period 300 years ago, the time when Lyly wrote his Grammar, when Ascham was teaching Lady Jane Grey and Queen Elizabeth to read Plato, and when the most important of our great grammar schools were founded. If you had in those days asked Erasmus or Sir Philip Sidney why Latin and Greek should hold this prominent, this almost exclusive rank, the reply would have been very easy. The books best worth reading in the world were written in those languages. If one wanted to see the best models of history, there were Thucydides and Livy; if he would know what dramatic art could be at its highest, he must read Sophocles and Euripides, or Plautus and Terence. If he would learn geometry, there was Euclid; rhetoric, he must read it in Quintilian or Aristotle; moral philosophy, in Plato or Cicero. "I expect ye," wrote Sir Matthew Hale to his grandchildren, "to be good proficients in the Latin tongue, that ye may be able to read, understand, and construe any Latin author, and to make true and handsome Latin; and though I would have you learn something of Greek, yet the Latin tongue is that which I most value, because all learning is ever made in that language." Modern literature was only just emerging into life, after the long darkness of the middle ages; and a certain flavour of barbarism and rudeness was held to belong to it. Chaucer and Dante had written, but it would not have occurred to any scholar of the sixteenth century to suppose that their books would repay critical analysis in the same sense as Homer or Ovid. Nearly all the literary wealth of the world, as it then was, was embodied in the language of Greece or that of ancient Rome.

Another reason for studying these languages was that they were the only languages whose grammar had been formulated and reduced to a system. Each of these languages was nearly homogeneous, with very few foreign ingredients. Each possessed an elaborate system of inflections and grammatical forms; and each had become a dead language—had ceased to be spoken popularly, and therefore to be subject to the sort of corruption which goes on in the case of a tongue freely used by an unlearned people. Both languages therefore presented examples of organized and philosophic grammar, and a fixed literature, in which the laws of

Their grammar.

grammatical structure were well exemplified and could be easily studied. On the other hand the languages of modern Europe were heterogeneous, full of anomalies, subject to phonetic decay, and in a constant state of fluctuation. No attempt had been made to fix their forms, to find out what grammatical laws were still recognizable in them, and they therefore offered little attraction or advantage to the student of language.

Purposes once served by Latin.

And besides all this, Latin, though a dead language for ordinary colloquial purposes, was an eminently living and vigorous language for many of the purposes recognized by a scholar. It had been accepted as the universal language of the Western Church. It was the common medium of communication among the ecclesiastics and among the scholars of Europe. Not only Bede and the earlier chroniclers, but Sir T. More, Buchanan, Bacon, Hobbes, Milton, and Newton found Latin the most appropriate channel for communicating their thoughts both to foreign scholars and to the educated of their own countrymen.

No longer served.

It is manifest that some of these reasons have either ceased to exist altogether, or have receded very much as to their relative importance. It cannot now be said that all the wisest and fairest productions of the human intellect are to be found in the Greek and Latin languages. A rich modern literature has sprung up. Many entirely new studies have come into existence. There is the science of historic criticism; there are new developments of mathematical science; there is the whole of the wonderful field of physical investigation; the modern languages, including our own, have become the subjects of philological and critical enquiry; and meanwhile the duration of human life has not been materially extended. It is evident, when we compare the books which are worth reading, and the subjects which can be studied to-day, with the books and the knowledge which were accessible in the days of Elizabeth, that the place occupied by Greek and Latin literature, however honourable, is relatively far less important than it was. This is now recognized by the ancient Universities themselves. The institution of the Law and Modern History schools at Oxford, and of the Natural Science Tripos and the Moral Science Tripos at Cambridge, are practical admissions that the word 'learning' must be extended in its meaning; and that *e.g.* an accomplished student of Natural Science, who knows little or no Greek, is as much entitled to rank as a scholar and to receive honourable recognition from the University, as a good Greek scholar who knows little or nothing of Natural Science.

And it is important also to remember that Latin has ceased to serve the purpose it once fulfilled of a common medium of communication among scholars. A modern Newton would not write his *Principia* in Latin. Our Sovereigns have no longer, as Cromwell had, a Latin secretary. Nor would any contemporary of ours who wished to vindicate the political action of the English people in the eyes of foreign nations carry on a controversy in the language employed by Milton and Salmasius. The occasions on which any educated Englishman, who is not a College tutor, or who does not take up learning as a profession, is called on to write in Latin are exceedingly rare. Few even of the most scholarly men in England are accustomed to think in Latin, or to use it often as a vehicle for expression. They read Latin books with more or less ease; they catch the flavour of the Augustan literature and the spirit of the Roman world, but the language which Tully and Horace spoke is no longer to them an instrument of thought.

Latin no longer the means of communication between learned men.

Or to any great extent an instrument of thought.

Yet it is still paramount in our higher instruction.

Nevertheless there is still a lingering and very potent tradition, stronger even in our Grammar Schools than in the Universities themselves, that Latin and Greek are in some way the staple of a gentleman's education; that he who has them and nothing else can claim to be called a scholar, and that he who has much other culture, and varied knowledge in other departments, and who has had no classical training, is an inferior being. It is not difficult to account for this sentiment. The men who make the public opinion of the country on these matters are for the most part those whose early education was carried out on this theory. One naturally values that which one knows best. Down deep in the mind of the successful statesman, the clergyman, or man of letters, who looks back on his years of toil over the Latin Accidence and the Greek Lexicon there is the half-expressed conviction, "The system must have been a good one because it produced *me*." It is very difficult for a man in later life to divest his mind of all the associations which give a certain dignity to the thought of a classical education, or to ask himself what might have been done with his faculties if they had been otherwise trained. Now and then a man has the boldness to put this question to himself, and the answer is not always satisfactory. Listen to Wordsworth's reminiscences of his College days. I was, he says,

> "Misled in estimating words, not only
> By common inexperience of youth
> But by the trade in classic niceties
> The dangerous craft of culling term and phrase
> From languages that want the living voice
> To carry meaning to the natural heart;
> To tell us what is passion, what is truth,
> What reason, what simplicity, what sense."
>
> *The Prelude.*

The testimony accumulated by the Schools Inquiry Commission of 1866 was conclusive not only as to the prevalence in the Grammar Schools of a belief in the supreme efficacy of Latin and Greek as means of mental training, but also as to the worthlessness of much of the result, and the heavy price we have paid in England for the maintenance of the Grammar School theory. It constantly happened to me when engaged as Assistant Commissioner on that enquiry to find an ancient Grammar School with 50 boys, of whom three-fourths had begun the Latin Grammar, about ten were learning the delectus, some four or five in the highest class of the school were translating Cæsar, and one or at most two at the head of the School were reading Virgil and elementary Greek, and gave some promise that they might perhaps go to the University. And an occasional success in preparing a boy for matriculation encouraged the master and trustees in describing this as a thoroughly classical school, and caused them to forget that at least 48 out of the 50 would never go to the University, and would never learn enough of Latin or of Greek to be able to read even a simple author. Meanwhile for the sake of the 'Classics' which had absorbed all their time they had been allowed to remain wholly ignorant of mathematics, they knew absolutely nothing of physical science, of French or German, or of the structure of their own language: they wrote, and even spelt, badly, and were often in point of general knowledge inferior to the children of a National School.

And often unfruitful of result.

This state of things is being slowly mended; and there can be little doubt that, ere long, all schools of this kind will have been modernized and improved. Other subjects are asserting their right to recognition; and perhaps the danger is that in the wholesome reaction against a state of opinion which gave to Latin and Greek an exclusive and hurtful predominance in a school course, we may come to make exactly the opposite mistake of unduly depreciating them. Meanwhile it is worth while for us to make up our minds on this question. What—having regard to the present boundaries of human knowledge and to the claims of modern life—is the right place for the ancient languages to hold, in a system of liberal education?

The future place of Latin and Greek in schools.

The answer to this question appears to me to depend entirely on the considerations which I tried to insist on in the second lecture, and particularly on the length of time which the student will probably devote to his course of instruction. You should keep in view roughly the three classes of learners—those who are likely to enter the Universities, and to aim at something like finished scholarship; those whose course of instruction will probably not be prolonged beyond 16 or 17 and who may be presumed to enter professions soon after; and those who only receive primary instruction ending at 13 or 14. Latin has indeed its relations to all three. But it is not Latin for the same purpose, or to be taught by the same methods. In an interesting and suggestive paper by Professor Ramsay, in *Macmillan's Magazine*, you will find that he would treat all these classes alike. Latin, he says, ought to be taught from the first as a living language. You are to aim at the power of varied expression and spontaneous thought by the help of Latin; you must learn the grammar very thoroughly, compose and recompose idiomatic phrases, long before you attempt to read an author. And all this he would seem to recommend alike for the boy who means to make scholarship the business of his life, and for the children of the Burgh and parish schools. But surely the reasons which justify the learning of Latin are so different in the different cases, that the same methods are not applicable to them all.

We may hope that means will always be found for encouraging genuine Greek and Latin scholarship in England. Considering the part which has been played by the ancient literature in forming the intellectual character of Europe, considering that nearly the whole of the best books which have been written in English are saturated through and through with allusions and modes of thought drawn consciously or unconsciously from classical sources; considering too the admitted value, the literary and artistic finish of the best books which have come down to us, it is evident that we shall sustain a great loss if ever this mine of wealth ceases to be explored or if we come to disregard it. And we may hope too that there will always be some students in England so devoted to the study of the ancient literature, that they will not neglect what may be called the niceties and elegancies, the refinements and luxuries of Greek and Latin scholarship. Even for these it may well be doubted whether Latin is ever likely to be used, as Professor Ramsay would have it, as a medium for free expression, or intellectual intercourse. It is only in a very limited sense that, even for them, Latin ought to be regarded as a living language. But we may admit that for them the training in versification and in Greek and Latin composition, to which so many years were devoted in the old grammar schools, has a meaning and a value. And in the sixth form of a public school, and in the case of all who are likely to reach it and to proceed to the Universities, let us by all means accept the University standard and work towards it. It is not within my province now to criticize that standard; or to say how you are to attain it. But I will ask you to consider the

(1) In High Schools.

case of those to whom this ideal is unattainable, and to enquire what part the study of Latin ought to play in their education.

(2) In Modern, Secondary, and Middle Schools.

For those scholars who, when at the University, are likely to select mathematics, natural science, or modern subjects as their special subjects, and for the far larger number who are never likely to proceed to the University, but who will enter professional or other active life at 16 or 17, the attempt to teach versification and the niceties of scholarship, or even to teach Greek at all, generally proves to be a mistake, for the reasons which have been already given, of which the chief is that the studies are not carried on to the fruit-bearing stage. Yet for such pupils, Latin has a real value. It can do much for them if the purpose with which it should be taught is carefully defined and kept in view.

Objects to be kept in view.

The substantial difference in the teaching of Latin to such pupils is that here you want them to read the language, but not to write it. You wish them to be familiar with the works of a few of the easier and more valuable Latin authors, and to make their contents intelligible. Besides, and even above this, you teach Latin to this class of pupils; (1) because in it you find the best practical illustration of the science of grammar and the laws and structure of language generally; (2) because it furnishes an effective instrument for examining the history, formation, affinities, and development of the English language, and (3) because it helps to explain much that would otherwise be obscure in our national literature, and to make intelligible the relation in which this literature stands to that of Greece and Rome.

How to be attained.

Now if these be the main objects contemplated, it will follow that much of the most laborious part of the orthodox Latin teaching in the grammar and public schools becomes, if not superfluous, of very secondary importance. These objects are attainable, within a very reasonable amount of time and without encroaching on the domain of other learning. And when it is once understood that they are worth attaining, it becomes evident that they are just as important in schools for girls as in those for boys. The tacit assumption in our old school plans that somehow Latin was a masculine and French a feminine study, is wholly indefensible. Both languages ought to be taught as essential parts of every school course which is likely to be prolonged to the age of sixteen, and unless it is likely to be prolonged beyond that age, more than these two languages ought not to be attempted.

And bearing in mind that the main reason for teaching Latin is because of its reflex action on the understanding of English, it is well from the first to teach the two languages together. A few elementary lessons on the necessary parts of an English sentence, and on the classification of English words, should precede the introduction of a pupil to the Latin grammar; but after such lessons have been well understood, it seems to me desirable to teach the two grammars together, comparing at every step English constructions and idioms with those of Latin. After all we must remember that the knowledge of grammar as a science is to be had, not from the study of any one language *per se*, but from the comparison and synthesis of two or more languages. It is not till we have seen the differences and the resemblances in the structure of two distinct grammars, that we can get the least perception of the difference between those principles which are accidental or distinctive of particular tongues, and those which are

By constant comparison of Latin with analogous English forms.

fundamental and common to all organized languages alike.

For instance how much clearer the nature of the difference between Personal and Demonstrative pronouns will be, if by some such table as that which follows, you point out (*a*) that our own language once recognized this distinction as clearly as the Latin, (*b*) that we have retained in modern use only those forms which are printed in capitals, and (*c*) that in the third person we have lost the plural forms of the Personal pronoun, and also most of the singular forms of the Demonstrative, and have pieced together the fragments, so as to make what we now call one pronoun, of which *he*, *she*, and *it* are the singular, and *they* and *their* the plural forms.

ENGLISH AND LATIN PRONOUNS.

FIRST PERSON.—

	Singular.		Dual.	Plural.	
Nominative	IC	*Ego*	Wit	WE	*Nos*
Genitive	MIN	*Mei*	Uncer	URE	*Nostri*
Dative	ME	*Mihi*	Unc	U's	*Nobis*
Accusative	ME	*Me*	Unc	Us	*Nōs*

SECOND PERSON.—

	Singular.		Dual.	Plural.	
Nom.	THU	*Tu*	Git	GE	*Vos*
Gen.	THIN	*Tui*	Incer	EOWER	*Vestri*
Dat.	THE	*Te*	Inc	Eow	*Vobis*
Accus.	THE	*Te*	Inc	Eow	*Vōs*

THIRD PERSON.—

	Singular.					Plural.	
	Masculine.		Feminine.		Neuter.		All genders.
Nom.	HE	*Is*	Heo	*Ea*	HIT	*Id*	Hi	*Ii*
Gen.	HIS	*Ejus*	HIR	*Ejus*	His	*Ejus*	Heora	*Eorum*
Dat.	HIM	*Ei*	HIR	*Ei*	Him	*Ei*	Heom	*Iis*
Accus.	Hine	*Eum*	Hi	*Eam*	HIT	*Id*	Hi	*Eos*

Comparison of Latin and English forms.

THIRD PERSON, DEMONSTRATIVE—

	Singular.						Plural.	
	Masculine.		Feminine.		Neuter.		All genders.	
Nom.	Se	*Ille*	Seo	*Illa*	Thæt	*Illud*	Tha	*Illi*
Gen.	Thæs	*Illius*	Thære	*Illius*	Thæs	*Illius*	Thara	*Illorum*
Dat.	Tham	*Illi*	Thære	*Illi*	Tham	*Illi*	Tham	*Illis*
Accus.	Thone	*Illum*	Tha	*Illam*	Thæt	*Illud*	Tha	*Illos*
Ablative	Thy	*Illo*	Thære	*Illâ*	Thy	*Illo*	Tham	*Illis*

INTERROGATIVE—

	Masculine and Feminine.	Neuter.
Nom.	Hwa	Hwœt
Gen.	Hwœs	Hwœs
Dat.	Hwam	Hwam
Acc.	Hwone	Hwœt
Ablative	Hwi	Hwi

It is important that lessons on grammar and on simple translation should proceed *pari passu* from the first. This is now recognized by all the best writers of elementary Latin books; but the principle though important is often lost sight of by teachers. They say, and quite truly, 'We must have our scholars well grounded in the grammar first of all.' But their notion of *grounding* consists in requiring a great deal of the grammar to be learned by heart, before it is understood or seen in any practical application to the actual construction of sentences. It is for this reason that the study is felt to be so dry and repulsive to school-boys. *By connecting translation with grammar from the first.*

We repel a scholar by forcing him to learn at the beginning the whole list of inflections and conjugations, containing many forms and distinctions of which he sees neither the meaning nor the use, and which he will not want for a long time to come. All such synopses are useful and indeed indispensable; but they should be reserved for a later period of the study when they will serve to collect and classify the knowledge which has been gradually acquired. With this view many good teachers object even to give the whole set of inflections in a noun to be learned by heart; but prefer to give a separate lesson on the genitive, or the accusative, to point out its various modifications and its exact meaning, and then to give a number of illustrative examples at once, so that theory and practice should go together from the first. Consider the difference in importance, and in immediate usefulness, between the accusative and the vocative case, consider how much more important the second declension is than the fourth, and you will then see how absurd is the method which obliges a boy to commit all these things to memory together at the same stage of his career. It is shocking to think of the heedless and unscientific use which many teachers have made of the mere verbal memory in treating this subject, keeping boys two or three years learning a great many bare abstractions, before allowing them to make any practical use of their knowledge or read a single line. It needs to be constantly repeated that memory is a faculty of association mainly, and that words and names without useful associations are of no value, and are soon rejected by a healthy intelligence.

How much of grammar need be learned by heart. The portion of the Latin grammar which, for the purpose now in view, requires to be thus gradually learned by heart is small, and may be comprised in a very few pages. It may consist of:—

(1) The five declensions including of course all adjectives and participles. Here of course you will not separate nouns from adjectives, and so go over the same forms twice. You will shew from the first the identity of the inflections in the two.

(2) The rules for gender, with one or two of the most notable exceptions.

(3) The four conjugations of verbs active and passive, with the substantive verb *esse*.

(4) The irregular verbs *volo, eo, nolo, mālo,* and *possum*.

(5) Three or four of the leading rules of syntax, and these only, when the time comes for applying them.

The simple rule of concord, between nominative and verb, and between noun and adjective, will come very early. Do not attempt to disjoin syntax and accidence as if syntax were an advanced part of the study.

And from the first, as sentences are formed, I would call attention to the corresponding form in English, or to the absence in English of some inflection which is present in Latin, and to the expedients by which in our language we supply the lack of a more complete accidence and inflection.

Many of the best teachers adopt the crude-form system of teaching the Latin and Greek accidence. They call attention to the stem of the word—to that part which is common to all forms, and is independent of the inflection, and they show how this stem is clothed with one garb after another, according to the use which has to be made of it. Such teachers would not speak of *rex* as the root for king, but *reg*, and would show how this root was disguised in the nominative case ; nor *porto, portare,* to carry, but *port;* nor ποὐς for foot but ποδ; nor πράσσω but πραγ.

The crudeform system.

"Ancient languages," said Lord Bacon, "were more full of declensions, cases, conjugations, tenses, and the like: the modern commonly destitute of these do loosely deliver themselves in many expressions by prepositions and auxiliary verbs : may it not be conjectured that the wits of former times were far more acute and subtle than ours are?"

We must not I think accept this inference too readily. For indeed the fact of the decay of inflections and of the substitution for them of prepositions and auxiliaries, may be accounted for on many other hypotheses than that of a decline in human acuteness, or in intellectual exactitude. Yet it is plain that by pointing out at each stage in learning the Latin grammar the difference between a given modification in the meaning of a word as expressed, say by an ablative in Latin, and by a preposition in English; by a future tense in Latin, and by the word *shall* or *will* in English; you are giving to the pupil a truer notion of the functions of grammar and the extent of its province than if you taught either of these forms by itself.

The Vocabulary. As to the vocabulary, I think we often put needless difficulties in the way by requiring every word to be separately hunted out in a dictionary. This is a very slow and wearisome process, and after all there is no particular value in it. It does nothing to encourage accuracy, and it certainly does not help to give any special love for the act of research. So in all early exercises it is well to bring the vocabulary specially needed in those exercises close under the eye of the learner so that he has not far to look for them. Later of course it is very desirable that he should know how to consult a dictionary, and should often use it; but if he has to make this reference in more, say, than one in ten of the words which occur in his lesson you are placing a needless impediment in the way of his progress.

Use genuine Latin sen- Again, it is desirable that as soon as possible you escape from the little graduated exercises in what may be called manufactured Latin;—the sort of Arnoldian exercise in which "Balbus strikes the head of the father of *tences, not those* the maiden;"—and get to real sentences, little narratives *manufac-* which have an interest of their own, and which are taken *tured for the purpose.* from good authors. Of course these should be so graduated, that the difficulties do not come all at once. But it is better to deal with a short passage, or a verse of an ode, which has a prettiness and interest of its own, even though there are one or two phrases in it a little beyond the reach of the learner's present grammatical knowledge, than to keep him too long on bald and meaningless sentences, merely because they illustrate a particular kind of grammar rule.

After a little progress has been made, a teacher may wisely select an easy ode of Horace, some passages from Ovid; the sentences from Cæsar descriptive of his visit to Britain; a few of the happier examples of characterization from the Catiline of Sallust, or some eloquent sentences from an oration of Cicero; and will make these first of all the subject of thorough grammatical investigation, postponing however any special difficulties and promising to recur to them hereafter. Then he will give a full explanation of the meaning, circumstances, and purpose of the extract, and finally after it has been translated carefully, will cause it to be learned by heart. This was Jacotot's method. *Tout est dans tout.* He required that some one interesting passage should be dealt with exhaustively, and should be made not only a specimen of the way in which a passage might be investigated, but a centre round which grammatical knowledge might cluster, and to which all new acquisitions might be referred by way of comparison or contrast. Nothing is more depressing and unsatisfactory than to arrange all authors in the order of their supposed difficulty, and to say, *e.g.* that one must spend so many months over Eutropius, and then another term on Cæsar, and afterwards proceed to Ovid and to Virgil, as if these books represented so many advanced rules in Arithmetic. A child properly taught Latin with the object I have indicated, should above all things be interested and made from the first to feel that the Latin language is like his own in the variety and attractiveness of its contents, and not a series of exercises in grammar and vocabulary only.

Literature should come early. For after all, one of your chief aims in teaching language at all is to make the scholar enjoy literature, and get an enlarged acquaintance with the meanings of words. The sooner we can bend our teaching towards these particular purposes the better.

One way of doing this will be to study some English classic *pari passu* with a Latin book or extract of a cognate kind. We have spoken of the simultaneous study of Latin and English Grammar. There is an equally good reason for the simultaneous reading of Latin and English literature. Side by side with the Latin lessons, or alternating with them, I would take good sentences from Classical English books and treat them in the same way. In the one lesson you will note down all Latin words which have supplied English derivatives, in the other all English words which have a Latin origin. You will make a list of them, illustrate their meaning and use, the way in which some portions of the original meaning have disappeared, and other shades or varieties of signification have become attached to the words since their introduction into English. By requiring these words to be collected in a special list you will at the same time be increasing your pupil's store of Latin words and will make him more accurately acquainted with the history and significance of words in his own language. Constant care should also be taken to secure that resemblances or differences in the idiom and structure of the two languages should be clearly apprehended, and free use should be made of note-books in order to promote thoroughness and accuracy. And as the pupil becomes further advanced, it is well to take up the parallel and simultaneous study of portions of an ancient and a modern author, *e.g.* with the *Ars Poetica* of Horace Pope's *Essay on Criticism* or Byron's *Hints from Horace* might be read; with a Satire of Juvenal, Johnson's imitation or some well-chosen passage from Dryden; with an oration of Cicero, a famous speech of Burke or Macaulay; with one of the *Georgics* of Virgil, an extract from Thomson or Cowper descriptive of rural life; with a passage from Livy or Tacitus, another passage from Gibbon or Froude.

This is a large subject, and no one of you can be more conscious than I am of the inadequacy of such few hints as can be given on it in a short lecture. Those of you who are engaged in teaching Latin or Greek, will find it necessary to read much and to think more, before you will attain a satisfactory course of procedure. By far the wisest and most suggestive of old books on the methods of teaching is Roger Ascham's *Scholemaster*, which explains fully his system of teaching by translation and re-translation. He would go through a Latin passage and translate it into English, writing the translation down carefully; then after an interval of an hour or two, he would give the scholar those English sentences for re-translation into Latin, and as he well shews, whether this be done by memory or by invention it is almost equally useful. I strongly advise also the reading of Mr Quick's admirable book on Educational Reformers, for that work not only summarizes well the main excellencies of Ascham's method, but it also gives an account of the methods of teaching Latin recommended by Milton, by Comenius, by Locke, and by others—subjects which it is beyond my province to discuss here. Nor ought I to omit the mention of Mr Henry Sidgwick's thoughtful paper in the *Essays on a Liberal Education*, and of Mr D'Arcy Thompson's *Day dreams of a Schoolmaster*, which is full of practical suggestion as to rational and simple means of teaching grammar.

The place of Latin in a Primary School.

In what I have said hitherto we have been chiefly concerned with the use which should be made of Latin in secondary schools. And this, as we have seen, does not aim at making what are called 'scholars,' nor at using Latin as a vehicle for the expression of the learner's own thoughts, but mainly at enabling him to understand the laws of language, and especially of his own language, better. Now what is the place, if any, which Latin should hold in a Primary school or in one whose course will probably terminate at 14?

There has been much contention as to the expediency of including in the Schedule of additional "Specific Subjects," attached to the Code of the Education Department, lessons on the elements of Latin Grammar. By some this is defended on the grounds that such knowledge will be serviceable to those promising scholars whom it may be worth while to encourage to go forward to a secondary school, and that in the open competition for admission to such schools Latin grammar is often one of the required subjects. But the truth is that at the age of 12 or 13 at which it is fitting to select such a pupil for an exhibition, Latin ought not to be required at all. It is of far more importance to secure that his intelligence shall have been quickened by the ordinary discipline of a good primary school, than that he should have been exceptionally trained for the exhibition, and he will learn Latin all the better and faster in the higher school for having received such discipline. Moreover the Primary school has no right to sacrifice the interests of the mass of its scholars to those of the exhibitioner; and in the interests of the mass, it is impossible to defend the teaching of a few fragments of Latin grammar which have no relation to anything else they are learning, or are likely to learn.

So I do not think it wise in Elementary Schools to attempt the formal study of Latin. But there is a sense in which the language has claims which should not be disregarded even here. Some lessons should be given showing that there *is* a Latin language, explaining who used to speak it, and how and why so many of our words are derived from it. Even in the humblest school-course the fact that other languages exist, and that there are many ways of expressing the same notion, ought to be understood. Then it is well to teach a few of the simpler tests by which words of Latin origin may be identified by terminations or otherwise; and to explain the more common of the phonetic changes which words undergo in becoming English. These should not be presented in the form of a list or table, but be brought out by induction from examples, of which some may be suggested by the teacher, but the most supplied by the scholars.

The Etymology of many Latinized words might be advantageously explained. But here a good deal of caution is needed. Tell a scholar who is not learning Latin that *commit* comes from *con* with, and *mitto* I send, or *perceive* from *per* and *capio*, or *obedience* from *ob* and *audio*, and you have simply given him a showy and unmeaning piece of knowledge, and rather

Derivations of English words.

hindered than helped his conception of the real significance of the English derivative. The only words in relation to which the mere learning of the Latin etymology by itself secures any useful purpose, are words like *submarine* or *soliloquy*, where the etymology brings out the meaning without the least ambiguity. But if you will take the trouble to show by a few examples what changes and modifications of meaning Latin words have often undergone in the process of becoming English, the etymological exercise will have a real value. In particular you will find it useful to trace out the changes by which words which have at first a literal and physical meaning come in time to have a metaphorical meaning. You take the word *fortis* and show it in *fortress* and afterwards in *fortitude* or *comfort*. So *Morsel* and *remorse*, *Effigy* and *fiction*, *Image* and *imagination*, *Pound* and *ponder*, *Refract* and *infringe*, *Integer* and *integrity*, give occasion for pointing out how the application of a word to some moral or spiritual truth is subsequent to its physical meaning, and that we may illustrate a moral truth by a physical image, but never a physical fact by an image drawn from the world of thought. A few of the most familiar Latin roots may then be taken, *e.g. pose;* and the pupils may be invited to supply words containing this syllable,—sup*pose*, ex*pose*, de*pose*, inter*pose*, re*pose*, and to show what is the common element of meaning in all of them.

Prefixes and affixes.

Afterwards it is well to call attention to the double signification of the Latin prefixes, to show, *e.g.* that they have a physical or prepositional meaning in some words, as in *trans*port, *in*vade, *ex*pel, *e*mit, *inter*collegiate, *re*gain, *extra*-mural, *per*forate; and an adverbial or derived meaning as *trans*figure, *in*complete, *ex*perience, *e*loquence, *inter*jection, *re*spect, *extra*vagant, *per*ish. In teaching these prefixes it is needful to show how inadequate a notion of their meaning is obtained by looking into a dictionary and simply taking their primitive signification as prepositions, without also taking into account their secondary meaning when they come to be used adverbially, in the composition of verbs.

If in these ways, Latin—not its formal grammar, but a part of its vocabulary, and such facts about the language as serve to explain the structure and meaning of English words—be recognized as a subject of study in the primary school, it will be found very stimulating and helpful to those who may afterwards have opportunities of learning more of the language; and at the same time, it will be of substantial value even to those who will enjoy no such opportunities, and is in no sense out of harmony with all else that is taught in the ordinary elementary course.

In teaching a modern foreign language the objects we are to have in view are not wholly identical with those we have already described. It is true French may in one sense serve the same purpose as Latin; if its grammar is taught side by side with that of English, and made the subject of constant comparison and contrast. But the structure of French grammar does not furnish either comparison or contrast quite so instructive as that of Latin for purposes of philological discipline, or for throwing light on the principles of grammar *per se*. The main reason for teaching French or German is that the learner may read books and converse in that language, and use it as an instrument of thought and communication. That therefore which is the first and main object of teaching Latin—the investigation of the logic of language, and the reflex action of its grammar on the structure

Modern foreign languages.

Their special purpose.

of other languages and particularly of our own—is only the secondary and subordinate object to be kept in view in the teaching of French. And that which is the principal reason for learning French, viz. that we may be able to think, to speak, and to write in it, is not, for purposes of ordinary education, contemplated in the study of Latin at all. And it is only by keeping this fundamental difference in view that we can arrive at right methods of teaching either.

How far they resemble Latin.

Obviously, some of the principles and methods already discussed apply equally to Latin and French. Both are foreign languages. In both we have to begin at the beginning, to learn vocabulary as well as grammar. In both it is essential to begin with a few nouns, to attach them first to verbs, afterwards to adjectives, afterwards to other nouns in the various case-relationships. In both it is equally important that new rules should be learned only if and when they are wanted, and should be seen in their applications and applied directly. In both there is the same necessity for kindling the interest of your scholar, by connecting the words he learns with living realities, with things and events within his comprehension. In both it is equally desirable to make constant reference to analogous usages and constructions in English.

How they differ from it.

But besides this, it is from the first necessary to treat French conversationally, to cause it to be talked as well as learned. It is not certain that lessons ever so careful on elementary sounds in French are the best helps to this. At first little familiar sentences are better. I have seen in one of the best schools in England what was called a 'parrot class,' in which little girls were learning to utter French phrases and nursery rhymes, with the right pronunciation and inflection as a whole, and were told roughly what was the meaning of them. This is what is often called the *Mastery System*. By it children are not at first allowed to see French written, but are made to acquire a thoroughly French pronunciation and intonation parrot-like, before they begin to have their attention directed to the sounds of separate syllables, to the meaning of separate words and idioms, or to translation and re-translation.

Such exercises are particularly useful. In talking we want to be trained to catch the meaning of a whole sentence without thinking of its particular parts, and the laborious synthesis of the various elements of a sentence is, as we all know, a rather slow process. Some therefore of the early work of teaching a young class French ought to correspond to the way in which a little child learns English from its mother or its nurse, *i.e.* in little sentences which at first carry the whole meaning with them, and are not thought of as capable of analysis. For the special purpose contemplated in teaching French, the sooner the child learns something which he feels a pleasure in committing to memory the better. *They should from the first be spoken rather than written.*

It is evident that talking in the language and learning by heart are much more important here than in Latin. No lesson in French which is confined to translation and reading is worth much, if it is not followed up by actual conversation. Even the simplest affirmative sentence admits of being turned into an interrogative, or furnishes the material for a question and answer of some kind, which however slightly varied, obliges the child to make the words his own. And unless the learner makes the words his own, and learns actually to use them, his progress is very unsatisfactory. Then we must remember that in seeking to get a store of vocables and words for use, it is not a large number of nouns and adjectives which we want first, but a few familiar locutions, the phrases for asking, for asserting, for denying, for enquiring; into which phrases nouns and adjectives soon fit themselves as fast as they are known. Mr Quick quotes from Marcel's *Study of Languages* a very significant sentence, "Half the knowledge with twice the power of applying it is better than twice the knowledge with half the power of application."

Latin for the eye. French for the ear.

To recognize the meaning and understand the grammatical forms of words as they are printed in a book suffices in learning Latin, and is itself a considerable achievement. It is the eye through which you want to approach the understanding in this case. The ear and the voice have little or nothing to do with it; for scarcely anybody ever has occasion to use a single sentence of spoken Latin, or to listen to Latin and interpret it at the same time. But in French or German it is the ear and the voice we want to cultivate quite as much as the eye, and much therefore of every good French lesson should go on with the books closed.

Audition.

It is especially important to use many exercises in what may be called *audition*—the listening to French sentences and rapidly interpreting them. In most schools, there is not even enough of dictation in French, which is obviously a simple and necessary exercise, and which of course you will not neglect. But even this does not suffice, for the measured careful utterance proper to a dictation lesson is very unlike ordinary speech, and many scholars will write a very good exercise from dictation, who would be quite unable to follow a conversation or even a sermon or oration delivered in the ordinary way. Is it not the painful experience of many of us who may be very familiar with book-French and able to read the language fluently; that when we

Invention and composition. 253

once cross the Channel, and hear it rapidly uttered we are confused, and cannot follow it fast enough. Here and there a word which happens to be the key-word or significant word in the sentence wholly escapes us; and this causes the entire sentence to be unintelligible. We wonder why people will talk so fast, forgetting that our own habitual speech is often just as rapid, just as full of contractions and elisions; and that after all we do not know a language for speaking purposes, unless we can think in it as fast as a person usually talks. Now the true remedy for this is constant exercise in listening either to reading or to speech, uttered at the rapid rate of ordinary conversation. And the power to make a right use of such an exercise is far more easily attained when very young, and when the mind is unencumbered by thoughts of analysis and grammar, than in later life. It should not therefore be postponed and treated as an advanced exercise, but frequently adopted from the beginning.

Mr Bowen, in an excellent paper read at the late Head Masters' Conference, recommended that with advanced scholars the occasional use of a French book of reference as an alternative for an English one is useful. He recommends reference to a good French gazetteer or dictionary, or to the *Biographie Universelle*, in addition to books of the same kind in English. To this it may be added that some of the scientific manuals by Guillemin or Papillon are as easily read by an elder boy who has learned French as English manuals, and often excel our books in style and in clearness of arrangement. The sooner you can make a French book of use for reference, or for learning a thing at first-hand, the more rapid will be the progress of your pupil.

Some exercises in invention and arrangement are given in most of the books, but not, as it seems to me, *Exercises in inven-*

tion and composition.

enough. There are French sentences to be translated into English and English into French. But there are not enough exercises in which learners are required to make sentences of their own. These however are very important. At first a noun, and a verb, and an adjective may be given, in order that two or three little sentences may be made out of them; afterwards a few nouns may be given, and the pupil told to put at his own discretion appropriate verbs to them. Then verbs or adjectives may be added and required to be added to suitable nouns. Afterwards particular idioms, or phrases may be given, and the pupil asked to construct sentences containing them. Thus at first you give the material for such sentences—but little by little, less should be given, and the scholars should be required to discover and supply words for themselves. And whether the required words are supplied from memory, or are hunted out and selected from a book, the exercise is equally valuable.

But although we thus dwell chiefly on the importance of the better cultivation of the ear and voice in teaching a modern foreign language, since these are just the points we are most in danger of forgetting, book-work being always more easy and seductive to teachers than the kind of oral practice which makes constant demands on your skill, your promptitude, and your memory; we must not of course overlook the fact that the language has also to be written, and its grammar thoroughly understood. You cannot therefore dispense with written exercises, especially in grammar and in composition, of the same kind as you would find necessary in teaching Latin. These however, are precisely the things which good modern books supply in great abundance.

The choice of teachers.

Lastly, a word may be said on the subject of the teachers of foreign languages. It is generally considered indispensable to have a Frenchman to teach French, and a German to teach German. But experience shows us that the power to speak French does not always co-exist with the power to teach it; that French ushers as a class are without the general liberal education which you look for in English assistants; and that as specialists, whose position renders them unable to look on the school work as a whole, they often fail to secure authority, or even to secure full knowledge for their own subject. It is obvious too that most of them are at a great disadvantage in the explanation in English of the meaning of the rules, and especially in comparing French idioms with English. Accordingly, in some of the best schools the modern language masters preferred are scholarly Englishmen, who have lived for a time abroad, and who have learned French or German well enough to think and converse well in it. And where such teachers are to be had, I should be disposed to prefer them. The objection to this is that the pronunciation is not likely to be perfect. But it is very easy to over-rate the importance of what is often so much vaunted in ladies' schools, the purely Parisian accent, and to pay too heavy a price for it. After all, this accent is not the first thing an Englishman wants. He will acquire it, if he goes abroad; and if he never acquires it, the power to express himself and to derive pleasure from reading French or German literature is much more important.

IX. THE ENGLISH LANGUAGE.

The relation of English to other linguistic studies.

WE have tried to elucidate in the last lecture these general truths, That all study of language is in itself disciplinal, and helps greatly the development of one particular class of mental power; That some of the reasons which justify the teaching of Latin and Greek, are identical with those which make us teach French or German, but that others are wholly different; That Latin is to be learned as a literary language, and with a view to grammatical and logical training mainly, and not for purposes of expression or intercourse; but That a modern language is learned mainly for the sake of expression and intercourse, and only incidentally and in a subordinate sense as a linguistic discipline. The questions arise now—Why and how should we teach English, our own language? What place in a complete scheme of instruction should the vernacular tongue as a separate study be made to occupy?

The answer to this question depends of course on the width and extent of your course, and on the nature of the other provision which that course affords for prosecuting the study of grammar as a science. It has been said that the true perception of that science is the result of the synthesis and comparison of two languages, and is well-nigh unattainable in the learning of one.

For that reason, I have already urged that in the teaching of Latin or of French, continual reference should be made to analogous forms and constructions in English. And no doubt in schools in which other languages are taught in this way, much of English is learned incidentally by comparison, analogy, and contrast, rather than in the form of intentional lessons on English, *per se*.

It is mainly in this incidental and indirect way, that most English scholars have come to learn their own language, and have very often come to learn it well. And hence it is not uncommon to hear English grammar spoken of as if it were wholly useless, and almost as if it were non-existent. And we are to enquire to-day whether this distrust of the value of conscious and systematic instruction in English is well founded, or whether such instruction can be made to serve a real educational purpose. We know that in France and Germany the study of the vernacular tongue is treated with more respect than with ourselves; that in France especially, exercises in the structure, logical analysis, and composition of French occupy a good deal of attention even in schools in which other languages are taught; and that it is probably to this cause we may attribute the greater ease and skill with which as a rule a Frenchman uses his own language, as compared with an Englishman of corresponding educational standing and advantages. The study of our own tongue appears to deserve more respectful treatment than it receives even in our higher schools. It certainly is a valuable, indeed an indispensable educational instrument in Primary schools, in which no other language is taught. *A Vernacular grammar often learned indirectly and incidentally.*

Of one thing, however, we may be sure from the first. It is not as a set of rules for enabling English people to speak correctly that English grammar has the least value. *Grammar as an Art.*

This is the popular conception of grammar, and it is a very erroneous one. Lindley Murray has expressed this in a definition. "Grammar is the art of speaking and writing the English language with propriety." Whoever tries to learn or to teach grammar with that object in view, is doomed to disappointment. No doubt there is a sense, and a very true sense, in which all careful investigation into the structure of words and their relations gives precision to speech. But this is an indirect process. The direct operation and use of grammar rules in improving our speech and making it correct, can hardly be said to exist at all.

Not to be acquired by rules. For we all learn to speak the English language in one fashion or another without the aid of books. Some of the best and purest speakers of the language have either never learned grammar, or are not in any way consciously guided to correct speech by a knowledge of grammatical rules. They have learned to use their own language *by using it*, by imitation and habit, and by the fine intuition which has led them to imitate good models rather than bad. If the 'art of speaking and writing the English language with propriety' is the one thing contemplated by learning grammar, the ordinary means are very imperfectly adapted to the end; for the study of grammar from a scholastic text book, even if the whole of it is learned from beginning to end, is very little helpful in improving the pupil's speech and writing. The faults which occur in speech, the confusions, the clumsy constructions, the misuse of words, and their mispronunciation, are not as a rule, sins against grammar, properly so called; and are not to be set right by learning English accidence or syntax. The rules given in books have little or no practical value. For instance, "Transitive verbs and prepositions govern the objective case." What does this mean? In English nouns, there is no objective case distinguishable from the nominative at all. In pronouns there are four or five survivals of old datives, which now serve both as dative and accusative, and may therefore be called objective. They are *me, thee, him, her, them,* and *whom.* And the rule in question amounts to an injunction that we should use these six words in their proper places, and not say, "Give *I* the book," or, "Send the money to *he.*" But these are faults which the most ignorant child is in no danger of committing, and against which no warning is needed. Considered therefore as a means of regulating our speech, this and the like rules are utterly valueless.

If therefore we have in view mainly the practical art of using the language in speech or writing with good taste and correctness, this particular result is probably best to be attained by talking to the pupil, by taking care he hears little but good English, by correcting him when he is wrong, by making him read the best authors, by practising him much in writing, and when he makes a mistake, by requiring him to write the sentence again without one. It will certainly not be attained by setting him to learn Murray's, or indeed any other grammar.[1]

Grammar, however, is a science as well as an art, and from this point of view, it investigates the structure of language, the history and formation of words, and the manner in which the mechanism of grammatical form is fitted to fulfil the great end of language—the just, subtle, and forcible expression of human thought. And if a book on grammar will help me to this end, and will

Grammar as a Science.

---

[1] "On n'apprend pas plus à parler, et à écrire avec les règles de la grammaire, qu'on n'apprend à marcher par les lois de l'équilibre." ST PIERRE.

reveal to me the laws and principles which underlie and account for the speech which I am using every day, then the study of such a book will have a scientific value for me quite apart from any practical help which it may give in avoiding solecisms, and in "speaking grammatically" as it is called. Such study of grammar, though it seems rather to have a theoretic than a practical character, will incidentally serve the purpose of making the speech more correct. If, however, that purpose is contemplated as the first which is to be served in teaching, we not only shall not attain it, but we shall fail altogether to achieve the much higher ends which may be reached by the teaching of grammar as a science.

Manuals of Grammar. Now the notable thing about manuals of English grammar until very lately was that they were all fashioned on the same model as a Latin or Greek grammar. There were Orthography, Etymology, Syntax, and Prosody. The learner begins with considering letters, and the whole alphabet is printed on the first page, and duly classified into vowels, consonants, semi-vowels, and diphthongs. Then he is conducted to Etymology, and to the separate study of words, which he is called on to classify and decline. Then comes Syntax, when he is invited to deal with sentences, and the relation of their parts, and to learn rules of concord and of government. Finally, he reaches Prosody, under which head he finds punctuation, metre, and other grammatical luxuries.

A vernacular language must be taught by analysis. But long before a child comes to the commencement of such a book, he has learned to speak, and to use his native tongue. He knows the meaning of sentences, and he thinks by means of the language. That which is in teaching French, the ultimate goal of your ambition, conversation and freedom in using words, is the very point of departure in the case of your own vernacular speech. Your pupil has already attained it. Hence the methods of teaching a native and a foreign language, are fundamentally different. The slow, synthetical process appropriate in the one case, of beginning with words—in the case of German and Greek, even with the alphabet, —and building up at first short sentences, then longer sentences, is wholly illogical and absurd in the case of the other. To a child a sentence is easier than a word, the cognition of a word is easier than that of a syllable as a separate entity; and the syllable itself is something easier than the power or significance of a single letter. And hence the way to teach English grammar is to begin with the sentence, because that is something known, and to proceed analytically. If other languages are to be learned by synthesis, our own should be learned by the opposite process of analysis; and whereas we learn a foreign language through, and by means of its grammar, we must learn and discover English grammar, through and by means of the language.

Grammar strictly defined is the logic of language in so far and in so far only as it finds expression in the inflections and forms of words. In Latin forms, you find this logic expressed with some fulness and scientific accuracy. In English it is expressed in an unscientific and very incomplete way. But the logic of language, which is the basis of all grammar, is discernible alike in both, and our business is to investigate that, whether it reveals itself fully in grammatical forms or not.

The main conclusions to which we have thus been led are four: (1) That of pure grammar there is very little in the English language. (2) That this little when discovered has scarcely any practical bearing on the improvement of our speech. (3) That nevertheless the study of the English language is worth pursuing, and if the expression 'English Grammar' be enlarged so as to connote exercises in the logic, history, formation and relation of words, it will designate one of the most fruitful and interesting of school studies; and (4) That whatever is to be learned of a vernacular language, must be learned by the method of analysis, and not by the synthetic process, which is proper in studying a foreign tongue.

We may now apply these conclusions in succession to several of the most useful forms of English exercise.

Classification. One of your earliest lessons consists of a view of the parts of speech. The books would have you begin by saying there are nine of them, and by requiring the pupil to learn by heart the definition and some examples of each. But it is surely a much more rational method to begin with a sentence which the scholar already understands, and so to draw from him the simple facts that in using language there are two essential conditions, viz.

(1) That we should have something to talk about;
(2) That we should have something to say.

You may illustrate this by taking a little sentence
The child sleeps
as a type, and you say that the former word is called the *Subject* or the thing talked about, and is a *Noun*, and the latter the *Predicate*, the thing said, and is a *Verb*.

Then you point out that each of these words admits of extension, and takes an attribute;
The *little* child sleeps *soundly*,
and you shew that the one word enlarges the subject and the other the predicate. You then invite the scholars to give you other sentences containing the same elements, and after a few examples you give names to the words which fulfil these two functions and call the one an *Adjective* and the other an *Adverb*.

Then you seek to attach other notions to the first, and you do this in two ways:

> The child sleeps *on* the bed.
> The child sleeps *because* he is tired.

In the former case you have added a word, in the latter a new sentence, the nature of the connexion thus established being shewn by the word in italics. Hence is deduced the necessity for two sorts of connective words, the *Preposition* which attaches a noun, and the *Conjunction* which attaches a sentence to what has gone before.

These are the six essential elements of organized speech, and the logical order of their importance is

Subject	*Noun.*
Predicate	*Verb.*
Adjunct to Subject	*Adjective.*
,, Predicate	*Adverb.*
Connective of Word	*Preposition.*
,, Sentence	*Conjunction.*

Then you go on to shew that you have not exhausted all the words in the language, but that there remain;

(1) The *Pronoun*, whose use you illustrate by examples. It is not a new element in language, but is simply used as a convenient substitute for a noun in certain cases.

(2) The *Article*, which is seen to be a kind of adjective used in a very special sense.

You shew that these two though useful are not indispensable, and that Latin did without the last altogether.

Lastly you point out that what is often called the ninth part of speech, the *Interjection*, is in fact not a part of speech at all; but as Horne Tooke called it "the miserable refuge of the speechless." It is the one form of human utterance which obeys no law, and is closest akin to the screams of a bird, or to the growling of a dog; and we never use it unless for a moment we part with the privilege of humanity, descend to the level of the lower animals, and cease to use organized language altogether.

Now all this could be well taught with varied illustrations in three lessons, and the outcome of it would shew itself in some such black-board sketch or summary as this :

ESSENTIAL PARTS OF SPEECH.

I.—Notional.

1. Words capable of forming the subject of a sentence. *Nouns.*
2. Words capable of forming the predicate . . *Verbs.*
3. Words capable of serving as attributes to Nouns . *Adjectives.*
4. Words capable of serving as attributes to Verbs . *Adverbs.*

II.—Relational or Connective.

5. Words connecting Nouns with sentences. . . *Prepositions.*
6. Words connecting sentences with sentences . . *Conjunctions.*

NON-ESSENTIAL BUT SERVICEABLE PARTS OF SPEECH.

7. Words capable of being used as substitutes for Nouns . . . . *Pronouns.*
8. Adjectives with a special and limited use . . *Articles.*

9. EXTRA-GRAMMATICAL UTTERANCES . . *Interjections.*

In further investigation of the use of each class of words you afterwards bring out by examples these facts :

Nouns may serve (*a*) with the verb "to be," as predicates; (*b*) with transitive verbs, as objects or completion of predicates; (*c*) with prepositions, as adjuncts either adjectival or adverbial.

A Verb of complete predication is Intransitive; one which makes an incomplete assertion is Transitive.

Pronouns which have in them a connective element of meaning are called *Relatives.*

So that instead of beginning with the definitions I should end with them. The process is one of induction and analysis from the first. You begin with the concrete whole—a sentence with which learners are already familiar, you work down to its parts, you seek to discriminate them carefully; then, and not till then, you give them names, and finally by way of clinching your lesson you ask for the meanings of those names, and after a few experiments of the Socratic kind, may succeed in evolving a good definition of each. In doing this explain if you like the significance of the name. But this is not always easy, and when easy not always helpful. Our grammatical terminology is so arbitrary, that an etymological enquiry into the meaning of the words *Preposition, Infinitive, Adjective*, will rather mislead than otherwise.

At this point you will find how useful it is to give examples illustrative of the way in which the same word may be used in very different ways : *e.g.*

(1) *Rest* comes to the weary. They *rest* from their labours.
(2) *Light* is diffused by reflection. This is a *light* room. They *light* the candle.
(3) *Reading* is a useful art. They have been *reading* for an hour. She has a *reading* book.

By a few tentative sentences of this kind you will shew that it is impossible to label a word with a name while it stands alone, that in fact it is not a part of speech at all until it is seen in a sentence. Follow this up by asking such a question as this; "take the word *Sound* and put it into a sentence so that it shall be a noun— an adjective—a verb." Much exercise in the making of sentences to illustrate each new distinction as it is pointed out, is indispensable.

You go back then to the *Noun*, the *Adjective*, and the *Adverb*, and shew that though each is generally expressed by one word, each may be expanded into a phrase or sentence which is equivalent to it.

e.g. (1) The *rainbow* appears . . . . *Simple noun.*
That *you have wronged me* doth appear
    in this . . . . . *Noun sentence.*

(2) The *small* house is mine . . *Simple adjective.*
The house *on the hill* is mine . . *Adjective phrase.*
The house *which you saw* is mine . *Adjective sentence.*

(3) She sings *sweetly* . . . . *Simple adverb.*
She sings *in the garden* . . *Adverbial phrase.*
She sings *when she is asked* . . *Adverbial sentence.*

Logical Analysis. When such preliminary exercises have been thought out the scholar will be ready for the more complete analysis of the parts of sentences and their relations to each other. This is an intellectual exercise of considerable value. It is not grammar, it is true; it is rather elementary logic; but it lies at the root of grammar; and when you have first taught your pupils to recognize the elements of a sentence and their mutual correlation, you will be in a position to ask how far each logical distinction has a grammatical or formative distinction to correspond to it.

As to the laying out of the result of such an analysis, there is of course no absolutely right or wrong method. But I would warn you against the common method of making a square diagram and trying to fit every sentence into it, *e.g.*

Subject.	Predicate.	Object, or completion of Predicate.	Extension.
The curfew	tolls	the knell	of parting day

This is something like the bed of Procrustes, and has a double disadvantage. It often leaves great vacant spaces, and it fails altogether to shew the real relations of words, phrases and sentences to one another.

Some sentences contain only one or two elements, and may be dismissed in two lines. Others require the statement of many more particulars than are provided for in such a diagram. The essential points in relation to the analysis are (1) That an account shall be given of every separate logical element in the sentence; (2) That the meaning and force of each of the connective words which are not strictly in the sentence but which indicate the character of subordinate sentences, shall be described; and (3) That the relation of the several sentences to each other whether as coordinate or subordinate shall also be clearly shewn. These conditions will be found to be fulfilled in the example on the next page.

After some exercises of this kind in logical parsing, or concurrently with them, it is useful to give the ordinary drill in grammatical parsing. *Grammatical Analysis.* But here it is necessary to distinguish between the proper province of logic and that of pure grammar. For instance, the difference between Common and Proper nouns is the logical difference between universals and particulars, and has no place in grammar whatever. And the distinction of sex is in no sense logical, and in English is hardly grammatical. It determines the form of our nouns and pronouns in only a very limited number of cases; and we have no conventional sex, as in Latin and French, which affects the concord of adjectives. Hence the enumeration of Gender among the attributes of English words has little to do with Etymology and less with Syntax, and in fact serves no grammatical purpose at all.

Specimen of Analysis.

But now farewell. I am going a long way
With these thou seest—if indeed I go
(For all my mind is clouded with a doubt)—
To the island valley of Avilion;
Where falls not hail, or rain, or any snow,
Nor ever wind blows loudly; but it lies
Deep-meadowed, happy, fair with orchard lawns,
And bowery hollows crowned with summer sea,
Where I will heal me of my grievous wound.
                                            TENNYSON.

		1 But	Particle connecting sentence with the preceding.
A.	{	2 now	Adverbial adjunct to 3.
		3 farewell	*Predicate.*
	⎧	4 I	*Subject.*
B	⎨	5 am going	*Predicate.*
	⎩	6 a long way	Adverbial adjunct to 5.
		7 with these	,, ,,
	⎧	8 [whom]	*Object.*
C.	⎨	9 thou	*Subject.*
	⎩	10 seest	*Predicate.*
		11 If	Particle introducing sentence D.
	⎧	12 indeed	Adverbial adjunct to 14.
D.	⎨	13 I	*Subject.*
	⎩	14 go	*Predicate.*
		15 For	Particle introducing sentence E.
	⎧	16 all my mind	*Subject.*
E.	⎨	17 is clouded	*Predicate.*
	⎩	18 with a doubt	Adverbial adjunct to 17.
Continu- ation of B.	{	19 To the island valley	Adverbial adjunct to 5.
		20 of Avilion	Adjectival adjunct to "valley" in 19.
	⎧	21 Where	=in which. Adverbial adjunct to 22.
		22 falls	*Predicate.*
F.	⎨	23 not	Negative adjunct to 22.
		24 hail	*Subject.*
		25 or rain	Alternative subject.
	⎩	26 or any snow	Alternative subject.

Specimen of Logical Analysis.

G.
- 27 nor — Particle showing relation of F to G.
- 28 ever — Adverbial adjunct to 30.
- 29 wind — *Subject.*
- 30 blows — *Predicate.*
- 31 loudly — Adverbial adjunct to 30.

32 But — Particle introducing co-ordinate adversative sentence to F and G.

H.
- 33 it — *Subject.*
- 34 lies — *Predicate.*
- 35 deep-meadowed — Adjectival adjunct to 33.
- 36 happy — ,, ,,
- 37 fair, with orchard lawns and bowery hollows — ,, ,,
- 38 crowned with summer sea — Adjectival adjunct to "hollows" in 37.

I.
- 39 Where — Adverbial adjunct to 41.
- 40 I — *Subject.*
- 41 will heal me — *Predicate.*
- 42 of my grievous wound — Adverbial adjunct to 41.

A. Principal sentence.
B. ,, ,, co-ordinate with A.
C. Adjective sentence to the word "these" in B.
D. Conditional sentence subordinate to B.
E. Causative sentence subordinate to D.
F. Adjective sentence to "valley" in B.
G. Co-ordinate sentence to F.
H. Co-ordinate sentence to G.
I. Adverbial sentence to 34 in H.

Note. The last sentence I. might be interpreted in the same way as F., as an adjective sentence qualifying 33.

A lesson on Auxiliary Verbs.   Let me now give you an illustration of another kind of lesson, in which, as indeed in all other enquiries into English, a knowledge of the elements of Old English Grammar will be of great help to you. Begin with a few examples of the use of Auxiliary verbs. You observe that there is no inflectional provision for Perfect, Pluperfect, or Future tense in English, nor for the Potential Mood, but these modifications of meaning are shewn by auxiliaries. The old grammars recognized a fundamental distinction between this method and that of accidence. In Ben Jonson's Grammar for instance, you will find the statement that the English Language has no Future tense but that its place is supplied by a Syntax. With this in view, it is worth while to give several special lessons on the peculiar function and use of auxiliaries in English. And in doing this, you will choose first examples of the use of these words not as auxiliaries, but as principal and independent verbs. 'Before Abraham *was* I *am*.' Here the verb *be* is independent and means existence. Afterwards and in ordinary modern use, it becomes a mere copula. 'He *was* going, I *am* a soldier.' Again 'I *have* a book, I *have* finished the book.' The first and independent meaning of the word 'have' is seen to be that of possession, the subsequent meaning that of completion. You shew that 'will' simply implies volition in such a sentence as "If I *will* that he tarry till I come;" but that in the sentence 'He *will* go,' it implies futurity. You ask why in merely stating a fact about a future act, you say 'I *shall* come;' but 'They *will* come;' yet that if you desire to express the same thing with more positiveness you change the form and say 'I *will*,' and 'They *shall*.' And having traced this *usus ethicus* by means of the analogous forms *should* and *would*, you come to the conclusion that though these two words have come in time to be auxiliaries, some faint reminiscence of their early signification still clings to them, and that even in their modern use, we can discern traces of the idea of volition in *will* and *would*, and of obligation in *shall* and *should*. The same thing is seen on examination to be true of all the auxiliary verbs. They have in becoming mere substitutes for inflection parted with much of their original meaning, but in all cases, some flavour of that original meaning remains. The result of these enquiries may then be tabulated in some such form as this:

English Auxiliary Verbs.

	Primitive Meaning.	Derived or Secondary Meaning.
BE *Beon*	Existence	Copula.
HAVE *Habban*	Possession	Completed action.
WILL *Wyllan* / WOULD	Volition	Futurity (1).
SHALL *Scealan* / SHOULD	Obligation	Futurity (2).
MAY *Magan*	Ability, Power	Permission.
CAN *Cunnan*	Knowledge	Ability.
MUST *Mot*	Compulsion	Obligation.
DO *Don*	Action	*

* Contributes by itself no additional meaning to the verb, but serves (1) to carry emphasis, as I *do* wish; (2) to furnish a place for a negative or other adverb, as I *did* not go; or (3) to help the construction of an interrogative sentence, as *Did* I forget?

Word-building and analysis—the investigation of the *Verbal Analysis.* parts of words and the separate significations of each part—form a most useful exercise. You take the word *Unselfishness* and decompose it. *Self* is seen to be here used as a noun. This noun becomes an adjective by the termination *ish*. The adjective thus formed is negatived by the prefix *un*, and this adjective *Unselfish* is converted into an abstract noun by the addition of the syllable *ness*. At each of these steps it is well to ask for a number of other examples of similar construction, to write them down, and to ask the pupils to make the generalization for themselves. Such a word as *Indestructibility* in like manner may be analysed, and the value and force of each separate syllable shown. And after this has been done, the result of the collocation of a number of examples, which will have been mainly supplied by the pupils, will appear in some such form as this. It certainly should not be presented at first in the form of a list to be learned from a text book, but should grow as the facts are elicited in successive lessons.

		ENGLISH.	LATIN.	GREEK.
NOUNS.	(a) From verbs	Do*er*	Spon*sor*	Acoust*ics*
		Learn*ing*	Subtrac*tion*	Catech*ism*
		Know*ledge*	Experi*ence*	*Hypo*thesis
	(b) From adjectives	Good*ness*	Puri*ty*	
		Tru*th*	Longi*tude*	Cyclo*id*
	(c) From other nouns	King*dom*		*Dia*meter
				Ilia*d*
		Duck*ling*	Retic*ule*	Aster*isk*
VERBS.	(a) From nouns	*Em*body	Fabric*ate*	*Meta*morphose
	(b) From adjectives	Sweet*en*	Fals*ify*	Christian*ize*
		*En*large	Celeb*rate*	
	(c) From other verbs	*Un*tie	*De*stroy	
		Wand*er*	*In*hale	
		*Be*have		
ADJECTIVES.	(a) From nouns	Child*ish*	Arbitra*ry*	*Eu*phonious
		Fruit*ful*	Graci*ous*	Cosm*ic*
		Rain*y*	Roy*al*	*Amphi*bious
		Week*ly*	Civ*il*	

	ENGLISH.	LATIN.	GREEK.
(*b*) From verbs	Read*able*	Aud*ible*	*Sym*bolic
	Will*ing*	Illustrat*ive*	
	Belov*ed*	Dec*ent*	
		Orn*ate*	
(*c*) From other adjectives			
	*Un*tidy	*Im*proper	*A*theistic
	Rud*er*	Superi*or*	
	Black*ish*		

Such a series of inductive lessons having been given, lists of illustrative examples prepared, and sentences framed to contain each of the less familiar words, the pupil will know something of the genesis both of words and of thoughts, and will be able on looking at many words to tell at once to what class they belong, from what sort of words they are immediately formed, and from what language they are derived. I know no lesson which when well given awakens more interest and mental activity even among young children than this.

It is well known that the part of English grammar which is usually considered most practical as an aid in correct speaking consists of the Rules of Syntax. But although it is useful to have at hand a compendium of such rules and to refer to them occasionally, experience shews that they have no value as guides. The true discipline in correct speech is to be found in the practice of composition, which should begin from the first. Short sentences should be prepared by the pupil to exemplify each new fact or distinction which you explain, and by degrees the sentences may become more complex.

Composition.

In the choice of subjects for composition exercises, let them be those on which the scholars have something to say. Do not ask your scholars to write on mere abstract themes. '*Virtus est bona res*,' 'Time is money,' and other arid generalities of that kind have little interest for scholars, and they do not know what to say about them. Let the composition exercises always refer to something of which a boy has the material at hand, an expedition he has recently taken, a story you have just read to him, a letter detailing some recent experience or well-known fact. It is probable that the number of solecisms in speech or in the formation of sentences which you will find among your pupils is very small, especially if they are in the habit of living and speaking with educated people at home. The chief difficulties which occur in actual composition are apt to shew themselves in connexion with the use of the relatives, and connective words, particularly in those sentences which are elliptical in form, and in which some part has to be supplied. You will deal with this form of fault partly by requiring as a rule that sentences should be shorter than young people are apt to make them; partly by requiring the *lacunæ* in elliptical sentences to be filled up, and partly by taking an involved or muddled sentence now and then, and setting scholars to parse or analyse it. This indicates where the difficulty of the construction lies, and helps to shew how the thought might by a rearrangement of words, or by the use of two sentences instead of one, be more concisely or more elegantly expressed.

Meanings of words. One essential object contemplated in the study of our own language is a knowledge of the meanings of its words. This, it is true, is not grammar, but it is closely connected with it. Definitions of words, however, must not be learned by heart, from dictionaries or lists, because the same word has not always the same meaning, and because the meaning is often determined by the context. Sentences, we have said, are to a child easier than single words, and it is often better to require a paraphrase of a short sentence, than to demand exact synonyms, which though right in the particular case will be wrong for others. Not until after much practice in giving the substance of short sentences in other language, is it useful to require exact definitions of particular words.

In fashioning lessons for Paraphrase, it will be well to adopt for yourselves and your pupils a few very simple rules: *Paraphrase.*

(1) Do not think that you have to find an equivalent for every word. But read the whole passage, turn it over in the mind; keep in view its drift and general purpose, and then rewrite it, so as to convey the collective meaning of the passage, not a translation of its words.

(2) Do not be afraid of using the same word, if it is clearly the best, and an equivalent cannot be found.

(3) Be sure that the sentences are short and simple, and guard with special care against the vicious use of relatives, participles, and connective words, and particularly of any constructions which you could not easily parse.

(4) Never use two words where one would suffice to express your thought; nor a hard word where an easy one would convey your meaning; nor any word at all unless you are quite sure it has a meaning to convey. At the same time, in dealing with very concise writers it is not necessary to try to make the paraphrase as short as the original.

(5) Do not translate all the metaphors, or all the poetry into prose. Slight change of figurative language is quite legitimate so long as the meaning is preserved.

(6) Keep in mind the general style of the extract, and, if it be grave or playful, maintain its character as far as you can, and be careful that the result shall be a perfectly readable piece of English, which would be

intelligible to those who had no knowledge of the original.

Examples. I will suppose that with these general rules in view you attempt to recast the following well-known passage from Bacon:

> Studies serve for delight, for ornament, and for ability. The chief use for delight is in privateness and retiring; for ornament is in discourse; and for ability is in the judgment and disposition of business. For expert men can execute, and perhaps judge of particulars one by one, but the general counsels, and the plots and marshalling of affairs come best from those that are learned. To spend too much time in studies is sloth; to use them too much for ornament is affectation; to make judgment wholly by their rules is the humour of a scholar. They perfect nature, and are perfected by experience. For natural abilities are like natural plants, that need pruning by study. And studies themselves do give forth directions too much at large, except they be bounded in by experience.
>
> Crafty men contemn studies, simple men admire them, and wise men use them. For they teach not their own use; but that is a wisdom without them and above them, won by observation.
>
> BACON'S *Essays.*

You first read it aloud, and point out that here the word 'studies' is used for learning generally. You call attention to the special sense in which for his present purpose Bacon uses the words 'ability,' 'discourse,' and 'crafty.' You shew how closely he has packed his meaning into a few words. And perhaps you arrive after this at something of this sort:

> I. Learning is valuable in three ways—as a source of pleasure, as a means of adding grace and beauty to life, and as an instrument for the discharge of duty. The first of these advantages is chiefly enjoyed in solitude; the second is found in social intercourse, while its third use is that it helps us to order and arrange the business of life. For although men of natural acuteness can perform good work and form right judgments about its details, yet the power to view things comprehensively, to group them together, and to

exercise a wise forethought in the arrangement of business is rarely possessed except by the well-instructed man.

It is a mark of indolence to give ourselves up wholly to the enjoyment of literature; it is a proof of self-conceit to value our reading only as a means of display; while to determine all questions by what books say is the sure characteristic of a pedant. Learning supplements and improves natural gifts, but itself needs to be further improved by the experience of life; for our natural gifts are like trees which need discipline and culture, and learning itself is apt to mislead a student, unless its conclusions are corrected by actual experience.

Learning is not unfrequently despised by the clever practical man; it is regarded with childish wonder by the foolish; but it is only truly appreciated by the wise. For learning does not teach its possessor how to employ it; the power to do this aright is a higher attainment than any scholarship, and can only come by thinking and observing.

Or you choose for an analysis of its meaning part of the opening passage of *Paradise Lost*.

> And chiefly Thou, O Spirit, that dost prefer
> Before all temples the upright heart and pure,
> Instruct me, for Thou knowest: Thou from the first
> Wast present, and with mighty wings outspread,
> Dove-like, sat'st brooding o'er the vast abyss,
> And mad'st it pregnant: What in me is dark
> Illumine; what is low raise and support,
> That to the height of this great argument
> I may assert Eternal Providence,
> And justify the ways of God to men.   MILTON.

It is not well to begin at once and try to paraphrase line by line. But the character of the invocations with which the Iliad and the Æneid commence may be pointed out; then Milton's classicalism, dominated as it was in this case by devout Christian feeling; then the passage in Genesis which was evidently in his mind; finally the mingling of humility in the presence of so vast an undertaking, with an inward consciousness of power to achieve it. Afterwards the meaning of the whole passage admits of being rendered on this wise;

> II. But most of all do I invoke Thine aid and teaching: Thou Holy Spirit, whose choicest dwelling place is the guileless and reverent human heart. Thou wast present at the beginning and like a dove with outstretch'd pinions didst hover over the void and formless infinite, and impregnate it with life.
>
> In so far as I am ignorant, enlighten me: when my thoughts are mean or poor, elevate and sustain them; that so I may be enabled to utter words not unworthy of my lofty theme, to speak rightly of the Divine Government and to vindicate the dealings of God with mankind.

In choosing passages for this purpose, it is well to have regard as much to the ease, the dignity, and the charm of the language as to the instruction which it may convey. And exercises of this kind, though more often in writing, may often with advantage be oral, and should almost always be made the subject of conversation and questioning before they are attempted.

Précis. With a view to correct the tendency to wordiness, which some forms of paraphrase are apt to generate, it is well to intersperse them with a few exercises on what is called in the public offices *précis-writing;* the condensation into a sentence or two of the main drift and purpose of a letter, an essay, or a formal document. The effort of mind required here in seizing upon the salient point among a number of particulars, of seeing the difference between the most relevant and the least relevant parts of a statement, and of stripping off all the dressing and circumlocution from the one chief purpose of a writer, is not only of special value in the after conduct of official business, but it is in itself of great value in promoting discernment and clearness of thought.

Versification. Considering how important a part is played by verse-making in the learning of Greek and Latin, it is remarkable that the composition of English verse is so seldom set as a school exercise. It must be owned that the Sapphics and Hexameters produced by school-boys do little to call out invention and literary taste. They are good exercises in grammar and prosody, and they guard the pupil against the one deadly sin of making false quantities;—a sin however, of which in the case of two languages which are seldom or never to be spoken,—it is very easy to exaggerate the seriousness. The effort is apt to prove a very mechanical one, and to be somewhat sterile in intellectual result; because the pupil is much more concerned with the length and shortness of the syllables, than with their meaning. Similar failure would result from exercises in English versification, if the making of rhymes, or the use of difficult metres were required. But when the pupil is familiar with some good passages from Shakespeare, Milton, and Wordsworth, and has caught the ring and movement of the English heroic measure, it is worth while to draw attention to the conditions which render that measure musical and effective, to the law of the recurrent accents, and to the necessity of making the structure of the thought, and the logical arrangement of the sentences fit in with the structure of the verse. Then it is a good exercise to give a subject, or a suitable extract from a book, and to require it to be reproduced in blank verse. This will be found to encourage the choice of a diction, elevated a little above that of ordinary life; to give practice in conciseness, and in the better arrangement of the thoughts; and to tune the ear to a truer perception not only of the melody of verse, but also of that of rhythmical prose.

And here it seems fitting to make some reference to English Literature as a branch of school instruction. *The study of English Literature.*

This is a comparatively new ingredient introduced of late years into the school course, and largely encouraged, and almost enforced by the influence of the Local and other University Examinations. A play of Shakespeare, or a part of Paradise Lost is taken as a theme, and read critically. In order to do this well several things are necessary: (1) To explain and trace to their origin all difficult and archaic words, (2) To hunt out all the historical and other allusions, (3) To elucidate the meaning and purpose of the book as a whole, (4) To analyse, paraphrase, and learn by heart, choice and characteristic passages, (5) To know something of the circumstances in which it was written, and the relation in which it stands, not only to the author's other writings, but to the literature of the period, and (6) To examine its style, and discover its merits or peculiarities as a work of literary art.

How to study the masterpieces of English. There can be no doubt that the reading of any one of the masterpieces of our literature in this way, is a very valuable and awakening exercise, and that rightly conducted it does much both to inform the pupil, and also to cultivate literary taste and a love of reading. But I think it essential if you would do this effectually, that you should not treat the book you are dealing with merely as something which has to be analysed, commented on, and picked to pieces; but also as a work of genius which has to be studied as a whole, and which the pupil must learn to appreciate as a whole. Before beginning to read the selected book piecemeal, the time of one lesson may be well devoted to a general and uncritical reading of the whole through, simply with a view to shew the scholar what it is about, and to kindle some interest in it for itself, and not as a lesson. A very skilful teacher of this subject complained to me that this was too often neglected, that pupils were invited to give their whole attention to the philological, historical, and antiquarian details, which were supposed to be useful in examinations, and that in this way all the enjoyment of the flavour and style of a book, as a great work of art, became impossible.

Indeed the complaint is not unfrequently made, that the habit of treating Macbeth or Comus as a lesson, taking it to pieces and putting them together again like a puzzle, is rather lowering and vulgarising in its effect, and calculated to destroy the freshness and interest with which the reader enjoys the book for its own sake. Now, this result is no doubt possible, but if it arises, I am sure it comes from bad and unskilful teaching.

It is surely a little inconsistent on the part of scholars, who profess to have formed their own literary taste by the close study of the Greek and Roman classics, and who do not admit that all the school exercises, the grammar, and the versification, have deadened their admiration for the beauties of Virgil and Homer, to say as they sometimes do that the study in an analogous way of an English poet, tends to deprave the literary taste, and to give disagreeable associations with our own classics. It would be truer to say, An Englishman can get discipline in taste and expression from reading Homer critically, although the language is ancient and unfamiliar. He ought also to get a like advantage from reading Shakespeare or Burke, though the language in which they wrote is his own. It is because English is our vernacular that a fuller knowledge of Shakespeare than of Homer is possible to an Englishman; and we should therefore set ourselves to attain it.

Listen here to a passage from one of Dr Arnold's letters.

"My delight in going over Homer and Virgil with the boys makes me think what a treat it must be to teach Shakespeare to a good class of young Greeks in regenerate Athens, to dwell upon him line by line, and word by word, in the way that nothing but a translation lesson ever will enable one to do, and so to get all his pictures and thoughts leisurely into one's mind, till I verily think one would after a time almost give out light in the dark, after having been steeped as it were in such an atmosphere of brilliance. And how could this ever be done without having the power of construing, as the proper medium through which alone all the beauty can be transmitted? because else we travel too fast and more than half of it escapes us."

There is here, as you see, a recognition of the fact that the slow process of construing, translating, and analysing line by line, is in the case of an author whose works are in a foreign language, very helpful to true literary insight and enjoyment. No doubt classic authors may be taught in so dull and soulless a way that pupils attach very unpleasant associations to the great names of antiquity, and their interest in them is permanently deadened. But no one who has ever had the good fortune to read a play of Æschylus, or a book of the Æneid with a thoroughly sympathetic teacher can doubt that Arnold is right, and that the literary and moral beauties of the writer, his images and pictures, may be thoroughly appreciated in the process of translation and analysis.

Critical analysis not destructive of literary enjoyment.

And if this be so with ancient writers, why not with our own? The faculty of criticism does not destroy the power of enjoyment in the case of an oratorio or a great painting. On the contrary, it greatly heightens it. It is the instructed man, whose perceptions have been trained to discern the difference between what is good and what is bad, and to know why one thing is good and another bad, who gets the most pleasure from the contemplation of a work of art[1]. And when we are taught to dwell on the exquisite fitness with which a great author has chosen his epithets, the appropriateness of his imagery, or the rhythm and balance of his sentences, all this is clear gain to us, and I do not see why any of that literary sensibility which comes from the sympathetic reading of a good book merely for our own delight should be sacrificed to it. Of course we must not be challenging admiration, or leading the pupil to express a pleasure which he does not feel. Still less must we fall into the ignoble habit of reading such a book with a view to examination only. It is however a great mistake to suppose that intelligence and perception are of less value in an examination than a few technical facts and dates. Nothing is more welcome to a good examiner than the discovery of any proof of originality or critical power, of strong opinion, or honest admiration, provided it goes with thorough knowledge of the substance of the book which is learned. The one thing which maddens an examiner is the mere routine of the text-books, the conventional critical judgments of the lecture-room mechanically reproduced, the use of second-hand estimates of books which the candidate has evidently never read. And so,

[1] "It is not the eye that sees the beauties of the heaven, nor the ear that hears the sweetness of music, or the glad tidings of a prosperous accident, but the soul that perceives all the relishes of sensual and intellectual perceptions; and the more noble and excellent the soul is the greater and more savoury are its perceptions. And if a child beholds the rich ermine, or the diamonds of a starry night, or the order of the world, or hears the discourses of an apostle; because he makes no reflex acts upon himself, *and sees not that he sees,* he can have but the pleasure of a fool or the deliciousness of a mule." JEREMY TAYLOR.

I would urge on you, when you have before you the two objects, first of enabling your pupil to understand and intelligently to admire an English classic; and then of enabling him also to get some credit for his knowledge at an examination: keep the larger and the nobler aim before you; disregard the second; and be sure nevertheless that this is the best way of attaining the second. There is not and ought not to be any real inconsistency between the two purposes.

The history of literature. With young students, the thorough and searching investigation of one or two fruitful books is of more value than lessons in what is called the history of literature. Of course it is desirable that the scholar should know the names of the greatest writers, when they lived, and what they wrote. But there is a certain unreality—almost dishonesty—in the mere appropriation of other men's opinions about books before we have read them. After all the best study of literature is to be found in literature itself, and not in what compilers of manuals have said about it. We are here especially bound to keep clear of all confusion between means and ends. What is the end which we propose to ourselves in all lessons on literature? It is to produce a permanent appetite for reading, a power of discriminating what is good from what is bad, and a conscious preference for it. "What a heaven," says Bishop Hall, "lives a scholar in, that at once and in one close room can daily converse with all the glorious writers and fathers, and single them out at pleasure! To find wit in poetry, in philosophy profoundness, in mathematics acuteness, in history wonder of events, in oratory sweet eloquence, in divinity supernatural delight and holy devotion, as so many rich metals in their proper mines, whom would it not ravish with delight?"

Now of course it would be unreasonable to expect you to convey to young learners anything like this scholarly enthusiasm. But if your teaching of literature is good and sound, it ought to convey at least the germ of such enthusiasm into a good proportion of the minds with which you deal. And this is the true test of your success in this department. For if your scholars do not acquire a positive love for reading, if they do not ask to be allowed to read the whole book or poem of which the extract you take as a lesson forms a part; if you do not find them voluntarily hunting in the library for the other works of some author whom you have tried to make them admire; if they do not feel a heightened admiration for what is noblest and truest in literature, and an increasing distaste for what is poor and flimsy and sensational, then be sure that there must be something incurably wrong in your method of teaching, and that all your apparatus of grammar, paraphrase, and logical and grammatical analysis, will have failed to fulfil its purpose.

True purpose of lessons in English literature.

X. ARITHMETIC AS AN ART.

Why Arithmetic should be taught.
BEFORE asking how we should teach Arithmetic it may be well to ask for a moment why we should teach it at all. There are two conceivable objects in teaching any subject. (1) Because the thing taught is necessary, or useful, and may be turned to practical account, or (2) Because the incidental effect of teaching it is to bring into play and exercise certain powers and capabilities, and so to serve a real educational purpose. As we have seen, some things we teach are justifiable on the one, and some on the other of these grounds. And it behoves us all, whatever be the subject we teach, to make sure which of these two purposes we are aiming at. For if lessons on any subject are not valuable, either for their obvious practical uses or for their disciplinal effect on the general power and capacity of the pupil, there is no justification for teaching that subject at all.

Both an Art and a Science.
But of Arithmetic we may safely say at the outset, that if rightly taught, it is well calculated to fulfil both purposes. Its rules become of real service in helping us to solve the problems of daily life; and its laws and principles, if rightly investigated, serve to set particular mental faculties in operation, and so to further the improvement and development of the learner. It is con-

spicuously one of those subjects of school instruction the purpose of which extends beyond itself. Its ideas and processes can be effectively applied to other regions of knowledge. You cannot measure its intellectual usefulness by looking only at its immediate aims. It is, in fact, both an Art and a Science :—an Art because it contemplates the doing of actual work, the attainment of definite and useful results ; a Science because it investigates principles, because he who unearths the truths which underlie the rules of Arithmetic, is being exercised, not merely in the attainment of a particular kind of truth about numbers, but in the processes by which truth of many other kinds is to be investigated and attained.

Now it is unnecessary to remind you that of these two aspects or uses of Arithmetic, the former is that which we usually associate with the name. It is not reasoning about numbers, but using figures for the purpose of calculation and working out sums, that we generally understand by the study of Arithmetic in schools. A text book of Arithmetic is often a book of exercises and problems, and nothing more. We all remember Goldsmith's schoolmaster, of whom it was said that

Often regarded as an Art merely.

"Lands he could measure, terms and tides presage,
And even the story ran that he could gauge."

Such a pædagogue, who could do sums of surprising length and intricacy, and set them down in beautiful figures in a book duly garnished with flourishes, passed then for the good arithmetician. The scholar who could work out the largest number of problems by the shortest and most dexterous methods was the winner of all the prizes, and so long as he produced right answers, the extent to which he had understood the processes he employed was a matter of small concern.

No doubt this notion of the place Arithmetic should hold in school-work, and of the object to be attained in teaching it, is still very prevalent. But it was not always so. Arithmetic, as taught in the schools of Athens or Alexandria; to the contemporaries of Socrates and Alcibiades; or later, when in the Middle Ages it shared with logic, geometry, grammar and rhetoric and music the distinction of forming one of the staple subjects of a liberal education, was taught in its principles, as a logical discipline; as something to be understood rather than as a series of devices for working out problems. It was however often mixed up with some wholly unsound and indefensible theories about the mystic properties of certain numbers; and numerical relations were supposed to furnish the key to certain moral and spiritual questions, with which we now think they have nothing to do.

It is interesting to turn to the oldest treatise in Arithmetic in our language and to see the spirit in which the subject was treated.

Robert Recorde's Arithmetick.
In Robert Recorde's *Arithmetick, or the Grounde of Artes*, dedicated to Edward VI., we have the first successful attempt to popularize the study of the 'Algorithmic science,' as it was then called, in England. It is written in the form of a dialogue, for, as the author quaintly says in his Preface, "I judge that to be the easiest way of instruction, when the scholar may aske any doubts orderly, and the master may answer to his question plainly." Accordingly, the book opens thus :—

Scholar. "Sir, such is your authority in mine estimation, that I am content to consent to your saying, and to receive it as truth, though I see none other reason that doth lead me thereunto: whereas else in mine owne conceite it appeareth but vaine to bestowe anie time privately on that which every childe may and doth learne at all times and hours.

Master. Lo, this is the fashion and chance of all them that seeke to defend their blind ignorance, that when they think they have made strong reason for themselves, then have they proved quite the contrary."

He goes on to vindicate his favourite study, and to shew its importance; and the docile pupil, whose function it is throughout the work to exhibit constant wonder and delight at the revelation of each new rule, soon expresses interest in the subject, and is conducted through the science in a spirit and temper which cannot be too much admired, if we may take the following fragment as an example:—

"*Scholar.* Truly, Sir, these excellent conclusions do wonderfully make me more and more in love with the art.

Master. It is an art, that the further you travell the more you thirst to goe on forward. Such a fountaine, that the more you draw the more it springes; and to speake absolutely in a word (excepting the study of divinity which is the salvation of our souls), there is no study in the world comparable to this, for delight in wonderfull and godly exercise: for the skill hereof is well known immediately to have flowed from the wisdom of God into the hearts of man, whom he hath created the chiefe image and instrument of his praise and glorie.

S. The desire of knowledge doth greatly incourage me to be studious herein, and therefore I pray you cease not to instruct me further in the use thereof.

M. With a good will, and now therefore for the further use of these two latter (multiplication and division) the seat of reduction."

In this way master and pupil proceed amicably together through integral and fractional Arithmetic, only pausing now and then to congratulate one another, and to offer devout thanksgivings to God for the beauty of the science, and for its marvellous uses. Recorde subsequently published an advanced treatise, entitled the "*Whetstone of Witte*, containing the extraction of roots, the Cossike practice, with the rule of equations, and the woorks of surd numbers." This book contains an admirable summary for the period, of the chief rules for the manipulation of algebraic quantities; but throughout both books it is the intellectual exercise, not the useful application, which seems to the author to be of chief interest and importance.

It must be owned however that if early writers thought little of the practical usefulness of the applications of Arithmetic our immediate ancestors and many of our contemporaries have thought of these practical applications almost exclusively. Since Recorde's time the majority of authors—from Cocker, and Wingate, and Vyse, and Dilworth, to Walkinghame and Colenso—have treated Arithmetic from the utilitarian point of view exclusively. Their books give few or no demonstrations of the theory of numbers, but are filled with what are called commercial rules. There are tare and tret, alligation, foreign exchanges, partnership with time, partnership without time (whatever that may mean), bills of parcels, the chain rule, a new method of finding the cubic contents of a cask, and so forth. The goal to be reached in the teaching of arithmetic is very clearly defined, and all the progress towards it is regulated accordingly. The successful arithmetician is to be a good computer, a skilful tradesman, a land surveyor, or an exciseman; and the whole object of the art is to fit him to perform one or other of these important functions.

The place of Arithmetic in a School course.

We are so accustomed to hear Arithmetic spoken of as one of the three fundamental ingredients in all schemes of instruction, that it seems like enquiring too curiously to ask why this should be. Reading, Writing and Arithmetic—these three are assumed to be of co-

The place of Arithmetic among School Studies. 291

ordinate rank. Are they indeed co-ordinate, and if so on what ground?

In this modern "trivium" the art of Reading is put first. Well, there is no doubt as to its right to the foremost place. For reading is the instrument of all our acquisitions. It is indispensable. There is not an hour in our lives in which it does not make a great difference to us whether we can read or not. And the art of Writing, too; that is the instrument of all communication, and it becomes, in one form or other, useful to us every day. But Counting—doing sums,—how often in life does this accomplishment come into exercise? Beyond the simplest additions and the power to check the items of a bill, the arithmetical knowledge required of any well-informed person in private life is very limited. For all practical purposes, whatever I may have learned at school of fractions, or proportion, or decimals, is, unless I happen to be in business, far less frequently available to me in life than a knowledge, say, of the history of my own country, or of the elementary truths of physics. The truth is, that regarded as practical *arts*, reading, writing, and arithmetic have no right to be classed together as co-ordinate elements of education; for the last of these is considerably less useful to the average man or woman not only than the other two, but than many others which might be named. But reading, writing, and such mathematical or logical exercise as may be gained in connexion with the manipulation of numbers, *have* a right to constitute the primary elements of instruction. And I believe that arithmetic, if it deserves the high place that it conventionally holds in our educational system, deserves it mainly on the ground that it is to be treated as a logical exercise. It is the only branch of mathematics which has found its way into primary

Two purposes to be served by it.

and early education; other departments of pure science being reserved for what is called higher or university instruction. But all the arguments in favour of teaching algebra and trigonometry to advanced students, apply equally to the teaching of the principles or theory of arithmetic to school boys. It is calculated to do for them exactly the same kind of service, to educate one side of their minds, to bring into play one set of faculties which cannot be so severely or properly exercised in any other department of learning. In short, relatively to the needs of a beginner, Arithmetic, as a science, is just as valuable—it is certainly quite as intelligible—as the higher mathematics to a university student.

Arithmetic has the same relation to a girl's as to a boy's education.

It is probably because the purely utilitarian or practical view of school Arithmetic has so generally prevailed that it has never been a favourite study in girls' schools. Mistresses, as a rule, do not take a strong interest in it, or seek to kindle their pupils' enthusiasm in it. Girls at school are, if not actually encouraged to dislike arithmetic, apt to take for granted that it is rather an unfeminine pursuit, that it is certainly unnecessary, and probably vulgar. And, no doubt, if the conventional notion about the purpose of Arithmetic is well founded, they are right. If cyphering means a collection of artifices for doing sums; if the great object of learning the art is to be fitted for the counting-house or the shop; then the instinct which makes governesses and their pupils shrink from Arithmetic is a true one. But if Arithmetic is a study capable of yielding intellectual fruit, if it helps to quicken and concentrate the attention, to bring under control the reasoning faculty, to shew by what method we can proceed from the known to the unknown, to enable us to perceive the nature of a fallacy, and to discriminate the two sides of the fine line by which the true is often separated from the false; if, in short, the study of Arithmetic is mainly helpful in shewing what truth is, and by what methods it is attained, then surely it bears just as close a relation to the needs of a woman's life as to those of a man. For she, too, has intellectual problems to solve, books to read, and opinions to form; and she will do all this to good purpose in just the proportion in which she brings to her work a trained and disciplined understanding, accustomed to analyse the grounds of belief, and to proceed by slow and careful steps from premises to inference.

So much will suffice for the present as to the greater purposes to be served in the teaching of Arithmetic. But the lesser purpose is not insignificant, and must not be overlooked. It is no slight thing to be a good computer, and to know how to apply arithmetical rules deftly and accurately to the management of an income, to the conduct of business, to statistics, to averages, to scientific and political data, and to the manifold problems which life presents. And even though the higher aims of Arithmetic are altogether overlooked, it cannot be said that time is wasted in achieving the lower aim. So much of arithmetical knowledge as is fairly tested by setting sums to be worked, and as is required in order to work them promptly and accurately, is well worth attaining. Its relative importance to genuine mathematical training may be, and often has been, exaggerated, but of its absolute importance there can be little question. *The practical side of Arithmetic.*

Thus then the two distinct uses of Arithmetic, (1) Its direct or practical use as an instrument for the solution of problems, and (2) Its indirect or scientific use as a means of calling out the reasoning faculty require to be separately apprehended, and I am intending to ask you to-day to look at the first, and in my next lecture at the second, and to enquire how each of the two objects thus to be kept in view can be best fulfilled. Of course two objects may be logically separable; and for purposes of discussion here may be treated apart; while as a matter of fact, they are pursued together. In attaining either object you cannot help doing something towards the attainment of the other. For you cannot teach practical arithmetic, even by mere rule of thumb, without giving *some* useful intellectual discipline; and you cannot make the theory and laws of Arithmetic clear to a boy's understanding without also giving him some serviceable rules for practical use. Still we may with advantage treat the two purposes of Arithmetic separately, and at present ask ourselves only how to teach Arithmetic as an *Art*.

Computation.

A really good computer is characterized by three qualities—promptitude, perfect accuracy, and that skill or flexibility of mind which enables him at once to seize upon the real meaning of a question, and to apply the best method to its solution. How are these qualities best to be attained?

Early exercises concrete not abstract.

Now the first thing necessary to be borne in mind is the familiar truth, that a child's earliest notions of number are concrete, not abstract. He knows what three roses, or three chairs mean before he can make abstraction of the number 3 as a separate entity. Hence it will be seen that the earliest exercises in counting should take the form of counting actual objects. For this purpose the ball-frame or abacus is generally employed, and with great advantage. He should count also the objects in the room, the panes of glass in the window, a handful of pebbles, the pictures on the wall, and the number of scholars in the class. It must not be set down as a fault if at first he counts with his fingers. Let him do so by all means if he likes. The faculty of abstracting numbers, and of learning to do without visible and tangible illustrations comes more slowly to some children than others. So long as they get the answer right, let them have what help they want till this power comes. It is sure to come ere long. At first, too, the little questions and problems which are given to children may fitly refer to marbles or apples, or to things which are familiar to them. But the mistake made by many teachers is to continue using these artifices too long; to go on shewing an abacus, or talking about nuts and oranges after the children have fully grasped the meaning of 6 + 5 in the abstract, and are well able to do without visible help. It is a sure test of a good teacher that he knows when and how far to employ such artifices, and when to dispense with them. The moment that concrete illustrations have served their purpose, they should be discarded.

Remember also that Arithmetic is one of the lessons in which discipline is more important than in any other. The amount of order and drill which may suffice for a good lesson in reading or geography will not suffice for arithmetic. Undetected prompting and copying are easier in this subject than in any other, and they are more fatal to real progress. It is important that in computing a scholar should learn to rely on the accuracy of his own work. If he has any access to the answer, and works consciously towards it; if he can get a whispered word or a surreptitious figure to guide him, the work is not his own, and he is learning little or nothing. It is therefore essential that your discipline should be such, that copying or friendly suggestion during the working of a sum shall be impos- *Strict discipline needed.*

sible. It is idle, in this connexion, to talk of honour. The sense that it is dishonourable to avail oneself of any such chance help as comes in one's way in solving a problem, is, after all, only a late product of moral training. You do not presuppose its existence in grown men at the Universities, who are undergoing examinations for degrees, or even for Holy Orders. You have no right to assume its presence in the minds of little children. They will at first copy from one another without the smallest consciousness that there is any harm in it. After all there is nothing immoral in copying until we have shewn it to be so. It is inconvenient to us, of course, and it happens to be inconsistent with genuine progress in Arithmetic, and it is for these reasons that it becomes necessary to stop it. The truth is that if you want to train children in the habit of doing their own work well, and depending on its accuracy, you must do habitually that which is done at all public examinations—make copying impossible. And this may be done by divers expedients, *e.g.* by giving different exercises to scholars as they sit alternately, so that no two who are together shall have the same sum, or by placing them in proper attitudes, and at needful distances, and under vigilant supervision.

Exercises given out in words, not figures. Again, I suggest that a good many sums should be given out in words, not in figures. Remember that the actual questions of life are not presented to us in the shape of sums, but in another form which we have to translate into sums; and that this business of translating the question out of the ordinary form into the form adopted in the arithmetic books is often harder than the working of the sum itself, *e.g.* Take 3018 from 10,000. In an ill-taught school a child is puzzled by this; he first asks what rule it is in. He next asks how to set it

Invention of Exercises. 297

down. Both of these are questions which he ought to answer for himself.

So long as a pupil finds any difficulty whatever in recognising an exercise in a given rule, under any guise, however unfamiliar, be sure he does not understand that rule, and ought not to quit it for a higher.

It is a very useful aid to this sort of versatility or readiness, not only to practise yourselves as teachers in the manufacture of new exercises, but also to encourage your pupils to invent new questions on each rule before you pass from it to the next. You will find a pupil's grasp of the real meaning and relations of an arithmetical rule much strengthened by the habit of framing new questions. Moreover you will find it a very popular and interesting exercise, which will kindle a good deal of spirit and animation in your class.

Never permit any reference to be made to the answer while the work is in progress. It would be a good thing if the printed answers to arithmetical questions could be concealed from pupils altogether. But I fear this is impossible. At any rate, teachers should be on their guard against the tendency of children before they get to the end of the sum to glance furtively at the answer, and to work towards it. Perhaps if the right answer is evidently not coming the pupil alters a figure, or introduces a new multiplier in order to bring it right. But a sum so wrought is a very unsatisfactory and delusive performance. *Answers to be kept out of sight.*

It is well at first rather to give a good number of short exercises irregularly formed, than to use those large symmetrical masses of figures, which the school books are apt to give us, and which are so much more convenient to the teacher, inasmuch as they take a good deal of time, and leave him a little more breathing space. *Numerous short exercises preferable to a few long ones.*

A large square addition sum, in which all the lines are of the same length, and all extend to hundreds of millions, is far less likely to be useful than "Add seventeen to a hundred and twenty, that to three thousand and ninety-six, that to twenty-seven, and that to five." Many children in fact who can do the first will be unable to do the second. Now and then, however, it is a good thing to give a very long exercise, to test sustained attention and continuity of thought, and to ensure accuracy.

Recapitulation. It is good also to take care that before proceeding to any new rule, you give a few exercises, which call out not alone the previous rule, but all the preceding rules. There is no true progress if any one of the elementary rules is allowed to drop out of sight.

I am often struck with the want of skill shewn in making sure at each step that all previous steps are understood. This arises no doubt from the way in which exercises are arranged in books, grouped under the heads of the various rules. A child gets a rule, works a number of sums all alike, and then leaves to go on to another. Whereas exercises ought to be so graduated, and sums so carefully framed as to bring into play all that has previously been learned, and to fix and fasten the memory of former rules. There is hardly any one text-book which I know that does this sufficiently. You should be supplied always therefore with a number of miscellaneous exercises, which you give the scholars from a book or manuscript of your own, and which they do not know to be illustrative of any special rule.

Writing out sums in books Making out a fair copy of a sum in a book, garnished with ruled red ink lines. and flourishes, is a favourite employment in some schools, and consumes a good deal of time. It has its utility, of course, as an exercise *not of much value.* in neatness and arrangement, and in the mere writing of figures. Moreover, it is liked by some teachers because it pleases parents, and is the only visible evidence of arithmetical progress, which can be appreciated at home. Yet as a device for increasing or strengthening a child's arithmetical knowledge, it is very useless. I venture to warn you, therefore, against the inordinate use of what are called "ciphering books;" believing as I do, that in just the proportion in which you teach Arithmetic intelligently, you will learn to rely less on such mechanical devices.

It will be well for us to consider, too, what use it is *Oral or mental Arithmetic.* which a pupil makes of a slate or a paper when he is working a sum. The object of all rules is, of course, to shew how a long or complex problem, which cannot be worked by a single effort of the mind, may be resolved into a number of separate problems each simple enough to be so wrought. As each separate result in multiplication, division, or addition is thus attained, we set it down as a help to the memory, and are thus at liberty to go on to the next. Now it is evident that the worth and accuracy of the general result depend upon the correctness with which we work out each of these single items. It is a good plan, therefore, to give a pupil some oral practice in the manipulation of single numbers, before setting him down to work a sum.

This Oral or Mental Arithmetic has long been a favourite exercise in elementary schools, but it has not been very generally adopted in schools of a higher class. One reason for this is to be found in the very restricted and technical use made of the exercise. In manuals of Mental Arithmetic, advantage is taken of little accidental facilities or resemblances afforded by particular numbers, and rules are founded upon them : *e.g.*

(1) To find the price of a dozen articles; call the pence shillings, and call every odd farthing three pence.

(2) To find the price of an ounce, when the price of 1 lb. is known; call the shillings farthings and multiply by three.

(3) To find the price of a score, call the shillings pounds.

(4) To find the interest on a sum of money at 5 per cent., for a year; call the pounds shillings, and for every additional month call the pound a penny.

(5) To square a number; add the lower unit to the upper, multiply by the tens, and add the square of the unit.

Its abuses. Each of these rules happens to offer special facilities in computation. But the occasions on which a question actually occurs in one of these forms are rare; and the student who has his memory filled with these rules, is not helped, but rather hindered by them when for example he wants to know what fourteen articles will cost, or what is the interest at 3 per cent., or how to multiply 75 by 23. All such rules are apt to seem more useful than they are, and when children, who have learned the knack of solving a few such problems, are publicly questioned by those who are in the secret, the result is often deceptive. I attended an exhibition or oral examination of a middle school of some pretensions a short time ago; and the teacher of Arithmetic undertook to put the scholars through a little testing drill. All his questions fell within the narrow limits of some of these special rules. He also gave one or two exercises in rapid addition which were answered with what seemed astonishing rapidity and correctness: *e.g.*

73 + 27 + 65 = Answer 165.
18 + 82 + 37 + 63 + 15 = Answer 215.

Not till six or seven such sums had been given did I notice that the first two numbers in each group amounted to 100, and the next two also; and that all the questions were framed on the same pattern. Many of the audience did not detect this, but of course the children were in the secret, and were, in fact, confederates with the teacher, in an imposture. It is because so much of what is called mental arithmetic consists of mere tricks of this kind, that the subject has been somewhat justly discredited by good teachers.

But the mental Arithmetic which is of real service *Its uses.* does not consist in exercise in a few special rules, but in rapid, varied, and irregular problems in *all* the forms which computation may take. It differs mainly from written Arithmetic, in that it uses small numbers instead of large ones. Before attempting to work exercises in writing in any rule, a good oral exercise should be given to familiarize the pupils with the nature of the operation. I will give a few examples to illustrate my meaning:

(1) *Addition and Subtraction.* Take the number 3, add it to 1 *Examples* and successively to the sums, up to 50. *of oral*
exercise.
1, 4, 7, 10, 13, 16, 19, 22, 25, 28, 31, &c. &c.
So with sevens: 1, 8, 15, 22, 29, 36, 43, 50, 57, 64, 71.
Then take 50 or 100 and go rapidly backwards taking away 3 every time, or seven, or eleven.

You will observe as you do this that there are certain combinations less easy than others. He whose turn it is to say 21 after 18; or to take away 3 from 32 will halt a moment longer than the rest. You observe this, and make up a series of questions in which these two particular numbers shall be brought into relation: 28 and 3, 48 and 3, 19 and 3, 3 from 42, 3 from 21, &c.

There are but nine digits, and if in succession you give nine short brisk lessons,—one on each,—requiring the number to be added and subtracted rapidly, you will come in succession upon every possible combination of these digits. You will bear in mind that when you yourself make an error in adding up a line of figures, you can trace it to some particular pair of units, say the 8 and the 7, or the 9 and the 5, which habitually give you more trouble than the rest. It is only practice which can set you right. So the moment you observe any hitch or difficulty in special combinations or subtractions, it is well to work at them till they become thoroughly familiar, till for example the sight of 8 and 7 together instantly suggests 5 as the unit of the sum, or the taking away of 6 from a number ending in 3 instantly suggests 7.

(2) *Money.* Little exercises on the arithmetic, first of a shilling, afterwards of half a crown, and afterwards of a sovereign are very interesting, and require no slate or book. The scholars should be practised in rapid adding, and subtracting, in dividing it into parts, in reduction to half-pence and farthings; in telling different ways in which the whole may be made up, *e.g.* a shilling into 7*d.* and 5*d.*, into 8*d.* and 4*d.*, into $3\frac{1}{2}$*d.* and $8\frac{1}{2}$*d.*, into $4\frac{1}{4}$*d.* and $7\frac{3}{4}$*d.*, &c., until every form of arithmetical exercise possible with this sum of money shall be anticipated.

(3) *Simple Calculations in time*, e.g. the time it will be 3 hours hence, 8 hours, 12, 24; the date and day of the week, three days, four weeks, seventeen hours, two months hence; and in like manner easy calculations respecting lengths and weights, may fitly precede all attempts to work sums in compound arithmetic by written exercise

(4) *Fractions.* The first oral exercises should be founded on familiar sums of money, and on the products already known in the multiplication table and may be graduated in some such way as this:

(*a*) The third of a shilling, the 8th, the 12th, the 4th, the 6th, &c. The fifth of 30, the ninth of 27, the third of 18, the twelfth of 72, &c.

(*b*) $\frac{2}{3}$ of 6*d.*, $\frac{5}{6}$ of 54, $\frac{4}{7}$ of 21, $\frac{3}{10}$ of 40, $\frac{5}{8}$ of 16.

(*c*) What number is that of which 5 is $\frac{5}{6}$; Of which 4 is $\frac{2}{7}$; Of which 10 is $\frac{5}{8}$; Of which 2*s.* is $\frac{4}{5}$; Of which 1*s.* 6*d.* is $\frac{3}{7}$?

(*d*) Find other fractions equal to $\frac{2}{3}$, to $\frac{4}{5}$, to $\frac{1}{2}$, to $\frac{5}{6}$, &c.

(*e*) $\frac{7}{12}$ of a foot, $\frac{5}{8}$ of 1 lb., $\frac{3}{7}$ of a week, $\frac{3}{15}$ of an hour.

By selecting your examples from fractions which present no complications or remainders, and by rapidly varying and often repeating them, it is easy to advance a considerable distance in the manipulation of fractions, before talking at all about numerators and denominators, or giving out what is called a rule.

(5) *Exercises on special numbers.* (a) Take the number 60. Its half. Its third. Its fourth. Its fifteenth. Its sixteenth, &c.

(b) Find two numbers which make 60; 24 and 36, 18 and 42, &c.
,, three numbers .... 11, 14 and 35; 21, 19 and 20; 7, 35 and 18, &c.

(c) Take from 60 in rapid succession, fours, sevens, elevens, eights, threes, &c.

(d) Find $\frac{3}{4}$ of 60, $\frac{2}{3}$, $\frac{4}{15}$, $\frac{8}{15}$, $1\frac{1}{2}$, $\frac{3}{8}$, $1\frac{9}{10}$, $\frac{17}{30}$, &c.

(e) Give the components of 60 pence. Of 60 shillings. Of 60 farthings. Of 60 ounces. Of 60 hours. Of 60 yards, &c.

(f) Find in how many ways 60 hurdles might be arranged so as to enclose a space, or in how many forms a payment of £60 might be made.

(6) *Proportion.* (a) Name other figures representing the same ratio as 5 : 7. As 3 : 8. As 15 : 21, &c. &c.

(b) Find a fourth proportional to 2 : 3 :: 4. To 5 : 6 :: 10. To 7 : 12 :: 6. 2s. : 2s. 6d. :: 4s. £3 : £1 5s. :: 6 oz.

(c) Find two pairs of factors whose products are equal, and arrange the whole four in several ways so that they shall form proportions: *e.g.* Because $5 \times 24 = 8 \times 15$, Therefore 5 : 15 :: 8 : 24 and 24 : 15 :: 8 : 5, &c. &c.

A good teacher will invent hundreds of such exercises for himself, and will not need a text-book. There is nothing unsound or meretricious in mental arithmetic of this kind. On the contrary, it will prove to be one of the most effective instruments in making your scholars good computers. It will give readiness, versatility, and accuracy, and will be found an excellent preliminary training for the working of ordinary sums in writing. Keep in view the general principle that the nature of each process should be made familiar by oral exercise before recourse is had to pen or pencil at all, and that the oral exercises should be of exactly the same kind as written sums, but should differ only in their shortness, and in the fact that each problem requires only one or at most two efforts of thought, and deals only with figures such as can be held in the mind all at once, without help from the eye. Much activity of mind is needed on the part of a teacher who conducts this exercise; and it is not its least recommendation that when so conducted it challenges the whole thinking faculty of the children, concentrates their attention, and furnishes capital discipline in promptitude and flexibility of thought.

The use of near and familiar objects as units of measurement.

In beginning to give lessons on money, weights, and measures, you may do well to make an occasional use of actual money, to give a few coins in the hand and to let them be counted. In French and Belgian schools, not only is a diagram shewing the form and proportion of the legal weights and measures displayed, but a complete set of the weights and measures themselves is deposited in every school: so that the children may be taught to handle and to use them, occasionally to weigh and measure the objects near them, and to set down the results in writing. The dimensions of the school-room and of the principal furniture should be known, and a foot or a yard, or a graduated line of five or ten feet should be marked conspicuously on the wall, as a standard of reference, to be used when lengths are being talked about. The area of the playground; the length and width of the street or road in which the school stands; its distance from the church or some other familiar object, the height of the church spire, should all be distinctly ascertained by the teacher, and frequently referred to in lessons wherein distances have to be estimated. Children should be taught to observe that the halfpenny has a diameter of exactly one inch, and should be made to measure with it the width of a desk or the dimensions of a copy-book. It constantly happens, that if I ask elder children, who have 'gone through' as it is called a long course of computation in 'long measure,' to hold up their two hands a yard apart, or to draw a line three inches long on their slates, or to tell me how far I have walked from the railway station, or to take a book in their hands and tell me how much it weighs, their wild and speculative answers shew me that elementary notions of the units of length and weight have not been, as they ought to be, conveyed before mere 'ciphering' was begun.

As to weights and measures, they are as we all know, a great stumbling-block. The books give us a formidable list of tables, and children are supposed to learn them by heart. But a little discrimination is wanted here. It is needful to learn by heart the tables of those weights and measures which are in constant use, *e.g.* avoirdupois weight, long measure, and the number of square yards in an acre; but it is not worth while to learn apothecaries' weight, cloth measure, or ale and beer measure, because in fact, these measures are not in actual or legal use; and because the sums which the books contain are only survivals from an earlier age when the technical terms in these tables, *puncheons, kilderkins, scruples,* and *Flemish ells,* had a real meaning, and were in frequent use. Keep these tables in the books by all means, and work some sums by reference to them: they are of course all good exercises in computation; but here, as elsewhere, abstain from giving to the verbal memory that which has no real value, and is not likely to come into use.

Weights and measures.

It seems hardly necessary to refer to the efforts some teachers have made to use Arithmetic as a vehicle for the inculcation of Scriptural or other truths. Such efforts have been commoner in other countries than our own. " How admirably," says an enthusiastic French writer on

Moral lessons in sums.

Arithmetic, "does this science lend itself to moral and religious training!"

Père Girard composed a manual of Arithmetic in which, for the most part, the problems given had a distinctly hortatory character, and were meant to embody economic and moral instruction. Here is an example.

"Un père de famille avait l'habitude d'aller tous les soirs au cabaret et laissait souvent sa famille sans pain à la maison. Pendant quatre ans qu'il a mené cette vie il a depensé la première année 197 fr., la seconde 204 fr., la troisième 212 fr., et la quatrième 129 fr. Combien de francs aurait epargné ce malheureux père s'il n'eut pas eu le gout de la boisson?"

And another French writer seeks on this wise to give a moral tone to his arithmetical lessons. He supposes the Curé to visit the school, and the teacher to say,

What does the number 7 remind you of?
The 7 deadly sins, the 7 sacraments, and the 7 golden candlesticks.
What have you tell me about the number 12?
The number of the Apostles, the number of the minor prophets and of the gates of the Apocalyptic Jerusalem."

And then he turns to the children, "*Mes enfants*," he says, "we have thus shewn to our worthy pastor that we establish true relations between the art of computing and the principles of virtue and religion. Who will say after this that Arithmetic is not a moral and edifying study?"— Who indeed? Of course sums founded on Bible facts, on the age of Methusaleh, or the length of Goliath's spear are innocent enough. But I suspect that all attempts of this kind to kill two birds with one stone, so to speak, are very unsatisfactory. Moreover it does not seem quite reverent to use books or names with which some of us have very sacred associations for the sake of manufacturing arithmetical puzzles for school boys. After all, in just the proportion in which children pay attention to the sum and do it well as a question in arithmetic they will disregard the moral or religious lessons which have been thus artificially forced into the exercise of counting. Arithmetic has indeed its own moral teaching. Rightly learned, it becomes a discipline in obedience, in fixed attention, in truthfulness and in honour. These are its appropriate lessons, and they are well worth learning. But if you want to deal with drunkenness and extravagance, or to teach Bible History, it is better to adopt some other machinery than that of an arithmetic lesson.

And touching one of these habits, that of fixed and concentrated intellectual attention, it may be well to bear in mind how greatly it is helped by exercises in rapid counting. Now and then it is a useful exercise to have a match, and to let the scholars work a given number of sums against time,—say so many within half an hour. One great advantage of this is that it keeps the scholar's whole power and faculty alive, and keenly bent on the one object. No irrelevant or foreign thought can for the time intrude into the mind. And quick work is not in arithmetic as in so many other subjects, another name for hasty and superficial work. In this one department of school life slowness and deliberation are rather ensnaring than otherwise. Intervals are here of little or no value for reflection. They merely give an opportunity for the thoughts to wander. The quickest calculators are those who for the time during which they are engaged on a sum shut everything else but the sum out of their thoughts; and they are for that very reason the best calculators. *Rapid computation.*

It must not be forgotten that arithmetic, like all the other exact sciences, has the advantage of dealing with results which are absolutely certain, as far as we can claim certainty for anything we know. In mathematical *Exactness.*

and purely logical deduction we always know when we get at a result that it is either correct or incorrect. There are no degrees of accuracy. One answer is right, and every other possible answer is wrong. Hence if we want to get out of arithmetic the training in precision and conscientious exactness which it is calculated to give, we must never be content with an answer which is approximately right; right for all practical purposes, or right in the quotient, but a little wrong in the remainder. The perfect correctness of the answer is essential, and I counsel you to attach as great importance to the minute accuracy of the remainder and what seems the insignificant part of the answer, as to the larger and more important parts of it. In mathematics no detail is insignificant.

Exercises in forecasting approximate answers. You will occasionally get answers not only wrong, but preposterously and absurdly wrong; *e.g.* you ask what per cent. of profit is gained, and receive some thousands of pounds for the answer; or you ask a question the answer of which has to be time, and the pupil brings it you in pence. It is well to check this by often asking a scholar to tell approximately, and before he does his sum, what he expects the answer to be,—about how much; why *e.g.* it cannot be so great as a million, or so small as twenty, or in what denomination the answer is sure to come. And if he has not expected anything, nor exercised himself in any prevision as to what sort of answer should emerge, you are in a position at once to discern that he is not making the best sort of progress, and when you see this to apply a remedy at once.

Ingenuity. In teaching the art of computation it is legitimate to devise special exercises in order to cultivate ingenuity. Such exercises may often be found in connexion with different methods of proving or verifying the answers to sums. When the answer has been found, the *data* and the *quæsita* should be made to exchange places, and the scholars may be asked to construct new questions, so that each of the factors in the original problem shall be made in turn to come out as the answer. Another method is to work out before the class in full a solution to a long and complex sum, and then invite the scholars to tell how the process might have been abridged; which of the figures set down was not essential as a means of obtaining the answer, or might have been dispensed with. Indeed the invention of contracted methods of working, whether by cancelling or otherwise, ought always to be at the suggestion of the scholar, and grow fairly out of his own experience in working by a needlessly long process. It should seldom or never be enunciated as a rule by the teacher.

Commercial rules.

It is perhaps hardly necessary to remind any one here that it is a mistake to measure the practical utility of the arithmetical exercises you adopt by their visible relation to commerce, and to the affairs of life. Of course it is important that many of the problems you set should be as like the actual problems of business as possible. Mere conundrums, obviously invented by the bookmakers, are apt to seem very unreal to boys and girls; and they prefer to confront the sort of difficulties which they are likely to meet with out of school. So I think it desirable that you should make sums out of the bills you pay, and bearing on what you know to be the rents of the houses, the income and expenditure of families of the class of life to which your pupils belong. You should keep your eyes open, and invent or take from the newspapers of the day little problems on the changing prices of goods, the weekly returns of births and deaths, the returns of the railway companies, or the fluctuations in the weekly wages of artizans. Simple examples of receipts, and of the use of a ledger and a balance-sheet, should also be given in connexion with the smaller transactions, with which the scholars are most familiar.

But do not suppose that exercises which have no ostensible relation to real business, are of inferior value even for practical purposes. What are often called commercial rules, such as discount, and tare and tret, are modified a good deal in the counting-house and bank, and are in their immediate application to business often far less serviceable than they seem. An eminent London Banker once said to me "The chief qualifications I want in a clerk are, next to good character and associations, that he should write a good hand, that he should have been taught intelligently, especially in Arithmetic, and that he should *not* have learned book-keeping. We have our own method of keeping accounts, and a pretentious system of school book-keeping has a number of technical terms which we do not use, and which hinder a lad from learning that method. But let him only have a good general knowledge of the principles of arithmetic and counting, and we will undertake to teach him all that is peculiar to the books of our house in less than a week." Perhaps this is an extreme case, but I am convinced that attempts to anticipate the actual application of arithmetic to the particular business in which a pupil may be hereafter engaged are generally mistakes.

Other forms of practical application.

The application of arithmetic to the solution of problems is often limited in the books to what is called business. But commerce is after all only one, though the most prominent, of the uses to which arithmetic has to be put in life. There are many interesting and varied applications to other purposes, which might be used with advantage : *e.g.*

The computation of the time of falling bodies.

The conversion of our weights and measures into French.

Finding the length of circumference and radii, and the area of circles and squares.

Actual measurement of the play ground or a neighbouring field, and elementary land surveying.

The right use of annuity and insurance tables, *e.g.* the tables at the end of the *Post Office Guide* will suggest many interesting forms of sums.

The use of logarithmic tables, and the solution of triangles by means of them: their application to the determination of the heights of mountains or spires or the breadth of rivers.

The difference of time between various places whose longitude is given.

The measurement of distances on a map which has a scale of miles attached to it.

The readings of the thermometer and the conversion of Fahrenheit to centigrade.

The statistics of attendance in the school itself, and the method of computing its average attendance.

Reduction of English money to decimals. One great help to the easy solution of money questions is the habit of using decimal equivalents, or reducing sums of money at sight to decimals of £1. We are at present far from the adoption of a decimal coinage in England; but we can by anticipation enjoy, in our accounts at least, many of the advantages of a decimal system of money, by the adoption of a simple rule. Let it be observed that two shillings = £·1, that one shilling = £·05, that sixpence = £·025, and that a farthing differs only from £·001 by a very small fraction; and it then becomes very easy to frame a rule for conversion of ordinary expressions for money into their equivalent decimal expressions.

Thus £17. 16s. 7¾d. = £17·832, because 16s. = 8 florins or £·8; 6d. = £·025, and 7 farthings = £·007.

In like manner £21·367 = £21 + 3 florins or £·3 + 1 shilling or £·05 + 17 farthings or £·017, or in all £21. 7s. 4¼d.

Half an hour's practice in conversion and reconversion in this way renders the process familiar. All questions in which the given sum of money does not extend to lower fractions than 6d. can evidently be solved with perfect accuracy by decimals, and without encumbering the mind with the ordinary reduction at all. Nearly all questions in Interest and many in Practice and Proportion can be wrought much more expeditiously by this than by any other method. Precaution is needed in those questions only in which odd pence and farthings occur and require to be multiplied.

Visible relation to business no test of real utility.
These various applications of arithmetic have different degrees of utility; but their value is not to be measured by inquiring which of them is most likely to be practically useful. The true aim in devising exercises in practical arithmetic is to cultivate general power, fertility of resource, and quickness in dealing with numbers; the habit of seeing at once all round a new problem, of understanding its bearings, and applying the best rule for its solution. Power of this kind is available, not only in all businesses alike, but in the intellectual and practical life of those boys and girls who are not likely to go to business. And this general quickness and versatility is just as well promoted, we must remember, by working problems which have an abstract look as by solving those in which the phraseology of the counter or the exchange is most ostentatiously used.

One other department of mathematics which has *Practical Geometry.* found its way into schools, resembles Arithmetic in being an Art and having useful practical applications, and also in furnishing disciplinal and purely intellectual exercise. Demonstrative Geometry has a value for this latter purpose, which, from the days of Plato and Archimedes, has been very generally recognised; but the claims of merely practical geometry as a useful part of both of primary and of secondary instruction appear to me to deserve more consideration than they generally receive. Every scholar should be taught to use the compass and ruler, and the quadrant and scale of equal parts. He should draw simple geometrical figures, as well as talk about them, and recognise their properties. He should know how to measure angles and lines, and to construct ordinary plane figures. In the best schools of Germany, France, and Switzerland, these simple things are taught to every scholar as matter of course. You may hear a teacher dictate to the class directions one by one as to the construction of a figure. "Draw a line 15 centimètres long, then another line upon it at an angle of 35 degrees, then another line of a given length to the right or left, &c., &c." until the class produces one after another figures which he has pre-determined, and of which the qualities and dimensions are afterwards explained and discussed in the class. The rules for practical geometry are comparatively few and simple; the exercise is interesting, and is a considerable relief from graver employment. It serves to familiarize the scholar with the properties of circles, of triangles, or of parallelograms, and so to make the future scientific study of geometry more intelligible. And for those who may never learn Euclid or even the modern system of demonstrative geometry which seems destined to supersede it, geometrical drawing will be found to have a value of its own in enabling scholars to judge better of heights and distances, and to know at least the chief properties of plane and solid figures.

Note on the form of Abacus. An ingenious modification of the Abacus, or ball-frame, in use in some of the French schools, possesses some advantages over the square Chinese frame with horizontal bars which is in common use in English schools. It is thus constructed:

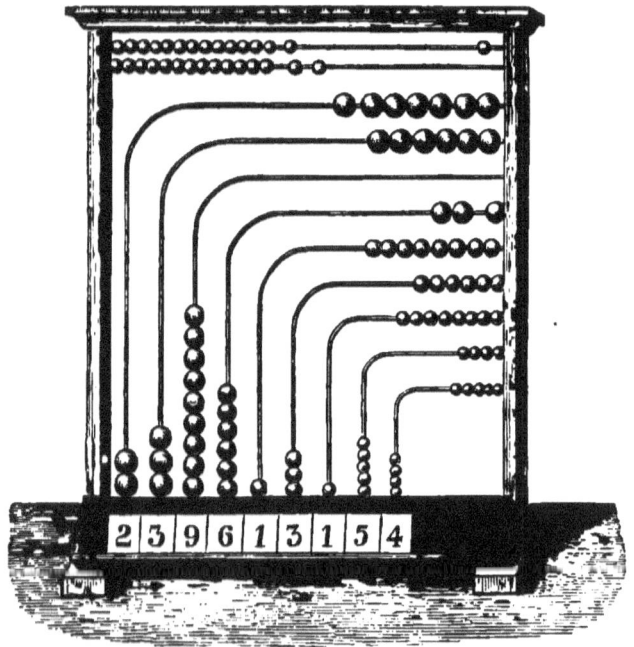

A much greater variety of exercises in subtracting and combining numbers can be made by means of this instrument; and the upright lines may be made very useful in explaining the principle of our notation, and the necessity for keeping hundreds, tens and units in columns.

XI. ARITHMETIC AS A SCIENCE.

HAVING sought to lay down some rules by which a teacher may be guided in making the mere arts of computation and measurement effective parts of education, it becomes necessary to consider more fully the claims of Arithmetic as a science, and the reasons for assigning to it as a disciplinal study, even a higher rank than would be due to its practical usefulness.

We should all be agreed that the main purpose of our *Science.* intellectual life is the acquirement of truth, and that one of the things we go to school is to learn how to acquire it. The mere accumulation of facts and information does not supply what we want. The difference between a wise man and one who is not wise consists less in the things he knows than in the way in which he knows them. We call arithmetic a science, and science, it may be said, means knowledge. But there is a good deal of knowledge which is not science. Science, properly so called, is organized knowledge, knowledge of things and facts and events in their true relation and co-ordination, their antecedents and consequences,—the recognition of every separate phenomenon in the shifting panorama of life as an illustration of some principle or law, broader, higher, and more enduring than itself. No number of facts or aphorisms learned by heart makes a man a thinker, or does him much intellectual service. Every particular fact worth knowing is connected with some general truth, and it is in the tracing of the connexion and collocation of particular and separate truths with general and abiding truths that science mainly consists. We may see hereafter that an historical fact is learned to little purpose unless it is seen in its bearing on some political, economic, or moral law. And we have already seen that a grammatical rule has scant meaning or use for us until it is seen as part of the science of language. This distinction runs through all sound and fruitful acquirement, and should always be present in the mind of a teacher. We must learn to see special facts and bits of experience in the light of the larger generalizations by which the world is governed and held together. We have so to teach as to develop the searching and enquiring spirit, the love of truth, and the habit of accurate reasoning. And if Arithmetic can be so taught as to serve this purpose, it has a value which greatly transcends what seem to be its immediate objects, and will be found to affect not the notions about number only, but also those about every other subject with which the understanding has to deal.

Induction and Deduction. Here it seems right to take the opportunity of referring to a distinction much insisted on in books on education, and on which I have yet said little or nothing; I mean the distinction between inductive and deductive modes of reasoning. In studying some subjects, the learner begins by acquiring separate facts, and as he goes on learns to group them, to see their resemblances, and to arrive at last at some larger statement of fact which embraces and comprehends them all. This process is called 'induction,' and is the scientific method or process with which Bacon's name is generally identified, though I need hardly say that it is a process as old as the human intellect itself. Bacon only insisted on its importance, and helped to formulate it as an instrument for the discovery of truth. On the other hand there are some subjects to be studied, in which you begin with the large, general, universal truth, and proceed afterwards to deduce from this a number of special and detailed inferences. Such subjects are said to be studied deductively. In the former the movement of the thoughts is from the perception of particulars to the recognition of the general law. In the latter it is from the statement of the general to the recognition of the particulars. One sees that his neighbour is dead, he remembers the death of his parents or friends, he reads the history of the past, and by putting these experiences together, he arrives inductively at the conclusion—that All men are mortal. He accepts this proposition. He muses over it. He adds, I too am a man. And he concludes, I therefore am mortal. Here the process is deductive. And sometimes in learning he must use one process, and sometimes another. And it is a great part of the business of education so to train the faculties that whichever process we adopt we should use it rightly, that our generalizations shall be valid and sound generalizations, and that our inferences shall be true, not hasty and illegitimate inferences, from the facts which may come before us.

Now Arithmetic and Geometry considered as sciences afford examples of both these kinds of learning. If I work out a few problems by experimental and chance methods, and having seen how the answer comes out, arrive at the conclusion that one method is best, I have *Arithmetic and Mathematics mainly but not wholly deductive.*

reached this result by the method of analysis or induction. But if I start from axioms and definitions, and afterwards apply these to the solution of problems, I am availing myself of the method of deduction. But the method of deduction is, after all, the characteristic mode of procedure in arithmetical as well as in all other departments of mathematical science. We shall see hereafter that the physical sciences furnish the best training in inductive reasoning, for there you have in fact no axioms or admitted truths to start from, and must in all cases begin by the observation of phenomena and the collocation of experience. But elementary truths about number and about space, which are respectively the bases of arithmetic and geometry, have the great advantage of being very simple and very evident. They lie quite outside the region of contingency or controversy, and they therefore furnish a better basis for purely deductive or synthetic logic than any other class of subjects in which the very data from which we proceed are often disputed, or at least disputable.

Mathematics a training in logic. Take a geometrical axiom—an elementary truth concerning the properties of space—"two straight lines cannot enclose a space;" or an arithmetical axiom, an elementary truth concerning the properties of number, "to multiply by two numbers successively is to multiply by their product," and we observe that the moment we state them we perceive their necessary truth; there is no room for debate or difference of opinion; to understand either statement is to accept it. And so with all other of the fundamental axioms of geometry and arithmetic. Whatever particular facts prove ultimately to be contained in these general or universal truths must be true. As far as we can be certain of anything we are certain of these.

Suppose then I want to give to myself a little training in the art of reasoning; suppose I wish to get out of the region of conjecture or probability, free myself from the difficult task of weighing evidence, and putting instances together to arrive at general propositions, and simply desire to know how to deal with my general propositions when I get them, and how to deduce right inferences from them; it is clear that I shall obtain this sort of discipline best, in those departments of thought in which the first principles are unquestionably true. For in all our thinking, if we come to erroneous conclusions, we come to them either by accepting false premisses to start with—in which case our reasoning, however good, will not save us from error; or by reasoning badly, in which case the data we start from may be perfectly sound, and yet our conclusions may be false. But in the mathematical or pure sciences,—geometry, arithmetic, algebra, trigonometry, the calculus of variations or of curves,—we know at least that there is not, and cannot be, error in our first principles, and we may therefore fasten our whole attention upon the processes. As mere exercises in logic, therefore, these sciences based as they all are on primary truths relating to space and number, have always been supposed to furnish the most exact discipline. When Plato wrote over the portal of his school, "Let no one ignorant of geometry enter here," he did not mean that questions relating to lines and surfaces would be discussed by his disciples. On the contrary, the topics to which he directed their attention were some of the deepest problems,—social, political, moral,—on which the mind could exercise itself. Plato and his followers tried to think out together conclusions respecting the being, the duty, and the destiny of man, and the relation in which he stood to the gods and to the unseen world. What had geometry to do with these things? Simply this: That a man whose mind had not undergone a rigorous training in systematic thinking, and in the art of drawing legitimate inferences from premises, was unfitted to enter on the discussion of these high topics; and that the sort of logical discipline which he needed was most likely to be obtained from geometry—the only mathematical science which in Plato's time had been formulated and reduced to a system. And we in this country have long acted on the same principle. Our future lawyers, clergy, and statesmen are expected at the University to learn a good deal about curves, and angles, and numbers and proportions; not because these subjects have the smallest relation to the needs of their lives, but because in the very act of learning them, they are likely to acquire that habit of steadfast and accurate thinking, which is indispensable to success in all the pursuits of life.

Arithmetic the mathematics of the School. What mathematics therefore are expected to do for the advanced student at the University, Arithmetic, if taught demonstratively, is capable of doing for the children even of the humblest school. It furnishes training in reasoning, and particularly in deductive reasoning. It is a discipline in closeness and continuity of thought. It reveals the nature of fallacies, and refuses to avail itself of unverified assumptions. It is the one department of school-study in which the sceptical and inquisitive spirit has the most legitimate scope; in which authority goes for nothing. In other departments of instruction you have a right to ask for the scholar's confidence, and to expect many things to be received on your testimony with the understanding that they will be explained and verified afterwards. But here you are justified in saying to your pupil "Believe nothing which you cannot understand. Take nothing for granted."

In short the proper office of arithmetic is to serve as elementary training in logic. All through your work as teachers, you will bear in mind the fundamental difference between knowing and thinking; and will feel how much more important relatively to the health of the intellectual life the habit of thinking is than the power of knowing, or even facility in achieving visible results. But here this principle has special significance. It is by Arithmetic more than by any other subject in a school course that the art of thinking—consecutively, closely, logically—can be effectually taught.

I proceed to offer some practical suggestions as to the manner in which this principle, if once recognised, should dominate the teaching of Arithmetic, and determine your methods.

You have first of all to take care that so much of our Arithmetical system, as is arbitrary and conventional, shall be shewn to be so, and not confounded with that part of Arithmetic which is permanently true, and based on the properties of number. We have for example adopted the number *ten* as the basis of our numeration; but there is nothing in the science of numbers to suggest this. Twelve or eight, or indeed any other number, might have served the same purpose, though not with quite the same convenience. Again the Arabic notation adopts the device of place to show the different values of figures: *e.g.* In 643 the 6 is shewn to mean 6 tens of tens, and the 4 to mean 4 tens, by the place in which they stand. But convenient as this arrangement is, other devices might have been adopted, which would have fulfilled the same purpose; and the Roman mode of representing the same number by DCXLIII may be with advantage compared; and its inconvenience practically tested by trying to work a sum with it. Again the

322   *Arithmetic as a Science.*

wholly artificial and accidental way in which our system of weights and measures has originated should, when the proper time comes, be explained, and a comparison be made with some other system, especially the French *Système Métrique*. Generally it may be said that when you find yourself confronted with any arithmetical devices or terminology which are arbitrary in their character, you will do well to shew their arbitrariness by comparing them with some others which are equally possible.

Illustration of the decimal method of notation.

The first occasion comes when you explain the decimal character of our common arithmetic, the device of distinguishing the meaning of the various multiples of ten and of the powers of ten, by their places and nearness to the unit; and the use of the cipher or nought (o). Here an appeal to some visible or tangible illustration will help you much. I take from an ingenious French book[1] an example of such an appeal.

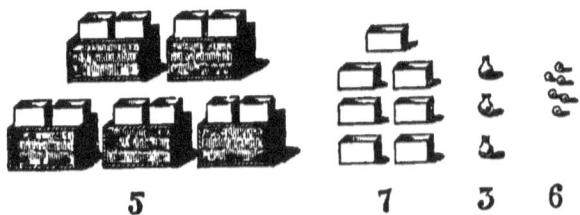

5   7 3 6

Here you observe small balls or marbles are used to represent units, bags containing ten of them to represent tens, boxes containing ten such bags to represent hundreds, and baskets containing ten boxes each represent thousands. When this has been shewn, you may further illustrate the nature of our notation by an addition sum: thus,

[1] L'Arithmétique du grand-papa; histoire de deux petits marchands de pommes, par *Jean Macé*. Paris, Collection Hetzel.

Illustrations of the decimal notation. 323

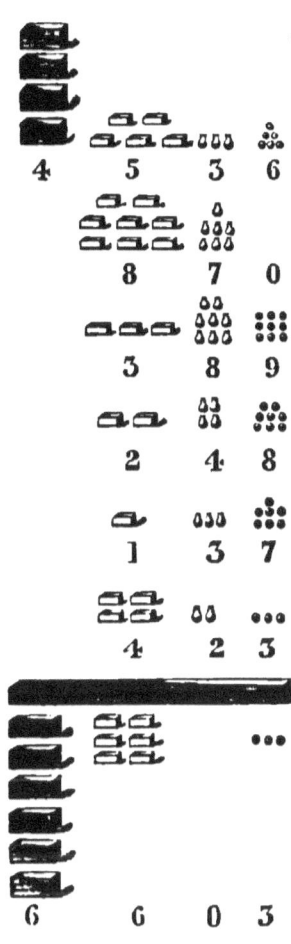

You require in succession that the numeration of each line should be explained orally, you call special attention to the need and special use of the o in the second line. It is seen that the first column makes 33, and that of them 30 may be included in 3 bags, and 3 remain. The addition of the next line gives 30, and shews the need of a device for marking the vacant place, and shewing that there are no odd tens. The 26 hundreds are then shewn to consist of 2 baskets full containing 10 boxes each, and of 6 boxes or hundreds remaining. These two baskets added to the four baskets represent six thousands.

Thus the fundamental parts of our system of notation—the device of place, the counting by tens, the use of the cipher, and the need of carrying, are all made clear to the eye and to the understanding of your pupil.

Many other forms of visible illustration have been devised, but it will be far better for you to exercise your own ingenuity in inventing them. Only bear in mind the rule of action already urged upon you. When

21—2

your box of cubes, your abacus, your number pictures, your diagrams representing collections of tens, have succeeded in making the subject intelligible; have the courage to cast them aside. Arithmetic is an abstract science, and the sooner scholars can see its truths in a pure and abstract form, the better. It is not an uncommon fault among Pestalozzian teachers to employ what are sometimes called intuitional methods, long after they have served their purpose, and when the pupil is quite ready to deal intelligently with abstract rules.

Scales of notation other than decimal. One very effective way of making the decimal notation clear is to assume some other number than *ten* as the possible base of a system of notation, and to invite the scholars to consider with you how numbers would have been represented on that system. It may be shewn that as a system founded on tens requires 9 digits and a cipher, so a *quaternary* system would have required three digits only, an *undenary* would have required one more digit than we use, say x; and that a *binary* scheme of notation applicable to the highest numbers would have been possible with one digit and a cipher only, since all large numbers would then have been gathered into *twos* and powers of two, instead of into *tens* and powers of ten.

By questions and suggestions you and your scholars come to frame on the black board some such table as this:

Decimal scale.	Scale of two.	Scale of six.	Scale of eleven.
1	1	1	1
2	10	2	2
3	11	3	3
4	100	4	4
5	101	5	5
6	110	10	6
7	111	11	7

Other Scales of notation.

Decimal Scale.	Scale of two.	Scale of six.	Scale of eleven.
8	1000	12	8
9	1001	13	9
10	1010	14	x
11	1011	15	10
12	1100	20	11
13	1101	21	12
14	1110	22	13
15	1111	23	14
16	10000	24	15
17	10001	25	16
18	10010	30	17
19	10011	31	18
20	10100	32	19

A few easy sums to be worked out in numbers arranged on these scales, and afterwards verified by conversion into ordinary numbers will do much to clear the mind of the pupil as to the wholly artificial character of the decimal notation.

When you come to Weights and Measures and before requiring tables to be learned by heart, it is well as I have said to give a short historical lesson shewing how our system grew up. The fact that we want fixed units of length, of weight, and of capacity to serve as the basis of all calculation; and the curious fact that nature does not supply by any single object a determinate and unalterable unit of any one of them, will partly account for the queer and irregular way in which we have from time to time based our calculations on grains of barley, on, the vibrations of the pendulum, or the length of Henry I.'s arm. With a good diagram, such as is in use in all the French schools, it may then be shewn how the unit of length, the *Mètre*, which forms the base of the metric system is obtained from the measurement of a definite part of the earth's meridian; how this unit squared gives the unit of surface, the *Are*, how the same

Lesson on the Système métrique.

unit cubed gives the units both of magnitude and of capacity, the *Litre* and the *Stère;* how a given bulk so measured of distilled water gives the unit of weight, the *Gramme;* how a certain weight of silver gives the unit of value, the *Franc;* and how all these units by a simple nomenclature, are subject to decimal multiplication and sub-division. It is only when a simple and scientific system like this is seen in all its details—and the whole of it may easily be explained and learned in one half-hour's lesson—that the real nature of the confusion and anomalies of our own system of compound arithmetic comes into clear light.

All rules should be demonstrated before they are learned or practised.

Every rule you teach should be first of all made the subject of an oral lesson and demonstration. The method of experiment and induction, will often enable you to arrive at the rule, and shew its necessity. One of the first rules in which the difference between a skilled teacher, and a mere slave of routine becomes apparent, is the early rule of Subtraction. You want for example to take 479 from 853, and the method of so-called explanation is apt to be like this:

853
479
———
374

"9 from 3 I cannot; *Borrow* 10. 9 from 13 leaves 4. Set down 4.

"*Carry* 1 to the 7. 7 and 1 are 8; 8 from 5, I cannot; borrow 10, 8 from 15 leaves 7. Set down 7.

"Carry 1 to the 4. 4 and 1 are 5. 5 from 8 leaves 3. Set down 3."

Subtraction.

Now, of course, if the object is to get the right answer that object is fulfilled, for 374 is undoubtedly correct. But as an exercise in intelligence I hope you see that this is utterly worthless. The word 'borrow' has been put into the children's mouths, but whence the ten is borrowed, why it is borrowed, or what sort of morality that is which permits you to 'borrow ten' in one direction, and pretends to compensate by 'paying back one' in another, are points which are left in obscurity. Language like this, which simulates explanation and is yet utterly unintelligible, is an insult to the understanding of a child; it would be far better to tell him at once that the process is a mystery, than to employ words which profess to account for it, and which yet explain nothing.

There are two ways in which, with a little pains, the reason of this rule may be made clear even to the youngest class. Thus:— *Method of decomposition.*

$$853 = 7 \text{ hundreds} + 14 \text{ tens} + 13$$
$$479 = 4 \quad,, \quad + 7 \,,, \quad + 9$$
$$374 \quad 3 \qquad\qquad 7 \qquad 4$$

"9 cannot be taken from 3; so borrow one of the tens from the 50 (in other words, resolve 53 into 40 and 13). 9 from 13 leaves 4. Set down 4 in the units' place.

"7 tens cannot be taken from 4 tens; so borrow 1 from the 8 hundreds (in other words, resolve 8 hundreds and 4 tens into 7 hundreds and 14 tens). 7 tens from 14 tens leave 7 tens. Set down 7 in the tens' place.

"4 hundreds from 7 hundreds leave 3 hundreds. Set down 3 in the hundreds' place."

Now here you will observe that the word "borrowing" is not inappropriate. But there is no paying back; for you have only borrowed from one part of your minuend 853 to another, and dealt with its parts in a slightly different order from that indicated by the figures. You have simply resolved 800 + 50 + 3, for your own convenience, into the form 700 + 140 + 13; and have left the subtrahend 479 untouched. I do not say this is the best method of working, but it is, at least, easy to explain; and the language you employ is self-consistent throughout.

Method of equal additions. The second method is a little harder to explain, but easier to work. It is that most generally adopted in schools. But before beginning to do a sum by it, it is worth while to explain to your class the very simple principle that "the difference between unequal quantities is not altered, if we add equal quantities to both." If I have five shillings in one pocket and seven in another, the difference is two $(7-5=2)$; but if I afterwards put three shillings into each pocket, the difference is still two $(10-8=2)$. By very simple illustration of this kind you may easily bring children to the conclusion, that if, for any reason, we think it convenient to add equal sums to two numbers whose difference we want to find, we are at liberty to do so without affecting the accuracy of the answer. When this has been explained, the sum may be thus worked :—

$$853 + 100 + 10 \qquad 8 \text{ hundreds, } 15 \text{ tens } 13$$
$$479 + 100 + 10 \qquad 5 \text{ hundreds, } 8 \text{ tens } 9$$
$$\overline{374} \qquad \overline{3 \text{ hundreds} + 7 \text{ tens} + 4}$$

"9 from three cannot be taken. *Add* 10 to the upper line. 9 from 13 leaves 4. Set down 4.

"Having added 10 to the upper line, I add ten to the lower. 8 tens from 5 tens cannot be taken. *Add* 10 tens to the upper line, 8 tens from 15 tens leaves 7 tens. Set down 7.

"Having added 10 tens, or 1 hundred to the upper line, we must *add* 1 hundred to the lower; 5 hundreds from 8 hundreds leave 3 hundreds. Set down 3."

But here it is observable that you have not performed the problem proposed. You have not taken 479 from 853; but you have added first 10, and afterwards 1 hundred to each, and the real problem performed has been to take $479+110$, or $500+80+9$ from $853+110$, or from $800+150+13$. But this, according to the principle first explained gives the same result as to take the first number from the second without the addition of the hundred and ten.

Yet the common phraseology employed about borrowing and carrying is equally inappropriate, and therefore equally bewildering, in both these processes. For by the first method there may be borrowing, but there is no carrying; and by the second, there is neither borrowing nor carrying, but equal addition.

Another device to which a good teacher resorts early is the making of the Multiplication Table in the presence of the class, and with its help. Generally the whole of that formulary is placed before the scholars, and they are required to learn it by heart, without knowing how it is formed or why. Now if the teacher says he is going to make up the table of multiplication by two's, and then writes 2 on the board, and requires the scholars to repeat the number, so that he writes down each result and records at the side the number of twos which have been added, he makes it clear to the scholars that multiplication is only a series of equal additions, and that the rule is only a device for shortening a particular form of addition sum. He will then deal in like manner with each of the 9 digits in succession, and afterwards efface what he has written and require the scholars to manufacture their own table before learning it.

Learners may make up their own tables.

One very effective way of making the theory of a process clear, is to adopt the method to which I may

Arithmetical parsing.

give the name of 'arithmetical parsing.' It consists in drawing out before the class the whole of a given process without abridgment, and then analysing it in such a way that a separate account shall be given of every figure in succession, shewing clearly how and why it plays a part in obtaining the final result. I take an example from Simple Division although almost every other rule would do as well I will suppose that by simple examples you have shewn what Division is, that you have deduced from the division of the parts—say of a shilling, and from some such example as this:—

Because $27 = 12 + 9 + 6$

Therefore the third of 27 or $\frac{27}{3} = \frac{12}{3} + \frac{9}{3} + \frac{6}{3}$ or $4 + 3 + 2$,

the general truth that 'we divide one number by another when we divide each of the parts of the first successively by the second, and add the quotients together.' It is then seen that when the dividend is a large number, it has to be resolved into such parts as can be dealt with one by one, in order that all the several results as they are obtained shall be added together to make the whole. An example may be worked thus: Divide 34624 by seven:

$$
\begin{array}{r}
7 \overline{)34624} \\
\hline
\end{array}
$$

$$
\begin{aligned}
4000 &= 28000 \div 7 \\
900 &= 6300 \div 7 \\
40 &= 280 \div 7 \\
6 &= 42 \div 7 \\
\tfrac{2}{7} &= 2 \div 7 \\
\hline
4946\tfrac{2}{7} &= 34624 \div 7
\end{aligned}
$$

This method of analysis is especially effective in what is called Long Multiplication, in Division, and also in Practice; for in these rules the answer comes out piece-

The teaching of Fractions.

meal, and it is both easy and interesting to challenge pupils for the separate significance and value of each line of figures as it is arrived at.

In the exercise just given it is well to call attention to the fact that the whole problem has not in fact been solved, for that all the dividend except 2 has been divided; but the seventh part of two remains undiscovered, and must for the present remain in the form $\frac{2}{7}$ or the seventh part of two.

Here then is the proper place to begin the explanation of fractions. They ought not to be postponed later, certainly not placed as they often are most improperly, after proportion. The remainder of a division sum suggests the necessity of dealing with the parts of unity. Here an appeal may be made to the eye: *Fractions should be begun early.*

and it may be demonstrated that one seventh of two inches is the same as two sevenths of one inch. I need not say that in your early lessons on fractions, the method of visible illustration is especially helpful, and that by drawing squares or other figures and dividing them first into fourths and eighths, then into thirds, sixths and ninths, or by the use of a cube divided into parts, you may make the nature of a fractional expression very evident even to young children, and may deduce several of the fundamental rules for reduction to a common denominator, and for addition and subtraction.

Fractions afford excellent discipline in reasoning and reflection. No one of the rules should be given on authority, every one of them admits of being thought out and arrived at by the scholars themselves, with very little of help and suggestion from their teacher. What for example can be more unsatisfactory than the rule for Division of Fractions if blindly accepted and followed. "Invert the divisor and treat it as a multiplier." This seems more like conjuring with numbers than performing a rational process. But suppose you first present the problem and determine to discover the rule. You here find it needful to enlarge a little the conception of what Division means. "What is it" you ask "to divide a number?" It is

(1) To separate a number into equal parts;

(2) To find a number which multiplied by the divisor will make the dividend;

(3) To find how many times, *or parts of a time*, the divisor is contained in the dividend.

It will have been shewn before, that this expression 'the parts of a time' is necessary in dealing with fractions, and involves an extension of the meaning of the word divisor as ordinarily understood in dealing with integer numbers. You may then proceed to give four or five little problems graduated in difficulty, e.g.

(1) Divide 12 by $\frac{1}{3}$. What does this mean? To find how many times $\frac{1}{3}$ is contained in 12. But $\frac{1}{3}$ is contained three times in 1, so it must be contained 3×12 times in 12. Wherefore to divide by $\frac{1}{3}$ is the same as to multiply by 3.

(2) Divide 15 by $\frac{3}{4}$. This means to find how many times $\frac{3}{4}$ are contained in 15. But $\frac{1}{4}$ must be contained in it 15×4 or 60 times. So $\frac{3}{4}$ must be contained in it one-third of 60 times or $\frac{4 \times 15}{3}$. Wherefore to divide by $\frac{3}{4}$ is the same as to multiply by $\frac{4}{3}$.

(3) Divide $\frac{5}{7}$ by $\frac{3}{4}$. This means to divide by the fourth part of 3. Let us first divide by 3. Now $\frac{5}{7}$ divided by $3 = \frac{5}{7 \times 3}$, or $\frac{5}{21}$. But since we were not to divide by three but by the fourth

Demonstration of Fractional division.

part of 3, this result is too little, and must be set right by multiplying by 4. Hence $\frac{4\times 5}{21}$ is the answer. Wherefore to divide $\frac{4}{7}$ by $\frac{3}{4}$ is the same as to multiply by $\frac{4}{3}$.

(4) To divide $\frac{5}{7}$ by $\frac{3}{4}$ is to find how often $\frac{3}{4}$ is contained in $\frac{5}{7}$. Let us bring them to a common denominator $\frac{5}{7}=\frac{20}{28}$, and $\frac{3}{4}=\frac{21}{28}$. The question therefore is how often are $\frac{21}{28}$ contained in $\frac{20}{28}$? Just as often as 21 shillings are contained in 20 shillings; that is to say not once, but $\frac{20}{21}$ of a time, for this fraction represents the number of times that 20 contains 21. Wherefore $\frac{5}{7}\div\frac{3}{4}=\frac{5}{7}\times\frac{4}{3}$.

(5) To divide $\frac{5}{7}$ by $\frac{3}{4}$ is to find a fraction which if multiplied by $\frac{3}{4}$ will make $\frac{5}{7}$. That means that $\frac{3}{4}$ of this unknown fraction will make $\frac{5}{7}$. But whenever A is $\frac{3}{4}$ of B, B must be $\frac{4}{3}$ of A. Hence the desired fraction must be $\frac{4}{3}$ of $\frac{5}{7}$. But this is the same fraction which would have been produced by inverting the divisor and treating it as a multiplier.

Wherefore to divide by any fraction is to multiply by its reciprocal, or

$$\frac{a}{b}\div\frac{c}{d}=\frac{a}{b}\times\frac{d}{c}.$$

Q. E. D.

I recommend that after each of these short exercises the numbers be altered, and the scholars required one by one to go through the demonstration orally. This will be found to serve exactly the same purpose as the proving of a theorem in geometry. It calls out the same mental qualities, demands concentration of thought, and careful arrangement of premisses and conclusion, and furnishes an effective though elementary lesson in logic and in pure mathematics.

The habit of registering the result of any such process, or embodying any truth you have ascertained in the shape of a formula in which the letters of the alphabet are substituted for numbers is a very useful one. The pupil makes a clear advance in abstract *The use of formulae.*

thinking; if, for example, after shewing that equal additions to two numbers do not alter their difference, and illustrating this by such examples as

Because $12 - 7 = 5$, therefore $(12 + 8) - (7 + 8) = 5$,

you help him also to see the truth of this:

If $a - b = c$, then $(a + n) - (b + n) = c$.

Do not suppose that this is algebra. No one of the notions or processes proper to algebra is here involved. It is simply the statement of an arithmetical truth in its most abstract form. It lifts your pupil out of the region of particulars into the region of universal truths. It helps him to see that what is true of certain numbers and what he has actually verified in the case of those numbers is necessarily true of all numbers. So I recommend the practice of embodying each arithmetical truth as you arrive at it in a general formula.

Use of arithmetical puzzles. There is not a single process in Arithmetic out of which you may not get real intellectual training as well as practical usefulness, if you will only set this before you as one of the objects to be attained. The plea that it takes time, and hinders progress, is, in my opinion, wholly invalid. What do you mean by progress? It is surely not hastening to what are called advanced rules. It is rather such increased mastery of the fundamental principles of arithmetic as will enable the pupil to invent rules for himself. And this he will attain if you set him thinking about the meaning of every process which you require him to use. Put before your class occasionally little facts about numbers, and ask them to find out the reasons for them. Here are two or three simple examples of what I mean:

(a) If the numbers in the following series progress by equal additions

1 . 3 . 5 . 7 . 9 . 11 . 13 . 15 . 17 . 19 . 21,

why is it that each pair of numbers, e.g. the first and the last, the second and the last but one, the third and the last but two, &c. equals 22, a number equal to twice 11, the middle term?

(b) If I take any number—say 732586, and any other composed of the same digits, say 257638, and subtract one from the other, thus:

$$\begin{array}{r}732586\\257638\\\hline 474948\end{array}$$ why is it that the digits of the remainder are sure to give me an exact number of nines $4+7+4+9+4+8 = 36 = 4 \times 9$?

(c) If I take four numbers in proportion or representing two equal ratios, e.g. 6 : 24 :: 5 : 20, why is it that 6 times 20 must equal 24×5?

In this last case you will do well to make the scholar deduce the equality of the two products as a necessity from the fact that the four numbers are in proportion. He sees that 24 and 5 make a certain product, and because *ex hypothesi* 6 is as many times less than 24 as 20 is more than 5, therefore that the product of 6 and 20 must equal that of 5 and 24. And when this is seen to be necessarily true of all proportions, the ordinary rule for finding one of the factors when the other three are given will readily be supplied by the pupils themselves.

Proportion, however, though it is a very interesting and valuable part of arithmetical science, and though its principles furnish excellent opportunities for exercise in logical demonstration, is of less practical utility in the solution of problems than the text books seem to assume. The Rule of Three is a great stumbling-block to learners. *Proportion.*

It comes much too early in the course, and learned empirically as it too often is, it is not readily capable of application to problems. Nearly all the questions usually set down under the head of 'Rule of Three' can be much better solved by simpler methods. Such a question as this for example :—

"If 17 articles cost £23. 10s., what will 50 such articles cost?"

ought not to be stated and worked as Proportion; but by the method of reduction to unity, thus :—

One article must cost £23. 10s. ÷ 17. Therefore 50 articles must cost $\frac{£23.\ 10s. \times 50}{17}$.

Thus the true place for the theory of proportion is after fractions, vulgar and decimal, have been well understood and seen in varied applications.

Extraction of roots. My last illustration shall be taken from an advanced rule, that for the Extraction of the Square Root. I will, as before, take an easy sum, and the directions for solving it, as given in the ordinary books.

Find the square root of 676, or the number which, multiplied by itself, will give 676.

```
       .
      676 ( 2
       4
  46 ) 276 ( 6
        276
        ---
```

RULE.—"Point off the alternate numbers from the unit, and thus divide the numbers into periods.

"Find the nearest square root of the first period, and subtract its square.

"(The nearest square root of 6 is 2; set down 2, and take twice 2 from 6.)

"Set down the remainder, and bring down the next period.

"(Set down 2 and bring down 76.)

The Square Root.

"Double the first figure, set it down, and use it as a trial divisor for the two first figures. Place the quotient thus found to its right, and then divide as usual. (Set down 6 after the 4 and multiply 46 by 6.)

"26 is the number sought, and is the square root of 676."

Really, as I recite it, the rule sounds more like a riddle, or a series of instructions in numerical *legerdemain*, than an appeal to the understanding. Whatever be the accuracy or worth of the result produced, it is certain that the process so described will do more to deaden than to invigorate the thinking faculty of any one who practises it. Moreover, as the rule appears utterly arbitrary, the memory will have great difficulty in retaining it, and without constant and toilsome practice, will probably not retain it at all.

Now before describing to you the rational process of attaining this result, I may remind you that in the earlier part of arithmetic the rules came in pairs. Thus, in Addition, you have the parts given, and are required to find the whole; and this rule is followed by Subtraction, in which you have the whole given and one of the parts, and are required to find the other part. So also in Multiplication, the factors are given, and you have to find their product; and then there is the inverse process of Division, in which the product and one of the factors are given, and you are required to find the other factor. In each case the former process is one of synthesis, or putting parts together, and the latter process one of analysis or decomposition of parts. But we all feel this order to be a natural and proper one. You would not teach Subtraction before Addition, nor Division before Multiplication; because unless a learner in this science first knows how to put the parts together to make the

The Synthetical before the Analytical Rule.

result, he is not in a position, with the result before him, to find out how that result is produced. Now the rule for finding the square root of a number is obviously a rule of decomposition or analysis, and is one of a pair of rules, analogous to Multiplication and Division, of which the one shews how to form the second power of a number out of the multiples of its parts, and the other shews how, when the second power of a number is given, to find the parts of that number of which it is the second power. But this rule for Evolution presupposes the rule of Involution; and cannot, in fact, be properly understood, unless that rule has first been learned. Yet in text-books of arithmetic, no mention is generally made of Involution, but the pupil is introduced at once to the Extraction of the Square Root.

Involution. Instead therefore of departing from the analogy of the earlier rules of arithmetic, and plunging at once into the rule for the extraction of roots, before we examine the formation of squares, let us begin by trying to find the second power of an easy number composed of two parts. Thus:

Because $11 = 7 + 4$; then $11 \times 11 = (7 + 4) \times (7 + 4)$.

But on multiplying each of these parts of eleven by each of the parts of eleven successively, and adding them together, I find I have four distinct products, of which the first is the square or second power of 7, the last is the square or second power of 4; and the remaining two are alike, each being the product of 7 and 4.

$$\begin{array}{r}7 + 4 \\ 7 + 4 \\ \hline (4 \times 7) + (4 \times 4) \quad = (7 + 4) \times 4 \\ (7 \times 7) + (7 \times 4) \quad = (7 + 4) \times 7 \\ \hline 7^2 + 2(7 \times 4) + 4^2 = (7 + 4) \times (7 + 4) \\ \text{or } 49 + \quad 2 \times 28 + 16 = 121 \end{array}$$

And in this way we may easily arrive at this general truth:—

"If a number consists of two parts, the second power of the whole number consists of the second power of the first part, together with the second power of the second part, together with twice the product of the first and second parts."

I will suppose that you have, by the help of varied illustration, made your pupils perfectly familiar with this proposition—and led them to recognise it under the general abstract formula:—

If $a = b + c$ then $a^2 = b^2 + c^2 + 2bc$.

You are now in a position to deal with the problem *Evolution* originally proposed: Find the square root of 676.

"Tens multiplied by tens give hundreds, therefore the square root of hundreds will be tens.

"The nearest square root to 600 is 2 tens.

"Take from 676 the square of 2 tens or 400.

"There remain 276.

"Therefore, the square root of 676 is greater than 20, and consists of 20 plus another number."

$$676 \big/ 20 + 6$$
$$400 \big(= 20^2$$
$$40 \big) \overline{276} \big/ 6$$
$$\underline{240} \big(= (40 \times 6)$$
$$\overline{36} = 6^2$$

But if so, the remainder 276 must contain *not only the square of that other number, but twice the product of the number* 20 *and that number*. With a view to find that number, try how many times twice 20 are contained in the remainder. The number 6 appears to fulfil this condition. See now, if 276 contains six times 40, together with 6 times 6, or 6 times 46 in all. If so, 6 is the unit figure of the required root. It has now been shewn that 676 contains the square of 20, and the square of 6, and twice the product of 20 and 6,

$$\text{or } 26^2 = 20^2 + 6^2 + 2(20 \times 6)$$
$$400 + 36 + 240 = 676.$$

The whole explanation of this inverse process is evidently deducible from the simple law of involution first described. The reason of the pupil follows every step, and acquiesces in a rule, otherwise *primâ facie* absurd, and therefore hard to remember. All this is of course very familiar and simple to the student of algebra; but I have never been able to understand why it should be postponed to algebra, or why the principles of arithmetic, requiring as they do for their elucidation no use of symbols, no recondite language, nothing but simple numerical processes, should not be taught on their own merits, and in their own proper place.

Analogous truths in Arithmetic and Geometry.   An appeal to the eye will greatly help the understanding of the rule for the extraction of the square root. A square may be erected on a line divided into two unequal parts, and it will be seen to be separable into four spaces whose dimensions correspond to the products just given. Afterwards a square on a line divided into three or more parts may be shewn, and the dimensions of the several parts may be expressed in numbers. In like manner every proposition in the Second Book of Euclid may be compared with some analogous proposition respecting the powers and products of numbers. But it is important here not to mistake analogy for identity. Some teachers seem to think they have proved the theorems in geometry when they have expressed the corresponding truths in algebraic symbols. The use of the word 'Square,' both for a four-sided figure and for the second power of a number, is a little misleading; and

Euclid's use of the terms Plane and Solid numbers in his Seventh Book would have further mystified students had it been commonly accepted. But since Geometry is founded entirely on the recognition of the properties of space, and Algebra and Arithmetic on those of number, it is necessary to preserve a clear distinction in the reasoning applicable to the two subjects. Except as shewing interesting analogies, the two departments of science should be kept wholly separate; and while the truths about the powers and products of numbers should be investigated by the laws of number alone, geometrical demonstrations should be founded rigorously on axioms relating to space, and should not be confused by the use of algebraic symbols.

Our attention to-day has been necessarily confined to the consideration of a rational way of treating Arithmetic, the one department of mathematics with which, in a school, the teacher is first confronted. But the same general design should be in the mind of the teacher, through Geometry, Algebra, Trigonometry, the Calculus, and all the later stages of mathematical teaching. While constantly testing the success of his pupils by requiring problems to be worked, he will nevertheless feel that the solution of problems is not the main object of this part of his school discipline, but rather the insight into the meaning of processes, and the training in logic. If Algebra and Geometry do not make the student a clearer and more accurate and more consecutive thinker, they are worth nothing. And in the new revolt against the long supremacy of Euclid, as represented in the Syllabus of the "Association for the Improvement of Geometrical Teaching," the one danger we have to fear is that the demonstrative exercises will be cut up into portions too small to give the needful training in continuity of thought.

Algebra and Geometry.

Euclid, with all his faults, obliges the learner to keep his mind fixed not only on the separate truths, but also on the links by which a long succession of such truths are held together. It is well to simplify the science of geometry, and to arrange—as the authors of the Syllabus have done—its various theorems in a truer order. But since it is not geometry, but the mental exercise required in understanding geometry, which the student most wants to acquire, a system of teaching which challenged less of fixed attention and substituted shorter processes for long would possibly prove rather a loss than a gain.

The true office of mathematical teaching. We return finally to the fundamental reason for teaching mathematics at all either to boys or men. Is it because the doctrines of number and of magnitude are in themselves so valuable, or stand in any visible relation to the subjects with which we have to deal most in after life? Assuredly not. But it is because a certain kind of mental exercise, of unquestioned service in connexion with all conceivable subjects of thought, is best to be had in the domain of mathematics. Because in that high and serene region there is no party spirit, no personal controversy, no compromise, no balancing of probabilities, no painful misgiving lest what seems true to-day may prove to be false to-morrow. Here, at least, the student moves from step to step, from premiss to inference, from the known to the hitherto unknown, from antecedent to consequent, with a firm and assured tread; knowing well that he is in the presence of the highest certitude of which the human intelligence is capable, and that these are the methods by which approximate certitude is attainable in other departments of knowledge. No doubt your mere mathematician, if there be such a person,—he who expects to find all the truth in the world formulated and demonstrable in the same way as the truths of mathematics, is a poor creature, or to say the least a very incomplete scholar. But he who has received no mathematical training, who has never had that side of his mind trained which deals with necessary truth, and with the rigorous, pitiless logic by which conclusions about circles and angles and numbers are arrived at is more incomplete still; he is like one who lacks a sense: for him "wisdom at one entrance" is "quite shut out;" he is destitute of one of the chief instruments by which knowledge is attained.

Nor is it enough to regard mathematical science only in its far-reaching applications to such other subjects as astronomy and physics, or even in its indirect efficacy in strengthening the faculty of ratiocination in him who studies it. There is something surely in the beauty of the truths themselves. We are the richer—even though we look at them for their own sakes merely—for discerning the subtle harmonies and affinities of number and of magnitude, and the wonderful way in which out of a few simple postulates and germinating truths the mind of man can gradually unfold a whole system of new and beautiful theorems, expanding into infinite and unexpected uses and applications. And as we look on them we are fain to say as the brother in Comus said of a kind of philosophy which was novel to him, and which perhaps he had hitherto despised, that it is indeed

> "Not harsh or crabbed as dull fools suppose,
> But musical as is Apollo's lute,
> And a perpetual feast of nectar'd sweets
> Where no crude surfeit reigns."

XII. GEOGRAPHY AND THE LEARNING OF FACTS.

Object to be kept in view.

IN considering the subject of Geography we shall do well to repeat our former question—Why teach it at all? What purposes do we hope to serve in including it in our course? We have seen in reference to the teaching of languages and of mathematics, that although there were two distinct purposes to be kept in view,—the practical and useful application of those studies on the one hand, and the indirect mental discipline afforded by them on the other,—in both cases the second object was more important than the first. Here, however, it is not so. Our main object in teaching Geography is to have certain facts known, because those facts, however learned, have a value of their own. We live in a beautiful and interesting world; one marvellously fitted to supply our wants and to provide us with enjoyment; and it seems fitting, if we would be worthy denizens of such a home,

It is mainly useful as information.

that we should know something about it, what it looks like, how big it is, what resources it contains, and what sort of lives are lived in it. To know these things is the first thing contemplated in teaching Geography. If there be mental exercise, and good training in the art of thinking and observing to be got out of these studies, they are the secondary not the primary objects which we want to attain. Yet even here in the one department of teaching in which mere information, as distinguished from scientific method or intellectual training, is relatively of the most importance, there are as in other subjects right ways and wrong, intelligent and unintelligent methods. The incidental and indirect effect of teaching on the formation of mental habits is not to be disregarded; and though much of the result we hope to gain belongs to the region of the memory only, we shall be all the better for enquiring whether there is not also room here for appeal to the judgment and to the imagination; whether in short, Geography may not be a really educational instrument, as well as a mass of facts which have to be mastered and committed to memory. *Yet partly as discipline.*

It is the more important to think thus about Geography; because I have observed that this is the favourite subject often with the worst and most mechanical teachers. It is in fact the one subject in which the maximum of visible result may be attained with the minimum of intellectual effort. To give a few names of places and point them out on the map, is the easiest of all lessons, and, what is more to the purpose, it makes a great show when it is learned. And when I ask a teacher what is the favourite subject of pursuit in his school and he answers Geography, and afterwards I find that what is called Geography merely means the knowledge of a number of names, and the power to identify their position on the map, I always draw a very unfavourable inference respecting the character of that school as a place of intellectual training; for I know that such information may have been imparted without the least exertion of educating power on the master's part; and that a good deal of such knowledge may easily *Geography generally considered easy to teach.*

co-exist, in the learner's mind, with complete mental inaction and barrenness.

Nevertheless, it would of course be wrong to undervalue the subject, (1) because, if rightly taught, it may be very stimulating and helpful to mental development, and (2) because it is better to have it taught wrongly than not taught at all. For even information as to the position of places on the globe is useful to everybody; useful especially to Englishmen, who are fortunate enough to be 'citizens of no mean city' and to belong to a race which dominates a larger portion of the earth's surface, and has more varied and interesting relations with distant parts of this planet, than any other people in ancient or modern times.

How to arrive at right methods. Now in considering how we should teach Geography, we may usefully fall back on a principle we have had before—that we should begin with what is known and what is near, and let our knowledge radiate from that as a centre until it comprehends that which is larger and more remote. This principle is specially applicable to the present subject. You want of course to give right general notions of the surface and configuration of the earth, and of the meaning and use of a map. The best way to begin is to draw a little ground-plan of the schoolroom; and put into it one after another, as the children watch you and make their suggestions, the desks, the tables, and other articles. Train them to observe you as you draw, and to correct you if you put a door into the wrong place, or make the line which represents a desk of disproportionate length. Then try a map of the surroundings of the school-room, its playground, the street in which it stands, the principal roads near, and put in one after another the church, the railway station, a river, a bridge, and other familiar objects, at the same time inviting each child to put into the map in its proper place his own home. Thus they will learn the meaning and right use of a map, and will feel a good deal of interest when they see it grow before them under your hand as you draw it on the board and fill in one detail after another. Without some such previous explanation and actual manufacture of a plan before the eyes of the children, an ordinary printed map of Europe or of the world is nothing but a coloured enigma.

So a lesson on Home geography (*Heimathkunde*) ought to be the first in a geographical course. Perhaps you will expect that I should be logical, and proceed in the same way, next to the general geography of the parish, afterwards to that of the county you live in, its physical features, its chief towns and industries, then to a description of England, afterwards to that of Europe, and finally to a general description of the world on which we live. But I am not prepared to push a theory—even one which is founded, as this is, on a true principle— to an impracticable and absurd extent. We must learn to think of the various parts of knowledge, not only in what seems their natural sequence, but also in the light of their relative importance. You cannot measure the value of geographical facts by a formula, or say that their importance diminishes as the square of the distance. The earliest geographical ideas may well be those derived from home and its surroundings; but these ideas require next to be properly localized, and shewn in relation to the size and form of the world itself. A good way of doing this is first to help the children to refer the map of the school and its surroundings to an ordnance map of the parish or division of the county; then to mark this larger division on a map of England, afterwards to shew England on a map of Europe, and then

Home Geography.

identify it on a globe. Thus by degrees you establish a sense of proportion, and help the child to see his bearings, so to speak, and the place he occupies in the universe. And this done, it is well to proceed at once, by the help of a globe, to give some very general notion of the shape and size of the earth, the distribution of land and water, the four cardinal points, and the meaning of the simpler geographical terms.

Lessons on earth and water. To make these lessons intelligible, you will need pictures or diagrams, or better still, you will mould before the class, in sand or soft clay, a rough representation of a range of mountains, or a group of mountains and valleys, and will then shew how water comes out from the glaciers or springs, and sometimes tumbles over steep rocks, and finds its way down the sides, and so forms a river or a lake. You will draw out from them that a river will be more rapid in a steep valley, more sluggish when it flows through a flat country; that it will increase in size as it goes on and receives affluents, and that the wide openings by which it enters the sea are often convenient places for the formation of harbours and for commercial stations, but that sometimes it cannot find free course, and is pent up between hills and rocks. Then you will explain the points of the compass, not of course in the way which some teachers adopt, of referring everything to a wall map, so that when you ask children to point to the North, they point up to the ceiling; but by leading them to know the actual bearings of their own school-room and the surrounding streets and buildings. This may be done most easily by inviting them to step out with you at 12 o'clock on a sunny day, and mark in the playground the line which the shadow of an upright stick projects. It is not a bad plan to have this line painted on a part of the floor of the school-room, so that the points of the compass shall be distinctly known, and every time N. S. E. or W. is mentioned the scholars shall be required to point to it. You will do well to have in the school a mariner's compass, and to draw attention (1) to the immense importance, especially to sailors, of knowing their bearings at times when neither sun nor stars are visible to indicate them; and (2) to the wonderful fact of the tendency of the magnetic needle always to point one way—a fact as you know wholly unique in the whole range of physical science, in itself inexplicable, and at the same time most curiously adapted to solve one practical problem in navigation, which as far as we know is absolutely insoluble by all the manifold resources of science in other directions.

These elementary lessons on the size and general conformation of the earth may at first include an explanation of the equator and the poles, and of the fact that the sun, though seen by us always to the south at noon, is seen by people on the equator over their heads, and by people living south of the equator to the north of them at that hour. But it is not at this stage expedient to include any details about meridians, or the measurement of latitude and longitude by degrees. Afterwards it seems best to proceed at once to the general geography of England, with especial reference to the county in which the scholar lives, to its boundaries, its hills and rivers and principal towns. Next in order should come a general description of the chief countries of Europe and of the chief British Colonies; afterwards the geography of Scotland and Ireland in detail, and then latitude and longitude and as much else in the way of descriptive geography as you have time to give. In French schools, little manuals of what we should call County

Order of geographical facts.

Geography are in extensive use. There is one for each Department; but a little prefatory chapter about the size and shape of the world, the points of the compass, and the position of France upon the globe, forms a common introduction to all the manuals alike. There is a map of the Department; an account of its name, size, limits, area, its chief industries and geological formation, its natural productions, the famous men it has produced, its historic associations, and a great number of details, administrative, statistical, commercial; besides engravings of the cathedral of the *chef-lieu*, and of any buildings, monuments, or scenes for which the Department is famed. The French child is generally expected to master this little manual of the part of the country in which he lives before he is asked to learn topographical details about more distant places.

No necessary sequence of difficulty or importance in this subject.

So much for the order which seems, on the whole, most reasonable for the teaching of geographical facts. You will not expect this order to be preserved in text-books, and there is no subject in which it is more necessary for you to emancipate yourselves from the domination of text-books, and to arrange your facts for yourselves. For in Reading and Writing there is at least a sequence of difficulty; in Grammar and Arithmetic a philosophical sequence; and in History the sequence of chronology. But in Geography there is no sequence at all. Except by accident or association, there is no one topographical fact which is more important than any other, or which can claim to be learned earlier. To every man his own home and his own work make the centre of the world; and the value for him of all information about the rest of the world is entirely relative. It is not absolute. Yet text-books, after all, cannot recognise this, and are bound to give in equal detail facts, some of which, from this point of view, are important and some unimportant. The compilers of such books must arrange their facts in a certain order so as to be easy of reference. So they are fain to begin with Europe, then to take Asia, then Africa, then America, and finally Australia; and in the hands of a mere routine teacher, the patient school-boy,—'for sufferance is the badge of all his tribe,'—is forced to learn a good deal about Denmark and the Caucasus, about the Burrampooter and the Lake Nyanza, before he knows anything of New York or of our colonies.

It is therefore essential that the teacher should exercise his own choice and judgment in respect to the order of importance and of usefulness in which geographical facts are related, and therefore to the order in which they should be taught. That order will not be always the same. At this moment the geography of the S. E. of Europe and the N. W. border of India is more useful to us than the geography of the Spanish peninsula. At the beginning of the present century it was otherwise. You have to ask yourselves not only what are the facts to which the books and the examiners assign prominence; but what are the facts which it behoves a well-instructed and intelligent person to know. A great many names and statistics are learned by school-boys which no educated person is expected to know, or would care to remember if he did. To some extent this is inevitable; but there would not be so large a discrepancy between the sort of knowledge a school-boy has from his lesson-book, and the sort of knowledge of which you yourself feel most the need when you mingle in society, or read a piece of contemporary history, if teachers thought oftener of the occasions on which geographical knowledge is wanted and the uses to which it has to be put.

The teacher to fashion his own order.

352   *Geography and the learning of Facts.*

I will add some miscellaneous suggestions about geographical teaching :—

Use of a globe.   Take care to have a globe always at hand to correct the erroneous impressions which are always produced by flat maps, because they are plane representations of parts of a spherical surface, and because they are almost necessarily on very different scales. A map of England hangs by the side of one representing Europe, and is generally quite as large, and there is no way of rectifying the impression except by shewing the position and relative sizes of both on the globe. The old globes in stands are far less useful than portable globes. I need hardly say that a celestial globe is utterly misleading. Use the globe also to shew how the sun comes on to the meridian of different places in succession at different times; and from the fact that the earth revolves round its axis in 24 hours, deduce a rough general rule for determining the times at different places, according to the number of degrees of longitude. For example you point out that in our Lat., $51\frac{1}{2}$ N., the value of a degree of longitude is to that of a degree of longitude on the great circle of the equator as 37 to 60. Say approximately then that as the great circle as well as all the parallels of latitude are divided into 360 degrees, and as the earth revolves in 24 hours, 15 degrees on any parallel represent an hour's difference of time; but $15°$ on the equator mean $\frac{1}{24}$ of a circumference of 24000 miles: hence on the equator 1000 miles E. or W. represent a difference of one hour in time. But in our latitude we may reckon that about 600 miles E. or W. represent an hour; and that thus a telegram from Constantinople which is about 30 degrees to our E. or about 1200 miles, and which has the sun on its meridian two hours before us, may be delivered in London apparently at an

The use of Maps.

earlier hour than that at which it is transmitted. At this moment, e.g. it is 2 o'clock here, it is 4 at Constantinople, and it is quite conceivable that a message transmitted thence and dated 4 p.m. might reach us by 3.

Call attention in every case to the scale of a map, and give exercises in judging approximate distances. Shew e.g. in a map of England what number of miles is represented by the length and breadth of the sheet respectively, and lead the scholars to exercise themselves in determining the approximate distances between towns or other places. In fashioning for yourself a map, such as has been described, of the parish or district in which the school is situated, seek to enlist the services of the children themselves; and invite them to suggest other objects or places, and when they make a copy of it, require each scholar to put into position and to mark specially the site of neighbouring buildings, as well as of the school, and their proper distances. *Judging distances.*

Do not rely wholly on maps with names printed on them. The habit of setting children to look vaguely for a place on the map, which merely means looking for a certain printed word, is very useless. Nothing is learned of the true position of countries by this means. The best maps are outline maps on a large scale without names; and best of all those which are drawn in outline by the teacher himself on a black board, and filled in item by item, as each new fact is elicited by questions or descriptions. And do not forget that the knowledge of the mere names and positions of places is worth little or nothing unless the scholar has some interesting associations with them. If you are asked to learn the name and position of a place *per se*, the memory refuses and rightly refuses to retain it, because it has no organic connexion with anything else you know or wish to know. The best know- *The use of Maps.*

ledge of mere topography is gained incidentally, in connexion with reading lessons, with lessons on history or familiar objects, with the tracing of imaginary voyages and travels. The map should be always at hand, and when referred to in order to identify a place, of which you are learning something else than its mere geographical position, is seen to serve a useful purpose and helps to impress a fact on the memory. Indeed every time a map is referred to for such a purpose, something is done to impress geographical facts on the eye. And this itself is a useful lesson.

Physical Geography. Connect from the first Physical geography with that which is called Political. By the former of course is meant the geography of the world as it would have been if man had never lived on it; by the latter, is meant all those facts which are the result of man's residence on the earth. But the second class of facts is nearly always to be accounted for by a study of the first. The earth is wonderfully designed for human habitation. It is our granary, our vineyard, our lordly pleasure-house. In some parts nature is bountiful, in others penurious; over some she sheds beauty, in others she offers material prosperity: at one place she hides treasure, at another she spreads it on the surface. In some places she invites neighbouring peoples to intercourse, in others she erects impenetrable barriers between them: in some she lures the inhabitants to peaceful prosaic industry, in others terrifies them by displays of awful and inexplicable forces. And even of those regions which she seems not to have designed for our use—the torrid desert, the lonely rocky mountains, and the mysterious ice-bound regions of the poles, may we not truly say, that they too are part of the bountiful provision she has made for our many-sided wants? For they impress and exalt our imagination, they minister to our sense of beauty; and yet at the same time they humble our pride, and make us feel that there is something more in the world than is immediately and easily intelligible to us. They give us in short a sense of the mystery, the vastness and the sumptuousness of the world, which is very necessary for a right estimate of our own true place in it.

And with such considerations before us we see how curiously the mere physical conditions in which man is placed determine his habits, the life he leads, the kind of societies he forms, the character and the history of different races. *Its influence on national character.* You think of our own fair island—'this precious stone set in the silver sea'—you turn the globe into the position in which England is at the top and in the centre, and you see how advantageously she is placed, in the middle of the hemisphere of land, near enough to partake of all the advantages of Western Europe, but far enough off to encourage in her people the sense of independence: with her extensive coasts, her excellent harbours, her hardy yet temperate climate—a climate of which Charles II. said that it allowed men to go about their work with less interruption and on a greater number of days than in any other country in the world; and you cannot dissociate the thought of our insular position, our climate and resources, from the character and history of our people. Take Holland as another example. It is low, flat, moist; hence suited for pasture rather than tillage; hence favourable for the rearing of cattle, for butter and for cheese; and because so low that the encroachments of the sea can only be prevented by enormous and costly dykes, and by incessant watchfulness, its inhabitants are distinguished by foresight and endurance, by thrift and industry; and because for these reasons the scenery is flat, dull and uninspiring, the inhabitants are *not* distinguished by the wealth of their imagination or the splendour of their literature.

Illustrations of the effect of physical conditions on national history. Look again at the vast alluvial plains watered by the Nile, the Euphrates, the Indus and the Yellow River. The soil is rich, the wants of the people few, the inducement to exertion small. There you have found in all ages of the world a teeming population, agricultural and stationary, attached to the soil, conservative in habits of thought, easily subjugated and kept in subjection; and there have been appropriately placed the great despotic monarchies. On the other hand look at small maritime states like ancient Phœnicia, Greece and Italy, separated by ridges of hills, inhabited by little communities, isolated, yet compelled sometimes to fight for their liberty; hence jealous of each other, and hence self-asserting, their history full of records of intestine divisions, and of heroic struggles for liberty. Here you cannot fail to see a connexion between the free vigorous life of early Rome and of the Etruscan and Greek republics, and the physical conditions under which the people lived.

Or contrast with the great communities which have formed the Egyptian, the Assyrian, and the Chinese Empires, the state of the people on the Great Tartar steppes where herbage is scanty, where a settled habitation is almost impossible, and where nomadic, and therefore restless, wild, suspicious and warlike races find an appropriate home. In like manner you may trace the influence of climate in some countries by the way in which it enervates the labourer, and in others by the way in which it impels him to exertion and calls out his higher qualities. You may even see how the aspects of nature affect the national character in many places: for where physical phenomena are equable and uniform as in temperate climates, and man has learned how to control nature, you find often a resolute self-reliant people, proud of their strength and encouraged to use it; but in regions subject to frequent earthquakes and convulsions, where the aspects of nature are formidable, and its phenomena on too vast a scale to be subject to human control, you will often find a timorous superstitious people, without enterprise or any of that cheerful hope which animates to intrepid discoveries and great inventions.

I must not stay now to pursue this line of enquiry. Those of you who would like to see how fertile such researches are, will do well to read the second chapter of Buckle, 'on the influence exercised by physical laws over the organization of society and the character of individuals,' and in that chapter you will find, amidst much which is crude and speculative, and a few unverified and hasty generalizations, many valuable truths and suggestive hints. In Mr Grove's excellent little book on Geography you will find similar material. But I want you to feel that physical geography is the basis of all true geographical teaching; that here, as in other subjects, it is not only the details which are of value, but also the tie that binds them together, and that all mere topography—all political administration and commercial geography must ultimately connect itself with a right understanding of such matters as soil, climate, shape, size, geology, and natural resources. An acquaintance with geology is especially helpful in making physical geography understood. A teacher who is skilled in this subject, and can make a right use of the comparison between a geological map and an ordinary map of the same country, will give new meaning to his lessons; will be able to say, e.g., how the presence of chalk or sandstone may be recognized by the contour of the hills.

Historical associations.

Another kind of tie by which mere geographical facts may be bound together is the historical. Associate therefore, as often as possible, the description of places with the memory of events which have happened in them. "The man," says Johnson, "is little to be envied whose patriotism would not gain force on the plains of Marathon, or whose piety would not grow warmer among the ruins of Iona." Association between the configuration of a region, and a great event that has happened in it, is a great help to the recollection both of history and geography too. Nobody can read Livy's account of Hannibal's passage over the Alps, Macaulay's siege of Londonderry, Mr Carlyle's account of Frederick the Great's campaign in Silesia, or of Cromwell's battle at Dunbar, without seeing a new meaning in geographical study. And if in the neighbourhood of your school, there is any spot or building rendered illustrious by its association with historical events, seek as far as you can to explain that association, and give interest to it.

Maps.

As to maps, the use of which is so obvious that they need no recommendation from me, I have only four observations to make: (1) That they are of more value after your descriptive lesson has been given than before; (2) That pupils should not always draw the whole maps as given in the books, but parts of them—say the south coast of England, or the county of Yorkshire—just so much of the map as is necessary to illustrate or fix the particular lesson you have given, such a map being often on a larger scale than that in the atlas; (3) That a physical map, one which merely represents the course of water, the position of coal, the prevalence of pasture land, or some one special fact, is often valuable; and (4) That it is never well to permit colouring or ornamentation of any kind until the outline has been carefully examined and found to be correct.

Further, the skilled teacher of geography ought to cultivate in himself the power of vivid and picturesque verbal descriptions of the aspect and contour of any country he has seen. You can only acquire this power by caring about such details. It is well known that Arnold's lessons to his Sixth Form on history, when he was reading Livy or the *Anabasis*, were wonderfully vivified by his striking descriptions of the country in which the events took place. When he travelled, he kept his eyes always open, and it is remarkable how often in his letters to old pupils, who had gone to some distant country, he wrote to them hinting at the kind of things which an observant man would do well to look for, and asking for the result of such observation for his own information and enjoyment. Here is part of such a letter written to Mr Gell, who had gone to reside in Tasmania: "I hope you journalize largely. Every tree, plant, stone, and living thing is strange to us in Europe, and capable of affording interest. Will you describe to me the general aspect of the country round Hobart Town? To this day I never could meet with a description of the common face of the country about New York or Boston, or Philadelphia, and therefore I have no distinct ideas of it. Is your country plain or undulating, your valleys deep or shallow, curving, or with steep sides and flat bottoms? Are your fields large or small, parted by hedges or stone walls, with single trees about them or patches of wood here and there? Are there many scattered houses, and what are they built of—brick, wood, or stone? And what are the hills and streams like—ridges or with waving summits,—with plain sides or indented with combs, full of springs or dry, and what is their geology? I can better fancy the actors when I have a notion of the scene on which they are acting."

Power of verbal description.

Illustrations of descriptive geography.

If you want to know how life-like the description of a country can be made, read the description in Scott's *Antiquary* of the sea in a storm, the account of the Western Hebrides in Johnson's *Journey*, or Black's *Princess of Thule*, Mr Bryce's account of his ascent of Mount Ararat, or some of the passages from Hooker's *Himalayan Journals*, from *Peaks, Passes, and Glaciers*, or Wills's *Wanderings in the High Alps*. In this department of teaching it is pre-eminently needful that the teacher should keep his mind open to the events which are going on around him, and try to utilize the information which newspapers and new books of travel and adventure will furnish. His own experience will also help him to give vividness to his lessons. After a foreign journey he will invite his class to have a lesson on the Rhine, on the aspect of the mediæval towns of Belgium or North Italy, on an Alpine ascent, on the English Cathedrals, or the English Lakes. Photographs and pictures from illustrated journals will all help to give reality to the impressions you want to convey.

Do not complain of all this as desultory and unscientific. Remember that this is the one subject in which you are least bound to preserve any predetermined order, and in which miscellaneous lessons, provided they are vivid and interesting, are quite legitimate, and serve the intended purpose well. That purpose is to increase the scholars' interest in the world in which they live, to awaken their observant faculties, and to help them to recognize the order, the wealth and beauty of the visible universe. If you do not do this, Geography is a very barren subject, even though your scholar knows with impartial exactness the populations, and the latitude and longitude of all the capital cities in the two hemispheres, and the names and lengths of all the rivers in the world. But if you do this, you may be well content with almost any portion of the subject which is thoroughly mastered. For he who has been led even by accident, or the course of your special experience, to examine one or two countries, to get a mental picture of their physical characteristics, and to see how those characteristics affect the situation of the towns, the nature of the products, and of the trade, the employments, the government, and even the idiosyncracies and the history of the inhabitants, will have in his mind a typical example of the way in which geography ought to be studied, and will—as the reading and experience of after life cause him to be interested one by one in other countries—know better how to obtain his information and to make a right use of it.

Although all these considerations point to the necessity of oral lessons, I am far from saying that you should be content with the somewhat vague and miscellaneous impressions which such teaching, if relied upon alone, is apt to leave. Text-books, catalogues, tables, statistical statements, and memory-work have their value, and must be resorted to by all who wish to give definiteness to such lessons. But the time to use them is after the oral teaching, not before it or instead of it.

Geography is a good type of that class of subject *Fact-lore.* which has its chief value as information useful in itself, and which has comparatively few ramifications into other regions of acquirement or of intellectual life. There is a large mass of serviceable knowledge which does not come within the ordinary range of school subjects, and which yet a school might help to impart—knowledge about the substances we see and handle, about the objects around us, about the things which are going on in the world. We must not, in our zeal for those parts of instruction which are specially educative, lose sight of the value of even empirical instruction about these things. To impart facts is not a teacher's highest business, but it is a substantial part of his business. It is so, not merely because it is disgraceful for a person to be ill-informed about common things. It is pitiable to measure the worth of any knowledge merely by the degree in which it is a credit to gain it, or a discredit to be without it. The best reasons for seeking to give to your pupils a good basis of facts are that the possession of them is very useful; that all future scientific generalization pre-supposes them; that they furnish *pabulum* for the thought and the imagination; and generally that life is rich and interesting in proportion to the number of things we know and care about.

So at every part of a school course provision should be made for instruction in matters of fact which lie outside the domain of the regular book-subjects. What is known in the German schools as *Natur-kunde* and *Erd-kunde* fulfils this description most nearly. But both terms are restricted as to the class of topics they include. The information or useful knowledge, now in view, can perhaps be best described by the hybrid term *Fact-lore*. It has, no doubt, a definite educational purpose, and may help to develop faculty in a useful way. But its main object is to supply facts, to excite an intelligent interest in the common objects and phenomena which surround the scholars, to teach them how to see and to handle, and to draw simple inferences from what the senses tell them, and to prepare the way for the later and more regular study of science.

Object lessons. In Infant Schools this aim is accomplished by means of what are called Object lessons. A teacher takes a piece of Coal in his hand and asks the children what it is. He asks them to look at it, and tell him what they can see, that it is black and shiny; to handle it, and to find out that it is hard, that parts of it are easily rubbed off, and that it is of a certain weight. He asks what would happen if he put it into the fire, and he finds that they can tell him not only that it burns, but that there is a gaseous flame at first, afterwards a duller burning, and finally nothing left but cinders. He makes them tell its familiar uses. Then he asks if they would like to know something more about it, and he proceeds to shew a picture of a coal mine, to describe the gloom, the heat of the pit, the mode of getting down to it and out of it, and the dangers to which miners are exposed. He tells them how many ages ago all this coal was vegetable matter; he produces a piece of coal, which he has chosen because its fossil character is well marked; he lets the children look at and handle it, and then he shews pictures of the various trees and plants which formed the material of which coal is formed. And at the end his black board presents a summary of the lesson, shewing in succession the qualities, the uses, and the history of coal, and the mode of procuring it.

All this is well, and in the hands of a good teacher fulfils valuable purposes. It has in it some of the characteristics we have insisted on for all good teaching. For it kindles the interest of children by dealing at first with what is fairly within the range of their own experience, and yet before it is finished it carries them into a new region distinctly beyond that range. It is well calculated to awaken curiosity and to stimulate the observing and enquiring faculty. But, then, like so many other good things, it is apt to degenerate. Pestalozzi, David Stow, and the Mayos have laid down rules; model lessons have been published, and accordingly it is

Their short-comings.

my lot to hear a number of so-called object lessons, which are very barren of any useful result whatever. Because Dr Mayo's book on object-lessons gives a list of the qualities of glass—*Brittle, Transparent, Hard, Fusible, Useful, Inelastic,* &c., one is doomed to hear one object after another treated in exactly the same way, and to see it solemnly recorded on a board that a cow is graminivorous, or that an orange is opaque. The blackboard exercise is a great stumbling-block to unskilful teachers. They are told beforehand at the Training Colleges that it should present at the end of the lesson a complete summary, arranged under heads, of all that the lesson contains, and so they exhibit throughout the lesson a much greater anxiety to get the matter on to the board than to get it into the understanding of the scholars. Moreover, lessons of this kind are apt to be desultory and unconnected, and to be given at irregular intervals. And although they occur in the Infant Schools with marked advantage under the name of 'object-lessons,' they are often discontinued altogether for the whole of the interval between the Infant School and the time when the regular teaching of Science begins.

Subjects for object and other collective lessons.

But through all that interval some conversational lessons on familiar objects should be regularly given. They are needed, as we have said, partly to keep up that habit of observant interest in what is going on in the world, which the Infant School tries to convey, and partly to furnish the materials for future reflection and generalization. The subjects available for this purpose are innumerable; it will suffice here to indicate a few of them :—

(a) *Common substances*—glass, iron, coal, silk, money.
(b) *Natural History*—trees, flowers, animals, wood.
(c) *Food and how to produce it*—wheat, wine, oil, meat, honey.
(d) *Manufactures*—glass, steel, cloth, pottery.

(*e*) *Natural phenomena*—wind, storms, change of seasons.

(*f*) *Forms of human employment*—farms, vineyards, life in a factory, a mine, a military station, a studio.

(*g*) *Construction of simple machines*—a hinge, a knife, a lock, a watch, a pump, a gas meter, a pulley.

(*h*) *Incidents of travel*—a voyage, a mountain ascent, a polar expedition, a shipwreck.

(*i*) *Local events*—a famine, harvest, an exhibition, a festival, the construction of a new railway.

(*k*) *Events in National and Municipal life*—the opening of Parliament, a general Election, the Assizes.

(*l*) *Buildings and public monuments*—their architecture and their history.

I am far from wishing to assign a prominent place in a school-course to miscellaneous topics like these. But some room should be reserved for them in your programme. One half-hour's lesson in the week will suffice, and if your assistants are encouraged to take their turns in preparing lessons on subjects with which they are specially conversant, and will carefully preserve their notes, with a record of the day on which the lesson was given, you will find many incidental advantages accrue both to them and to the school.

In forming a plan for such a course for a term you will do well, without making it so inelastic as to exclude any interesting topic which may unexpectedly arise, to have in view that most of the lessons of this kind ought to serve as helps and preliminaries to the ultimate teaching of science, and should therefore be given in a pre-determined order, and with distinct reference to the regular instruction in science which is intended to be taken up hereafter. The scientific spirit and the scientific method should be present, but should not be obtruded. Scientific nomenclature should be sparingly used, and then *They should have a definite though not a visible scientific purpose.*

only when the need for it has become apparent. It is well that children should be made, even in the lowest classes, to think about the formation of a glacier, the boiling of water, or the making of iron into steel. But each separate fact of this sort should be correlated with some other which is like it, so that an elementary perception at least may be gained of the nature of physical law.

They should have unity.

Be careful to consider beforehand how much can be reasonably taught in the thirty or forty minutes you mean to devote to the lesson. The great fault of most of these lessons is that they attempt too much. Consider well that you have need at the end of each division of the subject to recapitulate very carefully, and to make sure that you have been followed; and that certain facts must be accentuated by repetition and by writing. Do not let any one lesson contain a greater number of new truths or thoughts than can be fairly grasped and remembered in one short effort; or than can be so fitted together as to leave on the mind a sense of unity and completeness.

Use of a black board.

Let your black-board summary grow up under your hand as the lesson proceeds, and use it rather for recording your principal conclusions, at the end of each division of your subject, than as a promise,—or menace,—beforehand of what you are going to do. I have often heard little collective lessons, in which the teacher says 'now we are going to speak of the "qualities;"' and then the word "qualities" is gravely written down on the board; and one by one various adjectives are evolved and written underneath it. All this chills and repels the child and destroys his interest in the lesson. He does not care about "qualities." He is not prepared to enter with you into an investigation of the qualities of a thing which at present he knows and cares little or nothing about.

But if you will first interest him in the thing and make him care about it; then discuss in succession its various parts, attributes and uses; there is no harm afterwards in recalling what has been learned, and saying "We have in fact all this while been finding out the qualities of this thing; and we will write them down." But it is not at all necessary to enumerate all the qualities of each object as it comes under review. When this is done, the lessons on objects soon become monotonous and very wearisome. Each object has some one quality which it illustrates better than another. Thus a chief characteristic of glass is its transparency, of india-rubber is its elasticity, of gold is its ductility; and in a lesson on each of these objects it is well to take the opportunity of calling attention to the one. or two technical terms which the particular object best illustrates.

No single lesson should have many technical or unfamiliar terms in it. But every good lesson should at least introduce the learner to two or three new technical words, and make a distinct addition to his vocabulary. Every lesson in fact brings to light some name or formula which is specially characteristic of the new knowledge you are imparting, and will form a good centre round which recollections will cluster and arrange themselves after you have done. All such characteristic terms, names and formulae, should be very distinctly written and underlined; special attention should be called to them, and *re*called at the end of the lesson; and the question may be asked "What use did we make of this word?" Not unfrequently too the half-dozen words which have been written down, may be usefully copied down to furnish material for the full notes that have to be prepared as home lessons, and to serve as a reminder of the order in which those notes are to be arranged.

Technical terms.

Arrangement of each lesson in sections. In thinking out the plan of any such oral lesson, it is very necessary to break it up into definite portions, that you may know at what points to recapitulate. But it is not necessary to reveal the whole of that plan to your scholars. Your lesson must have a beginning, a middle and an end; and will be mapped out in your mind with this view; but there is no need to divide it ostentatiously into parts beforehand, and say what you are going to do. A logical division of the subject is necessary for you as part of your plan of workmanship, but the consciousness of this division is not always helpful to the learner. He is not concerned with the mechanism of teaching or with the philosophy of your art. He has to be interested, to be led by ways which he knows not, but which you know, and have clearly predetermined. But to begin with any display of the logical framework of your lesson is to begin at the wrong end. Not to speak it profanely, do not some of us,—patient hearers in church—feel a little rebellious when a preacher announces beforehand his intention to divide his discourse into three parts, and then to conclude with an appeal and application. We feel instinctively that the whole mechanism of firstly, secondly, and thirdly, was perhaps very useful to him when marshalling his own thoughts in his study beforehand, but that it is no business of ours. We are very ready to welcome the facts, the teaching, the reasoning, the inspiration, it may be, which he has to give; but the more he can keep his homiletic apparatus in the background the better.

To go back for a moment to our main subject and recapitulate. We have had before us *Descriptive* Geography, which aims at helping learners to realize the aspects of nature; *Commercial* Geography, which concerns itself with manufactures and cities, with population and productions; and *Physical* Geography which seeks for the truths and general laws underlying these mundane phenomena. The first addresses itself to the imagination, and is the most interesting and attractive. The second appeals to the memory, and is the most serviceable in the intercourse of life. The third alone enlists the aid of the understanding, and is for this reason the most valuable as a part of disciplinal education,—the only branch of the subject in fact which deserves to rank as science. We are to keep these three forms of geographical teaching separately in view and to take care that each receives the consideration which is due to it and no more.

The recognition of this distinction will not be without its value in connexion with the whole class of information of which Geography may serve as a type. I hope hereafter to say something more as to the place which physical and inductive science should hold in a high or complete course of instruction. Here, however, I must be content to have left on your mind the impression that even in the lower department of school life, the claims of such knowledge ought to be distinctly recognized, and that they are best recognized by planning out in regular series conversational and pictorial lessons on useful and interesting facts, and on what the Germans call *Natur-Kunde*, but what we may more fully describe as the phenomena of common life, observed and taught in a scientific way.

XIII. HISTORY.

Purpose of historical teaching.
IT is clear that there is a sense in which a large part of the History taught in schools belongs to the region which we have designated *Fact-lore;* because it is learned mainly as information interesting and serviceable *in se*. But the proportion of lessons in History which have a disciplinal, moral, and reflex value as part of education is somewhat larger than in Geography. We shall all be agreed that history is not a mere narration of facts in their chronological order; but that to know it is to know events in their true causes and connexion, to have our judgment exercised about the right and wrong of human actions as well as the sequence of events, and to recognize some principles underlying the mere facts.

"History," says Fuller, "maketh a young man to be old without either wrinkles or grey hair, privileging him with the experience of age without either the infirmities or the inconveniences thereof." But the history that will correspond to this description must be something which far transcends in its scope the scanty record of royal alliances, of wars, and of dynastic struggles, which constitute the staple of school text books. So unsatisfactory is the intellectual result of much of the labour spent on teaching history to children, that many authorities of great weight advocate the omission of the subject from the course of school instruction altogether. Herbert Spencer says, "That kind of information which in our schools usurps the name of History—the mere tissue of names and dates and dead unmeaning events—has a conventional value only : it has not the remotest bearing on any of our actions, and is of use only for the avoidance of those unpleasant criticisms which current opinion passes on its absence." And he proceeds to shew that the fundamental objection to such masses of facts as children are often required to learn is that they are undigested and unorganizable, that there is no unity about them, and therefore no scientific value in them. Now for my part, I do not think this a reason for omitting the study of History from a school-course, but simply for inquiring how the facts can be so taught, as to serve a real educational purpose.

Nothing is easier than to begin by denouncing the school-books. No doubt they are all more or less unsatisfactory. Yet it is difficult to know how if they honestly fulfil their intended purpose they could be otherwise. They must, of course, be crammed with facts; and as style must always be more or less sacrificed to the desire for excessive condensation, they are seldom very readable or interesting. Moreover, since the writer of a school-book naturally strives to narrate as large a number of authentic facts as his space will contain, it is often unavoidable that important and unimportant facts will be recorded with the same amount of elaboration, and that thus, much which is of little value will be minutely set forth. The more systematic text-books also attempt a classification of the main facts of each reign, under such heads as " birth and parentage of the sovereign, eminent men, wars," etc. Now, although this looks methodical, *Text-books.*

and is, indeed, very helpful to the utility of the book considered as a work of reference, it destroys its value as a book to be read. Nobody acquires a knowledge of historical facts in this formal way. To begin with classification of this kind, is to begin at the wrong end. It is only after a general interest has been awakened in the story of the reign, and after some of the important facts have laid hold upon the mind, that the use for such classification arises, or the necessity of it is felt.

Books useful, but to be subordinate to oral teaching.

In spite, however, of these drawbacks, the use of textbooks is a necessity, if you would avoid vagueness and teach history methodically. Let the book, however, be treated as supplementary and wholly subordinate to oral lessons, and be used for reference and home study mainly, and then it falls into its proper place. But if it be used in class at all let it be read aloud, explained, amplified, commented on, and made vividly interesting, before you require any of it to be learned as a lesson. Then by way of giving concentration and definiteness to what you have taught, it is not unreasonable to expect the bare facts as given in your school manual to be got up, copied out and remembered, though not of course to be learned by heart in the precise words of the book.

Two distinct aims.

These two objects (1) To make history stimulating to the imagination, and suggestive to the thought of the scholar, and (2) To furnish a good basis of accurate and well arranged facts for future use and generalization, will be before you. To care about the first object exclusively is to incur the risk of a relapse into slovenly teaching, and vague picturesque impressions. To be satisfied with the second only is to incur the yet greater risk of turning the most interesting and humanizing of all studies into a dull and joyless mnemonic, and so of giving your pupil a distaste for History which will last for life.

Has it ever occurred to you to ask how it is that so many of us have a much clearer knowledge of the history of the Jews, than of our own annals? Is it not because the Bible is in one respect the model of all history? Look at it without reference to its higher claims, simply as a piece of narrative. Consider how it is that it conveys to its readers so clear and full a knowledge of Jewish history during many centuries. There is, for example, a period of about one thousand years, from Abraham to Rehoboam, and how is the history of the time told? We have first the story of the patriarch's personal career. We are led to understand his character and his motives; we see him as the centre of a scene in which pastoral life is attractively portrayed, and which affords us glimpses of the patriarchal government, of life and manners, and of the social and domestic conditions of the time. In like manner we see Isaac and Jacob with their families and their environments; and then the narrative, disdaining to go into details about lesser matters, expands into a copious biography of Joseph, whose personal history and fortunes make us incidentally acquainted with the state of Egypt, its government, its political economy, and many facts of great interest, which, had they been tabulated in a book of outlines, we should not have cared to learn. The history then passes over a long uneventful period of nearly 400 years with scarcely a sentence, and again becomes full and graphic about the Exodus and the journey in the wilderness, investing even the details of legislation with a special interest by connecting them with the person, the character, and the private life of the lawgiver, Moses. And thus the story is continued, sometimes passing over a long interval of inaction or obscurity with a few words of general description, or a list of names; but fastening here and there on the name of Joshua, of Gideon, of Samuel, of Saul, or of David, and narrating the history of the times in connexion with the circumstances of his life. The current of human events, as it is described in the sacred writings, is not like that stream of uniform breadth and depth which text-books seem to describe, and which we see often depicted in chronological charts. It rather resembles a picturesque river, diversified in its aspect as it glides along; now feeble and narrow, now broad and swelling; hemmed in at one part of its course by overhanging rocks, and at another spreading out into a vast lake; becoming again contracted, or like the Arcadian river of Alpheus disappearing altogether from view, then re-appearing, and yet flowing ceaselessly; now past a fair city or a noble castle, and anon through a vast region which is flat and comparatively barren; continuous but irregular; possessing unity but not uniformity; inviting the traveller to glide rapidly along at one time, and to linger long and tenderly over some memorial of vanished greatness at another.

Because it concentrates attention on fixed points.

Who does not see that such a narrative precisely corresponds to the real picture of a nation's history? In the life of a people there are always great epochs of change and activity occurring at irregular intervals, and so marked and characteristic, that if they be once understood, all the lesser details and the intermediate events become intelligible through their means. Moreover, the Scriptural story of the people of Israel curiously resembles the actual knowledge which even the most accomplished historical scholar possesses. That it is adapted to the needs and conditions of the human understanding will be evident to any one who will take the trouble to recal his own experience, and will remember how he has secured one after another certain fixed points of interest, has grouped round them, little by little, the facts which he has subsequently acquired, filled up the intervals of time between them by slow degrees, but to the last has continued to retain his hold on these fixed points, and to refer every new acquisition to some one or other of them.

I do not say that it is possible or even desirable that school-books on English History should be made to conform to the Bible type in this respect. It is not safe to leave to the compilers of such books the task of determining what part of our annals shall be overlooked, and it is quite necessary that teachers should themselves exercise some discretion in this matter, selecting and adapting their historical lessons according to the age and capacity of the children, and to the probable duration of their stay at school. But if it be, indeed, certain that careful readers of the Bible obtain a truer insight into the character and polity, the manners, progress, and national life of a people than is to be secured, with the same degree of attention, from a modern compendium of English history, the fact is certainly a significant one, and will be found to suggest some important practical inferences.

Of these the most obvious is, that it is better to master the great and eventful periods than to go on continuously in the way suggested by the form of a text-book. We said in Geography that there was absolutely no sequence for mere topographical facts; that no one such fact had any real priority over another except in so far as accident or association rendered it useful to the learner. Hence it was expedient for the teacher to emancipate himself completely from the text-books, and to teach the mere facts of political Geography in any order he liked. But in history there is of course a natural order, that of

The great epochs should be learned in detail first.

chronological sequence; and if life were long enough, and if all events and periods were equally worth studying, this would be the true order of teaching. But as a matter of fact the order of the relative significance and value of events, is of far more importance than their chronological order; and does not in any way correspond to it.

The first lessons.

How then should we begin to teach English History? Not certainly by plunging at once into the story of Julius Cæsar and the Druids; nor by giving a number of dates to be learned, to form a framework for pictures we mean to paint. I should first give a short series of lessons either orally, or from a well-written reading book if I could find one, with a view to make some simple and fundamental historical ideas intelligible—a *State*, a *nation*, a *dynasty*, a *monarch*, a *parliament*, *legislation*, the *administration of justice, taxes, civil and foreign war*. Scholars would thus see what sort of matter History had to do with, and would be prepared to enter on the study with more interest. Then a general notion should be given of the number of centuries over which our History extends. A general outline of the period of time to be covered is necessary in order that each fact as it is known may be localized and referred to its due position among other facts. Thus a sort of Time-map divided into 19 centuries is roughly constructed, on the same principle as that which would lead the teacher to lay down the meridian lines of a geographical map before he drew it and filled in all its parts. But as soon as this is done the task of selection begins. He is by no means bound to follow blindly the course prescribed by the text-book. On the contrary it will be far better to fix upon the most characteristic periods, to cause them to be studied with fulness and exactness, and to reserve the chronicle of the less notable reigns until afterwards. The times of Egbert, of the Conqueror, of Elizabeth, of the Protectorate, of Anne, and of George III., are turning-points in our history. The person who understands these well is, as far as history is concerned, a well-informed man, even though he is unable to repeat in due order the list of sovereigns, and to tell their relationship to each other. For all the higher purposes contemplated in the study, a thorough acquaintance with the state of England in one or two of the most eventful periods is of far more value than a superficial knowledge of the entire history. The latter may be forgotten. There is no germinating power in it; it will neither grow when the pupil carries it with him into the world of books, and of news, and of conversation; nor furnish material for reflection in solitary hours. But the former serves as a nucleus for future acquirement. A learner who has been led to pay special attention to one period, and to master all its *differentiæ*, carries away with him from school not only a fund of knowledge which will hold together and retain its place in the mind, but also right notions of what historical investigation really is, and of the manner in which the annals of a period should hereafter be studied. In short, it is by no means necessary that a pupil should take with him into the world all the facts of a school-history, but it *is* necessary that he should be provided with a taste for historical reading, and with both the power and the disposition to study the subject systematically for himself. And this object is far more likely to be obtained by judiciously selecting and dwelling on the prominent epochs than by the ordinary routine method.

A good deal is often said as to the value of chronology, which some have called one of the eyes of History.

Chronology.

Mr Fearon says dates are to History what the multiplication table is to Arithmetic. I am not quite prepared to admit the analogy in this case. The multiplication table has two characteristics: It is constantly wanted in every sum we work; and every fact in it is of equal value. That 7 nines are 63 is just as liable to be wanted in Arithmetic as the fact that 2 sixes are 12. But of dates we may safely say that there are many degrees of usefulness in them, some being very valuable and others very worthless. And if the principle I have tried to lay down is a true one in regard to the study of periods of history, that principle will lead us to discriminate between the dates which we may wisely take some trouble to retain as fixed points in the memory, and those dates which none but a pedant would value, and which even a well-instructed man would not care to remember. I may confess to you—though with real deference to the judgment of many who think differently—that I do not see much use in knowing the date of an event, without knowing something about the event itself. If we learn dates as and when we study the events, the two together have a meaning and a value; but the date itself and apart is of little worth. If we examine our own mental history a little we shall find that such chronology as we thoroughly know and has become part of our permanent possessions connects itself with prominent and interesting events and has been added to piecemeal as our knowledge of history increases. We study a fact, become sensible of its importance, and *then* we remember the date.

Dates to be learned as facts are known, not independently.
For example, in English History the dates of Julius Cæsar, the first Christian mission, Alfred, the Conquest, John and Magna Charta, Edward III. and Chaucer, Henry VIII. and the Reformation, Elizabeth and the Armada, the execution of Charles I., the Restoration, the

Revolution of 1688, the great year of Minden and Quebec, the loss of America, the French Revolution, Waterloo, are the fixed centres round which a large part of our annals may be said to revolve.

I know an admirable teacher of History who relies most on good oral lessons for teaching this subject; but who has adopted the plan of printing on a card, and placing in the hands of every boy, a list containing in bold type about twenty of these dates. There is thus a sort of *carte du pays* under the eye of the scholar, and as each fact is named, it is identified with one of the dates. Then for an advanced class, there is a larger card, which contains some 50 dates in all, the original 20 being in somewhat larger type, and the minor or new dates smaller. In the highest class a third card is used with about a hundred dates, or 50 in addition to those already known; the whole being printed in three kinds of type to mark the different degrees of importance in the events. Thus certain fixed landmarks are put before the scholars. As each event is discussed and learned, they associate the date with it; and as they read more of history, they establish fresh halting places, put each new fact into its proper interval, and so these intervals become smaller and smaller. This seems to me to be the rational way of learning dates, as adjuncts to our historical knowledge, as helps in systematizing and arranging facts which we already know, not as facts or pieces of knowledge of any value in themselves. *Practical use of this principle.*

Observe to what absurd devices we are led when we accept chronology as a thing to be learned *per se*. One teacher maps out the ceiling of a room, and associates dates with particular portions of a diagram, the form of which is supposed to be printed on the learner's brain. Another invents a *memoria technica*, in which certain *Mnemonic systems of chronology.*

letters stand for figures. Thus you have the first syllable of a sovereign's name, and then a syllable made up of letters representing the date of his accession. And in some ladies' schools I have met with systems of metrical chronology, short rhymed couplets so formed that the initial letters either of the alternate words or of the nouns shall represent the years in which the facts occurred. e.g.

> "The Saxon is doomed, a Duke England obtains
> And the second William ascendancy gains,
> Tyrrel's arrow attacks and the Sage acquires sway,
> Then Adela's offspring the men long obey."

In this doggrel the initial consonants in each line give respectively the dates 1066, 1087, 1100 and 1135. You will observe the extreme difficulty which hampers the poet in the construction of lines like these; and that after all the result is not only almost unintelligible but even the names of the two monarchs Henry and Stephen referred to in the latter lines are not given. It would be easy to multiply examples of these systems of artificial memory, but to me they all seem open to one fatal objection. We are establishing with the names of historical personages a number of associations, some absurd, some unmeaning and all false, and burdening the memory of children with something in itself confessedly useless, for the sake of something useful supposed to be embodied in it. We assume that the mechanical contrivance will keep the date in the mind, and that afterwards the date will remain fixed, and the mere mechanism drop out of sight altogether. Now experience shows that the opposite result happens. Persons who have been taught on these mnemonic systems have often told me in later life that they have remembered the doggrel verses, or the queer syllables, but have forgotten the key. So the end has not been attained after all. On the whole therefore I have little faith in any device for remembering dates, except becoming interested in the events to which the dates relate.

An obvious inference from the view of historical *Biography.* study here presented is, that Biography is too much neglected, and its value as an adjunct to history too little regarded among schoolmasters. Yet every one knows how much more attractive is the life of a person than the history of mere events. There is a sympathy and a human interest awakened, when the career of a man is discussed, which can never be excited in any other way. The great charm of the Bible history as we have seen lies in the fact that it is a series of biographies, held together by a thread of narrative, it is true, but deriving its main interest from the circumstance that we see human fortunes in progress, human passions at work, and real human characters, whom we can love, or criticise, or admire. Our knowledge of the Bible history is primarily a knowledge of Moses, or David, or Paul, and only incidentally of the political and social condition of the people among whom they lived. Yet, though incidental only, this knowledge is very real, and is none the less valuable because it is held in the mind by its association with what we know of the chief personages, and their character and career. A good teacher will therefore do well occasionally, when his scholars are reading the history of a given period, to interrupt the regular course, and to select some representative man of the epoch, gather together from all sources particulars respecting him, and give two or three special lessons on his life. Suppose, for example, that the life of William of Wykeham is taken to illustrate the reign of Edward III. Let the pupils be led by a brief sketch to take an interest in the man, to follow his fortunes, to estimate his character. Let them see pictures of the buildings which he erected, be reminded of Winchester, of Windsor, of New College, Oxford, and of Saint Cross, and so get a glimpse of the educational machinery, the architecture, and the social habits of the period. Let them be directed to books in the library, in which anecdotes and illustrative matter may be found. Let them investigate the public and political questions with which his life was associated, and then be desired to prepare a sketch as full as possible, and in a narrative form, embodying all they have learned about Wykeham.

The result of such an exercise will be found to justify the interruption of the ordinary historical lessons for one or two weeks. A pupil who, in this way, has been directed successively to the biography of Alfred, of A'Becket, of Chaucer, of the Earl of Warwick, of Cecil, of Bacon, of Cromwell, and of Pitt cannot fail to have an extensive acquaintance with the current history of the times in which these men lived; while the form in which that knowledge is acquired will be found better adapted than any other to retain a permanent hold on his mind. In the selection of the typical man of each age, the teacher will be guided, partly by his own tastes, and partly by the materials at his command and the books to which he has access. It is of more importance that he should choose some one man in whom he is himself interested, and whose biography he has the means of making copious and lifelike in his lessons, than that he should be guided by any selection which another could make for him.

Examples of studies in biography. The materials for such biographical lessons are very abundant in our language, and may be found with little trouble. Our literature is rich in admirable monographs, such as Bacon's Henry VII., Lucy Hutchinson's Memoir of her Husband, Johnson's Sir Francis Drake, Earl Russell's Life of his ancestor Lord Russell, Fox's James II., Carlyle's Cromwell, Southey's Nelson, John Forster's Five Members, Leslie Stephen's, or Mrs Oliphant's Sketches of the 18th Century, Trevelyan's Life of Macaulay. In Walton's exquisite book of Lives, in Fuller's Worthies, in Macaulay's Biographies, in Lord Brougham's Statesmen of the Time of George III., in Miss Strickland's Lives of the Queens, and in Mignet's Mary Queen of Scots, also, abundant material for pleasing and graphic pictures of life and manners may be found. Very often, too, a diligent teacher will find that by piecing together the facts stated in two or three different books about some one person, he will be able, without difficulty, to prepare a short lecture or oral lesson, the preparation and arrangement of which will be as useful to himself as it will prove beneficial to his pupils. If this practice be occasionally adopted, it will surprise him to find how the facts relating to the history of an age will cluster and organize themselves round a great man's name, and how systematic the knowledge of history will thus become. I have already referred to the use of a library for these purposes and to the way in which after the teacher has given a brief sketch of the life he may set his pupils to fill up that sketch in writing, with all the particulars they can glean from different sources, until they have, in fact, partly produced the biography themselves. He will afterwards require the information thus given to be reproduced by the class in a regular form, with the facts arranged chronologically, or tabulated under various heads, besides an estimate of the character of the person whose life has been selected.

Lessons on great writers.

A very interesting series of lessons might be given on great books; their influence on History, and their value (1) as indicative of the thought and intellectual movement of the age which produced them, and (2) as helping to shape the thought or the policy of the age which succeeded: *e.g.*

Bede.	Spenser.	Dryden.	Addison.
Langland.	Shakespeare.	Hume.	Burke.
Chaucer.	Bacon.	Adam Smith.	Fox.
Sir P. Sidney.	Milton.	Gibbon.	De Foe.
Raleigh.	Algernon Sidney.	Swift.	Southey.
Hooker.	Locke.	Johnson.	Brougham.

There is not one of these whose life, with a notice of his most important books would not throw much light on the political history and the social life of the time in which he lived. So a series of lessons on great inventors: as

Roger Bacon, Newton, Stephenson, Boyle, Watt,

would serve a like purpose.

Historical readings.

As another means of giving life and reality to lessons on this subject, occasional Historical Readings may deserve a prominent place. The teacher may advantageously assemble his class once a week or fortnight, and give to them a half-hour's reading from some book which illustrates the period to which the recent historical lessons refer. Such readings should generally be anecdotal and dramatic in their character, as it is more necessary that they should deepen and intensify the impression of some one characteristic incident of the time, than merely go over the ground which has been covered by the historical lessons. If a teacher in his own private reading keeps his eyes open for passages such as will serve this purpose; if he will systematically mark them, or make a memorandum of the places in which they occur, it will surprise him to find how they will multiply upon him. Not only in books ostensibly written as histories, but in many others, there will often occur a striking and effective passage, which will, if well read, be sure to excite interest.

It would be an endless task to point out the passages in Palgrave, Hume, Macaulay, Froude, Clarendon, Carlyle, Freeman, Miss Martineau, Guizot, or Mr Knight, which are characterized by special interest or pictorial beauty, and which, if read to a class that had been recently engaged in accumulating the dry details of a given period, would be sure to help the imagination, and stimulate the intellectual activity, and strengthen the memory of the pupils. A teacher's own taste will generally be a safer guide in the adaptation of his readings to his ordinary teaching, than any formal list which could be set down here. But in making his selection he need on no account confine himself to grave books of history; one of the Paston Letters, a *naïf* anecdote from Froissart, a gossiping letter of Horace Walpole, a paper from the Spectator, an extract from Evelyn's Diary, a chapter of De Foe's History of the Plague, or even a passage from one of honest Pepys' grotesque confessions, will, if wisely chosen, and read at the right time, be found to play an important part in fastening the record of some great event on the mind. Nor should the stores of our poetical and dramatic literature be overlooked. What a freshness and life will be given to the dry bones of an ordinary narrative of the Wars of the Roses, if the teacher treats the learners at the end of their task with two or three well-selected scenes from Shakespeare's Henry IV. or VI. Who would not understand the whole life, costume, occupation, and *morale* of Edward III.'s contemporaries all the better for hearing

Examples of historical Readings.

Chaucer's inimitable description of some of the Canterbury Pilgrims, or even a page of Sir John Mandeville's quaint book of Travels? I cannot expect a mere routine teacher to take all the trouble I am recommending, but to all who desire to give to English history that place in their pupils' affection and interest which it deserves, I would say, Make your own miscellaneous reading tell upon your school lessons. This is a good rule in relation to all subjects. Attention to it serves to widen the range of illustration at command, and to impart vivacity and force to all the teaching of a school. But in history the rule is especially applicable. Let a teacher read one or two of Wordsworth's sonnets about the introduction of Christianity into England after his class has learned the story of Augustine's mission; or Macaulay's poem on the Spanish Armada, when that subject has been studied; or a pungent passage from Dryden's Absalom and Achitophel, or Milton's sonnet on Cromwell, or a ballad from Percy's *Reliques*, and the advantage of the practice will soon become apparent to him. Within the range of such reading also may fairly be included good extracts from Ivanhoe or Waverley, from the Last of the Barons, from Westward Ho, or Henry Esmond. It may be said, perhaps, that all this is not history; that children come to school to learn facts, not fictions, and that there is danger of relaxing the bonds of intellectual discipline by introducing into the school-room material of so unscholastic a character as a play of Shakspeare, or a novel of Sir Walter Scott. But to this it may be easily replied that my recommendation only extends to the contrivances by which school-book work of the ordinary kind is to be supplemented, not to any device for superseding it. We are not to use the imagination as an alternative, but as a help to the memory.

Nevertheless, there is one sense in which poetry embodies as much historical truth as history itself. We ought to know, not only what can actually be verified as fact but what has been believed to be fact. That Romulus and Remus were suckled by a wolf, that Agamemnon sailed against Troy, that Numa was instructed in the art of kingship by the divine Egeria, that Arthur gathered a goodly fellowship of famous knights at the Round Table at Caerleon, that William Tell shot at the apple on his son's head, may, or may not, be authentic facts which will stand the test of historic criticism. But they were for ages believed to be facts. The belief in their truth helped to shape the character and the convictions of after-ages. They had therefore all the force of truths, and they deserve study just as much as facts which can be historically verified. From this point of view Sophocles is as true and profound as Thucydides; Shakespeare as true as Bacon, and Chaucer as Froissart. Schiller in his *Wallenstein* is as much a historian as in his *Thirty Years War*. Thackeray when he wrote *Esmond*, after taking pains to saturate his own mind with the literature, the manners, and the history of the eighteenth century, was as true a historian, as when he prepared his more matter-of-fact critical estimates of the lives of Addison and Steele and their contemporaries. When Ben Jonson wrote *Catiline and Sejanus*, or Shakespeare *Julius Caesar* and *King John*, they were historians, in even a truer sense, than if they had sought without the aid of the vivifying imagination to give a bare narrative of such facts as could stand the test of destructive criticism. Considered as a picture of real life, is not Sir Walter Scott's Marmion or Ivanhoe as true a thing as his History of Napoleon? When the author wrote the last as mere task-work for the booksellers, he very conscien-

The poetry of history.

tiously consulted his authorities, and sought to produce an orderly and connected narrative. But when he wrote Ivanhoe, he studied the manners and incidents of the age, and sought to penetrate his own fancy with a picture of its doings, and habits, and modes of thinking. We will not stop to inquire which is the more interesting production: that is a question which has long been settled. But which, for all practical purposes, is the truer book, and the more important contribution to our history? Surely there is a higher truth than the truth of mere detail, and that is just what the compiler of annals misses, and the man of poetic genius seizes and retains. The power to recognize this truth, and "to show the very age and body of the time, his form and pressure" without concealment and without exaggeration is a rare one; it requires not only knowledge of actual occurrences, but philosophic insight enough to distinguish between characteristic and exceptional events, and imagination enough to select and adapt the materials, and to give unity and verisimilitude to the whole picture. And it is surely as important to us, and as helpful to the studies of our pupils, to know what impression the history of an age has conveyed to a man of genius, as to know what facts a laborious compiler may have collected about it[1]. Do not let us, then, despise the help which

---

[1] On this point Archdeacon Hare has a pregnant remark:—
"The poet may choose such characters, and may bring them forward in such situations as shall be typical of the truths which he wishes to embody, whereas the historian is tied down to particular actions, most of them performed officially, and rarely such as display much of character unless in moments of exaggerated vehemence. Indeed, many histories give you little else than a narrative of military affairs, marches and counter-marches, skirmishes, and battles, which, except during some great crisis of a truly national war, afford about as complete a picture of a nation's life as an account of the doses of

poets and even novelists can afford us in history. They appeal, in a way in which no mere historian can, to the imagination of children, and to that love of pictures and of dramatic incident, which is so strong in early youth. If judiciously and occasionally used, they make the story of the past a more real, living thing, and they may do much to increase the interest and pleasure which is felt by pupils in historical study.

And so it will be seen that of the two modes of teaching history; that which relies mainly on the dry bones of a text-book and that which seeks to clothe these bones with flesh and blood, and give to them vivid and picturesque reality, I greatly prefer the second. But we must not be insensible to the faults of this method if it is pursued alone. It may easily become loose and desultory, it is apt simply to awaken interest and animation, without taking means to secure that this interest serves a real educational purpose. We have before shewn that picturesque teaching sometimes leads the pupil to mistake interesting general impressions for real knowledge; and worst of all that it encourages him to indulge in sweeping historical generalization without knowing accurately the data on which it is founded. All this should be known and guarded against. It can only be effectually prevented by localizing each fact as it is learned in your Time-map, and by building up a fabric of dates, names, Acts of Parliament and other details, which will sustain and justify the historical impressions you wish to convey.

Dangers of relying on picturesque teaching only.

Keeping this in view, you may be well content to set before yourself, as the main object in teaching History, the kindling of a strong interest in the subject, rather than the covering of a large area of mere information.

physic a man may have taken, and the surgical operations he may have undergone, would be of the life of an individual."

For if you do the second and not the first, your pupil will not be likely to pursue the subject for himself. But if you do the first and not the second, all the rest may be safely left to his own discretion and reading. History we may observe is the one subject of school instruction in which your pupil can do best without your aid, and which when you have once kindled an appetite for it, you may most safely drop out of your regular course, and leave to take care of itself.

Lessons on the government and constitution of England.

Lastly, I would urge upon you the importance of lessons on the government and constitution under which we live. It is absurd to find children knowing about the Heptarchy and the Feudal System, and yet not knowing how our present Parliament is constituted, and what are its duties and functions. Not unfrequently I find in examining candidates for the public service students who really possess a good deal of book-knowledge about the Constitutions of Clarendon and the Act of Settlement, shewing lamentable ignorance as to the way in which laws are made at this moment; telling me *e.g.* that all Acts of Parliament originate with the Commons and must go to the Upper House for sanction.

Lessons on the duties as well as the rights of citizenship.

In giving a series of special lessons on our laws and constitution you will not be content with Hallam and Creasy and the constitutionalists who seem to think that the whole of the History of England resolves itself into a struggle between Crown and people, and into the gradual assertion of the right of representation, and of what Carlyle cynically describes as the 'liberty to tax oneself.' That indeed is a very important part of English History but it is not the whole. The removal of the impediments to printing and to the diffusion of knowledge; the history of Slavery and of its abolition; the gradual disappearance of religious disabilities, economic and commercial reform, the imposition and working of the Poor Law; the provision for National Education in the form of ancient endowments, and afterwards by public grants; the reform of the representation; the growth of literature, the extension of our Colonies—all these subjects deserve to be looked at separately, and to furnish the material for special lessons in the lecture form. Indeed I am disposed to recommend that concurrently with the study of history by periods, you should arrange a series of lessons, according to subjects, on this wise:

The Crown and its prerogatives.	Taxes.
The House of Lords.	A general election.
The House of Commons.	Treason.
The history and progress of an Act of Parliament.	The Army.
	The Navy.
Ministers.	The Civil Service.
Judges.	Public Trusts.
Magistrates.	The administration of towns and parishes.
Municipal Corporations.	
Juries.	Guardians of the poor.

Such a course, carefully prepared, and well illustrated by historical examples, will have the incidental effect of making the scholars sensible of the responsibility which will hereafter devolve upon them as members of a free community; a state which asks the voluntary services of her citizens in the administration of justice, in the management of public trusts, and in the conduct of public business. Every boy should be made to feel that unbought services will be required of him as member of parliament, magistrate, guardian or trustee, and that it will be honourable to render them. This sense of civic duty seems to me the necessary correlative to that consciousness of civic rights which Hallam and the constitutional writers are apt to dwell on so exclusively. You will find materials for such lessons not only in Hallam and Creasy, but also in Bagehot, and in Sir Erskine May.

Patriotism. Nor ought we to overlook the necessity for so teaching as to inspire our scholars with a love and admiration for the country we live in and for the institutions by which we are governed. It used to be the fashion much more than now, for Englishmen, especially after dinner, to talk much of our glorious and unrivalled constitution in Church and State. No doubt there was in all this an element of insular boastfulness, and perhaps a little selfishness and vulgarity. But after all patriotism is one of the things which our teaching ought to cultivate—a rational and affectionate regard for the country in which we have been born, and for the privileges we enjoy in it:

> "It is the land that freemen till,
>   That sober suited Freedom chose,
>   The land where, girt with friends or foes,
> A man may speak the thing he will.
>
> A land of settled government,
>   A land of just and old renown,
>   Where freedom broadens slowly down
> From precedent to precedent.
>
> Where faction seldom gathers head,
>   But by degrees to fulness wrought
>   The strength of some diffusive thought
> Hath time and space to work and spread."

And in every English school something at least should be done to make the scholars proud of this glorious heritage, and to animate them with a noble ambition to live lives and to do deeds which shall be worthy of it.

XIV. NATURAL SCIENCE.

It ought to be frankly premised here that I have had no special teaching experience on the particular subject of this lecture such as gives me any right to dogmatize upon it. Nevertheless, we may with advantage consider the reasons for including such studies in our school-course, and the place they ought to hold in it, for it is, after all, out of such considerations that all discovery of right methods ought to arise. The skilled teacher must look at the whole of the large domain of the inductive sciences, those which depend on observation and experiment, and ask himself how they are related to his special work. Until recently studies of this kind were rarely or never recognized as necessary parts of a liberal education. Even now they are fighting the way to recognition by slow degrees and against some opposition. The staple of school and university instruction down to our own time has consisted of the study of language and that of pure science, including mathematics and logic. On the part of the great majority of educated men in England, whose own minds had been formed in this way, there has been a strong feeling that all true intellectual training was to be had in connexion with these time-honoured studies. It is true that new and most fertile fields of investigation have been discovered and explored. Geology has brought to light marvellous facts respecting the history of our

The place of physical science in school education.

earth, electricity and magnetism have been applied in unexpected ways to the comfort and convenience of man, biologists have investigated the conditions and resources of life, astronomers have discovered by *spectrum analysis* the nature, and even the chemical composition of the heavenly bodies; the chemist, the physicist, the botanist have each in his turn revealed to us some hidden forces in nature, and taught us how those forces may be made available in enriching, beautifying and ennobling the life of man on the earth.

The triumphs of science not largely due to school or university teaching.

It must be owned however that these researches have owed little to the direct influence of our schools and colleges. It is not by academically trained men, as a rule, that the great physical discoveries have been made. Those who have made these discoveries have broken away, so to speak, from the traditional life of a student and a scholar; have quitted the study of books and betaken themselves to the study of things. They have come face to face with the realities of life, have seen and handled the materials of which the visible world was composed, and thus have in time formulated an entirely new body of knowledge, very different in kind from that which is to be found in the books which are called learned. And hence, there has been for a time an apparent antagonism between the men of learning and the great discoverers, inventors and experimenters in the world of physical science. Centuries ago Socrates taught that the only studies which were of real value to man were those which related to his own nature and destiny, to his duty as a member of a family or a state, to the culture of his own faculties and to the relation in which he stood to the gods and to his fellow men. As to investigations into the order of the heavens or into the nature of physical laws, he thought them presumptuous and sterile. The gods, he thought, had purposely concealed such knowledge from men, while in regard to the means whereby the material comfort of man might be increased he would certainly have dismissed such considerations as mean and ignoble, fit only for a tradesman or mechanic, but unworthy of a philosopher.

Some such feeling has survived among learned men, even down to our own time. You may find it in such utterances as 'The proper study of mankind is man.' It is shewn in the greater importance assigned to metaphysics and philology, to logic, to mental, moral and theological speculation, and to pure or deductive science, in all systems of academic instruction; and in the distrust felt by many, even down to our own time, of experimental science as something material, loose, and just a little commercial and vulgar.

In all the recent investigations into the condition of the great Grammar Schools nothing was more striking than the position of complete inferiority occupied by the study of the physical sciences, even in the rare cases in which they were recognized and admitted into the curriculum. The head-master was generally what is called a classical man, and naturally regarded success in his own department as the best test of a boy's possession of a gentleman's education. The teacher of physical science was only an occasional lecturer, poorly paid and little considered, and boys who devoted much time to that branch of study were understood to have lost caste in some way, and to fall short of the best ideal which the school sought to set up for its scholars. Nor can it be wondered at, that cultivated men felt a little reluctance to admit the physical sciences to honourable recognition as an integral part of the school course. For much of what called itself science was essentially unscientific in its

Position of natural science.

character and in its methods of investigation. The teachers were often mere specialists, entirely deficient in that general cultivation which alone enables a man to see his own subject in true perspective and proportion, and to teach that subject in the most effective way. A series of lectures illustrated by an orrery, on the "sublime science of Astronomy" in ladies' schools, or a few amusing experiments in chemistry in boys' schools have often represented the teaching of science, and have been regarded very justly by head-masters and mistresses with a little contempt. "May I ask you," said Lord Taunton, as chairman of the Schools Inquiry Commission to a schoolmaster who in his evidence was giving rather unusual testimony to the interest his boys took in physical science, "what department of science interests the scholars most?" "I think," was the reply, "it is the chemistry of the explosive substances." Of course, a bright light and a noise are amusing to schoolboys, but their interest in such phænomena is no very strong proof that they are learning science in any sense, or for any really valuable purpose.

Modern views as to the claims of this subject.

And all this time there has been an increasing number of thinkers and students, who, while not destitute of that general intellectual training which is to be got in the old beaten track of classics and mathematics, have gone out into the wide domain of physical research and found it more fruitful than they expected. And they say to those who live in the academic world—the world of books and of scholarly traditions, "You are mistaken in supposing that this is a merely material and practical region, while yours is essentially intellectual. There is here a body of truth, of the highest practical utility no doubt, but also of the greatest value for educational purposes. The laws and principles by which the facts of the material world may be explained and co-ordinated are quite as uniform, quite as beautiful, and as far-reaching in their applications as any of the laws of language or the truths of mathematics. Moreover, the processes of thought required in the study of these questions are just as rigorous, just as stimulating, stand in just as close a relation to the intellectual needs of a well-instructed man as those involved in the older studies. You can make the teaching of physical science as fruitful, as thoroughly disciplinal for all the higher purposes contemplated in a liberal education as the teaching of Greek or of geometry if you will only first recognize the possibility of making it so, if you will encourage skilled and accomplished men to take up this branch of instruction, and are ready to give them the same *status* and encouragement which you now give to accomplished teachers of philology or history. Enlarge your conception of what a liberal education means. Let that conception include some acquaintance with the actual constitution of the world we live in, of the forces which surround us, of the framework of our own bodies and the laws of matter and of life, and make provision for these things, as well as for those facts and speculations which are to be found only in books, and which have hitherto usurped the name of scholarship."

There is surely great force in this appeal, and no one of us who has any power of controlling the education of the young can properly disregard it. We may wish, for our own parts, that some Huxley or Tyndall had enunciated this message before we ourselves went to school, for then we might discuss with greater advantage the true claims of physical science and the place it should hold in a school course. But of the legitimacy of those claims there can be no doubt, and it may be well for us to try to analyse them.

Reasons for these claims.

(1) *The utilities of physical truths.*

For, consider in the first place the immense practical usefulness of some knowledge of physical science and the number of unexpected applications to the use and service of man which are found to grow out, not only of every new discovery, but of every honest effort to submit old discoveries to the test of new observation and experiment. One man studies carefully the nature of light, tries experiments with refracting media, with reflecting instruments, separates the rays, ascertains the chemical effect of certain rays on certain substances. He does all this perhaps from mere interest in the discovery of new and beautiful truth, and has no suspicion that speculative experiments of this kind can serve any immediate practical purpose. But soon it appears that what he has done enables us to find some new illuminating power, or that out of it grows the whole art of photography, with all its wonderful developments, its power to record what is beautiful, to represent to us a beloved countenance, to register the phænomena of nature, and even to aid in the detection of crime. It would not be difficult to shew that almost every new and valuable invention from the spinning-jenny to the telephone, which has increased the control of man over nature, economized his time or added to his comfort, is the product of scientific knowledge, and often of experiments and researches which had at first no merely utilitarian purpose, but were undertaken with the sole and simple object of discovering the secrets of nature, and revealing truth. And there is not a single lesson by means of which you can convey to a child a strong interest in any one department of physical science which may not develop itself, as it works and germinates in his mind, into results and discoveries of unexpected value, and add enormously to the resources and to the enjoyments of mankind.

A second reason for giving to a learner some acquaintance with nature and with the laws which govern her phænomena is the extreme beauty of the truths themselves. Even if nothing useful were to be gained by the study of science, it would be a shame to pass our lives in this well-ordered and harmonious world, and catch no echoes of the music of its laws; to be surrounded every day by mysteries, none of which we ever tried to penetrate; to possess a body fearfully and wonderfully made, and to cast no thoughts on its structure, its physiology, the functions of its parts, the marvellous adaptation of means to ends; to find oneself conveyed 60 miles an hour through the agency of steam, and one's thoughts conveyed a thousand times faster by the agency of electricity; and yet to know nothing of the nature of these forces or the laws of their action; to walk amid flowers and rocks, glaciers and avalanches, and to remain uninstructed and untouched by them. · But it is mainly by the conscious and systematic study of natural science that we learn to notice all these things and to draw right inferences from them. It must be *knowledge* of nature after all that is at the basis of a true enjoyment of her works, and a true reverence for her Author.

(2) *Their beauty and intellectual attractiveness.*

"Is it not," says Herbert Spencer, "an absurd and almost a sacrilegious belief that the more a man studies Nature, the less he reveres it? Think you that a drop of water, which to the vulgar eye is merely a drop of water, loses anything in the eye of the physicist who knows that its elements are held together by a force which if suddenly liberated would produce a flash of lightning? Think you that what is carelessly looked upon by the uninitiated as a mere snow-flake does not suggest higher associations to one who has seen through a microscope the wondrously-varied and elegant forms of snow-crystals? Think you that the rounded rock marked with parallel scratches, calls up as much poetry in an ignorant mind as in the mind of a geologist who knows that over this rock a glacier slid a million of years ago? The truth is, that those who have never entered on scientific pursuits are blind to most of the poetry by which they are surrounded. Whoever has not in youth collected plants and insects, knows not half the halo of interest which lanes and hedge-rows can assume. Whoever has not sought for fossils, has little idea of the poetical associations that surround the places where imbedded treasures were found. Whoever at the seaside has not had a microscope and aquarium, has yet to learn what the highest pleasures of the seaside are"

(3) *The disciplinal value of the inductive process.* But after all, the main reason for teaching some branch of physical science is to be found in considering the sort of processes by which the truths of such science are investigated, and the faculties of mind which are exercised in the course of physical investigations. For in the first place a student of any branch of natural history or science must learn to observe carefully, to use his eyes and to know the difference between facts which are abnormal and facts which are typical. Then he must come into actual contact with realities, must handle objects, must try experiments, must question matter and nature closely, must wait and watch, must invent new forms of test until he is quite sure that he has hold of the true answer. And when he has observed the phænomena, he has to reason from them inductively, and pass from particular facts to the general laws which underlie and comprehend them. We saw in considering the subject of mathematics that certain axioms and data being postulated the reasoner proceeded deductively, and out of them unfolded in due sequence an orderly series of particular truths. We saw that mathematics afforded a discipline in pure logic in passing from premiss to conclusion, in detecting fallacies in reasoning, and generally in deducing special inferences from wide, comprehensive and admitted truths. But in the physical sciences the mind proceeds in exactly the opposite direction. You begin with the particulars, you combine and co-ordinate them, and at

last, when you have enough of them, you arrive at some general proposition which includes them all. This generalized truth, which is the starting-point in mathematics, is the goal in physics; and whereas researches in the physical sciences tell you how to get at your major premiss, or your universal truth, it is the business of mathematics and of logic to tell you what inferences you may deduce from such a truth when you have got it. So all investigations into the phænomena of nature must begin by the observation of facts. The observer must put his facts together, must group them according to their resemblances and differences, and see what they have to say for themselves. He must have no prepossessions, no wish to twist the facts into a particular direction. His theory or final generalization when it comes must have been actually suggested by the facts.

This kind of procedure is very different from that by which the mind acts in syllogistic reasoning; and it is not wonderful that in the middle ages, when people began to study the nature of matter and of force, they should have imagined that all truth about these things was to be obtained in the same way as the truths about geometry, by the methods of Aristotelian logic. Hence, even the early physicists hampered themselves with certain dogmas, or first principles, which seemed to them self-evident, that "nothing can act where it is not," that "nature abhorred a vacuum," that there was somewhere in the world a substance which would transmute all metals into gold, that some source of perpetual motion could be discovered, or that "out of nothing nothing can come." It was against this kind of assumption that Bacon and Newton protested. *Hypotheses non fingo* — said the one. "Man," said the other, "is the minister and interpreter of nature." It is his business to find out what she actually says and

Inductive reasoning.

does, and when he has thus acquired data and facts enough he may construct upon them a theory that shall fit the facts, but not before.

The search for causes, A well-known line of a Roman poet expresses the desire of mankind to know the causes of things, "Felix qui potuit rerum cognoscere causas." You naturally wish to know causes; but it may be that nature will not reveal causes to you at all—but only facts. I take up something in my hand. What happens when I take it up? One set of muscles contracts and allows my fingers to stretch and to open; another set of muscles contracts as I grasp the object. Why do these muscles contract? Because they were affected by nerves. How came the nerves to convey the impulse? The impulse was given from the brain with which the nerve is connected. How did this impulse originate? In a wish that I formed. Do all the motions of the body originate in acts of consciousness or in acts of will? No, for some muscles, those of the heart, and digestive apparatus, for example, alternately expand and contract with great regularity without any volition of ours, indeed we could not by an act of will keep up these motions if they stopped, or stop them when they were going on. Are these automatic motions then produced by nervous impulse? Yes. But whence then does the impulse originate? Not in this case from the brain, but from other nervous centres or *ganglia* situated in the spinal cord. Is it then so, that movements which are conscious, and are produced or controlled by the will, come from nerves which communicate with the brain, and that automatic and unconscious muscular movements originate in other and inferior centres of nervous action? Yes.

Observe in all this, I have been seeking to know the cause. But I am no nearer knowing the cause at the end than at the beginning. Why and how a thought or wish of mine which seems wholly spiritual and mental should produce the physical result of setting a particular nerve in tremulous motion, and why that motion should in turn cause a muscle to contract, is as great a mystery to me as ever. The only answers to my questions have been statements of fact. *It is so.* Such a circumstance is always followed by such another circumstance. There is the antecedent and its uniform consequent. That is all. Of the hidden *nexus*, or necessity which should cause the particular antecedent to be followed by the particular consequent, I know nothing.

Take another example. I let this pen drop out of my hand. Why does it fall? Because I did not prevent it. But why should it move in that particular direction, when I gave it no impulse but merely ceased to hold it? Because all objects when disengaged tend to fall to the earth. But why should bodies fall towards the earth? Because the earth is a very large mass of matter, and smaller bodies are always attracted to large ones. But why and how do large bodies become thus attractive? Well, it is observed that throughout nature all masses of matter exercise mutual attraction and that the extent of this attraction is determined partly by their mass or density, and partly by their distances from each other. Is this true of the planets, and of the Sun? Yes. There is one broad statement which Kepler formulated in reference to this great fact of gravitation. It may be expressed thus, Gravity = Mass ÷ The Distance squared, and is often called the law of gravitation. *and for reasons.*

Now you will notice here again that at each step I have asked the question Why? and that at no step have I received an answer. The answer I have obtained in each case is the statement of a fact only; but then each *Not causes nor reasons but facts.*

fact was one broader, more comprehensive and general, than that which preceded it. The first fact was single; it was within the range of a little child's experience—that the pen fell. The last statement of fact, the great truth of gravitation, was far-reaching, sublime, co-extensive with the whole range of the universe so far as man can know anything about it all—a statement of fact which includes in its generalization the explanation—so we call it—of the movements of the atmosphere, of the rising and falling of the tides, and of the march of the planets on their heavenly way. But as a matter of fact, nothing has been explained or accounted for, no mystery has been solved. Each single fact derived from observation has been referred to some larger fact derived from wider observation, and the mind has been led to correlate a number of separate and diverse experiences under one comprehensive statement, to detect unity where there was apparent diversity; to substitute a great generalization for a little one, a great mystery for a little one. That is all.

Large truths instead of little ones. And surely that is much. Is it not a large part of the education of all of us to be enabled to lift up the thoughts from what is petty and transient and exceptional and to recognize in its stead what is vast, and typical, permanent and universal? Truly we are the richer for the perception of the larger truth, even though it is just as mysterious and inexplicable to us, as the smaller truth was to the little child. "In wonder," says Coleridge, "all philosophy begins, and in wonder it ends." The infant looks up into the sky with awe and bewilderment. The wisest man, when he knows all about the stars and their sizes and their distances and their chemical constituents, is fain to say, "When I consider Thy heavens the work of Thy fingers, the moon and the stars which Thou hast ordained, what is man that Thou art mindful of him and the son of man that Thou so regardest him"?

It is also to be observed that the ultimate object to be attained in the pursuit of physical science is the perception of what is called a *law*. We speak of the Law of gravitation or of the correlation of forces. But the word Law is here used in a very special sense. In the sphere of morals and religion, it implies prescription and authority on the one side, obedience and obligation on the other. But in physics the word is simply used to describe some statement of ascertained fact, some general truth derived from observation. It is not a law in any other sense. We may talk loosely and popularly of obeying the laws of nature. But what we mean is simply this —that there are the observed facts; that experience leads us to conclude that what has proved to be uniform within the range of our experience, will continue to be uniform under the same conditions; and that in planning our own actions, in inventing, contriving, and adapting the forces of nature for our own purposes, we must take these facts for granted, and not expect them to be modified to suit our will. *What are Laws of Nature?*

And if this be a correct description of the way in which truth relating to natural and experimental science is attained; we cannot fail to see how important is the mental discipline through which the student must pass in arriving at such truth. He must begin by noticing the phænomena, must put together and register the results of his observation; must hesitate to generalize too soon, must suspend his judgment, until he has facts enough, must verify each hypothesis by new experiments; must learn how to make a legitimate generalization from a multitude of particulars; must hold his generalized truth, even when he has it, only provisionally, knowing that it *Processes of thought required in physical studies.*

too may possibly require to be corrected, or at least absorbed by some larger generalization. And even when he recognizes a grand and apparently universal law such as that of gravitation he must leave room in a corner of his mind for the possibility of the existence of systems and regions "somewhere out of human view" to which the law of gravitation haply does not extend.

These processes available in all the intercourse of life.

And do you not see that the processes of mind thus brought into action, are very nearly akin to those by which we are every day forming our judgments about men and women, about political events, about the right and wrong of human actions? When we go wrong on these points it is more often through hasty and unauthorized inductions than from any other cause. "I do not like foreigners," says one; "I have been in some parts of the Continent where the people were very brutal and dirty." "I do not think University examinations any true test of power," says another. "I knew a man who had taken high honours and he turned out a complete failure." "Macaulay was very inaccurate, look at the mistakes he made about Penn." Do we not see in cases like this, illustrations of what Bacon was wont to call the *inductio per enumerationem simplicem*, the generalization too wide and sweeping for the facts; the inability to discern the difference between the act or event which is exceptional and that which is typical? Do we not feel, that what are wanted here are temper, reserve, breadth of mind, observation wide enough to comprehend a great many special details before arriving at large general assertions? And these are precisely the qualities of mind which the study of physical science generates and encourages. They are not brought into special activity either by the study of language or by the study of mathematics, valuable as both of them are in their place. For the logic of pure synthesis may shew you how to detect fallacies in drawing conclusions from general truths; it is by the inductive process that men must form the fixed and general principles on which they reason and act. And since for once that a man goes wrong through reasoning badly on given data, he goes wrong ten times through accepting data which are unsound and unverified; inductive reasoning is at least as useful a part of mental training for the duty of life, as the deductive process to which the name logic was once exclusively applied.

Such are some of the weightiest reasons for desiring to see experimental and inductive science included in every scheme of liberal education. Other reasons might easily be multiplied. "Scientific teaching," say the Public School Commissioners in their Report of 1861, "is perhaps the best corrective for that indolence which is the vice of half-awakened minds and which shrinks from any exertion that is not like an effort of memory, purely mechanical." A still more practical and obvious reason was urged in the Report of the Parliamentary Committee of 1863, "A knowledge of the principles of science would tend to promote industrial progress by stimulating improvement, by preventing costly and unphilosophical attempts at impossible inventions, diminishing waste, and obviating in a great measure ignorant opposition to salutary changes."

Practical and commercial considerations like these must of course not be kept out of view. They have a very intimate bearing on the education of primary schools and on the welfare of the industrial classes generally. One hears of the want of knowledge often evinced by artizans; of the trade rules which practically forbid a man to put special ability or enthusiasm into his work, and which seem designed to reduce the working power of

The bearing of scientific knowledge on skilled trades.

the intelligent mechanic to the level of that of the unintelligent. Laments are often heard of the decay of the old custom of apprenticeship, by which a master undertook to give a youth systematic instruction in the art and mystery which he practised; and in consequence of these shortcomings it is said that English workmen are less successful competitors than they once were with the skilled craftsmen of other nations. The gravity of these facts is unquestionable, though it is not within our present province to discuss them, except in their bearing on school education. Closely connected with every form of handicraft there is some kind of elementary science—it may be of mechanics, or of chemistry, of the properties of matter, or the nature of forces—which explains and justifies the rules of that particular handicraft and the knowledge of these things would be useful to the workman, not only in enabling him to do his work better, but also in calling out his sympathy and transforming him from a mechanical drudge into an intelligent worker. It is a humiliating thing to see a grown man content to employ year after year methods and forces which he does not care to understand. No one who earns his living under such conditions can get any enjoyment out of his work. Still less is he capable of discovering new methods by which in his own special department future workers may be helped to economize time, and to do work in a more artistic and thorough manner.

A partial remedy for this evil would be found if the study of natural phænomena were included in some form in the course of every primary school. One at least of the specific subjects of advanced instruction for which in the higher classes the Education Department makes special grants, should always be attempted in those classes. That subject should be chosen rather because the means exist for teaching it well, than because of its supposed relation to the particular calling likely to be followed by the scholar. Any one branch of physical science will serve to stimulate the appetite for further knowledge, and to suggest right methods of investigation in other and more practical directions. But when the one branch has been chosen, care should be taken that it shall not be treated as a new and special accomplishment—a *purpureus pannus* attached by way of ornament at the end of the school-studies, but rather as an organic part of those studies, in preparation for which a well-arranged series of *fact-lessons* shall have been regularly given in the lower classes. The results of introducing children in the last year of their school-life to the study of entirely new subjects and to little text-books full of technical terms, have proved to be very unsatisfactory.

But the further measures towards the true preparation for the calling of a skilled workman lie outside the ordinary domain of school life. It is in special technical schools, that the craftsman should be helped to study the philosophy of his own trade. Such schools under the name of "Écoles d'Apprentis" in France, or of Technical and Trade Schools in Switzerland and Germany, have long existed and done excellent work. But with the exception of the Trade School at Bristol founded by the late Canon Moseley and the Trade School established under the Endowed Schools Act at Keighley, very few such institutions have thriven here. Now that the old system of apprenticing to masters has died out, the best substitute for it is to be found in the establishment of schools which shall be accessible to the scholars who have left the primary schools, and in which the instruction in manual arts, though based on science, shall be consciously directed to practical ends.

Technical or Trade Schools.

The function of a Trade or Technical School is rather industrial than educational. It is to teach science in its application to industry and with a special view to the needs of the skilled artizan. Its course should include applied mechanics, experimental physics, electricity, magnetism and heat, chemistry, descriptive geometry, the properties of matter, measurement of planes and solids, and the principles of construction generally. There should be a workshop, a museum of tools and implements, a chemical and physical laboratory in which the learners can perform experiments under supervision; and the classes should be so arranged and divided that the learner may obtain an insight into the scientific basis and the practical rules of the particular craft which he intends to follow.

The best modern substitute for the old apprentice system.

There should be no difficulty in the establishment of such schools in all our great industrial centres; nor even in devising a liberal system of inducements by way of scholarships or otherwise to encourage the most promising scholars from the primary school to devote a few months to such special studies before entering on the business of their lives. Enormous sums have been bequeathed in England for the purpose of apprenticing boys to trades. They are the survivals from a time when the word 'apprentice' had a real meaning, and when the provision of such funds was one of the wisest forms of benevolence. But the conditions of our industrial life are so altered that these large funds have ceased to serve their intended purpose, and are too often only disguised doles of a very mischievous kind. The disposition of such funds which will be most nearly akin to the intentions of the original donors is obviously the establishment of technical schools and of such bursaries or scholarships as may facilitate access to them.

Here, however, we revert to the consideration of scientific teaching, not for immediate use in trade or commerce, but as a permanent factor in a liberal education. And from this point of view it matters very little what branch of such science you select—whether astronomy, mechanics, optics, general physics, botany or animal physiology—so long as you keep in view the purposes which have to be served in teaching them, and the kind of mental discipline which rightly taught they are able to give. You cannot attempt in a school course to teach all, or indeed half of these things. You may well be reconciled to this conclusion, when you reflect that to teach any one of them well, so as really to kindle the inquisitive and observant spirit, and to create a strong interest in watching, recording and co-ordinating the facts in some one department of the physical world, is to do much to stimulate the desire for further acquisition of the same kind when your scholar leaves school; and to bring into play one set of faculties, which are not sufficiently exercised in any other part of your school-course. *Subjects of physical inquiry most suited to schools.*

So it will be well to consider in what department of science you or any one of your assistants feel the strongest interest, or for what kind of teaching you have the best material and facilities at hand, and to select that. For that is after all the best subject for you to teach. And if you are in the country, or dependent on the services of visiting teachers, and Mr A. undertakes to give lectures on Astronomy and Mr B. on Physiology, I would have you decide between these rivals, not by asking which of the two subjects is most likely to prove suitable for your scholars, but which of the two lecturers is the abler man, the person of wider general culture, the more skilful and enthusiastic teacher, the one most likely to kindle in your pupil the wish to make further researches for himself. *Grounds of choice relative not absolute.*

Differentiation of studies for boys and girls.

Nor do I think it at all desirable in selecting a subject of experimental science for school purposes to be strongly influenced by considering whether your pupils are boys or girls, or what particular uses they may happen to make of the knowledge hereafter in the business of life. At first sight it seems obvious that mechanics for example is a specially masculine study, that it connects itself with many of the occupations which boys are likely to follow. But, after all, the number of men who require in their business or profession to be skilled in practical mechanics is very small; and the true reason for teaching such a subject at all is that the learner may know something of the properties of matter, the nature of statical and dynamic forces, and the way in which knowledge about the facts of the visible world ought to be acquired. And all these things have just as close a relation to the needs of a woman's life as to those of a man. Again, to a superficial observer, botany seems as if it were specially a feminine pursuit. There is a very obvious and natural association between girls and flowers. It is pleasant to think of young maidens in trim gardens culling posies:

"The rose had been washed, just washed in a shower,
Which Mary to Anna conveyed."

But such associations do not at all prove that botany is a specially appropriate study for young ladies; botany considered as a science, the investigation of the parts, the structure and functions of plants. There is nothing exclusively feminine in it. The truth is that mechanics and botany are both equally fitted in the case of either boys or girls to serve the purposes which experimental science is meant to serve. All depends upon the way in which the subject is taught.

Scientific terminology.

One very effective *crux*, or test, by which the difference between a good and a bad teacher of such subjects is to be detected, is to be found in the use he makes of scientific terminology. To hear some teachers of Botany or Chemistry you would suppose that to give a thing a hard name was to explain a fact, and that the learning how to label things with technical words was the learning of science. The note-books of students are sometimes found to contain little else but nomenclature and lists of terms. Such terms are of course indispensable, but their true value is to fix and crystallize facts and distinctions already perceived and explained in the first instance without their help. A technical term is a sign of distinction and classification, and presupposes that you have already something to distinguish and to classify.

A good teacher first explains the principle of his classification or distinction in untechnical phraseology; then shews the need of some word or phrase to describe what has been thus seen, and *then* introduces and explains his scientific term. It is only when in this way the learner comes to see the need of technical phraseology before he is invited to make use of it, that you can hope to make the terminology of science serve its proper and subordinate purpose, and to be a means rather than an end. Thus, as Mr Henry Sidgwick says, "The student is taught not only how to apply a classification ready made, but also to some extent how to make a classification; he is taught to deal with a system where the classes merge by fine gradations into one another, and where the boundaries are often hard to mark; a system that is progressive, and therefore in some points rudimentary, shifting, liable to continual modification; and along with the immense value of a carefully framed technical phraseology he is also taught the inevitable inadequacy of such a phraseology to represent the variety of nature[1]."

How and when to employ it.

---

[1] *Essays on a Liberal Education*, p. 195.

Practice as well as book-work.

Having chosen your subject you will do well in this department to rely not wholly on book-work, nor too largely on oral exposition and demonstration, but on the actual work of the pupils. They must be brought into close contact with the facts and phænomena of nature, and must be shewn how to handle objects and investigate their properties, to make mistakes, and to correct them for themselves. It is becoming more generally accepted every day by good teachers, not only of Chemistry but of Physics, that the best teaching is given in the laboratory rather than in the lecture-room. It is not merely by seeing experiments tried, but by trying them, that the properties of objects, their structure and organization, are best to be learned. But here it must be borne in mind that the discipline you want to give must be definite and exact; it is not seeing and handling only, but careful measurement if it be mechanics, careful observation if it be Botany or Physiology, and whatever it be, careful notes and recordation of the results of each experiment as soon as it is made.

Scholars to bring and make their own illustrations.

As far as you can, enlist the services of the scholars in the manufacture, collection and invention of the objects used in illustration of experimental lessons. Boxes of classified models and specimens which are prepared by manufacturers, and which are often very costly, are far less effective than collections of objects which the scholars themselves have helped to form, illustrations of the flora and fauna of the district, its geological formation, or manufacturing processes. In two of the best grammar schools which I have visited, and in which the greatest attention is paid to Natural Science, I found there was a carpenter's shop in which the boys themselves made their own apparatus for the illustration of mechanical powers and for other departments of science. Within certain limits, of course, you want all the help which Prof. Huxley or Balfour Stewart or Mr Lockyer can give you in the form of books, or which the ingenious producer of diagrams, and cabinets of selected models and objects, can invent for you. But these things are all supplements to true teaching and investigation, not substitutes for them.

After all, no teaching deserves the name of science which is a teaching of facts and operations only. In science you must have facts, but you must also have ideas. Unless the facts are presented in such a way as to group themselves together, throw light on one another, and reveal some general law of correlation or of sequence in nature, they are not science at all. It is perhaps a misfortune that the word 'science' has become popularly appropriated to a particular kind of information, and that astronomy, physics and a group of like subjects should have usurped the name of science. But as I have already reminded you the word 'science' does not refer to a particular class of facts, but to the method of investigating them. It does not mean knowledge, but knowledge obtained on right principles, and in a particular way. You may give a lesson on the future tense which shall be in the highest degree scientific, and you may give a lesson on the thermometer or on the satellites of Jupiter which shall not be science at all.

We cannot attach much educational value to lessons on familiar objects and occurrences, unless they are given with a distinctly scientific aim, and in a scientific manner. It is a frequent subject of complaint that children though learning a great many recondite things in school are very ignorant of things out of doors, that they do not know, *e.g.*, the difference between wheat and barley, or what are the names of common birds and

Lessons on 'Common things' not necessarily scientific.

flowers. Even in a book otherwise so valuable and so pregnant with important suggestions as Mr Herbert Spencer's book on Education you will find a formidable indictment, running indeed throughout all his pages, against schools, because they give book-learning and grammar and other pedantries, and do not shew the scholar how to get a living, nor to preserve their health, or what will be their future duties as parents and as citizens.

Such complaints often originate in a certain confusion of mind, as to what is the proper business of a school. Many things are very well worth knowing, which it is not the business of a school to teach. The world is a great school in which we are to be learning all our life, and he who brings into it quickened faculties will learn its lessons well by actual experience. But a child does not come to school to be told that a cow has four legs, that fishes swim, or that bread is eatable, nutritious, soft, white and opaque. Nor does he come there to learn the special business of a farmer, or of an engineer, or of a shoemaker. He is there to learn precisely those things which could not be so well learned out of doors, and to gain that sort of capacity and awakening which will enable him to acquire readily the lessons of common life and to turn them to the best account.

If you want to know what is the proper province of the school, consider a little what sort of lives your scholars lead, and the sort of homes they come from. In the houses of the very poor, there is probably little talk going on such as would draw the attention of children to the most interesting facts of nature and of daily life. So in schools for the poor, conversational lessons on common things, on birds and beasts, and on every-day events, are very useful and even necessary. If children live in towns and seldom see green fields, occasional lessons on the crops, the aspects of nature and on rural life are legitimate parts of a school course. But if children come from orderly and intelligent homes, in which they daily hear subjects discussed which are worth talking about, and if they know something about the country, lessons of this kind are less necessary. Bear in mind that anything you can do to make the knowledge derived from daily observation more exact and more useful, is worth doing, because it helps to make the future study of science easier. But do not imagine that everything of which it is a shame for a child to be ignorant, is necessarily your business to teach. The right rule of action appears to me to be this. It is no concern of ours to teach in schools that which an observant and intelligent child would learn out of doors; but it is our concern so to teach him as to make him observant and intelligent.

Training not special but general. Nor is it incumbent on teachers to anticipate the requirements of future life by giving the knowledge suited to this or that employment or profession. To do that would not only be to do grave injustice to the child who did not mean to adopt the particular calling; but it would injure him who did, by prematurely specializing his knowledge and directing his thoughts into a certain money-making groove. The duty of the school is to call forth such activities and to give such knowledge as shall be available alike in all conceivable professions or employments; and it can do this rather by considering oftener what intellectual wants are human and universal, than what is the way in which any particular child is to get his livelihood. A well educated English gentleman does not it is true know so much about a steam engine as an engineer, nor so much about the rotation of crops as a farmer, nor so much about book-keeping as a city clerk, but he knows a great deal more about all three than any one of them knows about the work of the other two; and this is simply because his faculty of thinking and observing has been cultivated on subjects chosen for their fitness as instruments of development, and not on subjects chosen with the narrow purpose of turning them to immediate practical use.

Scientific teaching of the future. There can be little doubt that in the education of the future, a larger space will be occupied than heretofore by the discipline of the inductive sciences, and it will be well if those of you who are entering the profession, will accept this as inevitable; and qualify yourselves both to meet the want, and to guide a movement which must for good or evil have important consequences. It is for you to take heed that the newer knowledge shall be not less educative and inspiring than the old, and that the word 'science' shall not degenerate into the symbol for what is empirical and utilitarian, nor for another kind of memory work. He who sets himself to do this has before him vast fields of usefulness. "Lift up your eyes and look upon the fields, for they are white already to the harvest." It may be that most of the teaching to be gained from Latin and Greek books has already been discovered; and that the capacities of the older forms of academic discipline have already been taxed to the uttermost. But in the direction we have been considering to-day, the prospect open before the wistful gazer is illimitable. Who can measure the possibilities of induction and experiment? Who knows what large generalizations may yet be possible respecting the course and constitution of nature, the tendency of history, the conditions of being and knowing on this earth, generalizations yet undreamed of either by the physicist or the philosopher? And how are these triumphs to be attained if the scientific temper,—the spirit of enquiry, of caution, of reticence, of hope, of enthusiasm, the delight in the perception of new truth, the careful and modest estimate of the worth of the truth when discovered,—is not fostered by our system of education? For the present it is in Natural Science, in Physics, in Chemistry or Botany, that we recognize the region in which these qualities can best be cultivated and displayed. It is the region nearest to us. But once understood and explained it has its relations not only to the *mundus visibilis* but to the whole *mundus intelligibilis*, to " worlds not quickened by the sun," to the interpretation of the history of man in the ages that are past, to the forecast of his indefinite improvement in the ages that are to come.

XV. THE CORRELATION OF STUDIES.

Review of the curriculum of school studies.

WE have considered in succession the principal instruments which are in a teacher's hands for forming the character, and training the faculties of scholars, and it may be convenient here to recall them. There are (1) the teaching of mechanical arts as Reading and Writing, and generally the training of the pupil to action. (2) Instruction in useful information or *Fact-lore*, with a view to give the pupil knowledge. Then come the studies which are specially intended to promote thought; (3) Language teaching, which gives command over the instrument of thought and of expression; (4) Mathematics, which gives the laws of ratiocination from generals to particulars; and (5) Inductive science which gives the habit of observation; and of generalization from particular experience.

We have said that all these ingredients in a school course should be within your view when you try to fashion a plan of study either for a primary or secondary school, for boys or for girls. We have also given some reasons for thinking that after a time both the first and the second kinds of teaching become relatively less important, and that in the main, and especially in the later stages of your course, the formative and disciplinal and therefore the best parts of school training will be found to be composed of the last three elements. But we may now go further and say that a reasonable regard to all three is more consistent with thoroughness in teaching than the limitation to one. The maxim, *non multa, sed multum*, has a plausible sound, and seems to furnish a justification to those whose ideal is to secure thorough scholarship in one department rather than many-sided culture. But in truth a pupil who leaves school, knowing only one language besides his own, and having learned it by comparison with his own, knowing also one branch of mathematics besides arithmetic, and one branch of Natural Science, is better educated—better fitted to receive all the subsequent knowledge which the experience of life may bring, and to know what to do with it, than the classical scholar, the mathematician, or the scientist pure and simple.

The good teacher seeks to give to each class of faculty a fair chance of development. He knows that it is impossible to determine with certainty very early in a scholar's career, what is the special department in which he is likely to achieve excellence. Nor is it at all necessary that you should know this too early. It has been often said that the ideally educated man, is one who knows something of many subjects, and a good deal of one subject. You are safe therefore in fashioning a somewhat comprehensive course so long as there is unity in it; and in making certain elements compulsory on all scholars, reserving alternatives and voluntary choice to the later stages of the school-life. You thus cast your net over a wider area, and prepare yourself to welcome a greater variety of abilities and aptitudes. You leave fewer minds to stagnate in apathy and indifference, and you discourage the tendency to attach an exaggerated value to particular subjects, and to indulge in the idle boast of learned ignorance. And if this be done, then when the time comes for specializing, and your pupil comes within sight of the University or of the business of life, you will be in a better position to determine in what direction and for what reason he will do well to direct his energies in a particular channel. And in helping the pupil to decide these questions it is well to have regard (1) to the probability that the study thus selected will be thoroughly assimilated, and will in his case be carried on far enough to become a factor of special value in his intellectual life, and (2) to the chance of his putting forth real effort in its pursuit. For *cæteris paribus*, that study is the best for each of us which calls out the largest amount of spontaneous exertion, and in which we are not recipients merely, however diligent, but willing agents.

Time not always proportioned to the importance of subjects. Although the threefold division of intellectual culture to which we have so often referred, should be clearly before the mind of a teacher, and dominate his plans, and though each division may well claim an equal share in his attention, it does not follow that the time available in a school course shall be given to these departments in equal proportions. It takes longer and harder work to achieve the desired intellectual result in some subjects than in others. A given amount of effort tells sooner in the early stages of science teaching than in those of language. You may make even a mathematical truth clear and effective for practical purposes, in a shorter lesson than would be needed for instruction of equal value on a difficult point in grammar. And hence it may be roughly said that if you have say 20 hours of a week available for the serious study of disciplinal subjects, it is not unreasonable to give nearly half of these to language and literature and subsidiary exercises, and of the remaining half, rather the larger portion to mathematics, and the smaller to experimental science.

These considerations may help us when we find ourselves confronted with the great difficulty of modern teachers—the claims of too many multifarious subjects. The right rule of action appears to be this. As each new subject demands attention, ask yourself to what department of school-work it belongs, and what present study in that department can be safely dropped, or rather absorbed and superseded by the higher or new study. Your scheme of study will not probably include more than two languages, say French and Latin, besides your own. Well if it becomes necessary to add German or Greek, that is a reason for setting aside for the present all special exercises in English, except those which arise incidentally out of the translation and treatment of other languages. If you want to begin a course of logic consider that this is the cognate subject to mathematics; that it addresses itself to the same side of the mind, so to speak; and take the time for it out of that which would have been given to some branch of mathematics. If you feel disposed to go through a course of lessons on Political Economy, or the elements of Political Philosophy, such a course may very wisely supersede for a time the formal study of History with which it is closely related. And as to the subjects of Physical Science, it is never wise to have more than two in hand at a time, and the introduction of any one new branch of Physics or Chemistry, may fitly take the place of another. The two principles to be kept in view are these. Do not permit your day's time-table to be cut up into fragments so small as to distract the attention of your scholars, and to interfere with due continuity of the studies; and take care that the general proportion of time and effort given to each of the formative or disciplinal branches of study shall not be substantially disturbed. We have before

The contending claims of too many subjects.

insisted on the need for unity of purpose throughout the school course and a regulated harmony in all its parts. This harmony is not disturbed when the scholar quits Arithmetic for Algebra, or Geometry for Trigonometry, or Botany for Geology, or Writing for Drawing; because in each case the new study is homogeneous with the old, and all that has been learned before is made available for new purposes. So long as a new subject is a fair intellectual equivalent for its predecessor, calls into action the same sort of force and utilizes former knowledge, we need not be afraid of introducing it, or of abandoning for a time the pursuit of some others which we value.

The convertibility of intellectual forces.

Even if we do not wholly succeed in this endeavour, it will be consoling to reflect, that after all, mental development though multiform in its manifestations, is at bottom one process, and that mental powers are not so sharply divisible into independent faculties as it would seem to us when we read books of psychology. In the physical sciences there are the doctrines of the conservation of energy and also of the convertibility of forces. You know that heat is a mode of motion, that when you can generate one kind of force—say electricity—it is capable of transmutation into light or some other kind of energy, and that radiant energy itself is said to be convertible into sound. And there is a similar law of convertibility in intellectual forces. Every piece of knowledge honestly acquired turns out to have unexpected relations with much other knowledge. Every kind of mental power, once evoked and applied to a worthy purpose, becomes available for other purposes, and is capable of being transformed into power of another kind. Only take care that what you evoke is really power, that δύναμις in your hands becomes true ἐνέργεια, that the subject you teach is so taught as to stimulate, to broaden, to reach out into regions beyond itself; and then the question of the number of subjects nominally included in your curriculum becomes of very small importance. It is only the dull and soulless mnemonic after all which is utterly barren of result. Compare an artist or musician who is a mere artist or musician with one who also brings to his work knowledge of other things, intellectual breadth and sympathy. All that the one has been helped to know and to feel in other regions than art becomes transfigured and absorbed into his work, and his work is more precious to the world in consequence.

Should any attempt be made to adapt training and teaching to the special tastes and capacities of children? This is a grave question and one which must often have occurred to you. There are those who complain not without seeming justice, that our plans treat all children alike, and do not sufficiently recognize inherent differences both in the amount of power and in the special direction of that power. George Combe spent his life in advocating this doctrine, and he taught that the true key to the idiosyncracies of children, and therefore to the right and philosophic treatment of various natures, was to be found in the study of the cranium and in what he called the science of Phrenology. He was a man of very clear purpose and strong will, and had the art of inspiring his disciples with much enthusiasm and admiration. But he never got so far as to induce one of them seriously to attempt the classification and teaching of a school on his principles, and the experiment yet remains untried. There are others who would urge you to study the temperaments of children, and to give to the lymphatic, the sanguine and the nervous scholars respectively, special and appropriate discipline. But I cannot counsel you to concern yourself much with such speculations.

Adaptation of the School course to individual wants and aptitudes.

For there is first the danger that perhaps your diagnosis of the case may be wrong; and then there is the further danger that even if it be right the treatment you adopt may not be after all the best. It is not yet proved either on the one hand that the child with a particular liking or talent, should have that tendency specially cultivated in his education, or on the other hand, that it is always wise to attempt to restore the balance by working at the development of those faculties in which he is deficient. By all means watch your pupils, see if experience shews any particular form of intellectual exercise to be burdensome or injurious to them; give prompt relief to those who seem in the smallest degree to be disheartened or overwrought; and having done this, devise the best course you can in the interest of the average scholar, and make all your pupils conform to it. Do you not in looking back on your own mental life, feel thankful that you were forced to learn many things for which at the time you had no special appetite, and which a scientific analyst of your yet unformed character and tastes might have declared to be unsuited to you?

Religious and moral instruction. In all this, I have said nothing of religious and moral teaching. But this is not because I disregard it, but simply because it is impossible to co-ordinate it with any of the subjects of which we have spoken. To say, for example, that so many hours should be given to grammar, so many to science, and so many to Biblical or moral lessons, would be difficult, and would not, whatever the proportion of time assigned, rightly represent our estimate of the relative importance of this last element. For "Conduct," as Mr Matthew Arnold says, "is three-fourths of life," and that a human being should do what is right and be animated by noble motives in doing it, is, as we must all feel, more important than that he should possess any given piece of useful information, or should have had his understanding trained in a particular way. But this does not at all imply that you should give in a school lessons on ethics and religion corresponding in length or number to your sense of the importance of those subjects.

Many of the best teachers feel that right moral guidance can only be had by direct didactic teaching, by the learning of formularies of faith and duty, and by lessons consciously directed to the enforcement of theological truths. Other teachers, with a no less profound sense of the importance of these things, have grave doubts as to the usefulness of school lessons on such subjects. They distrust the practice of teaching children in the sphere of religion to do what they would not be asked to do in any other department of their studies—to affirm what they do not understand. They dread, above all things, exacting from a young child vows or professions of religion which cannot possibly correspond to his actual convictions and experience. Such teachers would be disposed to rely more on the habits which were formed in school, on the spirit in which its work was done, and on the sort of moral and religious principles which may be learned indirectly in a high toned school, and are seen to penetrate all its corporate life, than on formal lessons in divinity. I shall not attempt here to pronounce an opinion on a controversial question which divides some of the most religious and high-minded teachers. Two considerations only shall be offered on this point.

Two views of the functions of a school in this matter.

The first of them is that the expediency of giving direct religious instruction depends a good deal on the character of your school, and on the life your scholars lead out of it. In a boarding school, where you have the whole control of the scholars' leisure and are *in loco parentis*, you will feel bound to provide for the religious instruction and worship, both on Sunday and on other days, which are usual in a well-constituted Christian family. And if you have the supervision of a Primary school, you cannot leave out of view the fact that many of the children come from homes in which the name of God is seldom heard, and in which the parents feel it no part of their duty to convey religious instruction to their children or to accompany them on Sunday to the house of worship. You will feel here that the only glimpse your scholar will have of the unseen world, the only teaching about his relation to a Divine Father, and the only introduction even to the morality and the poetry of the New Testament, are to be had in the school. On the other hand, if your school is a day-school of a higher kind, and the scholars have parents who are accustomed to concern themselves about the religious training and conduct of their children; or even who deliberately object to the inculcation of dogma at so early an age, your responsibility is greatly lessened. There is in such a case no moral obligation on a master, unless he is required to do so by the governors, to make the school a propaganda for his own or any other distinctive religious tenets. The principle of a 'conscience clause,' I may remind you, is not only recognized in all recent University legislation; it is embodied in the Endowed Schools Act, in the Elementary Education Act, and is in fact enforced on all schools to which public legislation has yet been extended in this country; it is founded on essential justice, and deserves to be yet more widely applied. It has certainly not proved in any way incompatible with the just influence of Christian teachers nor with the maintenance of the religious character of English schools.

Nor must we too hastily conclude that a school is a godless school, because for any reason no direct didactic religious lessons are given in it. Some of the weightiest lessons which we can learn in regard to the formation of our own character are not learned by way of direct instruction, but they come to us incidentally in seeing how religious principle shapes the conduct of others, and what it is worth when tested by the exigencies of life. The ordinary history of a school presents many such exigencies—many opportunities for effective moral teaching. Cases of misconduct arise which if dealt with calmly, seriously, and by a reference to a true and high standard of duty, have a very great effect upon the tone and feeling of the school. You will not be satisfied always to employ mechanical remedies for moral evils; but will direct attention from time to time to principles of conduct which have been illustrated or violated within the knowledge of your scholars.

When such incidents occur in the school life, they should be utilized. But they will occur rarely, and they will be all the more impressive if they are rare. It is not in the explicit didactic form in which older people expect to see ethical truths and maxims expressed, that moral duties can be best made intelligible to a young scholar, and binding on his conscience. Much more effective work is done in his case by taking care that his surroundings are right and healthful; by watching carefully, though without actually removing them, such temptations to evil as come within his reach, and by seeing that his daily life gives due scope and opportunity for the exercise of boyish virtues. And the school-master, who has a high sense of responsibility in this matter, will often ask himself "Are the arrangements of my school calculated to promote truthfulness, manliness, the sense of honour, the

The moral lessons taught by the daily discipline of a school.

feeling of moral obligation? Are the relations of my pupil to me such as to encourage him to treat me with confidence? Do they furnish him with occasions of being helpful to others? Does he take advantage of such occasions? Is he being trained in my school not merely to obey when the pressure of authority is upon him, but also to use freedom aright when he is a law unto himself? Is the virtue of courage taught not as an abstract lesson, but silently in the discipline and habits of the school?" For we may not forget what Aristotle has taught us that courage is, in one sense, the first of all virtues, because it is the one virtue which makes all others possible, without which indeed, many others are well nigh impossible. For all untruth is traceable to cowardice. All idleness, desultory reading, extravagance, self-indulgence—nearly all in fact of the faults which you most desire that schoolboys should avoid,—come from lack of boldness to say 'No' when the temptation comes, and to make a resolute effort to do what is known to be right. Trace out the consequences of a nerveless soft and too indulgent discipline, when it comes to bear fruit in afterlife. Consider what a man is likely to be worth who has not resolution enough to resist the public opinion of his class, to refuse to pronounce the Shibboleths of his party, to abstain from display and expense which he cannot afford, to emancipate himself from usages which he feels to be narrow and selfish, in his profession or trade. And when you think of these things you will see that in the microcosm of a good school there should be real training in courage and self-restraint, and that such training is often as effective when it is connected with the actual difficulties and temptations of school life, as when it forms part of a formal scheme of ethical or theological teaching.

Further, it must be borne in mind that every one of the departments of secular teaching with which we deal in schools carries with it its own special ethical lessons, holds them in solution, so to speak, and concerns itself in its own way with some important aspect of human character. We saw in considering the practice of simple arts, and in all the mechanical drill which they involve, how the scholar learned obedience, exact attention to rule, self-subjugation, deference for others, and the habit of losing sight of his individual claims, while working towards the attainment of results in which others besides himself had a common interest. The study of Language too, when rightly conducted, is essentially a discipline in veracity, in careful statement, in abstinence from exaggeration, in thinking before we speak. Chaucer's host says: *The ethical teaching embodied in School lessons.*

> "Eke Plato sayeth, whoso can him rede
> The wordes moste ben cosin to the dede;"

and George Herbert,

> "Lie not, but let thy heart be true to God,
> Thy mouth to it, thy actions to them both."

And the ideal in the mind of both poets you see is the perfect correspondence in a man's character between the thing thought, the thing done, and the thing said. There is no truer test of a consistent and noble type of life than this; and there is no intellectual training better fitted to develope such a type, than wise discipline in the use and meaning of language. In like manner Mathematical science has its own special moral lessons, none the less real because they are learned by implication only and are not formulated in precepts. It is a discipline in exactness, in perfect honesty, in patience. And of natural science and of all the studies pursued by the method of induction, have we not seen that they are a check on rash and hasty conclusions, that they teach fairness, breadth of mind, reticence, suspension of our judgment while the data for forming it are insufficient; and that these qualities are very necessary in the right conduct of life? As to History; it is full of indirect but very effective moral teaching. It is not only as Bolingbroke called it 'Philosophy teaching by examples,' but it is Morality teaching by examples. What, for instance, can be of higher value than the training it gives in the estimation of human character? We are called on to form judgments of men in very difficult positions, and we find a flippant and confident historian dismissing them with a single sentence, giving his estimate on one or two incidents in their lives, or summing up their characters in an epigram. Well, we look into ourselves, and we think of the people by whom we are surrounded, and we know that neither their characters, nor our own, admit of being fairly summed up in an epigram or a single sentence, that he who would know us thoroughly and judge us fairly, should know something of our powers and opportunities, our surroundings and temptations and of the circumstances in which our opinions have been formed. History may thus become to those who study it a lesson in charity, and a training whereby we may learn how to form right estimates of each other. It is essentially the study which best helps the student to conceive large thoughts, 'to look before and after,' and to appreciate, as Mr J. M. Wilson has wisely said, the forces of genius, of valour, of wisdom and of enthusiasm by which the world is moved.

There is yet another sense in which it is impossible to over-value the moral teaching of History. One looks back over the annals of our race, and recalls the past

The echoes of far-off contests and of ancient heroisms come down to us through the ages. "We have heard with our ears, and our fathers have declared to us the noble works which God did in their days, and in the old time before them." We hear of Philip Sidney, thirsty and dying on the field of Zutphen, refusing the cup of water and giving it to a poor soldier with the words, "Thy necessity is greater than mine." We recall the image of the saintly Bishop Ken, on the eve of the Declaration of Indulgence, as he stood with six other bishops before James in the presence chamber at Whitehall, "We have two duties to perform, our duty to God, and our duty to our king. We honour your Majesty, but we *must* fear God." Or we think of Wolfe the young soldier, on the heights of Quebec, spent and wounded after a hard fight, aroused by the cry, "They run." "Who run?" "The French." "Then I die happy." And as we realize these scenes, we know that this world is a better world for us to live in because such deeds have been done in it; we see all the more clearly what human duty and true human greatness are, and we are helped by such examples to form a nobler ideal of the possibilities even of our own prosaic and laborious life.

And thus it is quite possible that in a school in which few formal lessons are given on morals and conduct, the sense of a higher presence, and the habitual recognition of the highest motives of action may suffuse the whole of the teaching, or run through its entire texture like a golden thread. You have many objects in view which cannot be set down and provided for in a timetable. You want most of all to exert a right influence over the character, and you want too to gratify the legitimate demands of a child's fancy, and to furnish

Indirect moral teaching.

food for his imagination. You want to regard him from the first as a being not only with duties to fulfil and a livelihood to win, but with a life to live, with tastes to be gratified, with leisure to be worthily filled. And hence you will never satisfy yourself by putting before him the usefulness of knowledge, the way in which it adds to the value of its possessor in the market of the world, the examinations it may help him to pass, the fortune or the credit it may help him to win; but you will rather try to help him perceive the beauty and worth of an intelligent life for its own sake. It has been profoundly said by Bacon that the light of heaven is not only precious to see by, but to see. And of knowledge too, it may be truly said that it is not only good to shew us the way; and to help us to solve difficulties. It is also good, even if we solve no difficulties with it, and if we turn it to no definite commercial or other account, good if we only delight in its radiance and feel its warmth, and have our souls enriched and gladdened by it. "Truly the light is sweet, and a pleasant thing it is for a man to behold the sun." And a school is a very unsatisfactory institution, and fails to fulfil its highest function, if, however it may succeed in imparting knowledge, it does not also succeed in imparting a thirst for more, or at least a dawning sense of the inward need for mental and spiritual cultivation, whether such cultivation bears any visible relation to success in life or not.

And so the ideally perfect school is not only characterized as we have said in former lectures, by strict order, by right methods of instruction, and by vigorous intellectual activity; it should also be pervaded through and through by high purpose, by the spirit of work, by a solemn sense of duty, and by the love of truth. Does this seem to some of you an unattainable ideal? The first condition of its being attainable, is that you shall believe it worthy of attainment. Look back upon your own school days, recall the memories you have of them. Look forward into the life of your pupils, and ask what recollections they will have—what recollections you would like them to have, of you and of your teaching. Those recollections will not all be of the lessons you have intentionally given. They will depend much upon the spirit in which your work was done, on the motives which were seen to actuate you, and on the degree in which you were known to love that knowledge of which for the time you were in the scholars' eyes the chief representative.

You remember well who it was who once stood by *Vocation.* the lake of Genesareth and beckoned Andrew and Simon away from their boats and their fishing tackle with the words, "Follow me, I will make you fishers of men." That is a great parable; significant of the way in which in all ages of the world, some are called out from the meaner and more mechanical employments of life, and invited to take a share in the noblest of all work—in fashioning the intellect, the conscience, the character, the destiny of future generations of men and women. The call is not audible to all of us in quite the same way. By some it is recognized in the circumstances and what seem the accidents of life. Some hear it in the whispered intuitions which tell of personal fitness and aptitude. To others the voice comes, as a weighty and solemn conviction of the importance and usefulness of the work itself. But in some way or other the sense of the call ought to be present in the mind of every teacher. Without it the highest achievements of his art will be unattainable to him. With it, he will be in a position to make use of all the resources within his reach; he will have before him a true conception both of the road he has to traverse, and of the goal towards which he moves. And he will ever possess within him one of the strongest of all motives to action; for while he is doing his work, he will habitually recognize and will teach his scholars to recognize the unseen presence in their midst of One who is the helper of all sincere learners, and the teacher of all true teachers.

UNIVERSITY PRESS, CAMBRIDGE.
September, 1888.

PUBLICATIONS OF

The Cambridge University Press.

THE HOLY SCRIPTURES, &c.

The Cambridge Paragraph Bible of the Authorized English Version, with the Text revised by a Collation of its Early and other Principal Editions, the Use of the Italic Type made uniform, the Marginal References remodelled, and a Critical Introduction, by F. H. A. SCRIVENER, M.A., LL.D. Crown 4to., cloth gilt, 21*s*.

THE STUDENT'S EDITION of the above, on *good writing paper*, with one column of print and wide margin to each page for MS. notes. Two Vols. Crown 4to., cloth, gilt, 31*s*. 6*d*.

The Lectionary Bible, with Apocrypha, divided into Sections adapted to the Calendar and Tables of Lessons of 1871. Crown 8vo., cloth, 3*s*. 6*d*.

The Old Testament in Greek according to the Septuagint. Edited by H. B. SWETE, D.D. Vol. I. Genesis—IV Kings. Crown 8vo. 7*s*. 6*d*.
Volume II. By the same Editor. [*In the Press*.

The Book of Ecclesiastes. Large Paper Edition. By the Very Rev. E. H. PLUMPTRE, Dean of Wells. Demy 8vo. 7*s*. 6*d*.

Breviarium ad usum insignis Ecclesiae Sarum. Juxta Editionem maximam pro CLAUDIO CHEVALLON et FRANCISCO REGNAULT A.D. MDXXXI. in Alma Parisiorum Academia impressam: labore ac studio FRANCISCI PROCTER, A.M., et CHRISTOPHORI WORDS-WORTH, A.M.

FASCICULUS I. In quo continen ur KALENDARIUM, et ORDO TEMPORALIS sive PROPRIUM DE TEMPORE TOTIUS ANNI, una cum ordinali suo quod usitato vocabulo dicitur PICA SIVE DIRECTORIUM SACERDOTUM. Demy 8vo. 18*s*.

FASCICULUS II. In quo continentur PSALTERIUM, cum ordinario Officii totius hebdomadae juxta Horas Canonicas, et proprio Completorii, LITANIA, COMMUNE SANCTORUM, ORDINARIUM MISSAE CUM CANONE ET XIII MISSIS, &c. &c. Demy 8vo. 12*s*.

FASCICULUS III. In quo continetur PROPRIUM SANCTORUM quod et Sanctorale dicitur, una cum Accentuario. Demy 8vo. 15*s*.

FASCICULI I. II. III. complete £2. 2*s*.

Breviarium Romanum a FRANCISCO CARDINALI QUIGNONIO editum et recognitum iuxta editionem Venetiis A.D. 1535 impressam curante JOHANNE WICKHAM LEGG. Demy 8vo. 12*s*.

The Pointed Prayer Book, being the Book of Common Prayer with the Psalter or Psalms of David, pointed as they are to be sung or said in Churches. Embossed cloth, Royal 24mo, 2*s*.

The same in square 32mo. cloth, 6*d*.

The Cambridge Psalter, for the use of Choirs and Organists. Specially adapted for Congregations in which the "Cambridge Pointed Prayer Book" is used. Demy 8vo. cloth, 3*s*. 6*d*. Cloth limp cut flush, 2*s*. 6*d*.

The Paragraph Psalter, arranged for the use of Choirs by B. F. WESTCOTT, D.D., Canon of Westminster. Fcp. 4to. 5*s*.

The same in royal 32mo. Cloth, 1*s*. Leather, 1*s*. 6*d*.

London: Cambridge Warehouse, Ave Maria Lane.

The Authorised Edition of the English Bible (1611), its Subsequent Reprints and Modern Representatives. By F. H. A. SCRIVENER, M.A., D.C.L., LL.D. Crown 8vo. 7s. 6d.

The New Testament in the Original Greek, according to the Text followed in the Authorised Version, together with the Variations adopted in the Revised Version. Edited by F. H. A. SCRIVENER, M.A., D.C.L., LL.D. Small Crown 8vo. 6s.

The Parallel New Testament Greek and English. The New Testament, being the Authorised Version set forth in 1611 Arranged in Parallel Columns with the Revised Version of 1881, and with the original Greek, as edited by F. H. A. SCRIVENER, M.A., D.C.L., LL.D. Crown 8vo. cloth. 12s. 6d. (*The Revised Version is the joint Property of the Universities of Cambridge and Oxford.*)

Greek and English Testament, in parallel columns on the same page. Edited by J. SCHOLEFIELD, M.A. *New Edition, with the marginal references as arranged and revised by* DR SCRIVENER. 7s. 6d.

Greek and English Testament. THE STUDENT'S EDITION of the above on *large writing paper.* 4to. cloth. 12s.

Greek Testament, ex editione Stephani tertia, 1550. Small Octavo. 3s. 6d.

The Gospel according to St Matthew in Anglo-Saxon and Northumbrian Versions. By Rev. Prof. SKEAT, Litt.D. New Edition. Demy Quarto. 10s.

The Gospels according to St Mark—St Luke—St John, uniform with the preceding. Edited by the Rev. Prof. SKEAT. Demy Quarto. 10s. each.

The Missing Fragment of the Latin Translation of the Fourth Book of Ezra, discovered and edited with Introduction, Notes, and facsimile of the MS., by Prof. BENSLY, M.A. Demy 4to. 10s.

Codex S. Ceaddae Latinus. Evangelia SSS. Matthaei, Marci, Lucae ad cap. III. 9 complectens, circa septimum vel octavum saeculum scriptvs, in Ecclesia Cathedrali Lichfieldiensi servatus. Cum codice versionis Vulgatae Amiatino contulit, prolegomena conscripsit, F. H. A. SCRIVENER, A.M., LL.D. Imp. 4to. £1. 1s.

The Origin of the Leicester Codex of the New Testament. By J. R. HARRIS, M.A. With 3 plates. Demy 4to. 10s. 6d.

THEOLOGY—(ANCIENT).

Theodore of Mopsuestia's Commentary on the Minor Epistles of S. Paul. The Latin Version with the Greek Fragments, edited from the MSS. with Notes and an Introduction, by H. B. SWETE, D.D. Vol. I., containing the Introduction, and the Commentary upon Galatians—Colossians. Demy Octavo. 12s.

Volume II., containing the Commentary on 1 Thessalonians—Philemon, Appendices and Indices. 12s.

The Greek Liturgies. Chiefly from original Authorities. By C. A. SWAINSON, D.D., late Master of Christ's Coll. Cr. 4to. 15s.

Sayings of the Jewish Fathers, comprising Pirqe Aboth and Pereq R. Meir in Hebrew and English, with Critical Notes. By C. TAYLOR, D.D., Master of St John's College. 10s.

London: Cambridge Warehouse, Ave Maria Lane.

Sancti Irenæi Episcopi Lugdunensis libros quinque adversus Hæreses, edidit W. WIGAN HARVEY, S.T.B. Collegii Regalis olim Socius. 2 Vols. Demy Octavo. 18s.

The Palestinian Mishna. By W. H. LOWE, M.A., Lecturer in Hebrew at Christ's College, Cambridge. Royal Octavo. 21s.

M. Minucii Felicis Octavius. The text newly revised from the original MS. with an English Commentary, Analysis, Introduction, and Copious Indices. Edited by H. A. HOLDEN, LL.D. Crown Octavo. 7s. 6d.

Theophili Episcopi Antiochensis Libri Tres ad Autolycum. Edidit, Prolegomenis Versione Notulis Indicibus instruxit GULIELMUS GILSON HUMPHRY, S.T.B. Post Octavo. 5s.

Theophvlacti in Evangelium S. Matthæi Commentarius. Edited by W. G. HUMPHRY, B.D. Demy Octavo. 7s. 6d.

Tertullianus de Corona Militis, de Spectaculis, de Idololatria with Analysis and English Notes, by GEORGE CURREY, D.D. Master of the Charter House. Crown Octavo. 5s.

Fragments of Philo and Josephus. Newly edited by J. RENDEL HARRIS, M.A. With two Facsimiles. Demy 4to. 12s. 6d.

The Teaching of the Apostles. Newly edited, with Facsimile Text and Commentary, by J. R. HARRIS, M.A. Demy 4to. 21s.

THEOLOGY—(ENGLISH).

Works of Isaac Barrow, compared with the original MSS. A new Edition, by A. NAPIER, M.A. of Trinity College, Vicar of Holkham, Norfolk. Nine Vols. Demy Octavo. £3. 3s.

Treatise of the Pope's Supremacy, and a Discourse concerning the Unity of the Church, by I. BARROW. Demy 8vo. 7s. 6d.

Pearson's Exposition of the Creed, edited by TEMPLE CHEVALLIER, B.D. Third Edition revised by R. SINKER, M.A., Librarian of Trinity College. Demy Octavo. 12s.

An Analysis of the Exposition of the Creed, written by the Right Rev. Father in God, JOHN PEARSON, D.D. Compiled by W. H. MILL, D.D. Demy Octavo. 5s.

Wheatly on the Common Prayer, edited by G. E. CORRIE, D.D. late Master of Jesus College. Demy Octavo. 7s. 6d.

The Homilies, with Various Readings, and the Quotations from the Fathers given at length in the Original Languages. Edit. by G. E. CORRIE, D.D. late Master of Jesus College. Demy 8vo. 7s. 6d.

Two Forms of Prayer of the time of Queen Elizabeth. Now First Reprinted. Demy Octavo. 6d.

Select Discourses, by JOHN SMITH, late Fellow of Queens' College, Cambridge. Edited by H. G. WILLIAMS, B.D. late Professor of Arabic. Royal Octavo. 7s. 6d.

De Obligatione Conscientiæ Prælectiones decem Oxonii in Schola Theologica habitæ a ROBERTO SANDERSON, SS. Theologiæ ibidem Professore Regio. With English Notes, including an abridged Translation, by W. WHEWELL. D.D. Demy 8vo. 7s. 6d.

Cæsar Morgan's Investigation of the Trinity of Plato, and of Philo Judæus. 2nd Ed., revised by H. A. HOLDEN, LL.D. Cr. 8vo. 4s.

London: Cambridge Warehouse, Ave Maria Lane.

Archbishop Usher's Answer to a Jesuit, with other Tracts on Popery. Edited by J. SCHOLEFIELD, M.A. Demy 8vo. 7s. 6d.

Wilson's Illustration of the Method of explaining the New Testament, by the early opinions of Jews and Christians concerning Christ. Edited by T. TURTON, D.D. Demy 8vo. 5s.

Lectures on Divinity delivered in the University of Cambridge. By JOHN HEY, D.D. Third Edition, by T. TURTON, D.D. late Lord Bishop of Ely. 2 vols. Demy Octavo. 15s.

S. Austin and his place in the History of Christian Thought. Being the Hulsean Lectures for 1885. By W. CUNNINGHAM, B.D. Demy 8vo. Buckram, 12s. 6d.

GREEK AND LATIN CLASSICS, &c.
(*See also* pp. 13, 14.)

Sophocles: the Plays and Fragments. With Critical Notes, Commentary, and Translation in English Prose, by R. C. JEBB, Litt. D., LL.D., Professor of Greek in the University of Glasgow.
Part I. The Oedipus Tyrannus. Demy 8vo. *New Edit.* 12s. 6d.
Part II. The Oedipus Coloneus. Demy 8vo. 12s. 6d.
Part III. The Antigone. Demy 8vo. 12s. 6d.

Select Private Orations of Demosthenes with Introductions and English Notes, by F. A. PALEY, M.A., & J. E. SANDYS, Litt.D.
Part I. containing Contra Phormionem, Lacritum, Pantaenetum, Boeotum de Nomine, Boeotum de Dote, Dionysodorum. Crown 8vo. **New Edition.** 6s.
Part II. containing Pro Phormione, Contra Stephanum I. II., Nicostratum, Cononem, Calliclem. Crown 8vo. *New Edit.* 7s. 6d.

The Bacchae of Euripides, with Introduction, Critical Notes, and Archæological Illustrations, by J. E. SANDYS, Litt.D. New Edition, with additional Illustrations. Crown 8vo. 12s. 6d.

An Introduction to Greek Epigraphy. Part I. The Archaic Inscriptions and the Greek Alphabet. By E. S. ROBERTS, M.A., Fellow and Tutor of Gonville and Caius College. Demy 8vo. 18s.

Aeschyli Fabulae.—ΙΚΕΤΙΔΕΣ ΧΟΗΦΟΡΟΙ in libro Mediceo mendose scriptae ex vv. dd. coniecturis emendatius editae cum Scholiis Graecis et brevi adnotatione critica, curante F. A. PALEY, M.A., LL.D. Demy 8vo. 7s. 6d.

The Agamemnon of Aeschylus. With a translation in English Rhythm, and Notes Critical and Explanatory. **New Edition, Revised.** By B. H. KENNEDY, D.D. Crown 8vo. 6s.

The Theætetus of Plato, with a Translation and Notes by the same Editor. Crown 8vo. 7s. 6d.

P. Vergili Maronis Opera, cum Prolegomenis et Commentario Critico pro Syndicis Preli Academici edidit BENJAMIN HALL KENNEDY, S.T.P. Extra fcp. 8vo. 5s.

Demosthenes against Androtion and against Timocrates, with Introductions and English Commentary by WILLIAM WAYTE, M.A. Crown 8vo. cloth. 7s. 6d.

Essays on the Art of Pheidias. By C. WALDSTEIN, Litt.D., Phil. D. Royal 8vo. With Illustrations. Buckram, 30s.

London: Cambridge Warehouse, Ave Maria Lane.

M. Tulli Ciceronis ad M. Brutum Orator. A Revised Text.
Edited with Introductory Essays and Critical and Explanatory
Notes, by J. E. SANDYS, Litt.D. Demy 8vo. 16s.

M. Tulli Ciceronis pro C. Rabirio [Perduellionis Reo] Oratio
ad Quirites. With Notes, Introduction and Appendices. By W.
E. HEITLAND, M.A. Demy 8vo. 7s. 6d.

M. T. Ciceronis de Natura Deorum Libri Tres, with Introduction and Commentary by JOSEPH B. MAYOR, M.A. Demy 8vo.
Vol. I. 10s. 6d. Vol. II. 12s. 6d. Vol. III. 10s.

M. T. Ciceronis de Officiis Libri Tres with Marginal Analysis,
an English Commentary, and Indices. New Edition, revised, by
H. A. HOLDEN, LL.D.. Crown 8vo. 9s.

M. T. Ciceronis de Officiis Libri Tertius, with Introduction,
Analysis and Commentary by H. A. HOLDEN, LL.D. Cr. 8vo. 2s.

M. T. Ciceronis de Finibus Bonorum libri Quinque. The
Text revised and explained by J. S. REID, Litt. D. *[In the Press.*
Vol. III., containing the Translation. Demy 8vo. 8s.

Plato's Phædo, literally translated, by the late E. M. COPE,
Fellow of Trinity College, Cambridge. Demy Octavo. 5s.

Aristotle. The Rhetoric. With a Commentary by the late
E. M. COPE, Fellow of Trinity College, Cambridge, revised and
edited by J. E. SANDYS, Litt.D. 3 Vols. Demy 8vo. 21s.

Aristotle.—ΠΕΡΙ ΨΥΧΗΣ. Aristotle's Psychology, in Greek
and English, with Introduction and Notes, by EDWIN WALLACE,
M.A., late Fellow of Worcester College, Oxford. Demy 8vo. 18s.

ΠΕΡΙ ΔΙΚΑΙΟΣΥΝΗΣ. The Fifth Book of the Nicomachean Ethics of Aristotle. Edited by HENRY JACKSON, Litt. D.
Fellow of Trinity College, Cambridge. Demy 8vo. 6s.

Pindar. Olympian and Pythian Odes. With Notes Explanatory and Critical, Introductions and Introductory Essays. Edited
by C. A. M. FENNELL, Litt. D. Crown 8vo. 9s.

— The Isthmian and Nemean Odes by the same Editor. 9s.

The Types of Greek Coins. By PERCY GARDNER, Litt. D.,
F.S.A. With 16 plates. Impl. 4to. Cloth £1. 11s. 6d, Roxburgh
(Morocco back) £2. 2s.

SANSKRIT, ARABIC AND SYRIAC.

The Divyâvadâna, a Collection of Early Buddhist Legends,
now first edited from the Nepalese Sanskrit MSS. in Cambridge
and Paris. By E. B. COWELL, M.A. and R. A. NEIL, M.A.
Demy 8vo. 18s.

Nalopakhyánam, or, The Tale of Nala; containing the Sanskrit Text in Roman Characters, with Vocabulary. By the late
Rev. T. JARRETT. M.A. Demy 8vo. 10s.

Notes on the Tale of Nala, for the use of Classical Students,
by J. PEILE, Litt. D., Master of Christ's College. Demy 8vo. 12s.

History of Alexander the Son of Philip the King of the
Macedonians. Syriac Text and English Translation by E. A.
BUDGE, M.A. *[In the Press.*

London: Cambridge Warehouse, Ave Maria Lane.

The Poems of Beha ed dīn Zoheir of Egypt. With a Metrical Translation, Notes and Introduction, by the late E. H. PALMER, M.A. 2 vols. Crown Quarto.
Vol. I. The ARABIC TEXT. 10s. 6d.; cloth extra, 15s.
Vol. II. ENGLISH TRANSLATION. 10s. 6d.; cloth extra, 15s.

The Chronicle of Joshua the Stylite edited in Syriac, with an English translation and notes, by W. WRIGHT, LL.D., Professor of Arabic. Demy Octavo. 10s. 6d.

Kalīlah and Dimnah, or, the Fables of Bidpai; with an English Translation of the later Syriac version, with Notes, by the late I. G. N. KEITH-FALCONER, M.A. Demy 8vo. 7s. 6d.

MATHEMATICS, PHYSICAL SCIENCE, &c.

Mathematical and Physical Papers. By GEORGE GABRIEL STOKES, M.A., LL.D. Reprinted from the Original Journals and Transactions, with additional Notes by the Author. Vol. I. Demy 8vo., cloth. 15s. Vol. II. 15s. [Vol. III. *In the Press*.

Mathematical and Physical Papers. By Sir W. THOMSON, LL.D., F.R.S. Collected from different Scientific Periodicals from May, 1841, to the present time. Vol. I. Demy 8vo. cloth, 18s. Vol. II. 15s. [Vol. III. *In the Press*.

A History of the Theory of Elasticity and of the Strength of Materials, from Galilei to the present time. Vol. I. GALILEI TO SAINT-VENANT, 1639–1850. By the late I. TODHUNTER, D. Sc., edited and completed by Prof. KARL PEARSON, M.A. Demy 8vo. 25s. Vol. II. By the same Editor. [*In the Press*.

A Treatise on the General Principles of Chemistry, by M. M. PATTISON MUIR, M.A. Demy 8vo. 15s.

Elementary Chemistry. By M. M. PATTISON MUIR, M.A., and CHARLES SLATER, M.A., M.B. Crown 8vo. 4s. 6d.

Practical Chemistry. A Course of Laboratory Work. By M. M. PATTISON MUIR, M.A., and D. J. CARNEGIE, B.A. Cr. 8vo. 3s.

A Treatise on Geometrical Optics. By R. S. HEATH, M.A. Demy 8vo. 12s. 6d.

An Elementary Treatise on Geometrical Optics. By R. S. HEATH, M.A. Crown 8vo. 5s.

Lectures on the Physiology of Plants, by S. H. VINES, M.A., D.Sc., Fellow of Christ's College. Demy 8vo. 21s.

A Short History of Greek Mathematics. By J. Gow, Litt. D., Fellow of Trinity College. Demy 8vo. 10s. 6d.

Notes on Qualitative Analysis. Concise and Explanatory. By H. J. H. FENTON, M.A., F.C.S. New Edit. Crown 4to. 6s.

Diophantos of Alexandria; a Study in the History of Greek Algebra. By T. L. HEATH, M.A. Demy 8vo. 7s. 6d.

A Catalogue of the Portsmouth collection of Books and Papers written by or belonging to SIR ISAAC NEWTON. Demy 8vo. 5s.

London: Cambridge Warehouse, Ave Maria Lane.

The Collected Mathematical Papers of ARTHUR CAYLEY, M.A., F.R.S., Sadlerian Professor of Pure Mathematics in the University of Cambridge. Demy 4to. [*In the Press.*

A Treatise on Natural Philosophy. Part I. By Professors Sir W. THOMSON, LL.D., D.C.L., F.R.S., and P. G. TAIT, M.A., Demy 8vo. cloth, 16s. Part II. Demy 8vo. 18s.

Elements of Natural Philosophy. By Professors Sir W. THOMSON and P. G. TAIT. *Second Edition.* Demy 8vo. 9s.

An Elementary Treatise on Quaternions. By P. G. TAIT, M.A. *Second Edition.* Demy 8vo. 14s.

A Treatise on the Theory of Determinants and their Applications in Analysis and Geometry. By ROBERT FORSYTH SCOTT, M.A., Fellow of St John's College. Demy 8vo. 12s.

Counterpoint. A practical course of study. By the late Prof. Sir G. A. MACFARREN, Mus.D. 5th Edition, revised. Cr. 4to. 7s. 6d.

The Analytical Theory of Heat. By JOSEPH FOURIER. Translated, with Notes, by A. FREEMAN, M.A. Demy 8vo. 12s.

The Scientific Papers of the late Prof. J. Clerk Maxwell. Edited by W. D. NIVEN, M.A. Royal 4to. [*Nearly ready.*

The Electrical Researches of the Honourable Henry Cavendish, F.R.S. Written between 1771 and 1781. Edited by J. CLERK MAXWELL, F.R.S. Demy 8vo. cloth, 18s.

Practical Work at the Cavendish Laboratory. Heat. Edited by W. N. SHAW, M.A. Demy 8vo. 3s.

Hydrodynamics, a Treatise on the Mathematical Theory of Fluid Motion, by HORACE LAMB, M.A. Demy 8vo. cloth, 12s.

The Mathematical Works of Isaac Barrow, D.D Edited by W. WHEWELL, D.D. Demy Octavo. 7s. 6d.

Illustrations of Comparative Anatomy, Vertebrate and Invertebrate Second Edition. Demy 8vo. cloth, 2s. 6d.

A Catalogue of Australian Fossils. By R. ETHERIDGE, Jun., F.G.S. Demy 8vo. 10s. 6d.

The Fossils and Palæontological Affinities of the Neocomian Deposits of Upware and Brickhill. With Plates. By W. KEEPING, M.A., F.G.S. Demy 8vo. 10s. 6d.

A Catalogue of Books and Papers on Protozoa, Coelenterates, Worms, etc. published during the years 1861-1883, by D'ARCY W. THOMPSON, M.A. Demy 8vo. 12s. 6d.

An attempt to test the Theories of Capillary Action, by F. BASHFORTH, B.D., and J. C. ADAMS, M.A., £1. 1s.

A Catalogue of the Collection of Cambrian and Silurian Fossils contained in the Geological Museum of the University of Cambridge, by J. W. SALTER, F.G.S. Royal Quarto. 7s. 6d.

Catalogue of Osteological Specimens contained in the Anatomical Museum of the University of Cambridge. Demy 8vo. 2s. 6d.

Astronomical Observations made at the Observatory of Cambridge from 1846 to 1860, by the late Rev. J. CHALLIS, M.A.

Astronomical Observations from 1861 to 1865. Vol. XXI. Royal 4to., 15s. From 1866 to 1869. Vol. XXII. [*Nearly Ready.*

London: Cambridge Warehouse, Ave Maria Lane.

LAW.

A Selection of Cases on the English Law of Contract.
By GERARD BROWN FINCH, M.A. Royal 8vo. 28s.

The Influence of the Roman Law on the Law of England.
Being the Yorke Prize Essay for the year 1884. By T. E. SCRUTTON, M.A. Demy 8vo. 10s. 6d.

Land in Fetters. Being the Yorke Prize Essay for 1885. By T. E. SCRUTTON, M.A. Demy 8vo. 7s. 6d.

Commons and Common Fields, or the History and Policy of the Laws of Commons and Enclosures in England. Being the Yorke Prize Essay for 1886. By T. E. SCRUTTON, M.A. Demy 8vo. 10s. 6d.

History of the Law of Tithes in England. Being the Yorke Prize Essay for 1887. By WILLIAM EASTERBY, B.A., LL.B. Demy 8vo. 7s. 6d.

An Introduction to the Study of Justinian's Digest. By HENRY JOHN ROBY. Demy 8vo. 9s.

Justinian's Digest. Lib. VII., Tit. I. De Usufructu with a Legal and Philological Commentary by H. J. ROBY. Demy 8vo. 9s. The Two Parts complete in One Volume. Demy 8vo. 18s.

Practical Jurisprudence. A comment on AUSTIN. By E. C. CLARK, LL.D., Regius Professor of Civil Law. Crown 8vo. 9s.

An Analysis of Criminal Liability. By the same Editor. Crown 8vo. cloth. 7s. 6d.

A Selection of the State Trials. By J. W. WILLIS-BUND, M.A., LL.B. Crown 8vo. Vols. I. and II. In 3 parts. 30s.

The Fragments of the Perpetual Edict of Salvius Julianus, Collected, Arranged, and Annotated by the late BRYAN WALKER, M.A., LL.D. Crown 8vo. 6s.

The Commentaries of Gaius and Rules of Ulpian. Translated and Annotated, by J. T. ABDY, LL.D., and BRYAN WALKER, M.A., LL.D. New Edition by Bryan Walker. Crown 8vo. 16s.

The Institutes of Justinian, translated with Notes by J. T. ABDY, LL.D., and BRYAN WALKER, M.A., LL.D. Crn. 8vo. 16s.

Grotius de Jure Belli et Pacis, with the Notes of Barbeyrac and others; an abridged Translation of the Text, by W. WHEWELL, D.D. Demy 8vo. 12s. The translation separate, 6s.

Selected Titles from the Digest, annotated by BRYAN WALKER, M.A., LL.D. Part I. Mandati vel Contra. Digest XVII. 1. Crown 8vo. 5s.

Part II. De Adquirendo rerum dominio, and De Adquirenda vel amittenda Possessione, Digest XLI. 1 and 2. Crown 8vo. 6s.

Part III. De Condictionibus, Digest XII. 1 and 4—7 and Digest XIII. 1—3. Crown 8vo. 6s.

Bracton's Note Book. A Collection of Cases decided in the King's Courts during the Reign of Henry the Third, annotated by a Lawyer of that time, seemingly by Henry of Bratton. Edited by F. W. MAITLAND. 3 vols. Demy 8vo. £3. 3s. (nett.)

HISTORICAL WORKS.

Life and Times of Stein, or Germany and Prussia in the Napoleonic Age, by J. R. SEELEY, M.A. With Portraits and Maps. 3 vols. Demy 8vo. **30s.**

London: Cambridge Warehouse, Ave Maria Lane.

The Architectural History of the University of Cambridge
and of the Colleges of Cambridge and Eton, by the late Professor
WILLIS, M.A., F.R.S. Edited with large Additions and a Continuation to the present time by JOHN WILLIS CLARK, M.A.
Four Vols. Super Royal 8vo. £6. 6s.
 Also a limited Edition of the same, consisting of 120 numbered Copies only, large paper Quarto; the woodcuts and steel engravings mounted on India paper; of which 100 copies are now offered for sale, at Twenty-five Guineas net each set.

The University of Cambridge from the Earliest Times to the
Royal Injunctions of 1535. By J. B. MULLINGER, M.A. Demy 8vo. 12s.
—— Part II. From the Royal Injunctions of 1535 to the Accession of Charles the First. Demy 8vo. 18s.

History of the College of St John the Evangelist, by THOMAS
BAKER, B.D., Ejected Fellow. Edited by JOHN E. B. MAYOR,
M.A., Fellow of St John's. Two Vols. Demy 8vo. 24s.

Scholae Academicae: some Account of the Studies at the
English Universities in the Eighteenth Century. By CHRISTOPHER
WORDSWORTH, M.A. Demy Octavo, 10s. 6d.

Studies in the Literary Relations of England with Germany
in the Sixteenth Century. By C. H. HERFORD, M.A. Crown 8vo. 9s.

The Growth of English Industry and Commerce. By W.
CUNNINGHAM, B.D. With Maps and Charts. Crown 8vo. 12s.

Chronological Tables of Greek History. By CARL PETER.
Translated from the German by G. CHAWNER, M.A. Demy 4to. 10s.

Travels in Northern Arabia in 1876 and 1877. By CHARLES
M. DOUGHTY. With Illustrations. Demy 8vo. 2 vols. £3. 3s.

History of Nepāl, edited with an introductory sketch of the
Country and People by Dr D. WRIGHT. Super-royal 8vo. 10s. 6d.

A Journey of Literary and Archæological Research in Nepal
and Northern India, during the Winter of 1884—5. By CECIL
BENDALL, M.A. Demy 8vo. 10s.

MISCELLANEOUS.

Kinship and Marriage in early Arabia, by W. ROBERTSON
SMITH, M.A., LL.D. Crown 8vo. 7s. 6d.

Chapters on English Metre. By Rev. JOSEPH B. MAYOR,
M.A. Demy 8vo. 7s. 6d.

A Catalogue of Ancient Marbles in Great Britain, by Prof.
ADOLF MICHAELIS. Translated by C. A. M. FENNELL, Litt.D.
Royal 8vo. Roxburgh (Morocco back). £2. 2s.

From Shakespeare to Pope. An Inquiry into the causes
and phenomena of the Rise of Classical Poetry in England. By
E. GOSSE, M.A. Crown 8vo. 6s.

The Literature of the French Renaissance. An Introductory
Essay. By A. A. TILLEY, M.A. Crown 8vo. 6s.

A Latin-English Dictionary. Printed from the (Incomplete)
MS. of the late T. H. KEY, M.A., F.R.S. Demy 4to. £1. 11s. 6d.

Epistvlae Ortelianae. ABRAHAMI ORTELII (Geographi Antverpiensis) et virorvm ervditorvm ad evndem et ad JACOBVM
COLIVM ORTELIANVM Epistvlae. Cvm aliqvot aliis epistvlis et
tractatibvs qvibvsdam ab vtroqve collectis (1524—1628). Ex
avtographis mandante Ecclesia Londino-batava edidit JOANNES
HENRICVS HESSELS. Demy 4to. £3. 10s. *Net.*

London: Cambridge Warehouse, Ave Maria Lane.

The Despatches of Earl Gower, English Ambassador at the court of Versailles, June 1790 to August 1792, and the Despatches of Mr Lindsay and Mr Monro. By O. BROWNING, M.A. Demy 8vo. 15s.

Rhodes in Ancient Times. By CECIL TORR, M.A. With six plates. 10s. 6d.

Rhodes in Modern Times. By the same Author. With three plates. Demy 8vo. 8s.

The Woodcutters of the Netherlands during the last quarter of the Fifteenth Century. By W. M. CONWAY. Demy 8vo. 10s. 6d.

Lectures on Teaching, delivered in the University of Cambridge in the Lent Term, 1880. By J. G. FITCH, M.A., LL.D. Cr. 8vo. New ed. 5s.

A Grammar of the Irish Language. By Prof. WINDISCH. Translated by Dr NORMAN MOORE. Crown 8vo. 7s. 6d.

A Catalogue of the Collection of Birds formed by the late HUGH EDWIN STRICKLAND, now in the possession of the University of Cambridge. By O. SALVIN, M.A., F.R.S. £1. 1s.

Catalogue of the Hebrew Manuscripts preserved in the University Library, Cambridge. By Dr SCHILLER-SZINESSY. 9s.

Catalogue of the Buddhist Sanskrit Manuscripts in the University Library, Cambridge. Edited by C. BENDALL, M.A. 12s.

A Catalogue of the Manuscripts preserved in the Library of the University of Cambridge. Demy 8vo. 5 Vols. 10s. each.

Index to the Catalogue. Demy 8vo. 10s.

A Catalogue of Adversaria and printed books containing MS. notes, in the Library of the University of Cambridge. 3s. 6d.

The Illuminated Manuscripts in the Library of the Fitzwilliam Museum, Cambridge, Catalogued with Descriptions, and an Introduction, by WILLIAM GEORGE SEARLE, M.A. 7s. 6d.

A Chronological List of the Graces, etc. in the University Registry which concern the University Library. 2s. 6d.

Catalogus Bibliothecæ Burckhardtianæ. Demy Quarto. 5s.

Graduati Cantabrigienses: sive catalogus exhibens nomina eorum quos ab Anno Academico Admissionum MDCCC usque ad octavum diem Octobris MDCCCLXXXIV gradu quocunque ornavit Academia Cantabrigiensis, e libris subscriptionum desumptus. Cura H. R. LUARD, S. T. P. Demy 8vo. 12s. 6d.

Statutes for the University of Cambridge and for the Colleges therein, made, published and approved (1878—1882) under the Universities of Oxford and Cambridge Act, 1877. Demy 8vo. 16s.

Statutes of the University of Cambridge. 3s. 6d.

Ordinances of the University of Cambridge. 7s. 6d.

Trusts, Statutes and Directions affecting (1) The Professorships of the University. (2) The Scholarships and Prizes. (3) Other Gifts and Endowments. Demy 8vo. 5s.

A Compendium of University Regulations. Demy 8vo. 6d.

Admissions to Gonville and Caius College in the University of Cambridge March 1558—9 to Jan. 1678—9. Edited by J. VENN, Sc.D., and S. C. VENN. Demy 8vo. 10s.

London: Cambridge Warehouse, Ave Maria Lane.

The Cambridge Bible for Schools and Colleges.

GENERAL EDITOR: J. J. S. PEROWNE, D.D., DEAN OF PETERBOROUGH.

"It is difficult to commend too highly this excellent series."—*Guardian*.

"The modesty of the general title of this series has, we believe, led many to misunderstand its character and underrate its value. The books are well suited for study in the upper forms of our best schools, but not the less are they adapted to the wants of all Bible students who are not specialists. We doubt, indeed, whether any of the numerous popular commentaries recently issued in this country will be found more serviceable for general use."—*Academy*.

"Of great value. The whole series of comments for schools is highly esteemed by students capable of forming a judgment. The books are scholarly without being pretentious: information is so given as to be easily understood."—*Sword and Trowel*.

Now Ready. Cloth, Extra Fcap. 8vo.

Book of Joshua. By Rev. G. F. MACLEAR, D.D. With Maps. 2s. 6d.

Book of Judges. By Rev. J. J. LIAS, M.A. 3s. 6d.

First Book of Samuel. By Rev. Prof. KIRKPATRICK, M.A. With Map. 3s. 6d.

Second Book of Samuel. By Rev. Prof. KIRKPATRICK, M.A. With 2 Maps. 3s. 6d.

First Book of Kings. By Rev. Prof. LUMBY, D.D. 3s. 6d.

Second Book of Kings. By Prof. LUMBY, D.D. 3s. 6d.

Book of Job. By Rev. A. B. DAVIDSON, D.D. 5s.

Book of Ecclesiastes. By Very Rev. E. H. PLUMPTRE, D.D., Dean of Wells. 5s.

Book of Jeremiah. By Rev. A. W. STREANE. M.A. 4s. 6d.

Book of Hosea. By Rev. T. K. CHEYNE, M.A., D.D. 3s.

Books of Obadiah and Jonah. By Arch. PEROWNE. 2s. 6d.

Book of Micah. Rev. T. K. CHEYNE, M.A., D.D. 1s. 6d.

Books of Haggai and Zechariah. By Arch. PEROWNE. 3s.

Gospel according to St Matthew. By Rev. A. CARR, M.A. With 2 Maps. 2s. 6d.

Gospel according to St Mark. By Rev. G. F. MACLEAR, D.D. With 4 Maps. 2s. 6d.

Gospel according to St Luke. By Archdeacon FARRAR. With 4 Maps. 4s. 6d.

Gospel according to St John. By Rev. A. PLUMMER, M.A., D.D. With 4 Maps. 4s. 6d.

Acts of the Apostles. By Prof. LUMBY, D.D. 4 Maps. 4s. 6d.

Epistle to the Romans. Rev. H. C. G. MOULE, M.A. 3s. 6d.

First Corinthians. By Rev. J. J. LIAS, M.A. With Map. 2s.

London: Cambridge Warehouse, Ave Maria Lane.

Second Corinthians. By Rev. J. J. LIAS, M.A. With Map. 2s.
Epistle to the Ephesians. Rev. H. C. G. MOULE, M.A. 2s. 6d.
Epistle to the Hebrews. By Arch. FARRAR, D.D. 3s. 6d.
General Epistle of St James. By Very Rev. E. H. PLUMPTRE, D.D. 1s. 6d.
Epistles of St Peter and St Jude. By Very Rev. E. H. PLUMPTRE, D.D. 2s. 6d.
Epistles of St John. By Rev. A. PLUMMER, M.A., D.D. 3s. 6d.

Preparing.

Book of Genesis. By Very Rev. the Dean of Peterborough.
Books of Exodus, Numbers and Deuteronomy. By Rev. C. D. GINSBURG, LL.D.
Books of Ezra and Nehemiah. By Rev. Prof. RYLE, M.A.
Book of Psalms. By Rev. Prof. KIRKPATRICK, M.A.
Book of Isaiah. By W. ROBERTSON SMITH, M.A.
Book of Ezekiel. By Rev. A. B. DAVIDSON, D.D.
Epistle to the Galatians. By Rev. E. H. PEROWNE, D.D.
Epistles to the Philippians, Colossians and Philemon. By Rev. H. C. G. MOULE, M.A.
Epistles to the Thessalonians. By Rev. W. F. MOULTON, D.D.
Book of Revelation. By Rev. W. H. SIMCOX, M.A.

THE CAMBRIDGE GREEK TESTAMENT
FOR SCHOOLS AND COLLEGES

with a Revised Text, based on the most recent critical authorities, and English Notes, prepared under the direction of the General Editor,
J. J. S. PEROWNE, D.D., DEAN OF PETERBOROUGH.

Gospel according to St Matthew. By Rev. A. CARR, M.A. With 4 Maps. 4s. 6d.
Gospel according to St Mark. By Rev. G. F. MACLEAR, D.D. With 3 Maps. 4s. 6d.
Gospel according to St Luke. By Archdeacon FARRAR. With 4 Maps. 6s.
Gospel according to St John. By Rev. A. PLUMMER, M.A. With 4 Maps. 6s.
Acts of the Apostles. By Prof. LUMBY, D.D. 4 Maps. 6s.
First Epistle to the Corinthians. By Rev. J. J. LIAS, M.A. 3s.
Second Epistle to the Corinthians. By Rev. J. J. LIAS, M.A.
[*Preparing.*
Epistle to the Hebrews. By Archdeacon FARRAR, D.D.
[*In the Press.*
Epistle of St James. By Very Rev. E. H. PLUMPTRE, D.D.
[*Preparing.*
Epistles of St John. By Rev. A. PLUMMER, M.A., D.D. 4s.

London: Cambridge Warehouse, Ave Maria Lane.

THE PITT PRESS SERIES.

I. GREEK.

Platonis Apologia Socratis. With Introduction, Notes and Appendices by J. ADAM, M.A. *Price 3s. 6d.*

—— **Crito.** With Introduction, Notes and Appendix. By the same Editor. *Price 2s. 6d.*

Herodotus, Book VIII., Chaps. 1—90. Edited with Notes and Introduction by E. S. SHUCKBURGH, M.A. *Price 3s. 6d.*

Herodotus, Book IX., Chaps. 1—89. By the same Editor. *3s. 6d.*

Homer. Oydssey, Book IX. With Introduction, Notes and Appendices by G. M. EDWARDS, M.A. *Price 2s. 6d.*

Sophocles.—Oedipus Tyrannus. School Edition, with Introduction and Commentary by R. C. JEBB, Litt.D., LL.D. *4s. 6d.*

Xenophon—Anabasis. With Introduction, Map and English Notes, by A. PRETOR, M.A. Two vols. *Price 7s. 6d.*

—— —— **Books I. III. IV. and V.** By the same Editor. *Price 2s.* each. **Books II. VI. and VII.** *Price 2s. 6d.* each.

Xenophon—Cyropaedeia. Books I. II. With Introduction and Notes by Rev. H. A. HOLDEN, M.A., LL.D. 2 vols. *Price 6s.*

—— —— **Books III. IV. and V.** By the same Editor. *5s.*

Xenophon—Agesilaus. By H. HAILSTONE, M.A. *2s. 6d.*

Luciani Somnium Charon Piscator et De Luctu. By W. E. HEITLAND, M.A., Fellow of St John's College, Cambridge. *3s. 6d.*

Aristophanes. Aves—Plutus—Ranae. By W. C. GREEN, M.A., late Assistant Master at Rugby School. *Price 3s. 6d.* each.

Euripides. Hercules Furens. With Introduction, Notes and Analysis. By A. GRAY, M.A., and J. T. HUTCHINSON, M.A. *2s.*

Euripides. Heracleidæ. With Introduction and Critical Notes by E. A. BECK, M.A., Fellow of Trinity Hall. *Price 3s. 6d.*

Plutarch's Lives of the Gracchi.—Sulla. With Introduction, Notes and Lexicon by H. A. HOLDEN, M.A., LL.D. *6s.* each.

Plutarch's Life of Nicias. With Introduction and Notes by the same Editor. *Price 5s.*

II. LATIN.

Horace. Epistles, Book I. With Notes and Introduction by E. S. SHUCKBURGH, M.A., late Fellow of Emmanuel College. *2s. 6d.*

Livy. Book XXI. With Notes, Introduction and Maps. By M. S. DIMSDALE, M.A., Fellow of King's College. *Price 3s. 6d.*

P. Vergili Maronis Aeneidos Libri I.—XII. Edited with Notes by A. SIDGWICK, M.A. *Price 1s. 6d.* each.

P. Vergili Maronis Georgicon Libri I. II. By the same Editor. *Price 2s.* **Libri III. IV.** By the same Editor. *Price 2s.*

P. Vergili Maronis Bucolica. With Introduction and Notes by the same Editor. *Price 1s. 6d.*

Caesar. De Bello Gallico Comment. I. With Maps and Notes by A. G. PESKETT, M.A. *Price 1s. 6d.*

—— **Comment. I. II. III.** *Price 3s.* **Com. IV. V.,** and **Com. VII.** *Price 2s.* each. **Com. VI.** and **Com. VIII.** *Price 1s. 6d.* each.

London: Cambridge Warehouse, Ave Maria Lane.

M. Tulli Ciceronis Oratio Philippica Secunda. With Introduction and Notes by A. G. PESKETT, M.A. *Price* 3s. 6d.

M. T. Ciceronis de Amicitia. Edited by J. S. REID, Litt. D., Fellow of Gonville and Caius College. Revised edition. 3s. 6d.

M. T. Ciceronis de Senectute. By the same Editor. 3s. 6d.

M. T. Ciceronis Oratio pro Archia Poeta. By the same Editor. Revised edition. *Price* 2s.

M. T. Ciceronis pro L. Cornelio Balbo Oratio. By the same Editor. *Price* 1s. 6d.

M. T. Ciceronis pro P. Cornelio Sulla Oratio. By the same Editor. *Price* 3s. 6d.

M. T. Ciceronis in Q. Caecilium Divinatio et in C. Verrem Actio. By W. E. HEITLAND, M.A., and H. COWIE, M.A. 3s.

M. T. Ciceronis in Gaium Verrem Actio Prima. With Notes by H. COWIE, M.A., Fellow of St John's Coll. *Price* 1s. 6d.

M. T. Ciceronis Oratio pro L. Murena, with English Introduction and Notes. By W. E. HEITLAND, M.A. *Price* 3s.

M. T. Ciceronis Oratio pro Tito Annio Milone, with English Notes, &c., by JOHN SMYTH PURTON, B.D. *Price* 2s. 6d.

M. T. Ciceronis pro Cn. Plancio Oratio, by H. A. HOLDEN, LL.D. Second Edition. *Price* 4s. 6d.

M. T. Ciceronis Somnium Scipionis. With Introduction and Notes. Edited by W. D. PEARMAN, M.A. *Price* 2s.

Quintus Curtius. A Portion of the History (Alexander in India). By W. E. HEITLAND, M.A. and T. E. RAVEN, B.A. 3s. 6d.

M. Annaei Lucani Pharsaliae Liber Primus. Edited by W. E. HEITLAND, M.A., and C. E. HASKINS, M.A. 1s. 6d.

P. Ovidii Nasonis Fastorum Liber VI. With Notes by A. SIDGWICK, M.A., Tutor of Corpus Christi Coll., Oxford. 1s. 6d.

Beda's Ecclesiastical History, Books III., IV. Edited by J. E. B. MAYOR, M.A., and J. R. LUMBY, D.D. Revised Edit. 7s.6d.

III. FRENCH.

Le Philosophe sans le savoir. Sedaine. Edited with Notes by Rev. H. A. BULL, M.A., late Master at Wellington College. 2s.

Recits des Temps Merovingiens I—III. Thierry. Edited by G. MASSON, B.A. and A. R. ROPES, M.A. Map. *Price* 3s.

La Canne de Jonc. By A. DE VIGNY. Edited with Notes by Rev. H. A. BULL, M.A., late Master at Wellington College. *Price* 2s.

Bataille de Dames. By SCRIBE and LEGOUVÉ. Edited by Rev. H. A. BULL, M.A. *Price* 2s.

Jeanne D'Arc. By A. DE LAMARTINE. Edited by Rev. A. C. CLAPIN, M.A. New Edition. *Price* 2s.

Le Bourgeois Gentilhomme, Comédie-Ballet en Cinq Actes. Par J.-B. Poquelin de Molière (1670). By the same Editor. 1s. 6d.

L'École des Femmes. MOLIÈRE. With Introduction and Notes by GEORGE SAINTSBURY, M.A. *Price* 2s. 6d.

La Picciola. By X. B. SAINTINE. The Text, with Introduction, Notes and Map. By Rev. A. C. CLAPIN, M.A. *Price* 2s.

London: Cambridge Warehouse, Ave Maria Lane.

La Guerre. By MM. ERCKMANN-CHATRIAN. With Map, Introduction and Commentary by the same Editor. *Price* 3s.

Le Directoire. (Considérations sur la Révolution Française. Troisième et quatrième parties.) Revised and enlarged. With Notes by G. MASSON, B.A. and G. W. PROTHERO, M.A. *Price* 2s.

Lettres sur l'histoire de France (XIII—XXIV). Par AUGUSTIN THIERRY. By GUSTAVE MASSON, B.A. and G. W. PROTHERO, M.A. *Price* 2s. 6d.

Dix Années d'Exil. Livre II. Chapitres 1—8. Par MADAME LA BARONNE DE STAËL-HOLSTEIN. By G. MASSON, B.A. and G. W. PROTHERO, M.A. New Edition, enlarged. *Price* 2s.

Histoire du Siècle de Louis XIV. par Voltaire. Chaps. I.—XIII. Edited by GUSTAVE MASSON, B.A. and G. W. PROTHERO, M.A. *Price* 2s. 6d. Chaps. XIV.—XXIV. By the same. With 3 Maps. *Price* 2s. 6d. Chap. XXV. to end. By the same. 2s. 6d.

Lazare Hoche—Par ÉMILE DE BONNECHOSE. With Three Maps, Introduction and Commentary, by C. COLBECK, M.A. 2s.

Le Verre D'Eau. A Comedy, by SCRIBE. Edited by C. COLBECK, M.A. *Price* 2s.

M. Daru, par M. C. A. SAINTE-BEUVE (Causeries du Lundi, Vol. IX.). By G. MASSON, B.A. Univ. Gallic. *Price* 2s.

La Suite du Menteur. A Comedy by P. CORNEILLE. With Notes Philological and Historical, by the same. *Price* 2s.

La Jeune Sibérienne. Le Lépreux de la Cité D'Aoste. Tales by COUNT XAVIER DE MAISTRE. By the same. *Price* 2s.

Fredégonde et Brunehaut. A Tragedy in Five Acts, by N. LEMERCIER. By GUSTAVE MASSON, B.A. *Price* 2s.

Le Vieux Célibataire. A Comedy, by COLLIN D'HARLEVILLE. With Notes, by the same. *Price* 2s.

La Métromanie. A Comedy, by PIRON, by the same 2s.

Lascaris ou Les Grecs du XVE Siècle, Nouvelle Historique, par A. F. VILLEMAIN. By the same. *Price* 2s.

IV. GERMAN.

Mendelssohn's Letters. Selections from Edited by JAMES SIME, M.A. *Price* 3s.

Benedix. Doctor Wespe. Lustspiel in fünf Aufzügen. Edited with Notes by KARL HERMANN BREUL, M.A. *Price* 3s.

Selected Fables. Lessing and Gellert. Edited with Notes by KARL HERMANN BREUL, M.A. *Price* 3s.

Zopf und Schwert. Lustspiel in fünf Aufzügen von KARL GUTZKOW. By H. J. WOLSTENHOLME, B.A (Lond.). *Price* 3s. 6d.

Die Karavane, von WILHELM HAUFF. Edited with Notes by A. SCHLOTTMANN, PH. D. *Price* 3s. 6d.

Hauff, Das Wirthshaus im Spessart. By A. SCHLOTTMANN, Ph.D., late Assistant Master at Uppingham School. *Price* 3s. 6d.

Culturgeschichtliche Novellen, von W. H. RIEHL. Edited by H. J. WOLSTENHOLME, B.A. (Lond.). *Price* 4s. 6d.

Uhland. Ernst. Herzog von Schwaben. With Introduction and Notes. By the same Editor. *Price* 3s. 6d.

London: Cambridge Warehouse, Ave Maria Lane.

Goethe's Knabenjahre. (1749—1759.) Goethe's Boyhood. Arranged and Annotated by W. WAGNER, Ph. D. *Price* 2s.

Goethe's Hermann and Dorothea. By W. WAGNER, Ph. D. Revised edition by J. W. CARTMELL. *Price* 3s. 6d.

Der Oberhof. A Tale of Westphalian Life, by KARL IMMERMANN. By WILHELM WAGNER, Ph.D. *Price* 3s.

Der erste Kreuzzug (1095—1099) nach FRIEDRICH VON RAUMER. THE FIRST CRUSADE. By W. WAGNER, Ph. D. *Price* 2s.

A Book of German Dactylic Poetry. Arranged and Annotated by WILHELM WAGNER, Ph.D. *Price* 3s.

A Book of Ballads on German History. Arranged and Annotated by WILHELM WAGNER, PH. D. *Price* 2s.

Der Staat Friedrichs des Grossen. By G. FREYTAG. With Notes. By WILHELM WAGNER, PH.D. *Price* 2s.

Das Jahr 1813 (THE YEAR 1813), by F. KOHLRAUSCH. With English Notes by the same Editor. *Price* 2s.

V. ENGLISH.

Theory and Practice of Teaching. By the Rev. E. THRING, M.A., late Head Master of Uppingham School. New ed. 4s. 6d.

The Teaching of Modern Languages in Theory and Practice. By C. COLBECK, M.A. *Price* 2s.

John Amos Comenius, Bishop of the Moravians. His Life and Educational Works, by S. S. LAURIE, A.M., F.R.S.E. 3s. 6d.

Outlines of the Philosophy of Aristotle. Compiled by EDWIN WALLACE, M.A., LL.D. Third Edition, Enlarged. 4s. 6d.

The Two Noble Kinsmen, edited with Introduction and Notes by the Rev. Professor SKEAT, Litt.D. *Price* 3s. 6d.

Bacon's History of the Reign of King Henry VII. With Notes by the Rev. Professor LUMBY, D.D. *Price* 3s.

Sir Thomas More's Utopia. With Notes by the Rev. Professor LUMBY, D.D. *Price* 3s. 6d.

More's History of King Richard III. Edited with Notes, Glossary, Index of Names. By J. RAWSON LUMBY, D.D. 3s. 6d.

Cowley's Essays. With Introduction and Notes, by Prof. LUMBY, D.D. 4s.

Locke on Education. With Introduction and Notes by the Rev. R. H. QUICK, M.A. *Price* 3s. 6d.

A Sketch of Ancient Philosophy from Thales to Cicero, by JOSEPH B. MAYOR, M.A. *Price* 3s. 6d.

Three Lectures on the Practice of Education. Delivered under the direction of the Teachers' Training Syndicate. *Price* 2s.

General aims of the Teacher, and Form Management. Two Lectures by F. W. FARRAR, D.D. and R. B. POOLE, B.D. 1s. 6d.

Milton's Tractate on Education. A facsimile reprint from the Edition of 1673. Edited by O. BROWNING, M.A. *Price* 2s.

London: C. J. CLAY AND SONS,
CAMBRIDGE WAREHOUSE, AVE MARIA LANE.
Glasgow: 263, ARGYLE STREET.
Cambridge: DEIGHTON, BELL AND CO. **Leipzig**: F. A. BROCKHAUS.

www.ingramcontent.com/pod-product-compliance
Lightning Source LLC
Chambersburg PA
CBHW022106300426
44117CB00007B/612